FROM STUDY ABROAD TO EDUCATION ABROAD

Language Proficiency, Intercultural Competence, and Diversity

Senta Goertler and Theresa Schenker

 Routledge
Taylor & Francis Group

NEW YORK AND LONDON

First published 2021
by Routledge
52 Vanderbilt Avenue, New York, NY 10017

and by Routledge
2 Park Square, Milton Park, Abingdon, Oxon OX14 4RN

Routledge is an imprint of the Taylor & Francis Group, an informa business

© 2021 Taylor & Francis

The right of Senta Goertler and Theresa Schenker to be identified as authors of this work has been asserted by them in accordance with sections 77 and 78 of the Copyright, Designs and Patents Act 1988.

Library of Congress Cataloging-in-Publication Data
A catalog record for this title has been requested

ISBN: 978-0-367-25987-7 (hbk)
ISBN: 978-0-367-25986-0 (pbk)
ISBN: 978-0-429-29089-3 (ebk)

Typeset in Bembo
by Taylor & Francis Books

This book is dedicated to all who welcome and support education abroad students around the world, and all who open their eyes, heart, and ears to new communities and new members in their communities.

CONTENTS

ACKNOWLEDGMENTS

We would like to thank those who supported and welcomed us abroad; the education abroad participants who allowed us to be a part of their journey; our colleagues and mentors; our families who cheered us on along the way; our tireless feedback giver and beloved colleague emeritus Pat McConeghy; the anonymous reviewers of our book proposal; the respondents to our education abroad survey; and Karen Adler and the entire editorial team at Routledge.

PART 1
TRENDS AND DEVELOPMENTS
IN EDUCATION ABROAD

My year abroad was the most momentous, changeful, eye-opening, enlightening, horizon-extending, humbling, frustrating, confusing, yet joyful twelve-month period of my life. I have spent the subsequent years trying to figure out what it meant for my life, and how to best make use of what I learned from being exposed to life outside the bubble of my life up until that time. The value of the experience went way beyond the purely academic curriculum. It was truly the capstone experience to a good liberal arts education. I believe I became a global citizen, a better American, a more interesting and interested person, and a more empathetic human because of my year abroad in Freiburg.

—*Tim, Junior Year in Freiburg, 1987–1988*

Chapter 1.1. Introduction

Education Abroad in the US Today

As language educators and program coordinators, we (the authors) often talk with students about education abroad. Especially for our first-generation in-state students, going abroad can seem overwhelming. During conversations with them, we summarize not just our own stories as education abroad students who never went back home or came back for more, but also those of our alumni. We have yet to meet a student who regretted having studied abroad or wished they had gone for a shorter duration. Far more often students share stories like that captured by an alumnus from the Junior Year in Freiburg program: The abroad program was a life-changing experience on an academic, personal, professional, and human level; and they wished they had gone longer or could return. Nicole, an Academic Year in Freiburg (AYF) alumni exclaimed: "Do it! Go for longer than you think you want to go!" AYF alumna Erica called it #BestYearEver.

Yet, few US students study abroad. Only one in ten US undergraduates participates in an academic program abroad (Institute of International Education, 2018c). This is the case despite repeated efforts by institutions of higher education and the government to encourage participation. Just recently, for example, the Senator Paul Simon Study Abroad Program Act, a bi-partisan senate bill (Senate Bill 1198, 2019) was introduced, which once again advocates for more financial support for education abroad (Nietzel, 2019). This book focuses on how to maximize learning outcomes, improve education abroad design, and diversify participation.

We purposefully will use the term "education abroad" rather than "study abroad," as we want to include academic experiences abroad that may not require enrollment in a course such as internships, service-learning, or research activities. Education abroad is any experience that contributes to a student's academic and career preparation, completed in a country different from the one in which a student is regularly enrolled. We do not include experiences abroad, which have no academic and career preparation component or those where students complete an entire degree abroad. While we draw mostly from the perspective of US students going abroad, many of the lessons learned from the types of programs and students we discuss in this book are applicable to other contexts and student populations.

The Development of Education Abroad in the US

Education abroad has a long history that dates back to the European Middle Ages (Hoffa, 2007). Modern-day education abroad in the US was established in the latter part of the 19th century with two of the US leaders being Indiana and Princeton University who had programs in Europe and China, respectively. By 1909, the first reciprocal exchanges began between England, Canada, and the

USA, and a year later between the USA and Scandinavia (Hoffa, 2007). In 1919, the Institute of International Education was established, which in its Open Doors reports provided the first statistics on the internationalization of US education. In 1923, the first US credit-bearing program was founded at the University of Delaware, which eventually became the first Junior Year Abroad (AAUP, 1995), i.e., a one-year study abroad program for juniors organized through a US institution and hosted at an institution abroad. It appears that initially the expectations of these programs were little more than providing participants a grand tour of Europe. But over time, the programs became more academically oriented and rigorous with an emphasis on progress toward degree, language proficiency, intercultural competence/global awareness, the development of professional skills and career preparation, as well as personal and social development (Norris & Gillespie, 2009).

The height of education abroad was in the 1960s (Hackney, Boggs, & Borozan, 2012) followed by a decrease in participation in the 1970s/1980s. Interest in language education and international engagement are always fueled by national as well as global politics and economics. To discuss the details of these connections exceeds the space of this book (for more information see for example Kramsch, 2005). Since the early 1990s, education abroad has seen a tremendous increase again, which was slowed only by the 2007/2008 economic crisis. While there have been steady increases in education abroad participation over the last decade, they were due to the growth of short-term programs, which was not matched by or may have been at the expense of growth in long-term programs (Farrugia & Bhandari, 2016). Naturally, the 2020 pandemic temporarily halted education abroad.

Where federal programs like the GI Bill expanded access to higher education for millions of returning soldiers, the establishment of government-sponsored organizations and scholarships (1946: Fulbright; 1991: David L. Boren; 2000: Gilman scholarship) likewise made education abroad possible and affordable for more students. A turning point in thinking about education abroad was the 2005 report from the Abraham Lincoln Study Abroad Commission. Although the bill arising from the report died in committee, it set the agenda for discussions that followed. The Commission had proposed to increase education abroad participation to one million students by 2016/2017, which represented 50% of BA/BS degree recipients at the time. In actuality, only 325,339 US undergraduates participated in credit-bearing education abroad programs in 2016/2017, which is not even a third of the proposed goal. Another boost to education abroad was the 2014 Institute of International Education's Generation Study Abroad initiative, which sought institutional pledges to double education abroad participation by 2020 (Institute of International Education, 2014). The IIE initiative was the inspiration for this book.

Over 800 institutions of higher education signed on to the Generation Study Abroad challenge and introduced mechanisms to internationalize the educational with important definitions of terminology used in education abroad discussions. In Chapter 1.2 we look more generally at participation trends in education abroad, followed by trends in program design in Chapter 1.3. In Chapter 1.4 we provide more detail on the JYA. In Chapter 1.5 we outline the challenges to education abroad in general and in particular long-term education abroad such as the JYA. Based on the previous chapters, we present an argument in Chapter 1.6 for revisiting long-term education programs and for strengthening them in higher education abroad portfolios.

Definitions

There are different ways to classify education abroad programs. Some prefer to classify them by the amount of immersion and study in the target community (Engle & Engle, 2003), while others classify by type of provider (Twombly, Salisbury, Tumanut, & Klute, 2012), program length (Open Doors Reports) or integration at a host institution (Norris & Dwyer, 2005). We divide programs in this book by length following the standards of the Institute of International Education as well as involvement in the target community: island, hybrid, and full immersion/direct-enroll (Norris & Dwyer, 2005). In this book, we will use the following terms to help define and categorize various forms of education abroad:

- *Additional language:* Otherwise known as foreign or second language, this is a language students are learning that is not considered one of their first languages. At times, we will also refer to it as L2 or target language.
- *Direct-enroll/full-immersion:* A cost-effective program, which is based on an exchange or other agreement between two universities, where students enroll at the host institution directly, and are supported only by in-country staff.
- *Excursions:* Group trips to explore the area which might not contain an explicit connection to an academic course or program.
- *Experiential learning:* An educational opportunity that provides students a practical experience in the community.
- *Field trips:* Day or overnight group trips in conjunction with an academic offering, e.g., visiting the European parliament as part of a European politics seminar.
- *Global-mindedness/global citizenship:* At times used synonymously with intercultural competence, it describes knowledge of culture, attitudes about culture, and skills in navigating and communicating across cultures. While Intercultural Communicative Competence (ICC) usually includes a language component, global-mindedness often does not. Global-mindedness often includes an international orientation as an additional aspect.
- *Heritage language:* A minority language spoken in a student's community and family, in which the student has good (at least passive) proficiency.

- *Home institution:* The student's institution in the country in which they are regularly enrolled as a degree-seeking student and/or the university that financially and academically oversees the education abroad program.
- *Host institution:* The institution in the host country that is affiliated with the education abroad program and at which students typically take classes.
- *Host language(s):* The dominant language(s) spoken in the community/ies, in which the participants are living.
- *Intercultural communicative competence:* The ability to communicate effectively with people from diverse cultural and linguistic backgrounds.
- *Internships:* Paid or unpaid work experiences intended to promote work or research skills, which may or may not be accompanied by course credit.
- *Island programs:* Programs in which one or more faculty members from the home institution take a group of students abroad and are in charge of instruction while in the host community/ies. There is limited interaction with the host community/ies or university, students may be housed together, and immersion is not a primary goal.
- *Long-term education abroad:* A program abroad that is longer than one semester, typically a year.
- *Medium-length education abroad:* A program abroad of 10–15 weeks duration.
- *Sheltered immersion:* A type of instruction that is focused on content but takes the needs of language learners into account.
- *Short-term education abroad:* A program abroad that is shorter than 10 weeks.
- *Third-party vendor:* An institution or organization independent of the host university which organizes and administers education programs in a host community and typically has agreements with the home institution for credit transfer.
- *Undergraduate research:* Research projects that are typically larger than a course paper, which students conduct semi-independently abroad.
- *University-sponsored:* An education abroad program, which is administered by the home university.

Mission of the Book

Education abroad, especially a year-long program, is often seen as a life-changing experience, yet unfortunately also as a luxury experience. In this book, we hope to present ways to make education abroad, especially long-term abroad programs, more attractive and accessible to a broader audience and provide recommendations to maximize impact.

Chapter 1.2. Trends in Education Abroad Participation

The Status and Importance of Education Abroad in the US

The latest Open Doors report (Institute of International Education, 2018c) shows a continued increase in education abroad participation. In fact, participation in credit-bearing education abroad opportunities has tripled over the last two decades. While around 100,000 students went abroad at the beginning of the 1990s, that number rose to 150,000 by 2000 and stands today at above 300,000. While the overall participation trends are encouraging, still only 10% of US students study abroad and only 15.5% of BA students (Open Doors, 2018b). Even though the trend in education abroad has been positive with more students going abroad, stakeholders in higher education, business, and government, as well as employers have called for more education abroad experiences to better prepare graduates for a global workplace (Daniel, Xie, & Kedia, 2014; Harder et al., 2015; Molony, Sowter, & Potts, 2011).

As a consequence, there have been two major initiatives during the last two decades to increase education abroad participation: The Abraham Lincoln Study Abroad Commission (Commission on the Abraham Lincoln Study Abroad Fellowship Program, 2005) from the US government and the Institute of International Education Generation Study Abroad Initiative (Institute of International Education, 2014), in addition to the current Senator Paul Simon Study Abroad Program Act mentioned above (Senate Bill 1198, 2019).

The Lincoln Commission's purpose was to find sustainable ways to support education abroad and develop the global competence of US citizens. In their final report (Commission on the Abraham Lincoln Study Abroad Fellowship Program, 2005) the commission recommended to increase education abroad to one million students by 2016–2017. There are many interesting elements in the final report and it is often cited in research as an important turning point in thinking about education abroad: "Greater engagement of American undergraduates with the world around them is vital to the nation's well-being" (Commission on the Abraham Lincoln Study Abroad Fellowship Program, 2005, p. v). They list several reasons for this need: (1) Globalization; (2) language development; (3) educational attainment; (4) intercultural competence. Additionally, the commission wanted to overcome the underrepresentation of minoritized students and students from community colleges. Diversification was argued to be beneficial because: (1) More people would have international experiences; and (2) there would be a more diverse representation abroad of what the US is.

Even though the proposal was not approved, the discussions surrounding it still appear to have had an impact in education circles, since participation rose to over 250,000 by 2010 (Institute of International Education, 2011). Yet in spite of an upward trend, the Lincoln Commission's goal of one million students by 2016/2017 has not been realized (Institute of International Education, 2019a). Even though some institutions made new pledges, the overall institutional commitment was still too low. The commission reported that the University of Minnesota had made a commitment to send 50% of its undergraduate students abroad, and that several other institutions, including Harvard, had made education abroad a requirement. These were promising signs but still far from the increase and the diversification in participants for which the report had hoped, which in large measure can be attributed to a lack of funding or financial commitments from government, higher education institutions, and other organizations.

The second initiative that has had a positive impact on education abroad participation was the Institute of International Education's Generation Study Abroad Initiative. The goal of the initiative is to secure commitments from educational institutions, teachers, governments, employers, and associations to assist in doubling participation in education abroad by 2020. By including a diverse set of stakeholders, the initiative has a better chance at success. As of 2020, 450 US universities and colleges joined the 2014 Generation Study Abroad pledge. The mission of the pledge is to "mobilize resources and commitments with the goal of doubling and diversifying the number of US students studying abroad by the end of the decade" (Institute of International Education, 2014). IIE has invested $2 million dollars toward the goal and is fund-raising to support scholarships for students and grants to institutions, thereby exemplifying the call to action proposed by the Lincoln Commission. In contrast to the Lincoln Commission, the Generation Study Abroad pledge has found a broad following (Open Doors, 2018a) and IIES has already awarded stipends (Institute of International Education, 2018a). The global pandemic has had an enormous impact on the current numbers of participants with such a high percentage of program cancellation and fears and concerns that may linger in future years, which may dampen some of the influences of the discussed initiatives, a sentiment echoed by practitioners we surveyed.

Participation Trends in Education Abroad

The majority of students in education abroad are white and female, major in the Humanities or Social Sciences, attend liberal arts colleges, are typically of traditional college age (Twombly et al., 2012) and prefer programs led by a familiar faculty member in a large city not too far from home conducted in English (Hackney et al., 2012). Minoritized students, students from community colleges, students with disabilities, non-traditional students, and students from certain majors are underrepresented in education abroad even though increases have been noted in recent years (Institute of International Education, 2019b).

Length

Participation in short-term programs contributes greatly to the overall rise in education abroad. 65% of all education abroad students participate in programs shorter than an academic term and only 2% participate in long-term programs of more than one term (Institute of International Education, 2019a). With the over-representation of short-term programs in the Open Doors reports, enrollment trends are primarily based on trends in these programs. Yet, since short-term program participation has grown significantly, trends also point to growth potential in long-term programs.

Destination

Still more than half of the students go to Europe (54%), with the UK, Italy, and Spain being the preferred destinations (Institute of International Education, 2019a). However, there has been a diversification of host countries and Europe has steadily decreased from 60% in 2004/2005 to 54% in 2015/2016. At the same time the Middle East and North Africa increased from 1% to 2% (even close to 3 % in 2010/2011), likely due to increases in funding for education abroad in this region through the US government. Asia increased from 8% to 11% (Institute of International Education, 2018c).

Institution

Liberal arts college students are over- and community college students are underrepresented in education abroad. Community colleges show a low level of internationalization (Green & Siaya, 2005), but steps have been taken to enhance education abroad offerings at community colleges and to provide funding for students (Raby & Valeau, 2007).

Disciplinary Background

Participants in education abroad come from more diverse disciplinary backgrounds today than before. The participation rate of STEM students is steadily increasing and now stands at 26%. Business students make up 21%, Social Science students 17%, Foreign Language and International Relations students 7%, and Arts students 7% of education abroad students (Institute of International Education, 2019a). Interestingly, Farrugia and Sanger (2017) report that STEM majors tend to participate in non-major specific programs, when we had assumed that the increase of STEM students aligned with an increase in STEM education abroad opportunities. Klebnikov (2015) reports that the majority of students participating in year-long programs come from three areas: The Humanities (27%), STEM (24%), and the Social Sciences (22%). There is research that suggests that students prefer programs that connect with their majors (Opper, Teichler, & Carlson, 1990).

Classmanship

As the name JYA implies, most students used to go abroad in their Junior year in college, at which point they were more comparable in their academic skills to

European college students. As program types have shifted, so have the enrollment trends. In 2004/2005, 34.2% of the students going abroad on any type of program were Juniors at their home institution, which decreased slightly to 33% in 2017/2018. Interestingly, there was a large increase during the same period for Seniors participating in education abroad from 19.8% to 28.2%. Current enrollment trends also show that between 2004/2005 and 2015/2016 there has been a decrease in the percentage of Associate degree students studying abroad from 2.7% to 1.7% (Institute of International Education, 2019b).

Individual Differences

Several individual differences also play a role in students' likelihood to participate in education abroad and learning outcomes such as emotional intelligence, openness, agreeableness.

Carter (2015) found emotional self-awareness and flexibility to be predictors of undergraduates' participation in education abroad. Some studies suggest that students with higher emotional intelligence have shown better cross-cultural adjustment in education abroad settings (J. K. Harrison & Voelker, 2008; Lin, Chen, & Song, 2012) and stronger intercultural growth (Gullekson & Tucker, 2012). Students who possess higher levels of openness are more likely to participate in education abroad, especially long-term programs, and view it as an exciting opportunity (Bakalis, 2004; Salisbury, Umbach, Paulsen, & Pascarella, 2009; Zimmermann & Neyer, 2013). Research has identified agreeableness, along with openness, as a factor that predicts students' choices to participate in education abroad (Niehoff, Petersdotter, & Freund, 2017) as well as a factor that predicts better adaptation to the university abroad (Bordovskaia, Anderson, Bochkina, & Petanova, 2018) or to another culture in general (Swagler & Jome, 2005). Burke, Watkins, and Guzman (2009) revealed that the trait of agreeableness helped students be personally disciplined and adjust to the living conditions in Mexico. Students who had high levels of agreeableness were also less likely to complain about the target country.

International Orientation

Nowadays, more students who go abroad have previously studied abroad in another program (Olson & Lalley, 2012). In fact, 29% of students in Olson and Lalley's (2012) study chose another education abroad option or internship later. In addition to students participating in multiple programs, we have also seen an increase in students who are international students at the home university, participating in education abroad programs in a third country.

Gender

Gender (im)balance in education abroad has remained stubbornly unchanged with around 65% of the participants reported as female and 35% as male (Institute of International Education, 2018c). Several studies on what impacts students' intent to study abroad identified gender as one factor and confirmed that men were less likely to plan to participate in education abroad than women (Niehaus & Inkelas, 2016; Salisbury, Paulsen, & Pascarella, 2010; Salisbury et al., 2009; Stroud, 2010). Shirley (2006) did not find a gender difference and Hurst (2019) found that socio-economic background interplayed with gender.

Additionally, men and women choose education abroad for different reasons. For example, one study concluded that women's intentions for studying abroad are less affected by achievement goals and more affected by their desire to help others and by ethnic heritage (Li, Olson, & Frieze, 2013). In order to find out why men participate in education abroad less often, Thirolf (2014) conducted interviews with twenty male students who had indicated interest in a global education summer abroad program but had ultimately not attended. A main reason for their choice against a summer program was their outcome-orientation. The students preferred internships or research opportunities that they felt would enhance their CV more than a summer abroad. Another deterrent for the men in this study was the need to make money over the summer. The study showed that many male students are influenced by stereotypical ideas about the role of men and women in society. Students were of the opinion that women do not have pressures to find specific jobs after graduation and therefore are at liberty to do summer abroad programs. These differing goals may have an impact on how the participants navigate the education abroad experience and thereby the outcomes. For example, men may focus on language-unrelated goals while abroad (Kinginger, 2011). Gutel (2008) compared the homestay experience of male and female students and found few differences. Female students tended to want a more emotional connection with the family. Male respondents evaluated their experience more often based on how adequate they perceived the service the family provided.

Gender and sexuality impact not only who participates in education abroad, but also their experience there. These factors have a differing degree of impact on education abroad depending on the gender roles in the host community and policies and attitudes towards LGBTQ+.

Some studies have found an effect of the gender roles of participants on immersion (e.g., Trentman, 2013), but Baker-Smemoe, Dewey, Bown, and Martinsen (2014) did not find such an effect, which had been observed in other studies where gender roles did restrict engagement with the community. Research, for example, points to the difficulty female students have immersing themselves fully in cultures which hold unequal views of men and women and women are legally or socially restricted from spaces (Talburt & Stewart, 1999; Trentman, 2013).

Race and Ethnicity

While gender distributions have stayed mostly consistent in education abroad, the participation of students of color participating in education abroad has increased. Unfortunately, they still only represent 30% of the education abroad students, up from 18% in 2007/2008. The percentage of white participants has decreased from 83% to 70% between 2004/2005 and 2017/2018. American Indian and Alaska Native participants remained stable at around 0.5%. It is encouraging to see that the percentage of other students of color in education abroad has consistently increased: Hispanic and LatinX increased from 5.4% to 10.6% possibly due to some programs also focusing on supporting heritage students; Asian, Native Hawaiian and Pacific Islander participation increased from 6.3% to 8.4%; Black or African-American from 3.5% to 6.1%; and Multiracial from 1.2% to 4.4% (Institute of International Education, 2019b). Students of color tend to prefer programs that allow them to connect to their ethno-racial identity (Anya, 2011; Tolliver, 2000) or their cultural or linguistic heritage (Kasravi, 2009; Jungeun Kim & Stodolska, 2013; Petrucci, 2007; Trentman, 2015).

Students of color are underrepresented in education abroad and often do not apply due to safety concerns and irrelevant destinations (Hourigan & Murray, 2010; McClure, Szelenyi, Niehaus, Anderson, & Reed, 2010). BaileyShea (2009) analyzed data from the Higher Education Research Institute's (HERI) 2002 Cooperative Institutional Research Program Freshman Survey and the 2006 College Senior Survey (CSS) and found that minoritized students who were involved in leadership training were more likely to participate in education abroad than those who were not. Black students also reported not finding their concerns (e.g., fear of racism abroad; access to Black people with experience with the host community; intimidating and overwhelming bureaucracy; unsupportive education abroad personnel) heard while applying for education abroad programs and a discomfort discussing race issues and questions with program personnel (Simon & Ainsworth, 2012). Simon and Ainsworth (2012) found that "Black students without a foreign-born parent are less likely to have social networks with study abroad experience and therefore are less likely to be exposed to the valuable information and advice they provide" (p. 12). When students of color go abroad, they often choose to study in countries to which they have ancestral links which has been shown to contribute to their identity development (Beausoleil, 2008; Comp, 2008; Penn & Tanner, 2009; Raymondi, 2005). Students strive for a culture that feels comfortable in their destinations, which is why white students tend to go to Western Europe and Black students to Brazil or African countries like Ghana (Simon & Ainsworth, 2012).

Students of color may experience racism abroad (Goldoni, 2013; Willis, 2015) as well as racism during their decision-making process at home (Simon & Ainsworth, 2012). While students of color are also confronted with racism at home, the mechanisms and histories of the racism in the host community may vary greatly from

which they could visit several countries while receiving academic instruction by a faculty member of their home institution. On such programs, language learning was not emphasized and coursework was usually done in English. Thus, aside from the travel opportunities, short-term summer abroad programs were academic in nature, consisting of coursework or independent research (Hoffa, 2007). Especially in the early stages of education abroad, participation was limited to those who could afford the program and academic credit was not always awarded. Many programs stopped operations or moved during World War II. After World War II, education abroad programs resumed and some new program types developed that were influenced by specific foreign policy priorities. International student exchange received increased interest from the government because of its potential in supporting peaceful relationships with other countries. One of the earliest and most important programs of this kind is the Fulbright program, which according to their website has sent more than 370,000 students and scholars abroad since it began in 1946 (see www.cies.org/about-us).

Volunteer programs also developed after World War II. Organization established various volunteer and service opportunities that sent US students to countries all over the world to help with reconstruction efforts after the war and other humanitarian endeavors. Furthermore, cross-cultural immersion programs began to develop in the postwar times as well. Several organizations, among them Youth for Understanding and Experiment in International Living, planned abroad experiences that often included homestays and immersed students in the target culture (Hoffa, 2007). While these programs usually did not award academic credit, they did provide students with unique insights into other cultures. After the 1960s, more and more programs developed and included, for example, taking a year out before, during or after college for studying at a university abroad, studying abroad through a faculty-arranged exchange, attending a university abroad for doctoral research or degree studies, attending overseas programs designed for exchange students by different institutions, and traveling programs (Hoffa, 2007).

As already alluded to, programs have developed to adjust to the needs and wishes of the students and other stakeholders. The preferences of students for education abroad today include short-term programs; English as the medium of instruction; a location not far from the home country and preferably in large cities; a cohort of peers from the home country; and a familiar faculty leader (Hackney et al., 2012). Because employers are looking for employees with previous international experience (Norris & Gillespie, 2009), students are increasingly interested in finding international programs that fit their specific career needs.

Timing and Length of Education Abroad

There are three aspects of program design related to time: The ideal time for a student to participate in the program during their course of study; the length of the program; and the time in the academic calendar during which the program takes place. We have seen a diversification in all three areas.

Classmanship

In an effort to boost participation, and "considering that Study Abroad should be an on-going and integral educational tool targeted to all students, it is essential that students at all levels should have opportunities to participate in these programs" (Quraeshi, Luqmani, & Veeck, 2012, p. 86). Timing for education abroad has become much less prescribed and programs are thus attracting students throughout their college education.

Originally, education abroad was conceived as a full-year program taken when students reached junior status, the JYA. The timing of education abroad now greatly varies. Some students go on a gap year before enrolling in college such as for example the Congress-Bundestag programs. Some students participate in first-year seminars in the summer before they enter college or in their first year of college. These latter programs are typically through the institution in which the student is already enrolled. Students tend to have more flexibility in their schedule and greater willingness to participate in education abroad in their earlier years of study (Chieffo & Zipser, 2001). Education abroad has been found to influence academic and career trajectory (Dwyer, 2004), which means that an early education abroad experience can help students identify their scholastic goals in time to complete a major without undue delay. A by-product of students completing a first education abroad program early in their college career or even before, is an observed trend of students participating in multiple programs: A short-term faculty-led program in a familiar location first and then a longer more independent experience in a less familiar place. Short-term education abroad therefore serves as an entry point (Archangeli, 1999).

Participating in education abroad later in one's college career is of particular advantage to students with clear career goals. They can purposefully select an education abroad program specific to their discipline, one that possibly even offers research, service-learning, or internship experiences that prepare them for their careers. Going abroad during the senior year has the advantage that graduating students can remain in the host community for additional and extended work experience after the program while they await their degree to be processed. Some programs include a full-time internship after the study abroad component, which can be particularly attractive for graduating seniors. Other students launch from their education abroad to a graduate program abroad.

Length

Students today can select from a variety of program-lengths from a week to several years. Programs can be as short as one week, during which students may even visit several countries (James, 2018), or as long as two years.

There are benefits to short- and long-term programs, but they necessarily address different needs. The most notable differences between long-term and short-term program outcomes lie in relation to intercultural competence development/global-mindedness and language proficiency. Before drawing the conclusion, however, that long-term programs are more likely to result in these outcomes, one must acknowledge that short- and long-term programs may attract completely different student populations. There is a body of research that shows that students who are more open are more likely to participate in long-term programs (Bakalis, 2004; Salisbury et al., 2009; Zimmermann & Neyer, 2013). Thus, participants in long-term programs may be self-selected to seek and desire these outcomes, which can skew research results.

While there is some evidence to suggest that participants in long-term programs have the potential for greater learning gains, especially in regard to language proficiency and intercultural competence (Dwyer, 2004), these benefits are of no use to students with obligations or goals that make it impossible for them to participate in such programs (Blake-Campbell, 2014). The biggest advantage of short-term programs is that they are much easier to fit into a packed academic schedule and integrate with other life plans and responsibilities (Blake-Campbell, 2014; Castañeda & Zirger, 2011). Short-term programs are often able to recruit a more diverse student population (Blake-Campbell, 2014), thereby contributing on a bigger scale to a nation's overall global preparedness. Additionally, since research has shown that a previous experience abroad increases the willingness to participate in education abroad in the future (Brockington & Wiedenhoft, 2009; Ingram, 2005), short-term programs can serve as an excellent introduction and springboard for additional or more extensive programs. Furthermore, short-term programs give students the ability to complete several programs in different places (Allen & Dupuy, 2013).

Blake-Campbell concludes:

> the significant impact of short-term study abroad programs on varying levels cannot be discounted [...] although a short-term program has limitations, it is still a viable option and a catalyst for transformative learning to shape ideas of ethics, empathy, and engagement for the path to global citizenship.
>
> *(Blake-Campbell, 2014, p. 69)*

Short-term programs can have value if they are embedded in the curriculum or are part of a course and carefully designed to address specific issues (Hulstrand, 2015). Effective short-term programs facilitate a "stimulating, thought-provoking, experiential, outcomes-based curriculum in one or more subjects or disciplines designed for a specific cultural context" (Pasquarelli, 2018, p. 35).

Short-term programs have not only been perceived as less advantageous for developing global citizenship, language proficiency, and intercultural competence, but many have also received criticism for creating consumer rather than educational experiences (Kortegast & Kupo, 2017). There is some concern over the value of short-term faculty led programs of less than 4 weeks that are in some cases seen more as educational tourism than actual education abroad (Woolf, 2007). While short-term programs are perceived as efficient ways to develop an international perspective and global skills, Kortegast and Kupo (2017) argue that many short-term programs only offer participants cultural tourism that positions them as passive consumers of culture who purchase a cultural experience rather than allowing them to engage actively in other cultures through independent and facilitated experiences, things which lead to actual global competencies. They go on to argue that such short-term experiences reinforce power dynamics and privilege between cultures and a post-colonialist perspective. Furthermore, such short-term programs often do not engage learners in the critical self-reflection about their own values, identity, and role in the world that is necessary to develop global citizenship. It is therefore even more crucial in short-term programs to carefully design the curriculum and co-curriculum to create a community-engaged, ethical, and culturally and linguistically rich experience. One can find a list of such carefully designed programs in Crawford and Berquist (2020).

To conclude, short-term programs play an important role in education abroad, yet without careful consideration of design features they may not lead to the desired outcomes and could in fact negatively impact them. Yet the lessons we can learn from the effective program design modification in short-term programs to increase participation and diversify participation can inform efforts to change the program design of the JYA to meet the needs of today's students.

Academic Calendar

One of the challenges of education abroad is to find the right time for an education abroad program. Some scholarships and financial aid have restrictions. Furthermore, scheduling summer or semester programs can be a challenge in that the host institution's calendar may not align with that of the home institution. If the home institution has a long winter break, Chieffo and Zipser (2001) described the benefit of using it as the time for short-term education abroad. They also suggest aligning semester-long programs with the home not the host community's academic schedule. Goode (2008) described an institution which operates on trimesters and education abroad then again takes advantage of the winter and the summer break. MSU's semester-long program in Jena follows the German academic calendar for their summer semester and counts it as MSU's spring semester. The advantage of that system is that students can complete internships in January through March, where internship spots might be more readily available than in the summer. A disadvantage for aligning semester-long Spring semester programs or year-long programs with another educational calendar, is that students typically then have a shorter break between the end of their program abroad and the restart of the new school-year at home. This can have a further negative impact on the reintegration process for students. Yet, being in sync with the host community's academic calendar may positively contribute to the integration in the host community.

Destinations

There has been a diversification of destinations in which students can spend their time abroad, although English-speaking countries and Europe still remain the top destinations for education abroad. In the years since 1965 the top ten destinations for education abroad besides Western Europe initially included Mexico, Canada, Japan, Israel. More recently students have selected Australia, New Zealand, Mexico, Israel and China (Ogden, Soneson, & Weting, 2010). Within Western Europe, France and the UK have been the leading choices, but Germany has also been among the top five destinations across the decades.

There has been a small but steady increase in students selecting programs in Africa. The highest increase was seen in education abroad in South Africa and Ghana. Many Asian countries have also increased education abroad enrollments strongly in recent years including China, Japan, Thailand, and India. With the fall of the USSR, more students have shown interest in different Eastern European countries most notably the Czech Republic. Latin America has always attracted a large number of students for education abroad and remains a popular destination today. Mexico is the most-selected country in Latin America for US students. Less of an increase is seen in destinations in the Middle East due to the perception of political problems and instability, with the exception of Israel, which remains a top 10 destination (Ogden et al., 2010).

Programs in smaller cities often lead to greater integration of the students in the local community than programs in larger cities (Castañeda & Zirger, 2011). Smaller cities, however, can pose logistical challenges and are often less attractive to students. Once Theresa Schenker changed Yale's German summer program to an eight-week program in Germany, it became clear that an initial four-week stay in a smaller community (Jena) allows students to adjust to the culture and language in a manageable community before they go to a metropolitan area (Berlin). Furthermore, program leaders observed that the students' opportunities to use German are greater in a smaller town than in a cosmopolitan city.

The host community's cultural sensitivity, cultural values, and beliefs impact the experience for some, if not all students. How students perceive the host community and how they are perceived by the host community impacts interaction in quality and quantity (Allen & Dupuy, 2013). Host community members may not be interested in engaging with education abroad participants (L. Brown, 2009) possibly due to effort required in communicating with those from other cultures and possibly with lower proficiency, or due to negative views about the home cultures of the participants. Participants therefore may have a hard time finding contacts and meaningful interaction with the host community (Kinginger, 2004). Becoming a member of the host community is difficult and takes time (Goldoni, 2013; Trentman, 2013). The degree of host receptivity (e.g., how welcoming hosts are) can significantly impact the access that newcomers have to local practices; this, in turn, can affect intercultural attitudes participants acquire while living there and their willingness to engage with the community (Jackson, 2008). Similarly, the ethnoracial composition of the community and the gender roles it finds acceptable influence the experiences learners have and those they have access to. Racial bias, gender issues, and the community's particular view of education and goals of education abroad may prevent participant integration into the host community (Goldoni, 2013). On the other hand, in times of globalization participants and host community members may get the false impression that differences between their cultures are not so large (Brockington & Wiedenhoft, 2009).

The similarity of one's home culture to the host culture plays a role in learning outcomes, impacting some positively, others negatively. For example, a culturally closer context may reduce some of the stresses of living abroad, while a more different context may lead to more misunderstandings and missed opportunities. Where the dissimilarities are significant in gender expectations, acceptance of LGBTQ+, racial inclusion, and accommodation for people with disabilities and their acceptance and inclusion, program personnel and the prospective student need to work together to prepare for potential challenges. It is important that advisors and education abroad staff assist students in finding a suitable program and/or developing strategies for navigating the cultural context abroad. In some locations, certain behaviors and interests would be expected and allowed for men but not women, and vice versa; homosexuality is illegal or LGBTQ+ do not enjoy legal protection; discrimination against students of color is so prevalent that they may not feel welcome or even safe (Calhoon, Wildcat, Annett, Pierotti, & Griswold, 2003; Covington, 2017; McClure et al., 2010); students with disabilities (including mental health) may find the policies and practices unsupportive for their circumstances (Hameister, Matthews, Hosley, & Groff, 1999).

Thus, broad cultural discrimination, racism, sexism, homophobia, and a lack of infrastructure to support students with disabilities may render some destinations and contexts not suitable for students. Students of color, women, LGBTQ+, and students with disabilities have likely experienced discrimination also in their home country. However, the format of the discrimination and the strategies to address such discrimination varies by culture.

Selecting a destination for education abroad includes many considerations. Language skills, program goals, cultural differences, cost, safety, and political stability in the host community are only a few of the aspects that students have to think about before deciding on a location. Lack of language knowledge may be the largest barrier to studying in some of the non-traditional locations where residents only communicate in the host language(s) and English is not used as a lingua franca (Ogden et al., 2010). Cost factors, on the other hand can work in favor of lesser known locations because travel and accommodation may be cheaper.

As Hoffa and DePaul summarize:

the historical perspective of the traditional focus on Western Europe, in the eyes of many experts, has severely curtailed the capacity of study abroad to prepare students, and by extension the nation itself, for the global forces and realities that will shape life in this century.

(Hoffa & DePaul, 2010, p. 2)

In order to meet the needs of a diverse student body, a careful examination of current program destinations and development of appropriate programs in locations that allow students to reach their intended educational goals is an important task for education abroad providers and universities today.

Some believe that education abroad in less-commonly selected destinations "provides unique opportunities for students to pursue a variety of personal, academic, linguistic, and professional goals" (Ogden et al., 2010). Research has also found a positive connection between personal growth, program satisfaction and nontraditional destinations (Hutchins, 1996). Specifically, one study found higher satisfaction in destinations in Eastern Europe and Latin America (Cook, 2004). However, destination may determine who signs up for the program, which can skew the research results. Research also indicates that the development of global-mindedness may be affected by program location; the more culturally different the destination is from a student's home country, the more they may be able to gain (Douglas & Jones-Rikkers, 2001).

One of the reasons why students of color often shy away from participating in education abroad is because they do not find the destinations relevant to their identity and goals (Calhoon et al., 2003; McClure et al., 2010). As education diversifies both in terms of student population as well as disciplinary offerings, it is important that education abroad also expands to address the needs of those populations and disciplines. Selecting new destinations should be driven by academic concerns and not simply by the desire to offer programs in unique destinations (Woolf, 2007).

While great efforts have been made to diversify the portfolio of education abroad destinations, students are often still driven by geographical desires (Kortegast & Kupo, 2017). MSU recently restructured their Education Abroad Office to a disciplinary rather than a geographical focus to help students see the connection of education abroad to their academic goals rather than their travel and consumer goals. It seems reasonable to assume that participants would have greater academic gains, if their destination had expertise in their discipline either at the host institution or in companies/NGOs in the area, as in the program described by Moseley (2009). Even greater outcomes in academic achievement and employability seem possible, if the destination also provides access to undergraduate research and/or internships or other experiential learning (see also below; Moseley, 2009). Third party providers such as IES have also capitalized on highlighting the local resources as assets to a program and show the unique character of their programs over generic programs (e.g., the IES Freiburg program on Environmental Studies).

No matter how diverse the offerings are, students may still opt for the three-week program in London outside of their discipline over the one-semester program in their discipline in Namibia. Additionally, even if we can convince students to opt for the ideal destination for their situation and learning goals, we cannot guarantee their experiences in that community no matter how carefully it was selected.

Program Language and Linguistic Landscape

With the diversity of programs and the spread of English as a lingua franca, one can no longer assume that an education abroad program in Tokyo will fully immerse students in Japanese. To make education abroad more accessible to a wider variety of people, some programs require no language skills in the local language and may not even provide students with an opportunity to learn the host language(s) or engage in meaningful ways with the host culture. Immersive experiences have decreased and more programs are partially or completely administered and taught in English.

Program Language

Program design cannot control the actions of individuals nor control the context, but it can set the expectations and create parameters. One issue in research reports on education abroad is that these parameters and expectations are often not described, yet they likely have an impact on the outcomes. Programs can make several design decisions when it comes to questions such as:

- Does the program require a certain level of language proficiency in the language(s) of the host community for admission into the program?
- Does the program require that the students take additional language courses to reach a particular language proficiency level?
- Is language learning listed and/or intended as a program goal?
- What language do program staff use with the students?
- Is there a language pledge in which students make a commitment to speak only in the host language(s)?
- What is/are the language(s) of instruction in program courses?
- What is/are the language(s) used at the host institution?
- Are students living with locals?
- Are students provided with immersive experiences?

In every context abroad, there are high-stakes and low-stakes interactions. When language proficiency is low, it may be important to navigate high-stakes interactions in English. For example, one of our informants shared the importance of having access to counselors and health and wellness professionals who have experience with US culture and speak English at a high level. Even students with high language proficiency may need English-medium interactions in high stakes health and wellness situations and emergencies. Similarly, advising and some instruction may need to be in English or facilitated through English for students with lower language proficiencies in order to maximize their academic outcomes.

Linguistic Landscape

While the host community linguistic landscape is not a design feature of the program, the linguistic landscape must be considered in program design as it relates to the learning objectives of the program. When language and culture learning are at the center of education abroad, students have greater chances of being immersed in the language in destinations that do not use English as a lingua franca in addition to the local language (Kinginger, 2009b). Kinginger (2010) pointed out that several national and international political trends shaped the discourse about education abroad in favor of non-language focused programs. International trends such as the Bologna Declaration have led to an increase in English-medium courses at host institutions, which are attractive options for students with limited language skills in the local language. Kinginger (2010) argues that globalization, internationalization of education in host countries, and the increasing use of English as a lingua franca are hindering immersion in the target language for students. English media prevalence in certain countries as well as the presence of other exchange students or study abroad participants who speak English further complicate immersion (Lapkin, Hart, & Swain, 1995). Host community members may prefer to converse with learners in English (Trentman, 2013). Tight housing markets may mean that dorm rooms are preferentially given to international students, who may use English rather than the host language as the lingua franca.

While the dominance of English as a lingua franca has been viewed critical by many education abroad researchers and practitioners, we support here the position taken by Tullock and Ortega, who point out:

> Until now, study abroad has been conceived in monolingual terms. Study abroad participants have been imagined as monolingual classroom learners of a foreign language or of English with no experience using an L2 for meaningful communication. Study abroad contexts, too, have been imagined as monolithic learning settings filled with only target language input and only target language speakers with whom to interact. The target language is imagined to be a standard, literate variety of the dominant national majority language. And the L1 has been usually viewed as an avoidance strategy that constraints sojourners' opportunities to interact in the target language, and hence a danger to be averted because it would diminish opportunities to

improve their language skills. In our scoping of the qualitative studies, we have found glimpses that help debunk this monolingual habitus in study abroad research.

(Tullock & Ortega, 2017, p. 15)

They conclude later: "there is a dire need to acknowledge the multilingual realities of both sojourners and host contexts and to investigate the multilingual dynamics that shape language learning during stays abroad" (Tullock & Ortega, 2017, p. 19).

In addition to the presence of English, communities may also be using a different dialect than the one students learned in school, which can be especially challenging in languages such as Arabic or Chinese. Multilingual communities may require the students to be able to speak more than one of the local languages. Furthermore, the language used by host community members with education abroad participants may be unauthentic. Community members may use more teacher talk, when interacting with international students (Allen & Dupuy, 2013). Community members may also jump at the opportunity to practice their English skills (Trentman, 2013).

Maximizing Language Learning and Intercultural Competence

Especially for language learning and the development of intercultural competence/global-mindedness, it is often easier for students at sites in small towns to establish contact with the local community (Castañeda & Zirger, 2011). However, students prefer locations in big cities (Hackney et al., 2012). Participants in summer and other shorter programs often do not engage in many interactions with members of the host community (Hernández, 2016) and therefore cannot benefit from extended exposure to the host language(s). The review of research findings by DuFon and Churchill (2006) indicated that learner engagement with the host community is a key factor in language acquisition during education abroad. Programs can design components and activities that engage learners with more target community members or that improve the quality of such interactions.

As language educators, we hope that the local language(s) is/are always part of the learning goals as it is essential for relationship building across cultures (Brockington & Wiedenhoft, 2009). To allow learners to maximize language learning, a pre-departure proficiency in the intermediate range is advisable. Creating and facilitating interactions in the host language with sympathetic interlocutors are key in program design (Baker-Smemoe et al., 2014). Programs which require students to use the host language for a certain or the entire amount of time outside of class motivate students to engage in more host language conversations (Dewey, Bown, Baker, & Martinsen, 2014). Dewey and colleagues also found that a social network that includes speakers with high levels of English proficiency are more beneficial than speakers without those mutual language skills (Dewey et al., 2014). Furthermore, we must let go off the native speaker ideal and the idea that education abroad communities are monolingual (Tullock & Ortega, 2017), as they are typically multilingual communities in which English plays a role. Furthermore, we also must acknowledge that for some learners the host community language may actually be their first language or a heritage language. The linguistic background of the students as well as the linguistic landscape of the host community necessarily influences how to best support high quantity and quality host language interactions within and outside the classroom to support further language development.

In regard to intercultural competence, research suggests that intentional interactions in the host language(s) allow for a deeper understanding of the culture (Brockington & Wiedenhoft, 2009). Limited host language proficiency is likely to hinder participants from engaging in such deeper interactions. In those cases, participating in English-medium courses or internships or other activities facilitated in English may be the key for developing intercultural competence. We will go into more detail about how to effectively design programs for language learning in Chapter 3.2. and intercultural competence development in Chapter 3.3.

Program Types

As education abroad options have diversified so have the providers of such programs. We differentiate here between program providers that are independent of a university (e.g., IES, Fulbright) and those that are administered by a university (e.g., faculty-led, exchange programs, direct-enroll programs). Although these two types of providers differ in many respects, participants in either may or may not have access to host educational experiences (e.g., internships, courses at an educational institution).

Direct-Enroll Programs/Exchange Programs

Students who choose direct-enroll programs may select their own destination and host university and apply directly to the institutions like any transfer or international student. At times, direct-enroll programs are offered and facilitated through the home institution, which is the kind we will focus on here. In direct-enroll programs participants receive no or minimal support from their home institution and are integrated at the host university (Norris & Dwyer, 2005). Depending on the institution, direct enrollment involves a language test and sometimes only students with advanced proficiency are eligible to participate in regular university courses. At times, there might be additional restrictions on enrollment. Since these types of programs cannot really be designed by a home institution as much of the control over the experience is with the host institution, we will not focus on these programs in this book.

There is a little bit more control with exchange programs, since they are based on a collaboration between two institutions. Today, some colleges offer exchange programs in partnerships with schools abroad, for example bilateral exchange agreements in which a certain number of students from each institution attends the partner school for a summer, semester, or academic year (Poehling & Nair, 2003). The partnership between Connecticut (CT) and Baden Württemberg (BW), Germany, for example allows students from Germany to study at one of the nine participating institutions in CT while students from CT can attend one of the ten partner institutions in BW (UCONN, 2019). The partnership includes options for graduate students, teaching opportunities in CT, as well as short summer programs for students of all majors and language levels. Some programs offer joint degrees such as for example the German Studies doctoral program from the University of Arizona and the University of Leipzig.

The direct-enroll programs we focus on here are those where students are taking courses at a host university and are primarily supported by the host university, which has some sort of agreement with the home institution to allow for credit transfer. Students have reported being able to take regular courses with members of the host community as crucial to their language and intercultural development. Students in direct-enroll programs developed stronger relationships to peers in the host country (Hendrickson, 2016; Norris & Dwyer, 2005). They were also more likely than their peers in hybrid programs to remain in contact with friends from the host country after the end of their time abroad.

Due to the different academic cultures and potential language barriers, academic progress can be challenging for direct-enroll students. Without the assistance of a program staff, students may not be able to succeed in the host university courses. Faculty teaching at the host institution may not be properly trained to support international students and accommodate to their language learning needs (Garbati & Rothschild, 2016) and host institutions may not have a vested interest in supporting education abroad students (Hanouille & Leuner, 2001). This lack of support may have also be an issue during internships. Unfortunately, only 23% of students who had directly enrolled abroad and completed internships felt that internships abroad impacted their career. This may in part be due to the fact that students had no opportunity to reflect on negative experiences and miscommunications with a cultural facilitator (Norris & Dwyer, 2005).

The independence required for direct-enroll programs has both advantages and disadvantages. As discussed above, the disadvantage is the lack of support and the need for the student to process everything independently. However, direct-enroll participants became significantly more academically autonomous and showed significantly higher changes on Career Planning, (Lathrop, 1999).

Hanouille and Leuner (2001) argue that direct-enroll programs can be too demanding for students due to differences in the academic culture. Vande Berg

(2007) also says that only a limited number of students are independent and self-sufficient enough to excel in direct-enroll programs and benefit from them. Woolf (2007) stresses that students often need more support in navigating the new linguistic and cultural environment than a direct-enroll program provides. Direct-enroll programs are an excellent choice for independent students, who are ready to navigate a sink-or-swim situation. For other students choosing direct-enroll programs, more intensive preparations at home might be needed or online facilitation from home.

Hybrid Programs

Hybrid programs, which may be administered by a home institution, a consortium, or a third-party vendor, combine the option to take courses at a host institution with the support of more sheltered courses and in the case of the JYA typically also include a faculty leader from the home institution. Hybrid programs often include assistance in day-to-day matters, housing, safety, health, as well as excursions by the home university or a third-party provider. They offer courses specifically for education abroad students alongside classes available at the host university (Norris & Dwyer, 2005). Several of these education abroad programs, such as for example the AYF program and the semester program in Rome organized by Dartmouth (Convertini, 2019), include a faculty member on-site. Similarly, the semester-long program in Siena, run by AHA International, has a US faculty member from one of the consortium schools of the Northwest Council of Study Abroad (NCSA) on the ground with the students (Chambers & Chambers, 2008). There are a few alternative models, for example a semester-long program in Mexico without a faculty member present at all times, but with a faculty member visiting the program location three times throughout the semester to observe and supervise students (Currier, Omar, Talarczyk, & Diaz Guerrero, 2000).

A large-scale multi-year study of Georgetown's education abroad program outcomes showed that intercultural learning was stronger for students who took classes with other US students and/or international students in comparison to direct-enroll courses (Vande Berg, Connor-Linton, & Paige, 2009). One can speculate that individuals feel more comfortable engaging in cross-cultural interactions with other international and US students and that they have an opportunity to reflect and discuss the experiences with students facing similar challenges.

Having a faculty member from home available for assistance can help students adapt and adjust to the new linguistic environment and culture, can help create a sense of community for all participants (Convertini, 2019), and can make students feel more at ease. Lathrop (1999) found that students in the hybrid program developed more strongly in the areas of tolerance and salubrious lifestyle. A longitudinal study which investigated assessments of former participants of the impact of their education abroad experience showed that those who had been in a hybrid program more often found international careers in private industry (Norris & Dwyer, 2005). Additionally, participants in hybrid programs had more often completed an internship during their time abroad as well, and nearly half of those students felt that this had impacted their career choices, a more positive experience than the internship experience of those in direct-enroll programs. Norris and Dwyer (2005) suggest that the hybrid program model has longer-lasting career impacts on participants. This goes back to the notion that in hybrid programs, students can be supported when necessary and encouraged to be independent when ready, whereas a direct-enroll student has to develop these skills alone.

Faculty-Led and Island Programs

Faculty-led programs are often made up of exclusively home university staff. For example, MSU's summer education abroad program in Mayen, Germany, is led by a faculty director, who is supported by a Graduate Teaching Assistant, who teaches a language course. Yale's summer program in Berlin and Jena is led by a faculty member per location and supported by a grader for the courses. Faculty-led programs with intensive travel schedules may include several home institution faculty or staff to help with logistics and in the case of emergencies. The more staff is brought from home, the fewer the interactions with the host communities. More staff also often correlates with higher costs for the programs (Wang, Gault, Christ, & Diggin, 2016).

The popular so-called island programs have been viewed with concern by language educators and scholars. The increase in island programs abroad that include little interaction with the target community are hindering the development of language proficiency and intercultural competence (Kinginger, 2010; Pedersen, 2010). There are programs that do not focus on language development or intercultural competence as learning outcomes, but rather they focus on different academic skills or pre-professional experiences (e.g., clinical experience, research skills), and such programs may well work best in an island program format for those learning goals. Island programs are very similar to home-country instruction with faculty members taking their courses to the target country. As Hanouille and Leuner (2001) suggest, island programs can provide students "international flavor in a more digestible form" (p. 4). Island programs exist in varying lengths and can be tailored to the needs of specific student audiences (Hanouille & Leuner, 2001).

Woolf (2007) outlines several benefits of island programs: (a) They are designed for the specific needs of the students, (b) faculty can be innovative and flexible in curricular design, (c) they are independent of the host community's academic calendar and requirements, and (d) can be in more non-traditional locations as knowledge of the local language may not be necessary. Hanouille and Leuner (2001) point out additional benefits of island programs such as: (a) They bring the home institution prestige, (b) they are usually a financial gain for the home institution, (c) they are safe havens for students, (d) courses automatically

Housing

There are several housing options for students going abroad, all impacting the students' immersion in the target community. Students can stay in dormitories or in shared apartments with other international students or with native speakers (Muñoz & Llanes, 2014) or in host families. Some programs, especially very short ones, have students stay together as a group in hotels (Frisch, 1990), hostels or rented vacation homes (Sachau, Brasher, & Fee, 2010), motels, or convents (Haloburdo & Thompson, 1998), or guesthouses of the university abroad (Malewski, Sharma, & Phillion, 2012). These types of living arrangements offer limited opportunities for interacting with host community members but are convenient for students in programs without a language component. Programs of at least four weeks typically house students in host families or dorms. Programs shorter than four weeks usually take advantage of commercial accommodation (hotels, hostels, etc.). The more immersed the housing options are, the greater the chances of participant interaction in the host language and community. However, simply living with host community members is not sufficient to impact learning outcomes (Trentman, 2013).

Homestay

Allen et al. (2006) summarize research on homestay, which provides evidence for both the advantage of a homestay as well as a homestay myth. The homestay provides the opportunity to meaningfully engage with host community members for culture and language learning, however, in the final analysis it is up to the family members and the student to take advantage of those opportunities for the desired outcomes to ensue.

In general, students tend to report a positive experience in homestays (Di Silvio, Diao, & Donovan, 2016; Diao, 2016; Gutel, 2008; Schmidt-Rinehart & Knight, 2004; Spenader, 2011) though Di Silvio et al. (2016) found that satisfaction differed by language with learners of Spanish having more positive experiences than learners of Russian and Chinese during one-semester abroad programs. Students often report that they thought that the host family played a vital role in their language development (Di Silvio, Donovan, & Malone, 2014; DuFon & Churchill, 2006; Gutel, 2008; Hernández, 2010; Magnan & Back, 2007) and their intercultural development (Gutel, 2008). But students have also reported negative experiences (Allen, 2010; Kinginger, 2009b; Pellegrino Aveni, 2005; Wilkinson, 1998a). Wilkinson (1998b) analyzes the experience of seven women in a summer program in France and notes that they experienced many instances of cross-cultural misunderstandings, which not only led to frictions with members of the host community but also to the formation of negative stereotypes. In some cases the families are not as welcoming as students had hoped and do not provide many opportunities for language or cultural learning (Wilkinson, 1998a). Adult participants also can struggle with being integrated back into a family and family rules as they have been used to more independence, which then can lead to a struggle, which hinders the learning benefit of living with host families (Gutel, 2008). Several difficulties can occur in homestay placements and students have, for example, perceived a lack of effort of the hosts to include them in activities, limited conversation opportunities especially in small families (Knight & Schmidt, 2004), or lack of support for their language learning (Sharon, 1998). Furthermore, some students view host families more as a service provider, since they often get paid and the students pay, and judge their experience based on whether the host family met their service needs (Gutel, 2008). On the positive side, Castañeda and Zirger (2011) found that the students described host families not only as reasons for their positive language and culture learning in their own right, but also as providing them with access to even more people and diverse cultural and linguistic situations.

Despite some of the negative research observations and reports of negative experiences by students, the host families surveyed by Di Silvio and colleagues mostly reported that students integrated into the families, were eager to learn, were open, talkative, and engaged (Di Silvio et al., 2014). Furthermore, when surveying the families, Di Silvio et al. (2014) found a language difference in how comfortable the host families thought participants were in their families with Spanish-speaking families than the others. The hypothesis the researcher formed about these language differences was that closer cultural proximity leads to a more positive experience. We will provide more recommendations for host family housing situations in Part 3.

Dorms

Tight housing markets can make finding host families difficult. Furthermore, for semester- and year-long programs, in which students attend (at least in part) a host university, living in dorms connects them more quickly and efficiently with their (potential) peers. Communication with peers in the host language is an important element for fostering language learning (Dewey, 2008; Freed, Segalowitz, & Dewey, 2004). In the beginning of JYA programs, it was more common for students, especially female students, to live with host families. Today students are more often in dorms (Dwyer, 2004). Naturally, the people living in the dorms and the structure of the dorm varies from location to location and may even vary within one location.

Kinginger and Wu (2018) found that learners of Chinese stayed in dorms with native speakers and had many opportunities for practicing the host language with their roommates. The authors conclude that residence halls can provide a good language learning environment for education abroad participants. Similarly, Diao (2016) found that conversations in the dorms can help students acquire specific L2 functions, such as sentence-final particle usage. In our own analysis of social integration of our year-long education abroad participants, we found that students who had at least one other student from the program in the apartment or nearby typically had a stronger host community social network and felt more integrated than students who were the only student from the AYF program in the dorm. The hypothesis we formed was, that students feel more comfortable interacting with the flatmates when they have a familiar buddy with them.

In general, it is not so much where students live, but how their relationships in their housing situations develop over time and who the people are they are assigned to live with. Participants and host families or flatmates can be better prepared by the program and given tasks that support their relationship building (see Part 3).

Curriculum

The curriculum for an education abroad program is made up of many components. In some cases, education abroad programs take advantage of the offerings of host country institutions (Chieffo & Zipser, 2001), in others the curriculum has been designed exclusively for the program. Short-term programs often have one set of offerings with little variation for all students, whereas longer programs may have more varied curricula or educational opportunities for students. Curricula ideally include pre-departure as well as post-sojourn components and in-class as well as co-curricular learning opportunities such as field trips, excursions, service-learning, internships, ethnographic tasks, research, etc. The curriculum may be implemented in the language of the local community or in English or a mixture thereof. Well-designed programs are well integrated into the home institution's overall curriculum and allow participants to fulfill multiple requirements (e.g., language, general education, experiential learning, major specific).

In addition to the course offerings, some programs also offer co-curricular opportunities intended to support the students and their learning. Such opportunities may include extra tutoring, tandem partnerships, workshops, field trips and excursions, and gatherings to celebrate local and home holidays. Some programs also offer experiential learning, service learning, and/or internship opportunities to students (Castañeda & Zirger, 2011). Allen and Dupuy (2013) stress the importance of integrating in-class and outside of class activities and curricular and co-curricular components so that students see the value in each aspect of the education.

Disciplinary-Specific, Multi-disciplinary, and Interdisciplinary Program Designs

Education abroad programs can be discipline-focused, inter/trans-disciplinary or without disciplinary restrictions/multidisciplinary. Once students have chosen a major, many students have little flexibility as far as elective coursework is concerned. To attract these students to education abroad it is therefore necessary that programs are offered that closely relate to their major. For others, a disciplinary focus is not necessary. In any given year MSU offers approximately 30 programs in Germany. These programs range from a short-term German language and culture summer program to a multi-discipline year-long program and include disciplinary programs designed specifically for certain majors, such as Mechanical Engineering students at a Technical University in Germany or a faculty-led program on sustainability.

The change in disciplinary backgrounds of students has coincided with a diversification in targeted disciplinary programs. These more targeted programs are easier to integrate into the overall curriculum and are popular among students. The primary goal of such programs is often professional preparation and less (if at all) language and intercultural competence. We argue here that a program that responsibly engages with the host community, must have a focus on intercultural (communicative) competence. There is no question, that differentiating programs for the expectations of students in different fields has been an important step in increasing overall education abroad participation, but we can and must do better.

Business students, for example, seem to have more pragmatic interests and search for programs that specifically enhance their job prospects. They are also more concerned about graduating on time than non-business majors (Toncar, Reid, & Anderson, 2005). Programs specifically designed for business majors are a great way to attract this population to education abroad, even if the majority of these programs are short-term such as the month-long program in London organized by the University of Southern Mississippi (Black & Duhon, 2006). Many business-related education abroad programs include a short stay abroad with an experiential learning component that may involve corporate visits (Sroufe, Sivasubramaniam, Ramos, & Saiia, 2014), lectures from local businesses while abroad (Opengart, 2018), and research on the distinct political and economic situation in the target country (Shostya & Morreale, 2017). Two main barriers to education abroad for business majors are the available locations for their programs and the transferability of credits from courses abroad.

Turning now to Engineering students, Iowa State University allows any six-week program abroad to fulfill its International Perspectives requirement for engineering students (Chumbley, 2017). Another attempt at increasing enrollments of engineering students is to provide short, two-week immersion experiences during the first year of studies as a way to entice them to pursue longer education abroad options in later years, as done at the University of Pittsburgh (Olson & Lalley, 2012). Direct curricular integration of an education abroad experience, such as at Worcester Polytechnic Institute, can also increase students' participation significantly (Demetry & Vaz, 2017). At WPI, 50% of the junior class now participates in a two-month-long assignment in Thailand that fulfills an engineering project requirement.

Similarly to engineering and business, other pre-professional degrees such as nursing have also found that short-term programs with a significant experiential or clinical component are a good solution for their students. Only 30% of nursing schools offered education abroad programs in 2006 and most of them were short-term, though a few semester-long options existed (Currier et al., 2000; Haloburdo & Thompson, 1998). Nursing education abroad options included two- to six-week clinical immersion experiences in Central and South America (Caffrey, Neander, Markle, & Stewart, 2005; Walsh & DeJoseph, 2003), Africa (Anita & McKenry, 1999; Johanson, 2006; Tabi & Mukherjee, 2003), Europe, or the Caribbean (Anita & McKenry, 1999). Some programs are as short as nine days (L. Harrison & Malone, 2004) and others take place only during spring break (Evanson & Zust, 2004). These programs include targeted content for nursing students (Currier, Lucas, & Arnault, 2009).

Specific programs have also successfully been designed for students in education and for pre-service teachers. Education abroad programs can include a teaching practicum in another country, such as the six-week Ecuador immersion for TESOL teachers (Smolcic & Martin, 2018). Another example of programs designed for language teachers are the professional development language and culture immersion experiences funded by the New Zealand government for in-service teachers lasting from one month to one year (Corder, Roskvist, Harvey, & Stacey, 2018). Structured field experiences for teaching abroad exist through a number of third-party vendors including the Consortium for Overseas Teaching and the International Teacher Education Program (Cushner, 2009). The education abroad options including teacher training components take place in a variety of destinations including China (Parkhouse, Turner, Konle, & Rong, 2016), Central and South America (Cunningham, 2019; Malewski et al., 2012), Africa (Kulkarni & Hanley-Maxwell, 2015), and Europe (Marx & Moss, 2011). The majority of them are short-term (Cunningham, 2019); only some of the programs for teachers are a semester long (Doppen & Diki, 2017; Marx & Moss, 2011). Other major-specific programs exist for mathematics (Futamura & Marr, 2018), accounting (Meier & Smith, 2016), agriculture (Morgan & King, 2013), communications (Orbe & Orbe, 2018), social work (Cotten & Thompson, 2017), and others. The majority of major-specific education abroad options are short-term programs.

Disciplinary programs are optimal for students who are certain about their academic and professional goals and are on a tight schedule to complete their degree. For these students, disciplinary programs also help establish an international network of professional contacts (Moseley, 2009), especially if the program includes internships or research projects. These programs provide students with a multicultural perspective on their discipline, while allowing them to advance their degree and gain professional experience.

Interdisciplinary education abroad offerings are an effective way of combining language and culture study with coursework in other majors such as the STEM fields (Torralba, 2019). One example is a course developed at the University of Georgia that combines teacher education, social work, clothing/textile, history and other disciplines in their program in West Africa (Lowe, Dozier, Hunt-Hurst, & Smith, 2008). Several travel courses combine two or more disciplines, such as French and history (James, 2018), French and marketing (Berger & O'Neill, 2002), dietetics and hospitality management (Kuczmarski & Cole, 1999), or Spanish and biology (Gorka & Niesenbaum, 2001). Interdisciplinary programs often allow participants to double-dip in fulfilling requirements and they develop competencies in multiple disciplines, ideally viewing a topic through multiple disciplinary lenses.

As is the case with most discipline-specific programs, especially for pre-professional degrees, the majority of interdisciplinary education abroad programs are short-term and may include experiential learning opportunities for students. In many, more could be done to embed the program and the educational learning in the local community through culture and language learning. At the same time, long-term programs can learn from these short-term programs how to make education abroad more relevant for participants in reaching their professional goals.

Interdisciplinary programs in general allow students to work across disciplines and gain an appreciation of different fields of study (Torralba, 2019), foster critical thinking skills (Cai & Sankaran, 2015), foster an interest in interdisciplinary questions (Lewis & Niesenbaum, 2005), and explore more fields which can help participants to develop their academic and professional trajectory. While not necessarily interdisciplinary in nature, JYA programs allow students to explore multiple disciplines, often with more flexibility than their at-home curriculum.

Coursework

Coursework during education abroad can vary greatly and depends on the program type. In short-term programs students typically participate in courses taught in the host or the home language on a topic closely related to the faculty-leaders expertise. Students in semester- and year-long programs typically have access to language courses and other courses for international students as well as courses at the host institution. In JYA programs students can usually access courses at the host university as well as courses specifically designed for them. Students have access to courses at the university on a guest student status, which may come with enrollment restrictions. JYA programs often also offer their own sheltered immersion courses taught by the accompanying US professor and/or staff hired locally. One sign that higher education around the globe is attempting to attract international enrollments is that more and more courses at host universities are taught in English. Individual education abroad programs may permit, encourage, or forbid such courses. Each of these course types come with their own benefits and challenges and often it is the role of the director/program coordinator - in consultation with the student and the home university – to design an adequate course plan that takes into consideration the student's language ability, academic competence, and academic needs. The goal is typically to have courses transferable to the US home campus in a way that it helps the student make progress toward their degree.

Courses Taught in English

Courses taught in English have the advantage that students regardless of their host community language proficiency can make academic progress or such courses may serve to provide the necessary background knowledge to understand the host community (e.g., Moseley, 2009). Furthermore, if the courses are at the host institution, students can more easily mingle with host community members, since their initial contact in the classroom is mediated through (one of) their dominant language(s) and their language expertise might be a resource for their peers from the host community.

Language Courses and Sheltered Immersion Courses

Language courses are often part of programs that have language development as one of their goals. These courses are taught by home institution faculty or subcontracted, which allows for curricular control and language instruction tailored to the students' needs. They may also be local courses for international students. These have the advantage that program students can form international friendships. However, the instruction is less tailored to their needs in comparison to courses taught by home faculty or subcontracted courses.

Intercultural Training Courses

In addition to assistance with language, students need assistance dealing with the intercultural challenges they face. One way to address this need is to offer an intercultural course about how to participate in the community as well as how to deal effectively with students' likely emotional responses (culture shock, othering and stereotyping, reverse culture-shock) (Jackson, 2018).

Host University Courses

An education abroad experience can be significantly augmented by access to host university courses. The option is open to students who enroll directly or students who have access by virtue of their participation in an education abroad program. Success in direct-enroll courses requires a threshold level of language proficiency and cultural understanding, especially an understanding of the academic culture. Students may not be able to understand lectures in host language courses (Kuo,

2011) or be able to participate in seminars (Wright & Schartner, 2013). In order for students to be successful, they may need to be supported by tutors (Kim, Dewey, Baker-Smemoe, & Ring, 2015) or study groups organized by the program or the host institution's International Office. If available, it can be helpful for students to read the English version of a textbook (or a similar textbook), in addition to the version used in the course. When properly supported, even students with intermediate language skills can be successful in direct-enroll courses, though they may not benefit as much from the content knowledge development as students at an advanced proficiency or higher. In addition to making progress towards their degree and learning the field through the lens of another culture, students taking direct-enroll courses are also surrounded by peers from the community.

Hybrid Courses

Hybrid courses can come in a variety of forms. For example, MSU used to have a teaching internship in Germany. Students participated in an internship in Germany while enrolling in an online course at MSU supported by an MSU faculty member. Another hybrid model is when students start out the program with sheltered immersion or discipline specific courses taught by home faculty for the first portion of the semester and then attend courses at the host institution later in the semester (e.g., Moseley, 2009) or a course where the abroad component is just one element of a course that is otherwise taught on the home campus (Lewis & Niesenbaum, 2005). Yet another hybrid model is when students take a course at the host institution, but are supported by a recitation or tutoring session facilitated by their education abroad program.

Reflection and Awareness Raising

Education abroad researchers and practitioners have found that simply sending students abroad does not magically immerse them in the local language(s) and culture and lead to intercultural (communicative) competence. In reality, participants are limited in their development of intercultural competence and even language proficiency without critical analysis, reflection, and guided experiential learning activities (Dunkley, 2009). Some programs have developed reflective activities as part of the program or a course within the program. Based on her integration of the IDI in education abroad, Pedersen concludes:

> if intercultural effectiveness is a goal of study abroad, we need to do much more than send students abroad to study. We need to add intercultural effectiveness as a learning outcome for students in study abroad and develop curriculum (regardless of academic content) that incorporates opportunities for such learning and development in students.
>
> *(Pedersen, 2010, p. 77)*

Reflection can be done through blogging and microblogging, as suggested by Downey and Gray (2012). Some programs do not integrate reflection throughout the time abroad of students but require participants to write a reflection paper once they have returned (Root & Ngampornchai, 2013).

To maximize cultural and language learning, coursework and program activities should not only provide students with opportunities to engage with the host community, but also ask students to reflect on those interactions, especially cultural and linguistic practices. As Engle and Engle (2012) proclaimed: "we must go beyond immersion and intervene in ways that will allow [students] to make meaning out of the new cultural and linguistic interface that they experience" (p. 285). Blake-Campbell (2014) concurs that reflection, critical reflection, and critical self-reflection are key to reach education abroad learning goals. Most research has focused on reflection before and especially during abroad, but it is equally important after education abroad (Allison, Davis-Berman, & Berman, 2012).

Some programs include activities to raise awareness of cultural and linguistic phenomena. Various researchers concluded that difficult aspects of language such as pragmatics (Shively, 2010) or phonological development (Avello & Lara, 2014) as well as intercultural development (Dunkley, 2009) require explicit awareness-raising activities and reflection before and during the program. Cohen, Paige, Shively, Emert, and Hoff (2005) conclude that strategy training, awareness-raising and reflective practice are necessary for linguistic and cultural gains.

Immersive and Experiential Components

Optimizing immersion in the daily life of the host culture is central to the goals of some education abroad programs; for others it is of little or no importance. Immersion is essential, if language development and intercultural competence are part of the learning goals.

Experiential learning components have become integral parts of education abroad as the focus has shifted from language and culture learning to academic and professional development. Including experiential learning components can address several goals: Integration into the target community, resume building, developing subject knowledge through hands-on experience, and language acquisition in out-of-class contexts. Experiential components range from excursions and academically focused field trips to service learning, internships and research projects. Experiential learning can assist students "in translating classroom knowledge into meaningful learning for their future" (Qualters, 2010, p. 95) because it "closely links academics and student transformation" (Zamastil-Vondrova, 2005, p. 48).

As education program offerings have diversified, we have seen programs that include more immersive and experiential experiences (such as those described in Crawford & Berquist, 2020) than ever before. However, the general trend is toward those that have limited or no experiential learning opportunities or immersion in the local community (such as criticized in Kortegast & Kupo, 2017).

Immersive Course Requirements

Overall, the intensity and amount of immersive and experiential components of programs appears to be decreasing and programs are creating a US environment abroad rather than confronting participants with the local cultural context (Kinginger, 2010). Lack of immersive components, which is particularly common in island programs, has several negative consequences:

- Students no longer have to negotiate between their old and new self (Kinginger, 2010).
- Intercultural competence/global citizenry development suffer (Kehl & Morris, 2008) (Kinginger, 2010; More & Greenwood, 2019; Williams, 2005).
- Stereotypes are reinforced (Mora, Piñero, & Díaz, 2019).
- Home community viewpoints are fostered (Allen & Dupuy, 2013).
- Students are hindered in their adjustment to the new environment and development within it (Nguyen, Jefferies, & Rojas, 2018).

Research and practice reports have been summarizing immersive tasks that are required parts of education abroad programs or courses. For example, Goertler (2015) assigned students various language analysis tasks and tandem conversations as part of a course. For their ten-week education abroad program Archangeli (1999) required a project in which students would interview two native speakers. More information will be provided in Part 3.

Research Projects

Students often have to conduct research projects as part of their courses. However, some programs require the students to complete an overarching research paper or a research project might be the main or the only component of the education abroad programs. Integrating intercultural learning and cultural adjustment before going abroad by designing a research project which is then carried out while abroad and analyzed upon return can be an effective way to help students understand and make sense of their learning experience (Marx & Moss, 2015).

There are several general advantages of engaging in research components or programs abroad. For one, students gain valuable research experience and can often insert themselves into an international research network. Furthermore, there is often additional financial assistance for these projects. In the following, we will briefly explain several types of research abroad options.

Research guided by faculty from home institution: Some students conduct independent research abroad under the supervision of a faculty member from the home institution. Such research opportunities allow students to make targeted progress toward their academic and career goals.

Overarching research project as part of the education abroad experience: Another form of research abroad project is one connected to an education abroad program that includes field trips, excursions, and coursework where the project is the culmination of all those aspects. Moseley (2009) describes a program in South Africa, where students first take a short course on the region taught by the faculty leader and a partner professor from the host institution. The course is rich in co-curricular learning. After the course, students enroll in host institution courses and complete a research project related to the education abroad program themes in the region. Another example was provided by Vahlbusch (2003), from an education abroad program in Germany, where students engaged in a variety of activities to expand their classroom learning that ranged from researching government agencies, to investigating proposals to expand the local river. Their work included archival research, interacting with locals and agencies, interviewing, and presenting their analysis in class. Another example of the integration of experiential learning with coursework is a three-week course in Ghana for students from DePaul University (Tolliver, 2000). During their short stay, students meet community leaders and important representatives of nongovernmental organizations but also community members including priests/priestesses, healers, village chiefs and others. Another example is a media course in St. Petersburg, in which students produce their own documentary films during a six-week stay in Russia offered by the College of William and Mary (Prokhorov & Therkelsen, 2015). Research projects that are community-focused or community-based are a great way to focus on professional, cultural, and linguistic learning outcomes.

Joining a faculty member from home on an abroad research project: Faculty-led research projects abroad can be beneficial for both the faculty member and the student. MSU, for example, has an education abroad program in Greece, in which students work with a faculty member from MSU on archeological research. At times these studies might be focused on the faculty leader's expertise and thereby targeted in helping students advance their understanding in that particular discipline. On the other hand, students may also come from multiple disciplinary backgrounds, which then raises the profile of the research project to an interdisciplinary endeavor.

Joining a research team abroad: Other students may individually or as part of a program participate in research in a host research team. The advantage of such programs is that students are connected with an international community of scholars in their discipline, which likely will include peers from the host community. However, such projects might not always be an ideal match for the student's research interests.

Independent research abroad: Some students use available scholarships to independently conduct research abroad without any supervision from faculty at home or abroad. Such research is more common for graduate students, who have more refined research skills and research agendas.

Any undergraduate research experience undoubtedly develops students' research skills, even if the project is in a slightly different area. Moseley (2009) reports many of the advantages of research education abroad opportunities. For example, such opportunities allow faculty and student to form a closer professional relationship that is mutually beneficial. Often it allows students and faculty to expand their international professional network. As Moseley reports, and Senta Goertler has also experienced, such projects can lead to co-authored presentations and publications with students and/or members of the host community. Working in multinational teams also allows students to develop cultural skills. Any research project that is situated in the local community like those described by Moseley also contribute to deeper cultural understanding. Ethnographic research abroad is especially beneficial in helping students make sense out of misunderstandings and positively influence their language and cultural competence development (Jackson, 2006a, 2006b; Jurasek, Lamson, & O'Maley, 1996; Kinginger, 2009a). To maximize learning outcomes, we strongly encourage education abroad programs to include research tasks or projects before, during, and/or after education abroad that focus or are based in the community.

Field Trips, Excursions, and Travel Courses

Another form of experiential and immersive experiences are excursions and field trips. These trips are either part of an at-home course that only goes abroad for the excursion portion, or excursions as part of the general education abroad program abroad or a specific course abroad. Examples are a geography course in Costa Rica (Houser, Brannstrom, Quiring, & Lemmons, 2011), a sustainable tourism course in Costa Rica (Ritz, 2011), a culinary course in Italy (Dewald, Jimenez, & Self, 2016), or a sports management class in Australia (Fairley & Tyler, 2009). The AYF program regularly offers a German history course which includes an excursion to Berlin to visit historic and political sites and museums.

Learning outcomes have been reported as:

- Content knowledge development, comprehension, and retention (Houser et al., 2011).
- Closer connection to the professor (Houser et al., 2011).
- Connecting the real world to class learning (Houser et al., 2011; Ritz, 2011).
- Research skills (Robson, 2002).
- Challenge own beliefs (Ritz, 2011).
- Critical thinking skills (Ritz, 2011).

Many other benefits of these experiences are similar to education abroad in general such as: Personal development, and an appreciation and understanding of other cultures (Robson, 2002) and a changed worldview (Walsh & DeJoseph, 2003).

Another type of education abroad offering with an experiential learning component is comprised of so-called travel courses, which take students for a short period of time to one or more countries abroad. The content of these courses often deals with the histories, politics, economics or cultures of the regions that are visited. Travel courses exist for many different disciplines such as literature (Coby, 2016), languages, history (James, 2018), business (Ornstein & Nelson, 2006), culture (Berque & Chiba, 2017), nursing (Wros & Archer, 2010), biology (Zervanos & McLaughlin, 2003) and others. One such example is the course on The Arts of Medieval and Renaissance Britain offered at Massachusetts College of Liberal Arts, which culminates in a 11-day trip to Great Britain. Ritz (2011) describes a trip to Costa Rica incorporated in a sustainable tourism development course and summarizes emotional and social development as the main goals for the experience. Another example from a liberal arts college is a three-week course on Japanese culture that includes a two-week trip to Japan (Berque & Chiba, 2017). Travel courses can be used to enhance an existing on-campus course by providing students first-hand experiences in the community about which they learned in class.

Depending on the design, field trips, excursions, and travel courses are othering the communities and their cultural products and practices are presented as consumer goods, which reinforce assumptions about the people and their culture (Kortegast & Kupo, 2017): "These staged cultural experiences create a false sense of cultural interactions and cultural understanding" (p. 160). These superficial engagements do not always provide deep insights into a new culture, but rather highlight social and cultural capital from the home culture, i.e., students are presented with experiences and activities that are valued at home rather than those that the host community would want to share. Kortegast and Kupo (2017) present a list of questions that a program should ask itself during the planning and the implementation phases of a program in order to ensure a deeper cultural learning experience.

Service Learning/Community Engagement

Service-learning components or community-engagement projects can enrich an education abroad program more meaningfully by allowing students to work with the community directly (Torralba, 2019). Service-learning can be defined as a service to the community that is combined with reflective activities (Jacoby, 2015). It is traditionally assumed that service-learning should be tied to a credit-bearing course; however, recent research suggests that even without academic credit students will benefit from service-learning opportunities and deeply engage with them because these projects present personal and professional enrichment for participants (Anderson, Boyd, Marin, & McNamara, 2019). The importance of community-engaged projects in contrast to many service-learning projects is a reciprocal relationship between the program and the community. Lengths of service-learning and community-engagement projects can vary greatly.

To improve engagement with the community and gain disciplinary understanding, service-learning projects have become an important part of the educational landscape both at home and abroad. Service learning can take on many different shapes such as assistance in after-school programs or other community institutions or organizations (Kinginger, 2009b). The benefits of service learning are mostly connected to the immersion in the host community. Benefits to learners include:

- Positive impact on intercultural competence development (Brandauer & Hovmand, 2013; Brockington & Wiedenhoft, 2009; Mora et al., 2019; Vahlbusch, 2003).
- Understanding of the complexities of culture and cultural engagement (Jurasek et al., 1996).
- Positive effects on language skills (Brockington & Wiedenhoft, 2009; He & Qin, 2017; Hernández, 2016; Salgado-Robles & George, 2019; Vahlbusch, 2003; S.-L. Wu, 2017) including dialects and sociolects (C.-H. Wu, 2018).
- Increased contact with members of the host community (Ducate, 2009; Martinsen, Baker, Dewey, & Bown, 2010).
- Investment in the community (Vahlbusch, 2003).
- Higher-quality interactions with host community members (Martinsen et al., 2010).
- Authentic language use opportunities (Curtin, Martins, Schwartz-Barcott, DiMaria, & Ogando, 2013).
- Greater language confidence (Curtin et al., 2013).
- Expansion of the social network (Goldoni, 2013; Isabelli-García, 2006; Martinsen et al., 2010).
- Reflection and self-reflection (Jurasek et al., 1996).
- Improved analytical and problem-solving skills (Brockington & Wiedenhoft, 2009).
- Higher levels of civic competence (Vahlbusch, 2003), understanding issues of social justice and globalization (Evanson & Zust, 2004).
- Better understanding of career goals (Evanson & Zust, 2004).
- Development of practical experience in chosen field, if connected (Byker & Putnam, 2018; Malewski et al., 2012; Sharma & Phillion, 2019).

An example of a service-learning project is described by Sachau et al (2010), which took students from Minnesota State University to South Africa where they worked in construction projects at a campus for ten days and then traveled for six days. Students engaged in fundraising activities before their trip as well as class-work that covered relevant readings to prepare their time abroad. The authors conclude that in spite of the short time abroad, the experience had increased students' knowledge and impacted their attitudes and future travel plans. The danger of such projects is that it could cause harm to the community, for example because the participants may not have the necessary skills to perform these tasks.

The danger of service-learning projects is that they can turn into voluntourism that does more harm to the community than good from poor or unskilled service (Chapman, 2016) to othering and discriminating the local community to perpetuating power structures and racism (Kortegast & Kupo, 2017). Hence, MSU has developed a framework for service-learning and outreach that focuses on community engagement, used both at home and abroad.

In their history of community engagement at MSU, Fear and McKnight Casey summarize the four guiding principles:

> Reciprocal relationship with community-based partners will characterize MSU's work. Community voice and expertise will be recognized and respected. Students will be educated about the reasons that led to establishing the partnership and why the effort is important from a community point of view. Benefits will be bidirectional and balanced – for the community and for the university.
>
> *(Fear & McKnight Casey, 2020, p. 5)*

Berquist and Milano (2020) contrast service-learning as a one-way process whereas community engagement as a two-way process.

An example of a community-engagement project that focuses on ethical and reciprocal service learning is the community-partnership and civic engagement education abroad program from MSU's Residential College of Arts and Humanities in Costa Rica on "Ethics in Tourism and Sustainable Development" (Delgado & Yoder, 2020). Students live with families, take Spanish classes and courses on ethics and civil engagement. After four weeks, students go in smaller teams to smaller communities to work with community organizations in rural areas.

Design features of service learning/community-engagement projects and the duration can have a significant impact on the learning outcomes of students and the impact on the host community. Short and one-way programs may not truly help participants understand the intricacies and complexities of the issue being studied in the host community.

Work and Internships

While abroad, students may also engage in independent or program-sponsored experiences such as part-time jobs or paid or unpaid internships within the restrictions of the local context. About a third of the AYF program participants for at least part of the year work in part-time jobs. They do so for a variety of reasons: Income, connection to host community, or work experience to name just a few. Abroad students increasingly also engage in internships either organized by themselves or through their program. Internships may not be supervised by the home institution and may not result in credits, or they might be supervised by a professor at the home institution remotely or be integrated into an existing education abroad program. Several third-party vendors and some universities also offer education abroad opportunities that consist primarily of an internship, possibly with a language course requirement.

Internships in contrast to service-learning or community-engagement projects tend to be longer and/or completed as individuals rather than in groups. Internships can be completed as part of a program, for example AYF students have the opportunity to complete an internship during their second semester, or can be the education abroad program such as for example the Berlin internship program offered through the College of Arts and Letters at MSU. Internships offered through the home institution typically provide credit to the students, whereas students organize international internships on their own or through a non-home-institution approved third-party provider might not count towards credits at the home institution. Internships can provide students with an opportunity to integrate more strongly into the target community and acquire valuable skills for their field and future careers. It is also a chance for them to try out career paths and explore their own interests (Vahlbusch, 2003). Regardless of the destination of an internship, they might be conducted in English or in a local language or a mixture thereof. Steeves (2006), for example, reported on an English-medium journalism internship in Ghana. The AYF program offers English and German internships. A recent participant with interest and experience in political leadership, completed an internship in the sustainability office in City Hall, where she helped prepare community events and prepare grant applications.

Work, service-learning, and internships increase contact with the host community (Ducate, 2009) and can have a positive influence on language learning (Davidson & Lekic, 2012; Hernández, 2016; Vahlbusch, 2003; S.-L. Wu, 2017). Yet some internships are conducted in English (Kurasawa & Nagatomi, 2006) and therefore do not necessarily have such results. Regardless, internships expand the social network of participants and can therefore contribute to language and cultural learning (Goldoni, 2013; Isabelli-Garcia, 2006; Martinsen et al., 2010).

If selected and designed carefully, internships can provide students with opportunities to improve their language skills, especially discipline specific language skills (DeWinter, 2007; S.-L. Wu, 2017). N. A. Brown (2014) emphasizes the positive effects internship placements can have on language skills, especially if they are embedded in coursework and include reflection.

Experiential learning components are increasingly important to students as they try to be efficient and effective in their pathway through college towards a career. Furthermore, when designed well, these components greatly enhance the learning outcomes of education abroad in comparison to a simple study abroad.

Curricular Integration

Education abroad is integrated differently at different institutions. Some institutions require education abroad across campus or for certain majors (Bathurst &

Brack, 2012), others do not require it at all. Even in majors or schools that require education abroad, integration with the curriculum is often lacking. According to Butler (2019), participants need to be supported and such support needs to be integrated before, during and after education abroad and needs to extend "beyond academic content, culture, and logistics to information and tools that benefit knowledge and identity development" (p. 146).

As programs have become more diverse, preparing students for their education abroad experience has become more crucial since there is no one-size-fits-all preparation program, yet it is often done briefly with a focus on risk management issues or organizational matters. Some programs have begun implementing more expansive pre-departure orientations through workshops (Lou & Bosley, 2012) or several orientation sessions (Bai, Larimer, & Riner, 2016) focused on issues such as global citizenship and challenges (Blake-Campbell, 2014). Other universities offer preparatory semester-long courses prior to a semester or year abroad (Goldstein, 2017). Yet other programs today include credit-bearing intensive intercultural training before and after the student has been abroad, workshop series, culture assignments, re-entry workshops, online courses or support as well as research projects related to the sojourn prior, during, and after the abroad experiences. Outcomes of these interventions will be discussed in Part 2 of this book and best practices will be summarized in Part 3.

During the time abroad, online journaling and peer feedback can be ways to support student learning, as summarized in a study by Gabaudan (2016). In the absence of on-site directors who can assist students in navigating their time abroad, Wu (2017) outlines a model of self-analysis and oral reports combined with Skype conferences to support individuals studying abroad on their own.

Some institutions have recognized that participants need more support post-sojourn to encourage continued learning, to apply their new knowledge, and reflect on and unpack the experience. Students often struggle with a host of emotional challenges upon their return (Gaw, 2000; Wielkiewicz & Turkowski, 2010). Re-entry workshops with reflection opportunities can help students orient themselves after a stay abroad. Post-return social events in person or online provide the social support for students. Another option is to organize focus groups in which returning students can share their experiences and discuss difficulties of readjusting to life back home together (Wielkiewicz & Turkowski, 2010). While research has suggested the importance of actual coursework to prevent attrition of learning outcomes and to reintegrate students back into the host institution, there are few programs that require such coursework and it typically comes in the form of a capstone. Jackson (2018) developed and outlined a post-return course "Intercultural communication and engagement abroad" which helped students during their return. Unfortunately, from our experience many students realize too late that they need support for their re-entry and even when made available, students often do not take advantage of the offerings.

University added other US institutions as partners to the JYF program. In 1996, as a result of Wayne State University's withdrawal from the program – it still offers its Junior Year in Munich – the JYF was reconfigured by some of the partners as the Academic Year in Freiburg and is now run out of the University of Wisconsin with consortium partners MSU, the University of Iowa, and the University of Michigan. To this day the program is still led by a faculty member from one of the participating institutions on an annually rotating basis, who is supported by a per-manent in-country Program Director, student workers, and local instructors hired on a course-by-course basis. It is also important to note that the program is actually based on an exchange agreement between the Albert-Ludwigs-Universität and the AYF consortium partners. This story already points to a few factors that helped the program succeed: (1) Bringing partners on board; (2) structuring the program as an exchange program; and (3) changing the name to a more inclusive label. AYF has space for 60 participants per year, maintained an average of 40.5 students per year after the change in 1996, and has averaged 31 students over the last five years. The biggest drop in participation came after the financial crisis in 2008, from an average of 47.5 participants to just 32. In Spring 2020 AYF was moved to a remote format and in Fall 2020 AYF was suspended due to the global pandemic.

AYF today still shares many of the features and components of an early JYA program. AYF students live in dorms at the host institution, although the host family option is no longer available. Students still take a mixture of classes that can be divided into the following categories: (1) Specialized language courses for AYF participants only, subcontracted to a third-party vendor; (2) sheltered immersion courses open only to AYF students taught by instructors hired by AYF; (3) courses for international students offered at the university's German as a Foreign Language Center; (4) regular university courses (some of which are taught in English and some in German); and (5) regular courses offered at the University of Education (some of which are taught in English and some in German). Depending on the students' language proficiency, their academic apti-tude, and their goals and credit needs, the Director of Academics advises them on an appropriate combination of courses. In the past, the program also included Teaching Assistants from the home institutions, a wonderful opportunity for graduate students. However, that position has been eliminated due to budgetary concerns after enrollments declined.

Looking at the AYF program and its development since the 1960s shows an expan-sion and a stronger integration with the host institution through greater course access and the elimination of the host family option. Moreover, there was a modification of the grand tour component (i.e., many expensive group-only excursions) to an immer-sive component which includes outreach activities, experiential learning opportunities, excursions tied to courses, and field trips to discover the region with alumni, locals, and sponsors. Lastly, the program expanded from simply offering study abroad to also offering outreach volunteer opportunities, work-study options, and internships. All of these changes in addition to the already mentioned structural changes allowed to keep program costs low and to integrate more and more resume-building activities while simultaneously better integrating the students into the local community.

Program Staffing

The traditional JYA has its own program staff as well as program support staff at home. A program typically includes a director (e.g., in the past often referred to as Resident Director or Director in Residence), an administrative staff person, and none to some administrative support staff, and none to some local instructors in the host community. The director position typically rotates every year or every few years. The director typically has a main appointment at the home institution and oversees the program on the ground and serves as Dean of Students and academic advisor. They may also teach a course. The administrative staff person or program manager is typically a person hired locally long-term who manages the day-to-day operations of the program. The two may be supported by student workers or other staff. Larger programs also subcontract local instructors for sheltered immersion courses only open to the students in the program.

Junior Year Abroad versus Other Year-Long Programs

There are a few key elements that separate the JYA from some or all other year-long abroad experiences for US undergraduates:

1. JYA are organized and supported by a US institution.
2. They have local and home university staff at the host site.
3. All arrangements are made by the program (e.g., visa, housing, enrollment, transcripts, health insurance, etc.).
4. Credits are guaranteed to transfer to the organizing US institution.
5. Students can select from different types of courses to accommodate different academic and linguistic needs and goals.
6. Co-curricular and curricular activities are especially designed for the student population.
7. Efforts are made to keep costs as low as possible given the support system and efforts are made to keep them the same as at-home costs and/or transfer credit costs for direct-enroll programs.
8. There are often agreements between educational institutions that form the structure for these programs, which means that both institutions contribute with personnel and financially.

The Junior Year Abroad Advantage

The justification for JYA constitutes two questions: (1) Why should one participate in a year-long abroad experience? And (2) why should one participate in a

JYA rather than one of the other year-long options? While the JYA is not necessarily superior to all other year-long options, it presents distinct advantages for students because their learning outcomes can be more effectively impacted through targeted interventions, program design, and control over staffing. Depending on students' goals and circumstances, the JYA may not be the best or most appropriate choice.

Typically, language learning and intercultural competence development are more advanced with longer stays (Behrnd & Porzelt, 2011; Dwyer, 2004). The most important argument that comes from our students is that they often need the entire first semester to get settled, and then can use the second semester to enjoy the experience, truly take advantage of opportunities, and learn from their mistakes from the first semester. The strongest argument for us is that we have never had a returning student tell us, that they wish they had gone shorter, but we often have students tell us that they wish they had gone longer, even if they already participated in a year-long program.

The Future of the Junior Year Abroad

It is unlikely that JYA will regain the market share in education abroad it held in the 1960s. As early as 1970, Schwaneger (1970) predicted that the period of expansion of the JYA was at an end, and especially smaller colleges would be unable to sustain their JYA offerings, and we expect this to be the case going forward. In order to increase the market share, JYAs have to diversify and modernize their offerings and provide more access for a broader audience. We will discuss these best practices in Part 3.

Chapter 1.5. Challenges to Education Abroad

Perceptions of Education Abroad

In spite of the low percentage of US students who chooses to study abroad for a semester or academic year today, most students perceive education abroad as a valuable experience (American Council on Education, 2008) through which they may enhance their education, experience new cultures, and increase job skills and marketability (Curtis & Ledgerwood, 2018; Roy, 2014). Students also regard time abroad as a fun experience that can be beneficial and practical for them (Albers-Miller, Prenshaw, & Straughan, 1999) and help them gain self-confidence (Beverly et al., 2016). Thus, overall, students appreciate and realize the potential positive outcomes of an education abroad on their personal, academic, social, emotional, and career development. Nonetheless, policy makers, institutions, advisors, and faculty often do not value and emphasize the importance of an education abroad enough. More students indicate wanting to go abroad, than end up going. Unfortunately, while in theory education abroad is seen as important, it is still marginalized in many educational policies (Gore, 2005) and remains on the periphery for most universities and consequently students (Nolan, 2009).

Throughout the history of education abroad in the US, female students have chosen to go abroad in much higher numbers than male students (Gore, 2005; Twombly et al., 2012). Similar patterns have emerged in an analysis of participants in the European ERASMUS study abroad programs (Böttcher et al., 2016). Kinginger (2010) hypothesizes that high female participation leads to education abroad not being considered academically rigorous, but rather a "decorative add-on to the education of elite women" (p. 219). Nonetheless, motivating factors for students as well as barriers to education abroad often do not differ significantly by gender (Lindsay, 2014; Shirley, 2006).

More than half of the students entering college (55%) express interest in education abroad but the actual percentage of those going abroad is small. Nolan (2009) argues that "students in most of our universities enter a learning environment in which international study is neither valued nor encouraged" (p. 271). Increasing student participation in education abroad, therefore, has to begin with changing the attitudes of faculty toward such experiences and in order to achieve that institutional changes have to take place, the curriculum has to be internationalized, and language learning needs to have a firmer place in the educational journey of students (Nolan, 2009).

Reasons for Education Abroad

There are many motivations for participating in education abroad. Those of prospective participants include:

- Seeking to improve their language skills (Douglass, 2007; Sánchez, Fornerino, & Zhang, 2006).
- Wanting to broaden their horizon and visit a specific place (De Jong, Schnusenberg, & Goel, 2010; Nyaupane, Paris, & Teye, 2010).
- Building friendships and finding opportunities for personal development (Badstübner & Ecke, 2009; Toncar et al., 2005).
- Expanding their academic knowledge (De Jong et al., 2010; Nyaupane et al., 2010).
- Increasing their job prospects (Curtis & Ledgerwood, 2018; Teichler & Steube, 1991).

Student motivations for choosing education abroad are varied and individual. Their interest and their actual participation can depend on:

- Their perceptions of education abroad programs (Bandyopadhyay & Bandyopadhyay, 2015).
- Perceptions of personal and professional benefits (Hackney et al., 2012).
- Academic relevance (Albers-Miller et al., 1999).
- Program duration (Bandyopadhyay & Bandyopadhyay, 2015).
- Program cost (Bandyopadhyay & Bandyopadhyay, 2015).
- Program destination (Albers-Miller et al., 1999).
- Demographic factors (Bandyopadhyay & Bandyopadhyay, 2015).
- Self-efficacy and intrinsic motivation (Hackney et al., 2012).
- Friends or family with international experience or previous international experience themselves (Hackney et al., 2012).
- Their own intercultural awareness (Bandyopadhyay & Bandyopadhyay, 2015) and ethnocentrism (R. I. Kim & Goldstein, 2005).
- Their language proficiency (Hackney et al., 2012).
- An interest in new experiences and travel (Jacobone & Moro, 2015).

When analyzing student motivations for studying abroad, identifying factors that prevent them from considering or participating in education abroad programs can also help program designers to better understand the needs of students and design programs to meet their needs.

Barriers to Participation in Education Abroad

Given the interest in education abroad and the low actual participation, there are obvious barriers that prevent students from participating in education abroad or what makes it more challenging. It is important to note that some of those challenges are based on misinformation and it is the responsibility of program stakeholders to actively work on dismantling such misconceptions.

Financial Challenges

Cost is the main deterrent to education abroad (Doyle et al., 2010; Naffziger, Bott, & Mueller, 2010; Walker, 2015; Warnick, Call, & Davies, 2018). This includes high program costs and lack of financial aid options (Kasravi, 2009; McKinley, 2014; Vernon, Moos, & Loncarich, 2017). A lack of information and knowledge about existing programs and funding options deters some students from choosing a program (Albers-Miller et al., 1999). Not surprisingly, students with lower socioeconomic backgrounds are less likely to participate in education abroad (Lörz, Netz, & Quast, 2016). Given that cost is the most frequently cited concern, it is no surprise that Peterson's (2003) analysis of roughly 250 student responses from a large state university revealed that scholarship and financial aid options was the most frequently mentioned information needed by students to make a decision about education abroad. Thus, raising awareness of the available financing options is one major step toward increasing participation in education abroad.

From our experience as practitioners, these financial concerns are often ill-founded since student loans and scholarships tend to apply to education abroad experience and additional scholarships specifically for education abroad are available. The misinformation and incorrect assumptions can at times be traced to parents or advisors. That being said, while education abroad should be affordable for all students (Rai, 2019), many programs are expensive and costs are increasing in connection with a general increase of higher education costs in the US in recent decades. It should be the goal of programs to focus financial expenditures on the core missions and goals of the program.

It was not until 1965 that financial aid for education abroad became available for US students (Hoffa, 2007). The Higher Education Act (HEA) of 1992 played an important role in the development of education abroad programs because it made it possible for students to receive financial aid for pre-approved programs in addition to providing the option to receive other types of loans and grants. Today, universities are required to allow financial aid recipients to use the money for education abroad programs (Rai, 2019).

In their comparison of increases of education abroad costs and higher education costs, Cressey and Stubbs (2010) noted that between 1976 and 2007 study abroad prices increased more slowly than overall higher education costs. Their analysis also revealed that for the period under investigation education abroad costs were higher than the equivalent time at a public university but were similar to the costs at private universities. Increasing costs of education abroad are also related to a demand for more services during education abroad such as trips and activities. Program administrators are faced with the balancing act of continuing to appeal to the largest number of students while not pricing those very students out of the market. Furthermore, many programs offer credit at the home institution where program fees cover the cost of those credits by charging home institution prices for them. Thus, the education abroad program costs are directly influenced by increases in tuition at home.

Today students can choose from a variety of financial aid, student loan, scholarship and grant options to finance their choice of abroad program. The US Congress funds some national scholarships, many institutions have created their own scholarships from donations or semester fees, and third-party providers also offer scholarships to attract students to their programs (Cressey & Stubbs, 2010). Additionally, prospective students launching crowd-fundraising has become more common and acceptable. The overall availability of scholarships is still small and more needs to be done to support students financially in education abroad, especially for enriching activities such as unpaid internships.

Fears and Concerns

In addition to financial concerns, there are many fear-based obstacles to education abroad (Quraeshi et al., 2012). Some of them are very valid concerns or fears, others might be based on misconceptions. Furthermore, some of the fears can be addressed through education and preparation and others do not have a simple solution. It is the program's responsibility to assist students in making an informed risk-assessment before they sign up for a program. Concerns include fear of navigating a new place and travel (Amani & Kim, 2018), fear of the unknown (Naffziger et al., 2010), being away from family and the support network, being inadequately prepared, experiencing negative academic consequences, concerns about their well-being in a culture which may have different perspectives and cultural norms surrounding ethnicity, sexuality, gender identity, and equality (Bryant & Soria, 2015).

In addition to these worries, there are some significant health and safety concerns. Especially students from underrepresented groups have safety concerns (Vernon et al., 2017). Minoritized students, for example, may feel uncomfortable in other cultures where they are the only person of color and may worry about racism (Dessoff, 2006; Murray Brux & Fry, 2010; Willis, 2015), and women may be anxious about living in countries with different gender roles and they may experience or perceive more sexism than at home (Rawlins, 2012; Talburt & Stewart, 1999). Similarly, LGBTQ+ participants may not feel safe in countries that openly harass and prosecute people for their sexual orientation and/or gender identity. It is important for programs to provide facts to prospective students about dangers based on identity markers.

Students with disabilities also often have legitimate health and safety concerns. According to a report by the American College Health Association (2018), over 31% of students reported having a disability such as a learning disability, blindness, speech disorder, or a psychiatric condition. Over 30% of students further reported having been diagnosed or treated for one or more mental health conditions in the previous twelve months. Participating in education abroad, especially semester- and year-long programs presents additional and unique challenges for students with disabilities (Dessoff, 2006). Certain locations may simply be inaccessible to students with restricted mobility, for example. Lack of information about the suitability of programs and the lack of assistance with services (Matthews, Hameister, & Hosley, 1998) have been the strongest deterrents to education abroad participation unique to students with disabilities. Students with intellectual disabilities encounter different barriers, which may range from difficulties with reading maps and problems navigating a different transportation system to time management and problem solving (Prohn, Kelley, & Westling, 2016). It is not surprising that students with disabilities remain underrepresented in education abroad (Hameister, Mathews, Hosley, & Groff, 1999; Institute of International Education, 2019c; Johnstone & Edwards, 2019; Scheib & Mitchell, 2008) especially those with mobile disabilities (MIUSA, 2018).

A large number of college students nowadays struggle with their mental health at one point or another during their education. This should not be a deterrent to education abroad participation. In fact, a study of US college students' mental health self-assessment before, during, and after study abroad, showed that the mental health of the 619 survey respondents was better while abroad than before and after (Bathke & Kim, 2016). Students who struggle with mental health issues do not always report these problems. Educators should encourage students to discuss any mental health concerns both before, during, and after education abroad with appropriate program personnel. If program staffing allows, it can be advantageous if that information is shared only with one program personnel not directly involved with their academic progress or made anonymously via the appropriate personnel at the home institution, so that privacy can be protected.

Depending on the country to which students are traveling, other specific health and safety concerns might play a role, including weather related worries or concerns over clean food and water (Hartjes, Baumann, & Henriques, 2009). Other health problems, including food allergies and dietary restrictions, can also prevent students from considering education abroad programs. However, with proper planning and preparation, students do not have to miss out on the unique learning experience of living and studying in another country (Hope, 2017).

Other general concerns about health and safety are often related to terrorism, political unrest, natural disasters, epidemics, and crime. Recent terrorist attacks in Europe, have raised parent and guardian's concerns about safety (Gleye, 2017) and the current pandemic likely is also increasing fears as our survey respondents suggested. Although it may seem that issues surrounding safety abroad remain a challenge that education abroad programs can do little about beforehand (Wanner, 2009), pre-departure orientations and trainings, including risk management courses, can raise awareness of potential challenges and security issues and teach strategies how to handle them successfully. Having a faculty member from home abroad with students can help to assuage students' and parents' concerns about safety (Rai, 2019). It is the program leaders' responsibility to educate prospective students, so that they can make informed choices before, during, and after education abroad.

Academic Obstacles

Academic obstacles also prevent students from participating, whether those are real or just perceived. In our recruiting efforts for AYF the most often expressed concern is that students do not feel that they will have time in their curriculum to participate. At times they were told this by their advisor and other times they assumed so simply by looking at their degree navigation tools online. Such concerns include:

- Concerns over graduating on time (Warnick et al., 2018).
- Concerns about transferring credits (J. Parkinson & Musgrave, 2014; Stern, 2004).
- Worries over effects on academic performance or GPA (Vernon et al., 2017).
- Curricular constraints and timing issues (McKinley, 2014; Murray Brux & Fry, 2010; Stern, 2004).
- Specific majors may come with their own deterrents to education abroad:

  a   Sports management majors, for example, list missing out on events on campus (Jenny, Almond, Chung, & Rademaker, 2019).
  b   For nursing students, lack of language skills was at the top of the list of barriers (Kelleher, FitzGerald, & Hegarty, 2016).
  c   STEM majors have a high number of required courses and universities are reluctant to counting courses taken abroad (Wainwright, Ram, Teodorescu, & Tottenham, 2009).
  d   Pre-professional degrees often have the expectation that students move through the program as cohorts, which allows for little flexibility to integrate education abroad.

These academic concerns lead students to shorter programs (Garver & Divine, 2007) and those more directly connected to their home university. Delays in graduation can have temporal (time to degree), financial (additional tuition expenses), and social (not graduating with cohort) consequences. Some of these delays can be prevented by planning for education abroad early and re-arranging the generic yearly model schedules accordingly in consultation with advisors. Some delays in graduation are simply a matter of delays in paperwork and programs might be able to find solutions.

According to Marcum (2001), when education abroad is integrated into the curriculum, it will not prevent students from graduating on time. Close collaboration among partners across campus is crucial in order to create mechanisms for opening up the curriculum and ensuring reliable and speedy credit transfer from the

Chapter 1.6. Outlook

Purpose of this Book

As stated in the beginning, in this book, we aim to: (1) Make an argument for education abroad, especially long-term education abroad; (2) identify ways to maximize learning outcomes for education abroad through program design; (3) identify strategies for diversifying and increasing education abroad, and (4) define strategies to invigorate JYA programs and adapt them to the needs of today's students.

Current Situation

To summarize, education abroad participation is increasing. However, the former staple of education abroad, the JYA, along with other long-term education abroad programs are steadily decreasing. Education abroad participants are more diverse (e.g., in regard to majors and ethnicity) than they were thanks to more appropriate programs and options (Stallman, Woodruff, Kasravi, & Comp, 2010). Unfortunately, there are still many underrepresented groups in comparison to their market share in US higher education. There has also been a diversification of education program design in terms of program length, program destination, program type, program provider, disciplinary foci, experiential learning components, curricular integration, and curricular and co-curricular activities (see also DeWinter and Rumbley, 2010; Ogden et al., 2010). There has been a shift in the primary motivations for students to go abroad from more humanistic goals such as culture and language learning to more professionally oriented goals such as advancement in their professional preparation. Challenges and hindrances continue to be costs, academic concerns, worries, fears about health and safety, and at-home commitments and responsibilities.

The Future

Growth in education abroad often focuses on making education abroad more feasible through shorter programs with fewer language requirements (Castañeda & Zirger, 2011). However, education abroad without a language component does not help the US catch up in multilingualism (Commission on the Abraham Lincoln Study Abroad Fellowship Program, 2005) and is less likely to lead to an international involvement later on (Norris & Gillespie, 2009) and intercultural competence in general (Kinginger, 2010). Thus, our efforts must not focus simply on growth but on continuing to offer meaningful experiences abroad.

The JYA is necessary because many of the fundamental expectations of education abroad cannot be fully met by short-term programs. Yet, without modernizing the JYA to meet the needs of today's students, the future of JYA is in danger. While institutions could choose to send their students to direct-enroll programs, many of our students are accustomed to a level of support they are unlikely to find there (Kinginger, 2010). Additionally, students often need facilitation in their intercultural and translingual interactions while abroad in order to produce significant learning outcomes and allow for maximal personal development (Castañeda & Zirger, 2011; Dunkley, 2009; Pedersen, 2010). These types of facilitations and accommodations are often not made available in independent education abroad programs. Hence, we argue that a modernized JYA would greatly enhance the education abroad landscape.

References

AAUP. (1995). Directing foreign study: The professor abroad. *Academe*, 81(5), 21–21. Retrieved from www.jstor.org/stable/40250872.

Ablaeva, Y. S. (2012). Inclusion of students with disabilities in study abroad: Current practices and student perspectives. Master of Arts thesis, University of Oregon. ProQuest 1516785.

Abrams, I. (1960). *Study abroad* (Vol. 6). Washington, DC: US Department of Health, Education, and Welfare.

Albers-Miller, N. D., Prenshaw, P. J., & Straughan, R. D. (1999). Study abroad programs: An exploratory study of student perceptions. *American Marketing Association Conference Proceedings*, 10, 65–72.

Allen, H. W. (2010). Language-learning motivation during short-term study abroad: An activity theory perspective. *Foreign Language Annals*, 43(1), 27–49.

Allen, H. W., Dristas, V., & Mills, N. (2006). Cultural learning outcomes and summer study abroad. In M. Mantero (Ed.), *Identity and second language learning: Culture, inquiry, and dialogic activity in educational contexts* (pp. 189–215). Charlotte, NC: Information Age Publishing.

Allen, H. W., & Dupuy, B. (2013). Study abroad, foreign language use, and the communities standard. *Foreign Language Annals*, 45(4), 468–493.

Allison, P., Davis-Berman, J., & Berman, D. (2012). Changes in latitude, changes in attitude: Analysis of the effects of reverse culture shock – a study of students returning from youth expeditions. *Leisure Studies*, 31(4), 487–503. doi:10.1080/02614367.2011.619011.

Amani, M., & Kim, M. M. (2018). Study abroad participation at community colleges: Students' decision and influential factors. *Community College Journal of Research and Practice*, 42(10), 678–692. doi:10.1080/10668926.2017.1352544.

American College Health Association. (2018). *American College Health Association—national college health assessment II: Reference group executive summary spring 2018.* Retrieved from www.acha.org/documents/ncha/NCHA-II_Spring_2018_Reference_Group_Executive_Summary.pdf.

American Council on Education. (2008). *College-bound students' interests in study abroad and other international learning activities.* Washington, DC: American Council on Education (ACE), Art & Science Group, and the College Board.

Anderson, K. L., Boyd, M., Marin, K. A., & McNamara, K. (2019). Reimagining service-learning: Deepening the impact of this high-impact practice. *Journal of Experiential Education*, 42(3), 229–248. doi:10.1177/1053825919837735.

Anita, S. C., & McKenry, L. (1999). Preparing culturally competent practitioners. *The Journal of nursing education*, 38(5), 228–234.

Anya, U. (2011). Connecting with communities of learners and speakers: Integrative ideals, experiences, and motivation of successful black second language learners. *Foreign Language Annals*, 44(3), 441–466.

Archangeli, M. (1999). Study abroad and experiential learning in Salzburg. *Austria Foreign Language Annals*, 32(1), 115–122. doi:10.1111/j.1944-9720.1999.tb02380.x.

Avello, P., & Lara, A. R. (2014). Phonological development in L2 speech production during study abroad programs differing in length of stay. In C. Perez-Vidal (Ed.), *Language acquisition in study abroad and formal instruction contexts* (pp. 137–166). Amsterdam: John Benjamins.

Badstübner, T., & Ecke, P. (2009). Student expectations, motivations, target language use, and perceived learning progress in summer study abroad program in Germany. *Die Unterrichtspraxis/Teaching German*, 42(1), 41–49.

Bai, J., Larimer, S., & Riner, M. B. (2016). Cross-cultural pedagogy: Practical strategies for a successful interprofessional study abroad course. *Journal of the Scholarship of Teaching and Learning*, 16(3), 72–81. doi:10.14434/josotl.v16i3.19332.

BaileyShea, C. (2009). Factors that affect American college students' participation in study abroad. Doctor of Philosophy dissertation, University of Rochester. ProQuest 3395372.

Bakalis, S. (2004). Participation in tertiary study abroad programs: the role of personality. *International Journal of Educational Management*, 18(5), 286–291. doi:10.1108/09513540410543420.

Baker-Smemoe, W., Dewey, D. P., Bown, J., & Martinsen, R. A. (2014). Variables affecting L2 gains during study abroad. *Foreign Language Annals*, 47(3), 464–486. doi:10.1111/flan.12093.

Bandyopadhyay, S., & Bandyopadhyay, K. (2015). Factors influencing student participation in college study abroad programs. *Journal of International Education Research*, 11(2), 87–94.

Bathke, A., & Kim, R. (2016). Keep calm and go abroad: The effect of learning abroad on student mental health. *Frontiers: The Interdisciplinary Journal of Study Abroad*, 17, 1–16.

Bathurst, L., & Brack, B. L. (2012). Shifting the locus of intercultural learning. Intervening prior to and after student experiences abroad. In M. V. Berg, R. M. Paige, & K. H. Lou (Eds.), *Student learning abroad. What our students are learning, what they're not, and what we can do about it* (pp. 261–283). Sterling, VA: Stylus.

Beausoleil, A. (2008). Understanding heritage and ethnic identity development through study abroad: The case of South Korea. Doctor of Education dissertation, University of California. ProQuest 333041.

Behrnd, V., & Porzelt, S. (2011). Intercultural competence and training outcomes of students with experiences abroad. *International Journal of Intercultural Relations*, 36(2), 213–223. doi:10.1016/j.ijintrel.2011.04.005.

Berger, K. A., & O'Neill, G. P. (2002). Culture in context: An interdisciplinary travel study course. *The French Review*, 76(2), 297–315. Retrieved from www.jstor.org/stable/3132710.

Berque, D., & Chiba, H. (2017). Evaluating the use of LINE software to support interaction during an American travel course in Japan. *Lecture Notes in Computer Science, 10281*, 614–623. doi:10.1007/978-3-319-57931-3_49.

Berquist, B., & Milano, J. (2020). Intersections between service learning and study abroad: A framework for community engagement abroad. In P. Crawford & B. Berquist (Eds.), *Community engagement abroad: Perspectives and practices on service, engagement, and learning overseas* (pp. 13–28). East Lansing, MI: Michigan State University.

Beverly, M. M., Kelley, S. F., Urso, P., Anderson, M. J., Leatherwood, J. L., & Stutts, K. J. (2016). 1757 Student perspectives on agricultural study abroad programs. *Journal of Animal Science*, 94(suppl. 5), 855–856. doi:10.2527/jam2016-1758.

Black, H. T., & Duhon, D. L. (2006). Assessing the impact of business study abroad programs on cultural awareness and personal development. *Journal of Education for Business*, 81(3), 140–144.

Blake-Campbell, B. (2014). More than just a sampling of study abroad: Transformative possibilities at best. *The Community College Enterprise*, 20(2), 6–71.

Boateng, A., & Thompson, A. M. (2013). Study abroad Ghana: An international experiential learning. *Journal of Social Work Education*, 49, 701–715. doi:10.1080/10437797.2013.812897.

Bordovskaia, N. V., Anderson, C., Bochkina, N., & Petanova, E. I. (2018). The adaptive capabilities of Chinese students studying in Chinese, British and Russian universities. *International Journal of Higher Education*, 7(4), 1–16. doi:10.5430/ijhe.v7n4p1.

Böttcher, L., Araújo, N. A. M., Nagler, J., Mendes, J. F. F., Helbing, D., & Herrmann, H. J. (2016). Gender gap in the ERASMUS mobility program. *PLos ONE*, 11(2), 1–8. doi:10.1371/journal.pone.014951.

Brandauer, S. C., & Hovmand, S. (2013). Preparing business students for the global workplace through study abroad: A case study of the Danish Institute for Study Abroad. *Journal of International Education in Business*, 6(2), 107–121. doi:10.1108/JIEB-05-2013-0018.

Brockington, J. L., & Wiedenhoft, M. D. (2009). The liberal arts and global citizenship: Fostering intercultural engagement through integrative experiences and structured reflection. In R. Lewin (Ed.), *The handbook of practice and research in study abroad: Higher education and the quest for global citizenship* (pp. 117–132). New York: Routledge.

Brown, L. (2009). The transformative power of the international sojourn. *Annals of Tourism Research*, 36(3), 502–521. doi:10.1016/j.annals.2009.03.002.

Brown, N. A. (2014). Foreign language study coupled with internship experience as an entrée to professional opportunities. *Russian Language Journal*, 64, 71–81. Retrieved from www.jstor.org/stable/43669251.

Bryant, K. M., & Soria, K. M. (2015). College students' sexual orientation, gender identity, and participation in study abroad. *Frontiers: The Interdisciplinary Journal of Study Abroad*, 15, 91–106.

Burke, M. J., Watkins, M. B., & Guzman, E. (2009). Performing in a multi-cultural context: The role of personality. *International Journal of Intercultural Relations*, 33(6), 475–485. doi:10.1016/j.ijintrel.2009.05.005.

Butler, P. E. (2019). Learning to navigate: Lessons from student development. In E. Brewer & A. C. Ogden (Eds.), *Education abroad and the undergraduate experience: Critical perspectives and approaches to integration with student learning and development* (pp. 132–148). Sterling, VA: Stylus.

Byker, E. J., & Putnam, S. M. (2018). Catalyzing cultural and global competencies: Engaging preservice teachers in study abroad to expand the agency of citizenship. *Journal of Studies in International Education*, 23(1), 84–105. doi:10.1177/1028315318814559.

Cadd, M. (2012). Encouraging students to engage with native speakers during study abroad. *Foreign Language Annals*, 45(2), 229–245. doi:10.1111/j.1944-9720.2012.01188.x.

Caffrey, R. A., Neander, W., Markle, D., & Stewart, B. (2005). Improving the cultural competence of nursing students: results of integrating cultural content in the curriculum and an international immersion experience. *The Journal of Nursing Education*, 44(5), 234–240.

Cai, W., & Sankaran, G. (2015). Promoting critical thinking through an interdisciplinary study abroad program. *Journal of International Students*, 5(1), 38–49.

Calhoon, J. A., Wildcat, D., Annett, C., Pierotti, R., & Griswold, W. (2003). Creating meaningful study abroad programs for American Indian postsecondary students. *Journal of American Indian Education*, 42(1), 46–57. Retrieved from www.jstor.org/stable/24398471.

Carter, M. J. (2015). Exploring the relationship between study abroad and emotional intelligence. Doctor of Philosophy dissertation, The University of Alabama. ProQuest 3719152.

Castañeda, M. E., & Zirger, M. L. (2011). Making the most of the "new" study abroad: Social capital and the short-term sojourn. *Foreign Language Annals*, 44(3), 544–564.

Chambers, A., & Chambers, K. (2008). Tuscan dreams: Study abroad student expectation and experience in Siena. In V. Savicki (Ed.), *Developing intercultural competence and transformation: Theory, research, and application in international education* (pp. 128–153). Sterling, VA: Stylus.

Chapman, D. D. (2016). The ethics of international service learning as a pedagogical development practice: a Canadian study. *Third World Quarterly*, 39(10), 1899–1922. doi:10.1080/01436597.2016.1175935.

Chieffo, L., & Griffiths, L. (2009). Here to stay: Increasing acceptance of short-term study abroad programs. In R. Lewin (Ed.), *The handbook of practice and research in study abroad* (pp. 365–380). New York: Routledge.

Chieffo, L., & Zipser, R. (2001). Integrating study abroad in the foreign language curriculum. *ADFL Bulletin*, 32, 79–85.

Chumbley, L. S. (2017). Materials abroad: Building a sustainable study abroad experience for materials engineers. *JOM*, 69(4), 620–621. doi:10.1007/s11837-017-2314-x.

Cleveland, H., Mangone, G. J., & Adams, J. C. (1960). *The overseas Americans*. New York: McGraw-Hill.

Coby, J. (2016). Open roads, open topics: The virtues of open-ended final assignments in contemporary American travel literature courses. *Teaching American literature*, 8(3).

Cohen, A. D., Paige, R. M., Shively, R. L., Emert, H. A., & Hoff, J. G. (2005). *Maximizing study abroad through language and culture strategies: Research on students, study abroad program professionals, and language instructors*. Final report to the International Research and Studies Program, Office of International Education, US Department of Education. Retrieved from https://carla.umn.edu/maxsa/documents/MAXSARe searchReport.pdf.

Commission on the Abraham Lincoln Study Abroad Fellowship Program. (2005). Global competence & national needs. One million Americans studying abroad. Retrieved from www.aplu.org/library/global-competence-and-national-needs-one-million-america ns-studying-abroad/file.

Comp, D. (2008). US heritage-seeking students discover minority communities in Western Europe. *Journal of Studies in International Education*, 12(1), 29–37. doi:10.1177/ 1028315307299417.

Convertini, T. (2019). The city as the classroom: Maximizing learning abroad through language and culture experiential strategies. In M. Fuchs, S. Rai, & Y. Loiseau (Eds.), *Study abroad: Traditions and new directions* (pp. 38–51). New York: The Modern Language Association of America.

Cook, L. A. (2004). The relationship between expectation-experience growth discrepancies and satisfaction among students participating in international service-learning programs. Doctor of Philosophy dissertation, Brigham Young University. ProQuest 3127097.

Corder, D., Roskvist, A., Harvey, S., & Stacey, K. (2018). Language teachers on study abroad programmes: The characteristics and strategies of those most likely to increase their intercultural communicative competence. In J. L. Plews & K. Misfeldt (Eds.), *Second language study abroad: Programming, pedagogy, and participant engagement* (pp. 257–298). Cham: Palgrave Macmillan.

Cotten, C., & Thompson, C. (2017). High-impact practices in social work education: A short-term study-abroad service-learning trip to Guatemala. *Journal of Social Work Education*, 53(4), 622–636. doi:10.1080/10437797.2017.1284626.

Covington, M. (2017). If not us, then who? Exploring the role of HBCUs in increasing Black student engagement in study abroad. *College Student Affairs Leadership*, 4(1), article 5. Retrieved from http://scholarworks.gvsu.edu/csal/vol4/iss1/5.

Crawford, P., & Berquist, B. (2020). *Community engagement abroad: Perspectives and practices on service, engagement, and learning overseas*. East Lansing, MI: Michigan State University Press.

Cressey, W., & Stubbs, N. (2010). The economics of study abroad. In W. W. Hoffa & S. C. DePaul (Eds.), *A history of US study abroad: 1965–present* (pp. 253–294). Carlisle, PA: Frontiers.

Cubillos, J., & Ilvento, T. (2018). Intercultural contact in short-term study abroad programs. *Hispania*, 101(2), 249–266. doi:10.1353/hpn.2018.0117.

Cunningham, H. B. (2019). Responding to what we notice: International student teaching as a pathway to cultural responsiveness. *Urban Education* 54(9), 1262–1289. doi:10.1177/0042085919860569.

Currier, C., Lucas, J., & Arnault, D. S. (2009). Study abroad and nursing: From cultural to global competence. In R. Lewin (Ed.), *The handbook of practice and research in study abroad* (pp. 133–150). New York: Routledge.

Currier, C., Omar, M., Talarczyk, G., & Diaz Guerrero, R. (2000). Development and implementation of a semester program in Mexico for senior nursing students. *Journal of professional nursing*, 16(5), 293–299. doi:10.1053/jpnu.2000.9456.

Curtin, A. J., Martins, D. C., Schwartz-Barcott, D., DiMaria, L., & Ogando, B. M. S. (2013). Development and evaluation of an international service learning program for nursing students. *Public Health Nursing*, 30, 548–556.

Curtis, T., & Ledgerwood, J. R. (2018). Students' motivations, perceived benefits and constraints towards study abroad and other international education opportunities. *Journal of International Education in Business*, 11(1), 63–78. doi:10.1108/JIEB-01-2017-0002

Cushner, K. (2009). The role of study abroad in preparing globally responsible teachers. In R. Lewin (Ed.), *The handbook of practice and research in study abroad. Higher education and the quest for global citizenship* (pp. 151–169). New York: Routledge.

Daniel, S. J., Xie, F., & Kedia, B. L. (2014). *2014 US business needs for employees with international expertise.* Paper presented at the Internationalization of US Education in the 21st Century: The Future of International and Foreign Language Studies—A Research Conference on National Needs and Policy Implications, Williamsburg, VA.

Davidson, D. E., & Lekic, M. D. (2012). Comparing heritage and non-heritage learning outcomes and target-language utilization in the overseas immersion context: A preliminary study of the Russian flagship. *Russian Language Journal*, 62(2012), 47–78.

De Jong, P., Schnusenberg, O., & Goel, L. (2010). Marketing study abroad programs effectively: what do American business students think? *Journal of International Education in Business*, 3(1/2), 34–52.

Delgado, V., & Yoder, S. (2020). Reexamining university–community partnerships in a civic engagement study-abroad program. In P. Crawford & B. Berquist (Eds.), *Community Engagement Abroad: Perspectives and Practices on Service, Engagement, and Learning Overseas* (pp. 131–144). East Lansing, MI: Michigan State University.

Demetry, C., & Vaz, R. F. (2017). Influence of an education abroad program on the intercultural sensitivity of STEM undergraduates: A mixed methods study. *Advances in Engineering Education*, 6(1), 1–32.

Dessoff, A. (2006). Who's NOT going abroad? *International Educator*, 15(2), 20–27.

Dewald, B., Jimenez, A. C., & Self, J. T. (2016). Comparing pre- and post-perceptions of studying abroad: an Italy programme case study. *Anatolia*, 27(4), 444–455. doi:10.1080/13032917.2016.1160415.

Dewey, D. P. (2008). Japanese vocabulary acquisition by learners in three contexts. *Frontiers: The Interdisciplinary Journal of Study Abroad*, 15, 127–148.

Dewey, D. P., Bown, J., Baker, W., & Martinsen, R. A. (2014). Language use in six study abroad programs: An exploratory analysis of possible predictors. *Language Learning*, 64(1), 36–71.

DeWinter, U. J. (2007). Study abroad: An open door to language learning. *ADFL Bulletin*, 38(1–2),22–26. doi:10.1632/adfl.38.1.22.

DeWinter, U. J., & Rumbley, L. E. (2010). The diversification of education abroad across the curriculum. In W. W. Hoffa & S. C. DePaul (Eds.), *A history of US study abroad: 1965 - present* (pp. 55–114). Carlisle, PA: Frontiers.

Di Silvio, F., Diao, W., & Donovan, A. (2016). The development of L2 fluency during study abroad: A cross-language study. *The Modern Language Journal*, 100(3), 610–624. doi:10.1111/modl.12343.

Di Silvio, F., Donovan, A., & Malone, M. E. (2014). The effect of study abroad homestay placements: Participant perspectives and oral proficiency gains. *Foreign Language Annals*, 47(1), 168–188.

Diao, W. (2016). Peer socialization into gendered L2 Mandarin practices in a study abroad context: Talk in the dorm. *Applied Linguistics*, 37(5), 599–620. doi:10.1093/applin/amu053.

Doppen, F. H., & Diki, K. (2017). Perceptions of student teaching abroad: Upon return and two years after. *Journal of International Social Studies*, 7(2), 78–97.

Douglas, C., & Jones-Rikkers, C. G. (2001). Study abroad programs and American student worldmindedness: An empirical analysis. *Journal of Teaching in International Business*, 13(1).

Douglass, K. (2007). From the learner's perspective: A case study on motives and study abroad. In S. Wilkinson (Ed.), *Insights from study abroad for language programs* (pp. 116–133). Boston, MA: Thomson & Heinle.

Downey, G., & Gray, T. (2012). Blogging with the Facebook generation: Studying abroad with gen Y. Retrieved from www.researchgate.net/publication/257483917_Blogging_with_the_Facebook_Generation_Studying_abroad_with_Gen_Y

Doyle, S., Gendall, P., Meyer, L. H., Hoek, J., Tait, C., McKenzie, L., & Loorparg, A. (2010). An investigation of factors associated with student participation in study abroad. *Journal of Studies in International Education*, 14(5), 471–490. doi:10.1177/1028315309336032.

Ducate, L. (2009). Service learning in Germany: A four-week summer teaching program in Saxony-Anhalt. *Die Unterrichtspraxis/Teaching German*, 42(1), 32–40.

Duff, P. (2017). Social dimensions and differences in instructed SLA. In S. Loewen & M. Sato (Eds.), *The Routledge handbook of instructed second language acquisition* (pp. 378–395). New York: Routledge.

DuFon, M. A., & Churchill, E. (2006). Evolving threads in study abroad research. In M. A. DuFon & E. Churchill (Eds.), *Language learners in study abroad contexts* (pp. 1–30). Clevedon: Multilingual Matters.

Dunkley, M. (2009). *What students are actually learning on study abroad and how to improve the learning experience.* Paper presented at the 20th ISANA International Education Association Conference Proceeding, Canberra (Australia).

Dwyer, M. M. (2004). More is better: The impact of study abroad program duration. *Frontiers: The Interdisciplinary Journal of Study Abroad*, 10, 151–163.

Engle, L., & Engle, J. (2003). Study abroad levels: Toward a classification of program types. *Frontiers: The Interdisciplinary Journal of Study Abroad*, 9, 1–20.

Engle, L., & Engle, J. (2012). Beyond immersion. The American University Center of Provence experiment in holistic intervention. In M. V. Berg, R. M. Paige, & K. H. Lou (Eds.), *Student learning abroad. What our students are learning, what they're not, and what we can do about it* (pp. 284–307). Sterling, VA: Stylus.

Evanson, T. A., & Zust, B. L. (2004). The meaning of participation in an international service experience among baccalaureate nursing students. *International journal of nursing education scholarship*, 1(1), 0–14. doi:10.2202/1548-923x.1070.

Fairley, S., & Tyler, B. D. (2009). Cultural learning through a sport tourism experience: The role of the group. *Journal of Sport & Tourism*, 14(4), 273–292. doi:10.1080/14775080903453823.

Farrugia, C., & Bhandari, R. (2016). *Open Doors: Report on international educational exchange*. Baltimore, MD: Institute of International Education.

Farrugia, C., & Sanger, J. (2017). Gaining an employment edge: The impact of study Abroad on 21st century skills & career prospects in the United States, 2013–2016. Retrieved from https://educationabroad.wvu.edu/files/d/fbd30891-5f37-4309-a9b9-9bde74bd52bf/gaining-an-employment-edge-the-impact-of-study-abroad.pdf.

Fear, F. A., & McKnight Casey, K. (2020). The story of place: What we learned about engaged study-abroad work at Michigan State University. In P. Crawford & B. Berquist (Eds.), *Community engagement abroad: Perspectives and practices on service, engagement, and learning overseas* (pp. 1–12). East Lansing, MI: Michigan State University.

Fornerino, M., Jolibert, A., Sáchez, C. M., & Zhang, M. (2011). Do values or goals better explain intent? A cross-national comparison. *Journal of Business Research*, 64(5), 490–496. doi:10.1016/j.jbusres.2010.03.007.

Foster, M. (2014). Student destination choices in higher education: exploring attitudes of Brazilian students to study in the United Kingdom. *Journal of Research in International Education* 13(2), 149–162.

Freed, B. F., Segalowitz, N., & Dewey, D. P. (2004). Comparing regular classroom, study abroad, and intensive domestic immersion programs. *SSLA*, 26, 275–301.

Frisch, N. C. (1990). An international nursing student exchange program: an educational experience that enhanced student cognitive development. *The Journal of Nursing Education*, 29(1), 10–12.

Futamura, F., & Marr, A. M. (2018). Taking mathematics abroad: A how-to guide. *PRIMUS*, 28(9), 875–889.

Gabaudan, O. (2016). Too soon to fly the coop? Online journaling to support students' learning during their Erasmus study visit. *ReCALL*, 28(2), 123–146. doi:10.1017/S0958344015000270.

Garbati, J. F., & Rothschild, N. (2016). Lasting impact of study abroad experiences: A collaborative autoethnography. *Forum Qualitative Sozialforschung/Forum: Qualitative Social Research*, 17(2), 1–18. doi:10.17169/fqs-17.2.2387.

Garver, M. S., & Divine, R. L. (2007). Conjoint analysis of study abroad preferences: Key attributes, segments and implications for increasing student participation. *Journal of Marketing for Higher Education*, 17(2), 189–215. doi:10.1080/08841240801912427.

Gaw, K. F. (2000). Reverse culture shock in students returning from overseas. *International Journal of Intercultural Relations*, 24(1), 83–104. doi:10.1016/S0147-1767(99)00024-3.

Gleye, P. (2017). Study abroad in a time of terror; US student experiences in Brussels. *Frontiers: The Interdisciplinary Journal of Study Abroad*, 29(1), 15–27.

Goertler, S. (2015). Study abroad and technology: Friend or enemy? *FLTMag*. Retrieved from https://fltmag.com/study-abroad-and-technology.

Goertler, S., & McEwen, K. (2018). Closing the GAP for generation study abroad: Achieving goals, improving articulation, and increasing participation. *ADFL Bulletin*, 44(2), 41–55. doi:10.1632/adfl.44.2.41.

Goldoni, F. (2013). Students' immersion experiences in study abroad. *Foreign Language Annals*, 46(3), 359–376. doi:10.1111/flan.12047.

Goldstein, S. B. (2017). Teaching a psychology-based study abroad pre-departure course. *Psychology learning and teaching*, 16(3), 404–424. doi:10.1177/1475725717718059.

Goode, M. L. (2008). The role of faculty study abroad directors: A case study. *Frontiers: The Interdisciplinary Journal of Study Abroad*, 15, 149–172.

Gore, J. E. (2005). *Dominant beliefs and alternative voices: Discourse, belief, and gender in American study abroad*. New York: Routledge.

Gorka, B., & Niesenbaum, R. (2001). Beyond the language requirement: Interdisciplinary short-term study-abroad programs in Spanish. *Hispania*, 84(1), 100–109.

Green, M. F., & Siaya, L. M. (2005). *Measuring internationalization at community colleges*. Washington, DC: American Council on Education.

Guerrero, E., Jr. (2006). The road less traveled: Latino students and the impact of studying abroad. Doctor of Education dissertation, The University of California.

Gullekson, N. L., & Tucker, M. L. (2012). An examination of the relationship between emotional intelligence and intercultural growth for students studying abroad. *Journal of the Academy of Business Education*, 13, 162–178.

Gutel, H. (2008). The home stay: A gendered perspective. *Frontiers: The Interdisciplinary Journal of Study Abroad*, 15, 173–188.

Hackney, K., Boggs, D., & Borozan, A. (2012). An empirical study of student willingness to study abroad. *Journal of Teaching in International Business*, 23(2), 1123–1144.

Haloburdo, E. P., & Thompson, M. A. (1998). A comparison of international learning experiences for baccalaureate nursing students: Developed and developing countries. *The Journal of nursing education*, 37(1), 13–21.

Hameister, B., Matthews, P., Hosley, N., & Groff, M. (1999). College students with disabilities and study abroad: Implications for international education staff. *Frontiers: The Interdisciplinary Journal of Study Abroad*, 5(2), 81–100.

Hanouille, L., & Leuner, P. (2001). Island programs: Myths and realities in international education. *E World Education News & Review*, 14(1), 1–6.

Harder, A., Andenoro, A., Roberts, T. G., Stedman, N., III., M. N., Parker, S. J., & Rodriguez, M. T. (2015). Does study abroad increase employability? *NACTA Journal*, 59(1), 41–48.

Harrison, J. K., & Voelker, E. (2008). Two personality variables and the cross-cultural adjustment of study abroad students. *Frontiers: The Interdisciplinary Journal of Study Abroad*, 17, 69–87.

Harrison, L., & Malone, K. (2004). A study abroad experience in Guatemala: Learning first-hand about health, education, and social welfare in a low-resource country. *International journal of nursing education scholarship*, 1(1), 0–15. doi:10.2202/1548-923X.1040.

Hartjes, L. B., Baumann, L. C., & Henriques, J. B. (2009). Travel health risk perceptions and prevention behaviors of US study abroad students. *Journal of Travel Medicine*, 16(5), 338–343. doi:10.1111/j.1708-8305.2009.00322.x.

He, Y., & Qin, X. (2017). Students' perceptions of an internship experience in China: A pilot study. *Foreign Language Annals*, 50(1), 57–70. doi:10.1111/flan.12246.

Hendrickson, B. (2016). Comparing international student friendship networks in Buenos Aires: Direct enrollment programs vs. study abroad centers. *Frontiers: The Interdisciplinary Journal of Study Abroad*, 27, 47–69.

Hernández, T. A. (2010). Promoting speaking proficiency through motivation and interaction: The study abroad and classroom learning contexts. *Foreign Language Annals*, 43(4), 650–670. doi:10.1111/j.1944-9720.2010.01107.x.

Hernández, T. A. (2016). Short-term study abroad: Perspectives on speaking gains and language contact. *Applied Language Learning*, 26(1), 39–64.

Hoffa, W. W. (2007). *A history of US study abroad: Beginnings to 1965*. Carlisle, PA: Frontiers.

Hoffa, W. W., & DePaul, S. C. (2010). Introduction. In W. W. Hoffa & S. C. DePaul (Eds.), *A history of US study abroad: 1965–present* (pp. 1–13). Carlisle, PA: Frontiers.

Hope, J. (2017). Support students with food allergies during study abroad. *Disability Compliance for Higher Education*, 22(12), 2–2. doi:10.1002/dhe.30318.

Hourigan, T., & Murray, L. (2010). Using blogs to help language students to develop reflective learning strategies: Towards a pedagogical framework. *Australasian Journal of Educational Technology*, 26(2), 209–225.

Houser, C., Brannstrom, C., Quiring, S. M., & Lemmons, K. K. (2011). Study abroad field trip improves test performance through engagement and new social networks. *Journal of Geography in Higher Education*, 35(4), 513–528.

Hulstrand, J. (2015). Best practices for short-term, faculty-led programs abroad. *International Educator*, May–June, 58–64.

Hunley, H. A. (2010). Students' functioning while studying abroad: The impact of psychological distress and loneliness. *International Journal of Intercultural Relations*, 34(4), 386–392.

Hurst, A. L. (2019). Class and gender as predictors of study abroad participation among US liberal arts college students. *Studies in Higher Education*, 44(7), 1–15. doi:10.1080/03075079.2018.1428948.

Hutchins, M. M. (1996). International education study tours abroad: Students' professional growth and personal development in relation to international, global, and intercultural perspectives. Doctor of Philosophy dissertation, The Ohio State University. ProQuest 9710583.

Ingram, M. (2005). Recasting the foreign language requirement through study abroad: A cultural immesion program in Avignon. *Foreign Language Annals*, 38(2), 211–222. doi:10.1111/j.1944-9720.2005.tb02486.x.

Innis-Klitz, S., & Clark, J. E. (2003). Study abroad consortia: Collaborative ventures among schools. In G. T. M. Hult & E. C. Lashbrooke (Eds.), *Study abroad: Perspectives and experiences from business schools* (pp. 209–226). Oxford: Elsevier Science.

Institute of International Education. (2011). Top 25 destinations of US study abroad students, 2008/09–2009/10. Retrieved from www.iie.org/Research-and-Insights/Open-Doors/Data/US-Study-Abroad/Destinations/Leading-Destinations/2008-10.

Institute of International Education. (2014). IIE generation study abroad initiative. Retrieved from www.iie.org/Programs/Generation-Study-Abroad.

Institute of International Education. (2018a). 2017–2018 generation study abroad travel grant. Retrieved from www.iie.org/Programs/Generation-Study-Abroad/UtilityNav/Funding/2017-2018-Recipients.

Institute of International Education. (2018b). Duration of study abroad. Retrieved from www.iie.org/en/Research-and-Insights/Open-Doors/Data/US-Study-Abroad/Duration-of-Study-Abroad.

Institute of International Education. (2018c). Host regions and destinations of US study abroad students. Retrieved from www.iie.org/Research-and-Insights/Open-Doors/Data/US-Study-Abroad/Destinations.

Institute of International Education. (2018d). Open Doors report: Duration of study abroad. Retrieved from www.iie.org/Research-and-Insights/Open-Doors/Data/US-Study-Abroad/Duration-of-Study-Abroad.

Institute of International Education. (2019a). Open Door infographics 2019. Retrieved from https://p.widencdn.net/5i0s78/OD19_graphics_handout-2019.

Institute of International Education. (2019b). Profile of US study abroad students, 2005/06–2017/18. Retrieved from www.iie.org/Research-and-Insights/Open-Doors/Data/US-Study-Abroad/Student-Profile.

Institute of International Education. (2019c). Students with disabilities. Retrieved from www.iie.org/Research-and-Insights/Open-Doors/Data/US-Study-Abroad/Students-with-Disabilities.

Isabelli-Garcia, C. (2006). Study abroad social networks, motivation and attitudes: Implications for second language acquisition. In M. A. DuFon & E. Churchill (Eds.), *Language learners in study abroad contexts* (pp. 231–259). Clevedon: Multilingual Matters.

Jackson, J. (2006a). Ethnographic pedagogy and evaluation in short-term study abroad. In M. Byram & A. Feng (Eds.), *Living in studying abroad: Research and practice* (pp. 134–157). Clevedon: Multilingual Matters.

Jackson, J. (2006b). Ethnographic preparation for short-term study and residence in the target culture. *International Journal of Intercultural Relations*, 30(1), 77–98. doi:10.1016/j.ijintrel.2005.07.004.

Jackson, J. (2008). Globalization, internationalization, and short-term stays abroad. *International Journal of Intercultural Relations*, 32, 349–358.

Jackson, J. (2018). Intervening in the intercultural learning of L2 study abroad students: From research to practice. *Language Teaching*, 51(3), 365–382. doi:10.1017/S0261444816000392.

Jacobone, V., & Moro, G. (2015). Evaluating the impact of the Erasmus programme: Skills and European identity. *Assessment and Evaluation in Higher Education*, 40(2), 309–328. doi:10.1080/02602938.2014.909005.

Jacoby, B. (2015). *Service-learning essentials: Questions, answers, and lessons learned.* San Francisco, CA: Jossey-Bass.

James, C. M. (2018). Mapping as orientation, support, and aide-mémoire in short-term travel courses. *International Journal of Humanities and Arts Computing*, 12(1), 71–80. doi:10.3366/ijhac.2018.0208.

Jenny, S. E., Almond, E. C., Chung, J. J., & Rademaker, S. M. (2019). Sport management majors' perceived motivators and barriers to participation in a college-sponsored international experience. *The Physical Educator*, 76(2), 547–567. doi:10.18666/TPE-2019-V76-I2-8255.

Johanson, L. (2006). The implementation of a study abroad course for nursing. *Nurse educator*, 31(3), 129–131.

Johnstone, C., & Edwards, P. (2019). Accommodations, accessibility, and culture: Increasing access to study abroad for students with disabilities. *Journal of Studies in International Education*, 0(0), 1–16. doi:10.1177/1028315319842344.

Jurasek, R., Lamson, H., & O'Maley, P. (1996). Ethnographic learning while studying abroad *Frontiers: The Interdisciplinary Journal of Study Abroad*, 2(1), 23–44.

Kasravi, J. (2009). Factors influencing the decision to study abroad for students of color: Moving beyond the barriers. Doctor of Philosophy dissertation, University of Minnesota. ProQuest 3371866.

Kehl, K., & Morris, J. (2008). Differences in global-mindedness between short-term and semester-long study abroad participants at selected private universities. *Frontiers: The Interdisciplinary Journal of Study Abroad*, 15, 67–79.

Kelleher, S., FitzGerald, S., & Hegarty, J. (2016). Factors that influence nursing and midwifery students' intentions to study abroad: A qualitative study using the theory of planned behaviour. *Nurse Education Today*, 44, 157–164. doi:10.1016/j.nedt.2016.05.019.

Kim, J., Dewey, D. P., Baker-Smemoe, W., & Ring, S. (2015). L2 development during study abroad in China. *System*, 55, 123–133. doi:10.1016/j.system.2015.10.005.

Kim, J., & Stodolska, M. (2013). Impacts of diaspora travel on ethnic identity development among 1.5 generation Korean-American college students. *Journal of Tourism and Cultural Change*, 11(3), 187–207. doi:10.1080/14766825.2013.827201.

Kim, R. I., & Goldstein, S. B. (2005). Intercultural attitudes predict favorable study abroad expectations of US college students. *Journal of Studies in International Education*, 9(3), 265–278. doi:10.1177/1028315305277684.

Kinginger, C. (2004). Alice doesn't live here anymore: Foreign language learning and identity reconstruction. In A. Pavlenko & A. Blackledge (Eds.), *Negotiation of identities in multilingual contexts* (pp. 219–242). Clevedon: Multilingual Matters.

Kinginger, C. (2009a). *Contemporary study abroad and foreign language learning: An activist's guidebook.* University Park, PA: Center for Advanced Language Proficiency Education and Research (CALPER).

Kinginger, C. (2009b). *Language learning and study abroad: A critical reading of research.* New York: Palgrave Macmillan.

Kinginger, C. (2010). American students abroad: Negotiation of difference? *Language Teaching*, 43(2), 216–227. doi:10.1017/S0261444808005703.

Kinginger, C. (2011). Enhancing language learning in study abroad. *Annual Review of Applied Linguistics*, 31, 58–73. doi:10.1017/S0267190511000031.

Kinginger, C., & Wu, Q. (2018). Learning Chinese through contextualized language practices in study abroad residence halls: Two case studies. *Annual Review of Applied Linguistics*, 38, 102–121. doi:10.1017/S0267190518000077.

Klebnikov, S. (2015). More US students are studying abroad, but is it enough? Retrieved from www.forbes.com/sites/sergeiklebnikov/2015/07/30/more-u-s-students-are-studying-a broad-but-is-it-enough/#7503d4d81f8f.

Knight, S. M., & Schmidt, R. (2004). The homestay component of study abroad: Three perspectives. *Foreign Language Annals*, 37(2), 254–262.

Kortegast, C., & Kupo, V. L. (2017). Deconstructing underlying practices of short-term study abroad: Exploring issues of consumerism, postcolonialism, cultural tourism, and commodification of experience. *The International Journal of Critical Pedagogy*, 8(1), 149–172.

Kramsch, C. (2005). Post 9/11: Foreign languages between knowledge and power. *Applied Linguistics*, 26(4), 545–567.

Kuczmarski, M. F., & Cole, R. P. (1999). Transcultural food habits travel courses. *Topics in Clinical Nutrition* 15(1), 59–71. doi:10.1097/00008486-199912000-00009.

Kulkarni, S. S., & Hanley-Maxwell, C. (2015). Preservice teachers' student teaching experiences in East Africa. *Teacher Education Quarterly*, 42(4), 59–81.

Kuo, Y.-H. (2011). Language challenges faced by international graduate students in the United States. *Journal of International Students*, 1(2), 38–42.

Kurasawa, I., & Nagatomi, A. (2006). Study abroad and internship programs: Reflection and articulation for lifelong learning. *Global Business Languages*, 11, 23–30.

Lapkin, S., Hart, D., & Swain, M. (1995). A Canadian interprovincial exchange: Evaluating the linguistic impact of a three-month stay in Quebec. In B. F. Freed (Ed.), *Second language acquisition in a study abroad context* (pp. 67–94). Amsterdam: John Benjamins.

Lathrop, B. J. J. (1999). The influence of study abroad programs on United States students' psychological development. Doctor of Philosophy dissertation, University of Georgia.

Lee, J., & Green, Q. (2016). Unique opportunities: Influence of study abroad on Black students. *Frontiers: The Interdisciplinary Journal of Study Abroad*, 18, 61–77.

Lewis, T. L., & Niesenbaum, R. A. (2005). The benefits of short-term study abroad. *Chronicle of Higher Education*, 51(39), B20.

Li, M., Olson, J. E., & Frieze, I. H. (2013). Students' study abroad plans: The influence of motivational and personality factors. *Frontiers: The Interdisciplinary Journal of Study Abroad*, 23, 73–89.

Lin, Y.-c., Chen, A. S.-y., & Song, Y.-c. (2012). Does your intelligence help to survive in a foreign jungle? The effects of cultural intelligence and emotional intelligence on cross-cultural adjustment. *International Journal of Intercultural Relations*, 36(4), 541–552. doi:10.1016/j.ijintrel.2012.03.001.

Lindsay, A. (2014). *The gender gap in study abroad*. SIT Graduate Institute, Capstone Collection. Retrieved from https://digitalcollections.sit.edu/capstones/2734

Lörz, M., Netz, N., & Quast, H. (2016). Why do students from underprivileged families less often intend to study abroad? *Higher Education*, 72, 153–174. doi:10.1007/s10734-015-9943-1.

Lou, K. H., & Bosley, G. W. (2012). Facilitating intercultural learning abroad. The intentional, targeted intervention model. In M. V. Berg, R. M. Paige, & K. H. Lou (Eds.), *Student learning abroad. What our students are learning, what they're not, and what we can do about it* (pp. 335–359). Sterling, VA: Stylus.

Lowe, T. B., Dozier, C. D., Hunt-Hurst, P., & Smith, B. P. (2008). Study abroad in West Africa: an interdisciplinary program of international education. *College Student Journal*, 42(3), 738–747.

Magnan, S. S., & Back, M. (2007). Social interaction and linguistic gain during study abroad. *Foreign Language Annals*, 40(1), 43–61. doi:10.1111/j.1944-9720.2007.tb02853.x.

Malewski, E., Sharma, S., & Phillion, J. (2012). How international field experiences promote cross-cultural awareness in preservice teachers through experiential learning: Findings from a six-year collective case study. *Teachers College Record*, 114, 1–44.

Marcum, J. A. (2001). Eliminate the roadblocks. *The Chronicle of Higher Education*, 18. Retrieved from www.chronicle.com/article/Eliminate-the-Roadblocks/21807.

Martinsen, R. A., Baker, W., Dewey, D. P., & Bown, J. (2010). Exploring diverse settings for language acquisition and use: Comparing study abroad, service learning abroad, and foreign language housing. *Applied Language Learning*, 20(1–2),45–69.

Marx, H. A., & Moss, D. M. (2011). Please mind the culture gap: Intercultural development during a teacher education study abroad program. *Journal of Teacher Education*, 62(1), 35–47. doi:10.1177/0022487110381998.

Marx, H. A., & Moss, D. M. (2015). Coming home: Continuing intercultural learning during the re-entry semester following a study abroad experience. *Journal of International Social Studies*, 5(2), 38–52.

Matthews, P. R., Hameister, B. G., & Hosley, N. S. (1998). Attitudes of college students toward study abroad: Implications for disability service providers. *Journal of Postsecondary Education and Disability*, 13(2), 67–77.

McCabe, L. (2005). Mental health and study abroad: Responding to the concern. *International Educator, Nov/Dec 2005*(52), 52–57. Retrieved from www.nafsa.org/_/File/_/InternationalEducator/EducationAbroadNovDec05.pdf.

McClure, K. R., Szelenyi, K., Niehaus, E., Anderson, A. A., & Reed, J. (2010). "We just don't have the possibility yet": US Latina/o narratives on study abroad. *Journal of Student Affairs Research and Practice*, 47(3), 367–387.

McKinley, K. E. (2014). Identifying barriers to study abroad program participation. Doctor of Education dissertation, Walden University. ProQuest 3617093.

Meier, H. H., & Smith, D. D. (2016). Achieving globalization of AACSB accounting programs with faculty-led study ebroad Education. *Accounting Education* 25(1), 35–56. doi:10.1080/09639284.2015.1118391.

Minton, M. R. (2016). Trio-eligible students and study abroad: Influential factors, barriers, and benefits. Doctor of Philosophy dissertation, Illinois State University. ProQuest 10131421.

MIUSA. (2018). Students with disabilities in education abroad statistics. Retrieved from www.miusa.org/resource/tipsheet/USstudentsatisfaction.

Molony, J., Sowter, B., & Potts, D. (2011). QS global employer survey report 2011. How employers value an international study experience. Retrieved from https://content.qs.com/qs/qs-global-employer-survey-2011.pdf.

Mora, E. I., Piñero, L. Á.-O., & Díaz, B. M. (2019). Developing intercultural competence in Seville outside the classroom. *Learning and Teaching: The International Journal of Higher Education in the Social Sciences*, 12(3), 73–87. doi:10.3167/latiss.2019.120305.

More, E. I., & Greenwood, D. J. (2019). Active learning and intercultural competence. *Learning and Teaching: The International Journal of Higher Education in the Social Sciences*, 12 (3), 1–17. doi:10.3167/latiss.2019.120302.

Morgan, A. C., & King, D. L. (2013). Improving undergraduates' exposure to international agriculture through experiential learning. *NACTA Journal*, 57(3a), 2–7.

Moseley, W. G. (2009). Making study abroad a win-win opportunity for pre-tenure faculty. *Frontiers: The Interdisciplinary Journal of Study Abroad*, 18, 231–240.

Muñoz, C., & Llanes, À. (2014). Study abroad and changes in degree of foreign accent in children and adults. *The Modern Language Journal*, 98(1), 432–449. Retrieved from www.jstor.org/stable/43651770.

Murray Brux, J., & Fry, B. (2010). Multicultural students in study abroad: Their interests, their issues, and their constraints. *Journal of Studies in International Education*, 14(5), 508–527.

Naffziger, D. W., Bott, J. P., & Mueller, C. B. (2010). Study abroad: Validating the factor analysis of student choices. *International Business: Research, Teaching and Practice*, 4(1), 72–81.

National Center for Education Statistics. (2019a). Characteristics of postsecondary students. Retrieved from https://nces.ed.gov/programs/coe/indicator_csb.asp.

National Center for Education Statistics. (2019b). Undergraduate enrollment. Retrieved from https://nces.ed.gov/programs/coe/indicator_cha.asp.

Nguyen, A.-M. D., Jefferies, J., & Rojas, B. (2018). Short term, big impact? Changes in self-efficacy and cultural intelligence, and the adjustment of multicultural and monocultural students abroad. *International Journal of Intercultural Relations*, 66, 119–129. doi:10.1016/j.ijintrel.2018.08.001.

Niehaus, E., & Inkelas, K. K. (2016). Understanding stem majors' intent to study abroad. *College Student Affairs Journal*, 34(1), 70–84. Retrieved from http://search.ebscohost.com/login.aspx?direct=true&db=ehh&AN=118904660&site=ehost-live&scope=site.

Niehoff, E., Petersdotter, L., & Freund, P. A. (2017). International sojourn experience and personality development: Selection and socialization effects of studying abroad and the Big Five. *Personality and Individual Differences*, 112, 55–61. doi:https://doi.org/10.1016/j.paid.2017.02.043.

Nietzel, M. T. (2019). More American students need to study abroad: Here's how congress can help. *Forbes*, June 3. Retrieved from www.forbes.com/sites/michaeltnietzel/2019/06/03/more-american-students-need-to-study-abroad-heres-how-congress-can-help/#3756794b36cb.

Nolan, R. W. (2009). Turning our back on the world: Study abroad and the purpose of US higher education. In R. Lewin (Ed.), *The handbook of practice and research in study abroad: Higher education and the quest for global citizenship* (pp. 266–281). New York: Routledge.

Norris, E. M., & Dwyer, M. M. (2005). Testing assumptions: The impact of two study abroad program models. *Frontiers: The Interdisciplinary Journal of Study Abroad*, 11, 121–142.

Norris, E. M., & Gillespie, J. (2009). How study abroad shapes global careers: Evidence from the United States. *Journal of Studies in International Education*, 13(3), 382–397. doi:10.1177/1028315308319740.

Nyaupane, G. P., Paris, C. M., & Teye, V. (2010). Why do students study abroad? Exploring motivations beyond earning academic credits. *Tourism Analysis*, 15, 263–267. doi:10.3727/108354210X12724863327920.

Ogden, A., Soneson, H. M., & Weting, P. (2010). The diversification of geographic locations. In W. W. Hoffa & S. C. DePaul (Eds.), *A history of US study abroad: 1965–present* (pp. 161–198). Carlisle, PA: Frontiers.

Olson, J. E., & Lalley, K. (2012). Evaluating a short-Term, first-year study abroad program for business and engineering undergraduates: Understanding the student learning experience. *Journal of Education for Business*, 87(6), 325–332. doi:10.1080/08832323.2011.627889.

Open Doors. (2018a). Current partners. Retrieved from www.iie.org/Programs/Genera tion-Study-Abroad/Our-Current-Partners.

Open Doors. (2018b). Open Doors 2017 executive summary. Retrieved from www.iie. org/Why-IIE/Announcements/2017-11-13-Open-Doors-2017-Executive-Summary.

Opengart, R. (2018). Short-term study abroad and the development of intercultural maturity. *Journal of International Education in Business*, 11(2), 241–255. doi:10.1108/JIEB-02-2017-0009.

Opper, S., Teichler, U., & Carlson, J. (1990). *Impacts of study abroad programmes on students and graduates*. London: Jessica Kingsley Publishers.

Orbe, M. P., & Orbe, I. P. (2018). Intercultural theorizing for a global communication curriculum: A short-term study abroad pedagogical template. *Journal of Intercultural Communication Research*, 47(5), 392–398.

Ornstein, S., & Nelson, T. (2006). Incorporating emotional intelligence competency building into the preparation and delivery of international travel courses. *Innovations in Education and Teaching International*, 43(1), 41–55. doi:10.1080/14703290500467442.

Parkhouse, H., Turner, A. M., Konle, S., & Rong, X. L. (2016). Self-authoring the meaning of student teaching in China: Impacts on first-year teaching practices. *Frontiers: The Interdisciplinary Journal of Study Abroad*, 28, 78–98.

Parkinson, A. (2007). Engineering study abroad programs: Formats, challenges, best practices. *Online Journal for Global Engineering Education*, 2(2), 1–15.

Parkinson, J., & Musgrave, J. (2014). Development of noun phrase complexity in the writing of English for academic purposes students. *Journal of English for Academic Purposes*, 14, 48–59.

Pasquarelli, S. L. (2018). Defining an academically sound, culturally relevant study abroad curriculum. In S. L. Pasquarelli, R. A. Cole, & M. J. Tyson (Eds.), *Passport to change: Designing academically sound, culturally relevant, short-term, faculty-led study abroad programs* (pp. 35–59). Sterling, VA: Stylus.

Pedersen, P. J. (2010). Assessing intercultural effectiveness outcomes in a year-long study abroad program. *International Journal of Intercultural Relations*, 34(1), 70–80. doi: doi:10.1016/j.ijintrel.2009.09.003.

Pellegrino Aveni, V. (2005). *Study abroad and second language use: Constructing the self.* Cambridge: Cambridge University Press.

Penn, E. B., & Tanner, J. (2009). Black students and international education: An assessment. *Journal of Black Studies*, 40(2), 266–282.

Peterson, C. F. (2002). Preparing engaged citizens: Three models of experiential education for social justice. *Frontiers: The Interdisciplinary Journal of Study Abroad*, 8, 165–206.

Peterson, D. L. (2003). The decision to study abroad: Contributing factors and implications for communication strategies. Doctor of Philosophy dissertation, Michigan State University. ProQuest 3092192.

Petrucci, P. R. (2007). Heritage scholars in the ancestral homeland: An overlooked identity in study abroad research. *Sociolinguistic Studies*, 1(2), 275–296. doi:10.1558/sols.v1i2.275.

Poehling, A., & Nair, R. D. (2003). Choosing partners and structuring relationships: Lessons learned. In G. T. M. Hult & E. C. Lashbrooke (Eds.), *Study abroad: Perspectives and experiences from business schools* (pp. 191–207). Oxford: Elsevier Science.

Posey, J. T., Jr. (2003). Study abroad: Educational and employment outcomes of participants versus non participants. Doctor of Philosophy dissertation, The Florida State University. ProQuest 3137474.

Prohn, S. M., Kelley, K. R., & Westling, D. L. (2016). Studying abroad inclusively: Reflections by college students with and without intellectual disability. *Journal of Intellectual Disabilities*, 20(4), 341–353.

Prokhorov, A., & Therkelsen, J. (2015). Visualizing St. Petersburg: Using documentary production in a short-term study abroad program to enhance oral proficiency, media literacy, and research skills. *Journal of Film and Video*, 67(3/4), 112–124.

Qualters, D. M. (2010). Making the most of learning outside the classroom. *Experiential Education*, 124, 95–99. doi:10.1002/tl.427.

Quraeshi, Z. A., Luqmani, M., & Veeck, A. (2012). Advancing the participation of business students in study abroad programs. *Global Journal of Management and Business Research*, 12(11), 81–92.

Raby, R. L., & Valeau, E. J. (2007). Community college international education: Looking back to forecast the future. *New Directions for Community Colleges*, 2007(138), 5–14. doi:10.1002/cc.276.

Rai, S. (2019). Emerging issues in study abroad. In M. Fuchs, S. Rai, & Y. Loiseau (Eds.), *Study abroad: Traditions and new directions* (pp. 144–156). New York: The Modern Language Association of America.

Rawlins, R. (2012). Whether I'm an American or not, I'm not here so you can hit on me: public harassment in the experience of US women studying abroad. *Women's Studies*, 41(4), 476–497.

Raymondi, M. D. (2005). Latino students explore racial and ethnic identity in a global context. Doctor of Education dissertation, State University of New York at Binghamton. ProQuest 3153765.

Redden, E. (2007). The middlemen of study abroad. *Inside Higher Ed*. Retrieved from www.insidehighered.com/news/2007/08/20/middlemen-study-abroad.

Redwine, T., Blackburn, J., Bunch, J. C., Greenhaw, L., Rutherford, T., Wingenbach, G., & Walther, D. (2017). Describing parents' perceptions, valuation, and support of study abroad programs at three Southern land-grant universities. *Journal of Agricultural Education*, 58(4), 240–253. doi:10.5032/jae.2017.04240.

Ritz, A. A. (2011). The educational value of short-term study abroad programs as course components. *Journal of Teaching in Travel & Tourism*, 11(2), 164–178. doi:10.1080/15313220.2010.525968.

Robson, E. (2002). "An unbelievable academic and personal experience": Issues around teaching undergraduate field courses in Africa. *Journal of Geography in Higher Education*, 26(3), 327–344.

Root, E., & Ngampornchai, A. (2013). "I came back as a new human being": Student descriptions of intercultural competence acquired through education abroad experiences. *Journal of Studies in International Education*, 17(5), 513–532. doi:10.1177/1028315312468008.

Roy, T. (2014). Student perception and the value of studying abroad. A look at Michigan State University undergraduate business students. Master's Degree in International and Comparative Education, Stockholm University. Retrieved from www.edu.su.se/polopoly_fs/1.181282.1403532122!/menu/standard/file/Travis%20Roy%20-%20Student%20 Perceptions%20%20The%20Value%20of%20Studying%20Abroad%20%28FINAL% 29.pdf

Sachau, D., Brasher, N., & Fee, S. (2010). Three models for short-term study abroad. *Journal of Management Education*, 34(5), 645–670. doi:10.1177/1052562909340880.

Salgado-Robles, F., & George, A. (2019). The sociolinguistic impact of service-learning on heritage learners sojourning in Spain: Vosotros versus ustedes. *Heritage Language Journal*, 16(1), 71–98.

Salisbury, M. H., Paulsen, M. B., & Pascarella, E. T. (2010). To see the world or stay at home: Applying an integrated student choice model to explore the gender gap in the intent to study abroad. *Research in Higher Education*, 51(7), 615–640.

Salisbury, M. H., Paulsen, M. B., & Pascarella, E. T. (2011). Why do all the study abroad students look alike? Applying an integrated student choice model to explore differences in the factors that influence white and minority students' intent to study abroad. *Research in Higher Education*, 55(2), 123–150.

Salisbury, M. H., Umbach, P. D., Paulsen, M. B., & Pascarella, E. T. (2009). Going global: Understanding the choice process of the intent to study abroad. *Research in Higher Education*, 50(2), 119–143. doi:10.1007/s11162-008-9111-x.

Sánchez, C. M., Fornerino, M., & Zhang, M. (2006). Motivations and the intent to study abroad among US, French, and Chinese students. *Journal of Teaching in International Business*, 18(1), 27–52. doi:10.1300/J066v18n01_03.

Scheib, M., & Mitchell, M. (2008). Awaiting a world experience no longer: It's time for all students with disabilities to go overseas. In T. Berberi, E. C. Hamilton, & I. Sutherland (Eds.), *Worlds Apart?: Disability and Foreign Language Learning* (pp. 202–217). New Haven, CT: Yale University Press.

Schmidt-Rinehart, B. C., & Knight, S. M. (2004). The homestay component of study abroad: Three perspectives. *Foreign Language Annals*, 37(2), 254–262.

Schwaneger, H. (1970). The junior year abroad: Then, now, and? *Die Unterrichtspraxis/ Teaching German*, 3(1), 154–159. doi:10.2307/3529383.

Senate Bill 1198. (2019). Senator Paul Simon Study Abroad Program Act of 2019, Pub. L. No. Senate Bill 1198, 116th Cong. Stat.

Shames, W., & Alden, P. (2005). The impact of short-term study abroad on the identity development of college students with learning disabilities and/or AD/HD. *Frontiers: The Interdisciplinary Journal of Study Abroad*, 11, 1–31.

Sharma, S., & Phillion, J. (2019). How study abroad experiences develop multicultural awareness in preservice teachers: An eleven-year multiple case study. In M. Fuchs, S. Rai, & Y. Loiseau (Eds.), *Study abroad: Traditions and new directions* (pp. 63–78). New York: The Modern Language Association of America.

Sharon, W. (1998). On the nature of immersion during study abroad: Some participant perspectives. *Frontiers: The Interdisciplinary Journal of Study Abroad*, 4(2), 121–138.

Shirley, S. W. (2006). The gender gap in post-secondary study abroad: Understanding and marketing to male students. Doctor of Philosophy dissertation, University of North Dakota. ProQuest 3233968.

Shively, R. L. (2010). From the virtual world to the real world: A model of pragmatics instruction for study abroad. *Foreign Language Annals*, 43(1), 105–137.

Shostya, A., & Morreale, J. C. (2017). Fostering undergraduate research through a faculty-led study abroad experience. *International Journal of Teaching and Learning in Higher Education*, 29(2), 300–308.

Simon, J., & Ainsworth, J. W. (2012). Race and socioeconomic status differences in study abroad participation: The role of habitus, social networks, and cultural capital. *ISRN Education*, 2012, article 413896. doi:10.5402/2012/413896.

Smolcic, E., & Martin, D. (2018). Structured reflection and immersion in Ecuador: Expanding teachers' intercultural and linguistic competencies. In J. Jackson & S. Oguro (Eds.), *Intercultural interventions in study abroad* (pp. 190–205). New York: Routledge.

Spenader, A. J. (2011). Language learning and acculturation: Lessons from high school and gap-year exchange students. *Foreign Language Annals*, 44(2), 381–398. doi:10.1111/j.1944-9720.2011.01134.x.

Sroufe, R., Sivasubramaniam, N., Ramos, D., & Saiia, D. (2014). Aligning the PRME: How study abroad nurtures responsible leadership. *Journal of Management Education*, 39(2), 244–275. doi:10.1177/1052562914560795.

Stallman, E., Woodruff, G. A., Kasravi, J., & Comp, D. (2010). The diversification of the student profile. In W. W. Hoffa & S. C. DePaul (Eds.), *A history of US study abroad: 1965 - present* (pp. 115–160). Carlisle, PA: Frontiers.

Steeves, H. (2006). Experiencing international communication: An internship program in Ghana, West Africa. *Journalism & Mass Communication Educator*, 60(4), 360–375.

Stern, G. M. (2004). Credit transference a key barrier to study abroad; Recommendations in new ACE report can ease path. *The Hispanic Outlook in Higher Education*, 14(25), 26–31.

Stroud, A. H. (2010). Who plans (not) to study abroad? An examination of US student intent. *Journal of Studies in International Education*, 14(5), 491–507.

Swagler, M. A., & Jome, L. M. (2005). The effects of personality and acculturation on the adjustment of North American sojourners in Taiwan. *Journal of Counseling Psychology*, 52(4), 527–536. doi:10.1037/0022-0167.52.4.527.

Tabi, M. M., & Mukherjee, S. (2003). Nursing in a global community: A study abroad program. *Journal of Transcultural Nursing*, 14(2), 134–138. doi:10.1177/1043659602250637.

Talburt, S., & Stewart, M. A. (1999). What's the subject of study abroad?: Race, gender, and "living culture". *The Modern Language Journal*, 83(2), 163–175. Retrieved from www.jstor.org/stable/330333.

Teichler, U., & Steube, W. (1991). The logics of study abroad programs and their impact. *Higher Education*, 21, 325–349.

Thirolf, K. Q. (2014). Male college student perceptions of intercultural and study abroad programs. *Journal of Student Affairs Research and Practice*, 51(3), 246–258.

Tolliver, D. E. (2000). Study abroad in Africa: Learning about race, racism, and the racial legacy of America. *African Issues*, 28(1/2), 112–116. doi:10.2307/1167071.

Tompkins, A., Cook, T., Miller, E., & LePeau, L. A. (2017). Gender influences on students' study abroad participation and intercultural competence. *Journal of Student Affairs Research and Practice*, 54(2), 204–216.

Toncar, M. F., Reid, J. S., & Anderson, C. E. (2005). Perceptions and preferences of study abroad: do business students have different needs? *Journal of Teaching in International Business,* 17(1/2), 61–80.

Torralba, J. A. (2019). Developing a service-learning component within a university-based study abroad program: Implications for university–community relations. In M. Fuchs, S. Rai, & Y. Loiseau (Eds.), *Study abroad: Traditions and new directions* (pp. 55–62). New York: The Modern Language Association of America.

Trentman, E. (2013). Arabic and English during study abroad in Cairo, Egypt: Issues of access and use. *The Modern Language Journal,* 97(2), 457–473. doi:10.1111/j.1540-4781.2013.12013.

Trentman, E. (2015). Arabic heritage learners abroad: Language use and identity negotia-tion. *Al-'Arabiyya,* 48, 141–156. Retrieved from www.jstor.org/stable/44654042.

Tullock, B., & Ortega, L. (2017). Fluency and multilingualism in study abroad: Lessons from a scoping review. *System,* 71, 7–21. doi:10.1016/j.system.2017.09.019.

Twombly, S. B., Salisbury, M. H., Tumanut, S. D., & Klute, P. (2012). *Study abroad in a new global century: Renewing the promise, refining the purpose.* Hoboken, NJ: Wiley.

US Department of Education's National Center for Education Statistics. (2018a). Table 233. Number of US students studying abroad and percentage distribution, by sex, race/ethnicity, academic level, host region, and duration of stay: 1996–97 through 2007–08. *Digest of Education Statistics.* Retrieved from https://nces.ed.gov/programs/digest/d10/tables/dt10_233.asp.

US Department of Education's National Center for Education Statistics. (2018b). Table 319.30. Bachelor's degrees conferred by postsecondary institutions, by field of study and state or jurisdiction: 2015–16. *Digest of Education Statistics.* Retrieved from https://nces.ed.gov/programs/digest/d17/tables/dt17_319.30.asp.

UCONN. (2019). Baden-Wuerttemberg – Connecticut exchange program. Retrieved from https://bwgermany.uconn.edu.

Vahlbusch, J. (2003). Experiential learning in the University of Wisconsin-Eau Claire's pro-gram in Wittenberg, Germany. *ADFL Bulletin,* 34(2), 33–35. doi:10.1632/adfl.34.2.33.

Vande Berg, M. (2007). Intervening in the learning of US students abroad. *Journal of Studies in International Education,* 11(3/4), 392–399.

Vande Berg, M., Connor-Linton, J., & Paige, R. M. (2009). The Georgetown consortium project: Interventions for student learning abroad. *Frontiers: The Interdisciplinary Journal of Study Abroad,* 18, 1–75.

Vernon, A., Moos, C., & Loncarich, H. (2017). Student expectancy and barriers to study abroad. *Academy of Educational Leadership Journal,* 21(1), 1–9.

Wainwright, P., Ram, P., Teodorescu, D., & Tottenham, D. (2009). Going global in the sciences: a case study at Emory University. In R. Lewin (Ed.), *The handbook of practice and research in study abroad: higher education and the quest for global citizenship* (pp. 381–398). New York: Routledge.

Walker, J. (2015). Student perception of barriers to study abroad. Honors in the Major Program in Marketing, University of Central Florida. Retrieved from http://stars.library.ucf.edu/honorstheses1990-2015/1890.

Walsh, L. V., & DeJoseph, J. (2003). "I saw it in a different light": International learning experi-ences in baccalaureate nursing education. *The Journal of Nursing Education,* 42(6), 266–272.

Wang, L. C., Gault, J., Christ, P., & Diggin, P. A. (2016). Individual attitudes and social influences on college students' intent to participate in study abroad programs. *Journal of Marketing for Higher Education,* 26(1), 103–128. doi:10.1080/08841241.2016.1146385.

Wanner, D. (2009). Study abroad and language: From maximal to realistic models. In R. Lewin (Ed.), *The handbook of practice and research in study abroad: Higher education and the quest for global citizenship* (pp. 81–98). New York: Routledge.

Warnick, G. M., Call, M. S., & Davies, R. (2018). *Understanding engineering and technology student perceptions: Barriers to study abroad participation.* Paper presented at the ASEE Annual Conference & Exposition, Salt Lake City, UT.

Wayne State University. (2015). Junior year in Freiburg (1960–96). Retrieved from www. jym.wayne.edu/junior_year_in_freiburg.html.

Whatley, M. (2017). Financing study abroad: An exploration of the influence of financial factors on student study abroad patterns. *Journal of Studies in International Education,* 21(5), 431–449.

Wielkiewicz, R. M., & Turkowski, L. W. (2010). Reentry issues upon returning from study abroad programs. *Journal of College Student Development,* 51(6), 649–664.

Wilkinson, S. (1998a). On the nature of immersion during study abroad: Some participant perspectives. *Frontiers: The Interdisciplinary Journal of Study Abroad,* 4(2), 121–138.

Wilkinson, S. (1998b). Study abroad from the participants' perspective: A challenge to common beliefs. *Foreign Language Annals,* 31(1), 23–39.

Williams, T. R. (2005). Exploring the impact of study abroad on students' intercultural communication skills: Adaptability and sensitivity. *Journal of Studies in International Education,* 9(4), 356–371. doi:10.1177/1028315305277681.

Willis, T. Y. (2012). Rare but there: An intersectional exploration of the experiences and outcomes of Black women who studied abroad through community college programs. Doctor of Education dissertation, California State University. ProQuest 3533746.

Willis, T. Y. (2015). "And still we rise …": Microaggressions and intersectionality in the study abroad experiences of Black women. *Frontiers: The Interdisciplinary Journal of Study Abroad,* 16, 209–230.

Woolf, M. (2007). Impossible things before breakfast: Myths in education abroad. *Journal of Studies in International Education,* 11(3–4),496–509. doi:10.1177/1028315307304186.

Wright, C., & Schartner, A. (2013). "I can't … I won't?" International students at the threshold of social interaction. *Journal of Research in International Education,* 12(2), 113–128. doi:10.1177/1475240913491055.

Wros, P., & Archer, S. (2010). Comparing learning outcomes of international and local community partnerships for undergraduate nursing students. *Journal of Community Health Nursing,* 27(4), 216–225.

Wu, C.-H. (2018). Intercultural citizenship through participation in an international service-learning program: A case study from Taiwan. *Language Teaching Research,* 22(5), 517–531. doi:10.1177/1362168817718573.

Wu, S.-L. (2017). The planning, implementation, and assessment of an international internship program: An exploratory case study. *Foreign Language Annals,* 50(3), 567–583. doi:10.1111/flan.12280.

Zamastil-Vondrova, K. (2005). Good faith or hard data? Justifying short-term programs. *International Educator,* 14(1), 44–49.

Zervanos, S., & McLaughlin, J. S. (2003). Teaching biodiversity & evolution through travel course experiences. *The American Biology Teacher,* 65(9), 683–688.

Zimmermann, J., & Neyer, F. J. (2013). Do we become a different person when hitting the road? Personality development of sojourners. *Journal of Personality and Social Psychology,* 105(3), 515–530. doi:10.1037/a0033019.

PART 2
GOALS AND OUTCOMES OF
EDUCATION ABROAD

My study abroad, though short term, had a lasting impact on my life. I was able to connect with the culture in a way that is simply impossible when you are not in the country. One of my successes was the meaningful relationship with my host family. [...] I also did drastically improve my language skills, and my study abroad helped me set a major life goal. The factors contributing to my success were an interest in the language and culture, an experienced host grandma who spoke no English, and great faculty from MSU leading the group. My challenges were thinking about the time too much as a party.

—Education abroad alumnus and survey respondent

Chapter 2.1. Introduction

We strongly believe in the benefits and merit of education abroad for the individual and communities. Here we will outline education abroad (aspirational) goals and research proven outcomes. As a reminder, most research on education abroad is on short-term programs, hence benefits of short-term programs are likely over- and benefits of year-long programs underrepresented in this summary.

Let us start with the aspirational goals of education abroad and turn back again to the Lincoln Commission report (Commission on the Abraham Lincoln Study Abroad Fellowship Program, 2005). The Lincoln Commission made some bold claims about the importance of education abroad for the US. They emphasize that "greater engagement of American undergraduates with the world around them is vital to the nation's well-being" (p. v). Further, they explain that "our national security and domestic prosperity depend upon a citizenry that understands America's place in the world, the security challenges it faces, and the opportunities and perils confronting Americans around the world" (p. ix). They list several reasons for this need. Firstly, globalization: (a) Economic, military, and diplomatic challenges are global; (b) business leaders want employees with global skills. Secondly, education abroad is essential for language development. Thirdly, there is a shown positive influence of education abroad on educational attainment and long-term learning. Fourthly, intercultural competence is needed to succeed in the 21st century. We agree with the Lincoln Commission that a community or nation today must have a globally aware, interculturally competent, well-educated, multilingual, skilled, and engaged workforce. We also agree that such a profile can be developed through well-designed, especially long-term, education abroad and will provide the research evidence in the following chapters.

While language learning and travel to a new region of the world were in the foreground at the beginning of education abroad (Hoffa, 2007), the four main goals today include curricular learning, cross-cultural development, career enhancement, as well as the development of the students' character and intellectual abilities (Hoffa & DePaul, 2010) or simply put individual maturation (Petzold & Moog, 2018). As we have already discussed, language proficiency development is less foregrounded today in favor of career enhancement. As language educators and multilingual and multicultural individuals, we continue to believe that language proficiency and language development are important contributors to all the other goals.

There are various research methodological issues that influence the generalizations and implications we can draw from the previous research. There are few long-term studies that take into consideration the post-sojourn retention of developments. Furthermore, studies typically investigate a sample of convenience (i.e., the ones that opt to do education abroad and either have no comparison group or compare them to the overall student population). This is an unfair comparison as the students who opt to go abroad may already be different from those who do not. Tullock and Ortega (2017) in their scoping review point out that there is too much variability in measurements and research is ignoring multilingualism in education abroad. Similarly, Kinginger (2010) argues that research is conducted and presented from an ethnocentric viewpoint and does not consider the local context. By drawing from a broad variety of research studies, we hope to bring a fuller picture to education abroad. As is common in education abroad research summaries, we acknowledge that certain data sets are overrepresented most notably Dewey's data and the IES alumni survey results. This is particularly problematic when talking about long-term effects and effects outside of language proficiency and intercultural competence, since many of those studies are based on the IES alumni survey, which – while very large – is not representative of overall education abroad participants and is based on self-perception not actual assessments of the reported learning outcomes.

The research-based outcome summaries are divided into four chapters along the following themes: Language development; intercultural competence development; academic, personal, and professional development; and impact on communities.

Chapter 2.2. Language Learning Outcomes

Assessment of Language Learning During Education Abroad

As language learning remains one of the primary goals of education abroad, especially in long-term programs, all language skills have received attention in research studies and a myriad of assessments have been employed to uncover the effects of education abroad on these skills.

Oral proficiency has been assessed most frequently and the most commonly used assessment is ACTFL's Oral Proficiency Interview (OPI). Other assessments include:

- Using native speakers to assess speaking samples based on provided criteria (Yager, 1998) or holistically (J. Kim, Dewey, Baker-Smemoe, & Ring, 2015).
- The Simulated Oral Proficiency Interview (SOPI) (Miano, Bernhardt, & Brates, 2016).
- The Oral Proficiency Interview by Computer (OPIC) (Godfrey, Treacy, & Tarone, 2014).

Often, researchers assess a variety of measures in oral speech samples of students, such as:

- Complexity (Leonard & Shea, 2017).
- Accuracy (Huensch & Tracy-Ventura, 2017) or tonal accuracy (J. Kim et al., 2015).
- Different measures of fluency (Huensch & Tracy-Ventura, 2017) including speech rate (Towell, Hawkins, & Bazergui, 1996), breakdown fluency through filled and unfilled pauses (J. Kim et al., 2015), and repair fluency through repetitions (Huensch & Tracy-Ventura, 2017).
- Vocabulary knowledge (J. Kim et al., 2015).

In addition to relying on students' individual speech samples, studies have analyzed speech in role-plays between language learners in order to evaluate language gains (Lara, Mora, & Pérez-Vidal, 2015).

Writing proficiency has been assessed using:

- ACTFL's Writing Proficiency Test (WPT) (Miano et al., 2016).
- The DIALANG test (Schenker, 2018).
- Samples of students' writings such as picture description tasks (Putra, 2014), argumentative essays (Sasaki, 2009) or students' e-journals (Stewart, 2010).

For reading and listening skills, studies have employed tests and assessments, such as:

- The Educational Testing Service Listening and Reading Tests (Rivers, 1998), replaced in 2004 by the online reading and listening tests by A-CLASS (Davidson, 2010; Hampel & Hauck, 2004).
- The DIALANG test (Schenker, 2018).
- The Defense Language Proficiency Test (Watson, Siska, & Wolfel, 2013).
- Their own tools, for example reading passages with different question types (Lapkin, Hart, & Swain, 1995), texts with comprehension questions (Borras & Llanes, 2020), a picture matching task based on audio descriptions (Llanes & Muñoz, 2009), or free-recall protocols (Dewey, 2004).

Vocabulary development has been assessed using:

- Measures of type/token ratios in speaking samples (J. Kim et al., 2015).
- Three-word association test (AV3T) (Ife, Vives, & Meara, 2000).
- Lexical decision tasks (Grey, Cox, Serafini, & Sanz, 2015).
- The Eurocentres Vocabulary Size Test (Milton & Meara, 1995).
- The Swansea Levels X-lex test (Tracy-Ventura, 2017).
- The Updated Vocabulary Levels Test (Borras & Llanes, 2020).
- Writing tasks to measure productive vocabulary (Borras & Llanes, 2020).

Grammar skills have been assessed with measures such as:

- Self-designed grammar tests with multiple-choice questions (Klapper & Rees, 2012).
- A holistic evaluation of accuracy in students' writing (Douthit, Schaake, Hay, Grieger, & Bormann, 2015).
- Analysis of specific grammar structures in students' speech or writing samples (Lindseth, 2016; Marqués-Pascual, 2011; Putra, 2014).
- Grammaticality judgement tests (Serrano, Llanes, & Tragant, 2016).
- Written scenarios with discourse tasks to be completed (Xu, Case, & Wang, 2009).
- Picture narration tasks (Arnett, 2013).

To assess other skill areas, a variety of distinct measures were employed, such as reading tasks for phonetic development (Bongiovanni, Long, Solon, & Willis, 2015; Diaz-Campos, 2004), or computerized pragmatic listening tests for assessing pragmatic development (Taguchi, 2008, 2011). Many studies also rely on students' self-assessments to evaluate the impact their time abroad had on their skills (Davie, 1996; Meara, 1994; Roskvist, Harvey, Corder, & Stacey, 2014). While generally showing positive results, studies based on students' perceptions only give a partial picture of the potential of education abroad to affect linguistic abilities and self-assessments often do not correlate to actual gains (Lapkin et al., 1995).

Due to the large variety of measures applied to assessing language learning outcomes in education abroad, inconsistent findings emerge, and generalizations and comparisons are not always possible. For example, a meta-analysis of education abroad research revealed that 31 studies of fluency made use of 75 different measures of the construct (Tullock & Ortega, 2017). Furthermore, many studies lack a control group or compare groups with different profiles. Weak statistical analyses in quantitative studies have also been criticized (Rees & Klapper, 2008). Additionally, Kinginger (2009) calls for the development of empirical tests that assess everyday speech in different languages to address the realities of the language students use and learn during education abroad. She emphasizes that none of the frequently used assessment tools, "capture the subtle changes occurring as language learners abroad enlarge their communicative repertoires" (p. 68).

Overall, results of language research on education abroad offer "an encouraging picture. [...] the research provides convincing, concrete, and detailed evidence to back up the impression that study abroad is especially useful" (Kinginger, 2009, pp. 208–209) in the domain of fluency development, starting and ending conversations, and developing native-like features. In general, education abroad has the potential to help learners increase in all areas of their linguistic abilities, but research often focuses on short-term program outcomes and students' speaking proficiency. Reading and listening skills have received limited attention in previous research and studies on year-long programs are scarce.

Short-Term Program Outcomes

Speaking

Studies analyzing the effects of short programs of eight weeks or less on students' target language speaking proficiency generally show positive results. Many short-term studies focus on US learners, usually native speakers of English. For example, 15 out of the 20 participants in a four-week program in Madrid improved their speaking skills by at least one step on the SOPI, with some improving by two levels (Hernández, 2016). Milleret (1991) also used an adapted OPI and found that the average gain was one step from Intermediate Mid (IM) to Intermediate High (IH). Another study, also focusing on a short five-week program in Spain, revealed that, from a qualitative perspective, students improved their ability for oral narration (Duperron & Overstreet, 2009). Using a picture–narration and role-play task to assess oral skills, Allen and Herron (2003) noted significant gains in all assessed areas (amount of communication, comprehensibility, fluency, and quality of communication) for their US participants in the six-week program in France.

Students studying for six weeks in Germany also significantly improved their speaking proficiency in all components that were measured by native speaker raters on a scale developed by the researcher. The components included fluency, accentedness, pronunciation, grammar and vocabulary (Hardison, 2014). Some short-term studies, on the other hand, showed no or little evidence of progress in speaking proficiency. In their 6–11-day programs for UK teenagers in France, Evans and Fisher (2005) noted "no general pattern of progress" (p. 180). Similarly, Martinsen (2010) only revealed modest changes in oral proficiency of US learners of Spanish after six weeks in Argentina as assessed by trained raters using a rubric.

Positive results were also found for learners outside of the US, such as Spanish students in short-term programs in England. Spanish teenagers improved significantly in their speaking proficiency as measured by an oral picture-telling task. Gains were strongest in the areas of fluency and moderate for lexical richness and accuracy (Serrano et al., 2016). Similarly, Spanish students of different ages who participated in 3–4-week programs in English-speaking countries improved on four out of the six oral proficiency measures included in a study by Llanes and Muñoz (2009).

Listening

Unsurprisingly, perhaps, short-term education abroad has shown to affect students' listening skills positively. In fact, one study that investigated the effects of a very short stay in France on British adolescents' French skills, showed that the listening skills improved the most along with writing proficiency (Evans & Fisher, 2005). Similarly, a 3–4-week program for Spanish speakers in English-speaking countries resulted in significantly higher scores on the post-listening test than on the pre-listening one (Llanes & Muñoz, 2009). In line with that, a four-week program for US students in Germany also resulted in significant gains in listening abilities moving the majority of students from A1 on the CEFR to A2, with some students even reaching the B2 level after their education abroad program (Schenker, 2018). Students in this study also performed significantly better than students taking the same courses at home. Positive results were also found in a study investigating students' gains after a six-week stay in France (Allen & Herron, 2003). Students' listening skills improved significantly, and their self-reported confidence in several listening tasks had also increased, although self-assessments of some abilities, such as understanding native speakers when speaking naturally, remained unchanged. Intensive four- and six-week summer immersion in China for US Air Force Academy Cadets also led to statistically significant increases in students' listening comprehension skills (Savage & Hughes, 2014).

A comparison of an intensive five-week education abroad course in France and the same course on the home campus, showed that both groups increased on two of the three sections of the listening test (Cubillos, Chieffo, & Fan, 2008), but there were no significant differences found between the groups. However, the study revealed that students at home and abroad used different listening strategies. While research has found gains in listening skills through education abroad, the study by Cubillos and colleagues puts into question whether those gains would have been greater than those of students staying at home.

Writing and Grammar

Few studies have investigated the effects of short-term education abroad on learners' writing and grammar skills, which typically also do not tend to be the focus of the experience. The aforementioned study by Evans and Fisher (2005) which investigated changes in the language skills of British teenagers as a result of short stays in France, identified writing as the most improved skill along with listening. Schenker's (2018) study on learners of German in a four-week program in Berlin also showed significant gains in the area of writing. While 11 students were on level A1 before the summer, only two remained at A1 after the summer. This program had included specific writing practice through daily blogging. A five-week program for future Spanish teachers in the US, which included a three-week stay in Mexico, showed significant differences in accuracy and amount of writing based on six participants' pre- and post-essays (Cubillos, 2004). However, based on a thorough review of previous literature, Serrano, Tragant, and Llanes (2012) conclude that short-term education abroad may not be sufficient for improving writing skills in significant ways.

Research on grammar skills and education abroad is equally scarce and the few existing results are mixed. Menard-Warwick and Palmer (2012) conducted a case study of three learners in a five-week program in Mexico and could not find evidence of development in their use of verbs. The authors also noted strong individual differences. Another study indicates modest advantages for grammar skill development of at-home instruction over short-term education abroad of three or four weeks for teenagers learning English (Serrano et al., 2016). In contrast, Schenker (2018) saw significant gains in grammar knowledge for her 43 learners of German in a four-week summer course in Germany, but did not see differences between the education abroad group and the students who had taken the equivalent course during the semester on the home campus. Additionally, a five-week program in Barcelona for US learners of Spanish led to significant improvements in grammar as measured on students' success on a grammaticality judgment test (Grey et al., 2015). Specifically, students improved on word order and number agreement but increases were non-significant for gender agreement. A study summarizing two short-term programs to Argentina (14 days) and Australia (10 days), in which students engaged in blogging or hand-written journaling, concluded that students were able to improve grammar, punctuation and spelling through blogging, more so than through hand-written journaling (Douthit et al., 2015). Once again it appears that what students do abroad has an influence on the impact of education abroad on skill development.

Reading and Vocabulary

Comparing gains in reading for students in an at-home program and a nine-week summer course in Japan, Huebner (1995) identified slight advantages for the education abroad group. This may be due to the fact that the students in Japan were surrounded by Japanese writing while the students at home had limited input in this area. The study also noted that individual gains differed more widely for the students in Japan. Similarly, an intensive immersion program in China for US Air Force Academy cadets led to significant improvements in reading comprehension (Savage & Hughes, 2014). Schenker's (2018) study also revealed significant gains in the areas of reading as well as vocabulary, but while the education abroad group gained more than students in the regular program at home, the at-home group outperformed the education abroad students in reading. In contrast, Dewey (2004) also compared Japanese progress in an education abroad and an intensive immersion context at home through the Middlebury program. The eleven- and nine-week programs, respectively, did not result in different outcomes for the at-home and education abroad group for free-recall and vocabulary knowledge though the means for both groups increased. However, the education abroad students self-assessed their reading comprehension more strongly, which points to the dangers of using self-assessment to make arguments about education abroad outcomes.

Even short programs abroad have been shown to produce measurable gains in students' vocabulary (Grey et al., 2015; Hardison, 2014). In their 5-week program in Spain, students improved their lexical accuracy, specifically in identifying non-words. Specific gains were identified for the acquisition of idiomatic phrasal verbs in English by Chinese learners, though variation between students' individual achievements was large (Conroy, 2016) and linked to their homestay experience. Spanish teenagers in Llanes and Muñoz (2009) significantly decreased their lexical errors as a result of their 3–4-week education abroad experience in an English-speaking country. Similarly, another study by Borras and Llanes (2020) also investigating Spanish teenagers learning English through short-term study abroad showed positive results for students' fluency in reading, reading comprehension, and receptive vocabulary. However, the three-week program did not produce measurable gains in productive vocabulary, specifically lexical fluency, lexical sophistication and lexical density.

In addition to the already mentioned outcomes, studies investigating short-term programs have shown positive results for students' pragmatic competence (Hassall, 2013; Reynolds-Case, 2013), phonetic knowledge (Bongiovanni et al., 2015) and pronunciation (Diaz-Campos, 2004).

Concerns in Short-Term Programs

Linguistic gains vary drastically from student to student and a large percentage does not show any improvements. For example, no phonological gains were

"speech rate, articulation rate, phonation time ratio, pause length, and native speaker rating" (Tullock & Ortega, 2017, p. 13). All in all, research on year-long education abroad outcomes consistently shows significant increases in oral proficiency, often measured by the OPI (Di Silvio et al., 2016; Iwasaki, 2007; Lindseth, 2010) or SOPI (Hernández, 2010a; J. Kim et al., 2015). Other measures were also employed to assess fluency in speaking samples or through interviews and results all in all show positive trends (Du, 2013; Marqués-Pascual, 2011; Stewart, 2010). Substantial gains in speaking proficiency are often found for participants in year-long programs (Carlson, Burn, Useem, & Yachimowicz, 1991) though even semester-long programs have led to measurable increases.

Long-term education abroad is especially useful in helping students reach advanced levels of speaking proficiency, which are often nearly impossible to achieve with just at-home classroom instruction. Brecht, Davidson, and Ginsberg (1995) found that without education abroad only 13% of students reach advanced levels of Russian, whereas with semester-long education abroad it was 40%. They conclude "that at least one semester of study in-country is required if any sizable percentage of students studying Russian is to reach at least a functional level of competence in speaking" (p. 55).

Spending an entire year or more abroad can also lead to pronunciation that shows patterns used by native speakers which is not achieved by students who never went abroad (Han, Hwang, & Choi, 2011). Students who spent a year abroad in Germany, for example, were rated as more native-like by native speakers of German in their pronunciation than students who had studied German in the US only (O'Brien, 2003). Thus, year-long education abroad can support students in sounding more native-like than their classmates who remained at home (Foster, 2009). In line with oral proficiency, education abroad also assists students in developing stronger narrative and discursive skills (Lafford, 2004). These skills were stronger than those developed by a comparative group who had stayed at home.

Writing

Another language area that can benefit from extended study in another country is the domain of writing, although it has not received as much attention as oral proficiency. Students who had spent a year abroad in various countries felt that their writing skills had seen only small improvements and quantitative analysis of data confirms that minor gains were made (Meara, 1994). The results of the Language and Social Networks Abroad Project (LANGSNAP) on 57 British undergraduates studying abroad in France, Mexico, or Spain for nine months showed slight improvements in written fluency for the French learners, as well as an increase in their ability to write in different genres (Mitchell et al., 2017). The Spanish learners showed significant increases in their written fluency which they maintained even after returning home.

Contrary to those findings, programs of only three months appear to cause positive writing gains that are, however, not maintained fifteen months after students return home. Pérez-Vidal and Juan-Garau (2009) analyzed the writing of English learners from Spain who studied for three months abroad. The results showed several improvements for the education abroad group who increased significantly in lexical diversity, as well as in accuracy, where the finding approached significance. Even students who spent only one semester abroad produced writing that was deemed more fluent both by native speaker raters and expert language instructors (Freed et al., 2003). However, comparing two and three months abroad led Baró and Serrano (2011) to conclude that an extra month abroad does not make a difference for students' writing. In connection to other studies on writing development, it appears that one semester may not be sufficient to develop certain aspects of writing performance.

Comparisons of education abroad and at-home students are favorable for the education abroad context. In a study by Sasaki (2004), which compared EFL writing of students who spent one or two semesters in an English-speaking country to students staying in Japan, the education abroad group showed significant gains in writing proficiency and the at-home group did not. In a follow-up study that traced Japanese students' English writing skills over a 3.5-year period, Sasaki (2009) found out that only students who had studied abroad improved their writing proficiency. The at-home group even performed more poorly in their senior than in their freshman year. Sasaki (2011) further revealed that only spending time abroad impacted students' motivation to continue to improve their EFL writing. The studies support Serrano et al.'s (2012) findings that more than one semester abroad seems to be necessary in order to achieve noticeable gains in writing. Other studies also show that writing measured globally develops more strongly in the education abroad context compared to students who stayed at home (Godfrey et al., 2014). However, looking at different components of writing showed that the at-home group made greater gains in fluency, while the education abroad group showed greater development in accuracy. The authors conclude that both groups made progress in writing over the course of one semester at home and in France, but they developed in different areas.

Vocabulary

Vocabulary knowledge can grow greatly through long-term education abroad programs (J. Kim et al., 2015; Pizziconi, 2017; Tracy-Ventura, 2017). Semester- and year-long education abroad has been shown to be highly beneficial for growing the range of students' vocabulary (Ife et al., 2000; J. Kim et al., 2015). Academic year abroad programs have also been shown to help students develop their lexical diversity (Mitchell et al., 2017) which they are showing higher levels of than students who study the language at home (Foster, 2009). Spending a year abroad, and "being exposed to the language on a daily basis in all manner of contexts, results in an enriched and networked lexicon which enables the learner to 'sound more natural'" (Foster, 2009, p. 105). While some studies suggest that low-proficiency learners benefit more in their vocabulary learning during education abroad (Milton & Meara, 1995), other research suggests that intermediate and advanced students also benefit in their vocabulary advancement during time abroad (Ife et al., 2000). According to Pizziconi (2017), however, considering Japanese learners' potential gains in a year abroad, low- and high-performing students achieve similar results. In fact, it has been suggested that the growth rate of vocabulary knowledge is four times higher during a semester abroad than during regular at-home instruction (Milton & Meara, 1995).

Perhaps not surprising, comparing vocabulary acquisition in education abroad contexts with students who stayed at home generally shows stronger gains for the education abroad groups who spent an entire year (Foster, 2009) or at least one semester (Dewey, 2008; Tanaka & Ellis, 2003) abroad, than the students who learned the language without studying abroad. In fact, students who spent an entire year abroad used language that was as diverse as that of native speakers (Foster, 2009). In contrast to the positive findings outlined above, Collentine (2004), who compared learning of students spending one semester abroad in Spain and those studying Spanish at home in the US, showed that the at-home group acquired more discrete lexical features. The study indicates that three months abroad is not a more suitable context for acquiring lexical skills than studying at home. Since studies on year-long programs (Pizziconi, 2017; Tracy-Ventura, 2017) show significant increases in how students use and know vocabulary items, it could be suspected that large gains are made after more than one semester abroad. This was confirmed by comparative research (Briggs, 2015; Ife et al., 2000).

Grammar

Year-long education abroad can help students make significant progress in their grammar skills as shown in a study by Klapper and Rees (2012) on UK students studying in Germany for a year, although strong individual differences were noted. In addition, Isabelli-García (2007) showed that students with one or two semesters of education abroad or other extended long-term residences in other countries benefited more from specific grammar instruction after their return. Specifically, they were able to use the subjunctive in Spanish more effectively after post-return instruction of this grammatical concept.

A small comparison of only two education abroad students in the US and two at-home students in Indonesia showed that the education abroad students developed their grammatical accuracy more strongly (Putra, 2014). However, other studies comparing at-home and education abroad contexts did not always find that the education abroad context produced stronger results. For example, Freed et al. (2003) noted that the at-home and education abroad group did not differ in their grammatical accuracy when comparing pre- and post-essays. Similarly, another study found that the at-home group developed better on discrete lexical and grammatical items than the group studying abroad for one semester (Collentine, 2004). Arnett (2013) found no differences on use of auxiliary for German past-tense or for accusative and dative forms between students in a semester program abroad and the at-home group. Likewise, Marqués-Pascual (2011) found that there were certain grammatical concepts that can be learned as well in at-home as education abroad contexts, but that other structures, such as the omission of thematic subjects in Spanish, are better learned through semester-long education abroad. Students in education abroad have been shown to develop a stronger socio-pragmatic awareness, such as when to use formal vs. informal address forms in French (Kinginger, 2008). Similarly to other language domains, pragmatic and grammatical competence improved more in longer stays (Xu et al., 2009).

Listening and Reading

Few studies have focused on the development of listening and reading skills during long-term education abroad. Nonetheless, the available studies point to the fact that listening as well as reading proficiency also benefit from a longer stay in the target culture (Davidson, 2010; Dyson, 1988). Learners themselves notice an increase in their listening proficiency after a year abroad (Aydin, 2012; Davie, 1996; Meara, 1994) which may not be surprising given the extended opportunities for hearing the language that a year abroad provides. In Aydin's (2012) study on pre-service teachers of English from Turkey who participated in the ERASMUS program, the participants noted improvements in their English reading, writing, listening, and speaking skills along with vocabulary knowledge and pronunciation improvements.

Kinginger's (2008) study of 23 American students on a semester-long program in France showed that, overall, students made significant progress in both reading and listening as measured by a standardized test. In spite of this result, twelve students did not gain enough to proceed to the next proficiency level. Looking at the scores for reading and listening separately, Kinginger (2008) notes that gains for reading were much lower than for listening where the gain scores were often substantial. This finding is echoed in the study by Lapkin et al. (1995) who also found that the semester-long program produced stronger gains in students' listening than in reading proficiency.

Tanaka and Ellis (2003) noted that although students improved their listening and reading proficiency after a fifteen-week program in Japan, the scores for overall proficiency gains were stronger than the individual progress made in listening and reading. Another study which focused on Spanish learners of English who spent a semester abroad revealed significant gains in listening proficiency which were maintained fifteen months after the end of the program (Beattie, Valls-Ferrer, & Pérez-Vidal, 2014). Additionally, the gains made in education abroad were stronger than those made by the students in the at-home context. In contrast to these positive findings, Watson et al. (2013) analyzed results of semester-long programs in various countries and languages for US Military Academy students and found that only about half of the 498 participants crossed a threshold to the next level in listening and reading proficiency. Several students showed a negative gain in reading and listening, which although found disturbing by the authors, could be attributed to the assessment tool that was used (the Defense Language Proficiency Test).

Long-term programs can help students become a full participant in exchanges in the host language(s) as shown in a study by Dings (2012). While learners abroad at first often interact from a novice learner standpoint with the native speakers acting as experts, toward the end of a year abroad, language learners are no longer seen as peripheral participants in conversations but as full conversation partners. Students who spent six or more months abroad realize that language skills will not develop automatically by being in the community but that contact with expert speakers of the language is crucial in order for them to improve their language proficiency. Most students realize that seeking out opportunities for interacting with expert speakers is their responsibility (Aydin, 2012; Bicknese, 1971).

Further language-related skills acquired by students in year-long education abroad settings include:

- Increased interactional competence (Dings, 2014; Masuda, 2011; Shively, 2015; Taguchi, 2015).
- Sociolinguistic competence (Barron, 2006; Howard, 2008; Regan, 1995, 2005; Regan, Howard, & Lemée, 2009).
- Socio-pragmatic competence (Barron, 2003; Matsumura, 2003).
- Pragmatic competence (Félix-Brasdefer, 2013; Hassall, 2013; Matsumura, 2001; Reynolds-Case, 2013; Schauer, 2007; Warga & Schölmberger, 2007).

Regan's (2005) study on the acquisition of sociolinguistic competence by learners of French showed that even a year after their year abroad, students were still using the investigated pattern in the same way as native speakers of French thus showing a long-lasting effect of year-long education abroad. Garbati and Rothschild (2016) found a long-lasting impact of long-term study abroad in metalinguistic awareness.

At-Home versus Education Abroad

Several studies show that education abroad promotes the acquisition of stronger skills than at-home instruction. Foster (2009) noted that students in year-long education abroad in London developed their lexical skills more strongly than their peers at home in Teheran. Nonetheless, there were several measures on which no significant difference was found such as some measures of fluency and accuracy.

When comparing education abroad to intensive at-home immersion, the outcomes are often more similar (Serrano, Llanes, & Tragant, 2011). However, Freed, Segalowitz, and Dewey (2004) compared a semester abroad in France to traditional at-home instruction and an intensive 7-week immersion summer course at home and found that the students in the immersion context showed gains on all fluency measures, whereas the education abroad group only showed gains on four out of the six. Overall, the results showed that the immersion groups' gains were largest, and the at-home groups made the smallest gains and actually had lower post- than pre-scores on several measures. Collentine (2004) showed that the at-home group performed better on certain grammar and lexical items, but the education abroad group developed stronger narrative abilities and used semantically denser language. The study underlines the importance of carefully monitoring education abroad program components and increasing students' opportunities for language learning while abroad. Simply spending a semester abroad will not result in stronger outcomes. In this study, the immersion group reported using the L2 more than the education abroad group and gains in fluency were connected to reported language use.

Based on the findings by Marqués-Pascual (2011), some features of language can be better acquired in an education abroad context, such as omission of the thematic subject, while others can be learned equally well in the at-home context, such as Spanish verb agreement morphology. A similar conclusion is drawn by Serrano et al. (2016). Based on a comparison of three-week program abroad and at-home classes, the at-home context was more effective for improving grammatical knowledge and the education abroad context produced better outcomes in oral lexical richness.

Program Design and Language Learning

Length consistently impacts language skills (Dwyer, 2004b; Félix-Brasdefer, 2013; Ife et al., 2000; Sasaki, 2009): Vocabulary (Briggs, 2015; Ife et al. 2000), lexical development (Collentine, 2004; Milton & Meara, 1995), and listening (Davidson, 2010). Davidson (2010) compared outcomes of summer, semester and year-long programs and confirmed that gains are strongly correlated to length of time spent abroad. Only year-long programs enabled students to reach Superior or Distinguished levels in Russian.

From a second language acquisition standpoint, it is no surprise that a longer stay which coincides with more input and output in the host community language results in greater language proficiency development. Research has confirmed that longer education abroad is more beneficial for language development

Segalowitz and Freed (2004) found that most interactions between participants and host families were short and formulaic and limited in topic scope. Tanaka (2007) and Wilkinson (1998) also found that there was limited interaction. Some host families use English rather than the community language with the program participants. Collentine (2009) found that host families use teacher talk with students, which has a negative impact on the participants' language learning. Similarly, Iino (2006) revealed that Japanese host families used simplified language and provided limited corrective feedback. All of these aspects of the quality of the interactions, can negatively impact the language and cultural competence development of participants. Lafford (2004) showed that the more time the students spoke with their host families, the more they focused on form rather than meaning. It could be that the positive impact of host families on participants' language learning does not set in until they feel comfortable with each other to also engage in language negotiations.

Di Silvio, Donovan, and Malone (2014) found that students who perceived themselves to have gained less language skill during their time abroad than they had hoped have a more negative view on their homestay than those who were satisfied with their progress. Interestingly, Di Silvio and colleagues found that the satisfaction with the homestay was more closely related with their satisfaction with their language learning than their actual language learning gains. Martinsen (2010) found no relationship between satisfaction with the homestay and language learning gains. Homestay's effectiveness can be improved through careful selection and preparation before education abroad, and communication tasks to support engagement and language learning during the stay abroad.

Curricular features can also impact language learning such as experiential components, immersive tasks, awareness-raising and reflective tasks. Language learning also benefits from awareness-raising activities (Goertler & the 369ers, 2019; Shively, 2010; Watson & Wolfel, 2015). Savicki and Price (2015) summarize a study which prompted students to write three reflective essays: one before, one during, and one after education abroad. In their writings, students were prompted to discuss academic expectations, cultural expectations, and psychological issues. The authors conclude that the specific prompts enabled students to not only reflect but also show cognitive complexity in their writings which demonstrated their attempt to process their experiences. They also recommend including even more student writings at a later time after their return to the US. The Center for Advanced Research on Language Acquisition at University of Minnesota created a collection of reflective activities for before, during, and after education abroad (Paige, Cohen, Kappler, Chi, & Lassegard, 2002), the implementation of which has revealed positive effects for both the development of intercultural competence as well as linguistic ability, especially pragmatics (Cohen et al., 2005).

When considering language learning effects, research shows that pre-departure language instruction can improve learning outcomes abroad, for example in the area of pragmatic awareness (Halenko & Jones, 2017). Pizziconi (2017) suggests that "going to Japan at a lower proficiency level following intensive pre-[study abroad] language training enables greater gains during the [study abroad] and possibly a long-term advantage in terms of attainment levels after four years" (p. 146). If so designed, language classes can also serve as a place to engage students in cultural simulations, practice ethnographic interviewing, and analyze cultural observations thereby preparing students with skills in addition to language that will be helpful once they are abroad (Kruse & Brubaker, 2007).

Students in direct-enroll or related programs with insufficient language ability are likely to require additional language courses before they can enroll in regular classes at the institutions abroad. Thus, pre-departure language abilities can also impact students' academic adjustment abroad. If they do not possess adequate language skills, they may not be able to understand lectures in the target language (Kuo, 2011) or participate actively in seminars, and may find it difficult to interact with host community members (Wright & Schartner, 2013), all of which will impact their adjustment and further language progress.

Individual Differences Impacting Language Learning

There are several specific internal factors that affect the language learning outcomes of education abroad, including students' intercultural competence, and the pre-departure language proficiency of students. There is no clear consensus about the ideal initial language proficiency for education abroad participants but the current research points to the existence of a threshold-level of grammatical competence that students should possess in order to benefit from education abroad (Lafford & Collentine, 2006; Llanes, 2011). As DeKeyser suggests, if students "know the rules of the language for communication, however haltingly, then they will become much better at using them through repeated practice abroad" (DeKeyser, 2007, p. 217). Results from previous studies suggest that learners with lower initial language proficiency show greater gains through education abroad (Avello & Lara, 2014; Beattie et al., 2014; Brecht et al., 1995; Collentine, 2009; Duperron & Overstreet, 2009; Freed, 1995b; Juan-Garau, 2014; Milleret, 1991; Mitchell et al., 2017; Tanaka & Ellis, 2003; Valls-Ferrer & Mora, 2014). A study on students with no prior target language knowledge showed that long-term education abroad of one year did have strong significant effects on their skills and students were able to reach IH levels or higher after the first five months abroad (Spenader, 2011).

While there is some evidence for a threshold level of grammar competence needed to benefit from education abroad, most studies also suggest that students make stronger linguistic gains during education abroad if they begin their sojourn with lower language proficiency (Brecht et al., 1995; Duperron & Overstreet, 2009; Freed, 1990, 1995b; Juan-Garau, 2014; Lapkin et al., 1995; Llanes & Muñoz, 2009; Milleret, 1991). This suggests that in addition to a threshold level, there might also be a ceiling effect. The trend is observed in all language skills including listening (Beattie et al., 2014), speaking (Juan-Garau, 2014), and grammar (Duperron & Overstreet, 2009).

Some studies, on the other hand, did not reveal stronger gains for low-proficiency learners. For example a study investigating vocabulary knowledge in semester and year-long education abroad showed that low-proficiency learners did not make stronger gains than more advanced students (Ife et al., 2000). Similarly, another study investigating reading development showed that students with low reading proficiency did not develop more strongly than those with average reading proficiency (Lapkin et al., 1995). However, students with very low proficiency may not benefit from education abroad due to insufficient prior knowledge. In DeKeyser's (2010) study, for example, students' lack of grammatical knowledge prevented them from making progress during a six-week stay abroad. Lapkin et al. (1995) support the threshold hypothesis based on their findings that students with especially low reading pre-scores did not achieve greater proficiency gains than students with medium pre-scores as a result of a three-month program. A threshold level also seems to exist for the development of grammatical competence. Lafford and Collentine (2006) suggest that "those students with a well-developed cognitive, lexical, and grammatical base will be more able to process and produce grammatical forms more accurately after their experience in a study abroad context" (p. 117). Similarly, without a certain level of grammatical knowledge, students in a six-week program abroad were unable to make measurable progress and felt frustrated over their lack of language gains. DeKeyser (2010) noted that "the promise of study abroad remains unfulfilled without adequate preparation in the form of proceduralized or at least declarative knowledge of the second language grammar" (p. 80). In the context of grammatical knowledge, DeKeyser (2010) suggests, that "the more they know, the more they can get better at using what they know through practice" (p. 90). This confirms findings of an earlier study that showed that better basic grammar knowledge was a predictor of stronger gains in reading, listening, and speaking proficiency (Brecht et al., 1995). The threshold hypothesis may be true for different language domains.

In general, students at different proficiency levels show different developmental patterns during education abroad (Marqués-Pascual, 2011). Similarly, a case study of British students abroad showed that strong gains can be made regardless of prior language ability (Mitchell et al., 2017). Based on her study of oral proficiency gains during a semester abroad, Lindseth (2010) suggests that sending students abroad when they have an IM proficiency may be the ideal time because it gives them a good chance of advancing to IH or Advanced Low (AL). Since students with extremely low pre-study abroad language levels generally do not improve as strongly, researchers conclude that a basic threshold level has to be achieved before students can make noticeable gains in education abroad (Llanes, 2011). Yet, the ideal time for students to go abroad depends on their individual goals as well as the program objectives so that different models need to be available for students.

In spite of the threshold hypothesis, even low-proficiency learners can benefit from education abroad because other factors such as personality and identity perceptions affect the learning outcomes as well. In connection to language skill development, Taguchi (2016) found that students with high levels of flexibility/ openness might be better equipped to develop their pragmatic competence abroad because of the underlying assumption that openness is accompanied by adaptability which is needed in order to adjust to different situational needs. She concludes, that "people who are more open-minded to differences might have an edge on pragmatic abilities because of the common underlying attributes of adaptability, flexibility, and variability" (p. 361).

Language proficiency and its development during education abroad has important effects on the outcomes of the sojourn in many domains. For example, students may feel insecure and uncomfortable to seek interactions with others while abroad if they perceive their language ability as not strong enough to have successful conversations (Tanaka, 2007). At the same time, the amount of contact with target member speakers affects how well students adjust and learn abroad and how they develop (Nguyen, Jefferies, & Rojas, 2018). Not only pre-departure language ability but also students' self-perceived L2 abilities affect learning during education abroad. Students who feel anxious about their L2 skills often underestimate their abilities (MacIntyre, Noels, & Clément, 1997) which may prevent them from seeking interactions in the host language(s). Additionally, language learning aptitude affects the linguistic progress during education abroad (Brecht et al., 1995; Davidson, 2010).

While Robson's (2015b) analysis of Asian learners in the UK revealed that self-perceived communication competence predicted learner engagement more strongly than self-perceived willingness to communicate (WTC), the study also revealed that instruction and class design can affect students' WTC in education abroad contexts (Mystkowska-Wiertelak & Pawlak, 2017; Robson, 2015a). One important variable, for example, is the role of the teacher in language instruction. As can be expected, students with higher levels of pre-departure WTC communicate more frequently in the host language abroad than their first language(s) (Yashima, Zenuk-Nishide, & Shimizu, 2004). Additionally, education abroad programs can positively impact students' WTC (De Poli, Vergolini, & Zanini, 2018). It must be pointed out that WTC alone does not guarantee that increased interactions with local community members will take place. As studies have shown (Kinginger, 2004), many participants in education abroad struggle to find meaningful engagement with host community members and this is sometimes attributed to a lack of interest from host community members to interact with international students (Brown, 2009a). While possessing high levels of WTC is an important factor for education abroad, students might need other strategies for establishing contact and interacting with members of the target community, which explains the impact of immersive tasks discussed in the previous chapter.

Even in long-term programs, students' linguistic gains are not equal and strong individual differences have been revealed (Klapper & Rees, 2012). While great developments in students' language skills can occur during year-long programs, this development is non-linear (Bacon, 2002; Warga & Schölmberger, 2007) and impacted by a variety of factors. As Freed notes, "as in all second language learning, there is great variation in student performance with a suggestion that individual differences may be yet more pronounced for those who have been abroad" (Freed, 1995a, p. 27). These differences have been attributed to students' emotional intelligence levels as well as the arbitrary experience of a year abroad which does not follow a standardized program (Klapper & Rees, 2012). Wang (2010) notes, "Whether study abroad can make a difference has to do with an infinite number of variables including the type and the quality of interactions the learners have with others and with the study abroad environment" (p. 57).

In their large-scale study about proficiency gains by students studying in Russia for one semester based on data from fifteen years, Brecht et al. (1995) identified several predictors of gains in reading and listening. For example, students with prior experience in Russia were more likely to gain in listening proficiency, as well as students with knowledge of other languages, students with higher pre-program reading proficiency, and younger students as well as male students. Age can be an advantage in language and in several contexts male students have more access to interactions. Gender can play a role in how fully students are able to participate in social interactions (Trentman, 2013; Walsh & DeJoseph, 2003). Female students also have challenges to establish a social network needed for language development (Kinginger, 2004; Polanyi, 1995). It should then be no surprise that in the study by Brecht et al. (1995) of education abroad in Russia men were more likely to reach Advanced Low proficiency than women.

Individual differences play a large role in language development of education abroad students (Collentine, 2009; Mitchell et al., 2017). Examinations of education abroad contexts have shown that students with higher processing speeds made stronger advances in complexity, fluency and accuracy in L2 speaking (Leonard & Shea, 2017). Similarly, Wright (2013) found that Chinese students studying in the UK showed L2 oral proficiency improvements that were affected by their working memory. Phonological memory has also been shown to contribute to oral proficiency gains during a semester abroad (O'Brien, Segalowitz, Freed, & Collentine, 2007). Faretta-Stutenberg and Morgan-Short (2017) investigated whether individual cognitive abilities affect learning and compared the contextual impact of at-home and a semester-abroad program and found some difference. Some students who return from education abroad have made little progress in their language skills which led Sunderman and Kroll (2009) to analyze whether a threshold of cognitive resources must exist for students to benefit from education abroad. Their results on accuracy in L2 production showed that a certain level of working memory has to be possessed by students in order to benefit from their education abroad experience. However, their threshold hypothesis was not confirmed for students' comprehension skills. The authors conclude that higher levels of working memory may allow students to pay attention to several factors in language production at the same time while suppressing their L1. Since we cannot change cognitive ability, this knowledge can help programs and individuals set more realistic language learning goals.

In education abroad contexts, it is suggested that higher levels of integrative motivation make students seek more interactions with community members which in turn may lead to stronger gains in language proficiency (Hernández, 2010a; Isabelli-García, 2006). Students with extrinsic motivation in programs abroad were shown to engage with the host culture less often than those with intrinsic motivation (Holtbrügge & Engelhard, 2016). Understanding students' motivations and goals can help those involved in advising for and during education abroad, to help students select an appropriate program for their interests and teach them strategies to achieve their goals.

In addition to pre-departure language proficiency and individual differences, Martinsen (2010, 2011) discovered that pre-departure levels of intercultural sensitivity predicted gains in language proficiency. Cultural sensitivity was identified as the strongest predictor of language gains in a study investigating learning in a variety of study abroad programs (Baker-Smemoe et al., 2014). Pre-departure language proficiency has also been shown to impact students' sociocultural adjustment while abroad and research concludes that students with higher language proficiency find it easier to adjust socioculturally (Basow & Gaugler, 2017; Ozer, 2015). In Spenader's (2011) study students who acculturated more strongly were those with higher language proficiency, whereas students with lower proficiency tended to be those who did not wish or attempt to integrate into the host community.

Conclusion

In summary, education abroad can have a positive impact on language development. The level of improvement depends on program factors, individual differences, and contextual factors. Research has suggested that there is a threshold proficiency level at the Intermediate level in order for participants to take advantage of the abroad environment for maximum language learning. Research has also suggested a ceiling effect for language development, meaning that those already at Advanced levels make less progress than those at lower levels. Students benefit from receiving language instruction prior to the departure that helps them achieve Intermediate levels (Lindseth, 2010). As one would expect, students with higher pre-departure language proficiency adapt easier socioculturally after arrival in the host country (Basow & Gaugler, 2017; Ozer, 2015; Spenader, 2011). Insufficient language skills also hinder students' ability to progress academically in host community courses (Kuo, 2011) and if one's self-perceived language proficiency is low it impacts one's willingness to communicate (Robson, 2015b). In addition to language instruction, students also benefit from intercultural training prior to the departure. During their time abroad, students improve their language learning through reflection and awareness-raising activities. More details will be provided in Part 3.

Chapter 2.3. Intercultural Competence and Global Citizenship

Introduction

Much of education abroad is hailed to improve intercultural sensitivity, intercultural competence, and preparation for a global world and workforce. These goals are the biggest unifying element of education abroad as it applies to additional language and first language programs. This chapter summarizes previous research on the effects of education abroad on intercultural competence, global citizenship, and cultural learning.

There is a lack of consensus on what precisely constitutes intercultural competence, intercultural communication competence, cross-cultural competence and adaptability, or intercultural sensitivity, because the concepts are complex and continuously evolving (Deardorff, 2006b). While a variety of terms, models and definitions exist, we define intercultural competence as "the ability to communicate effectively and appropriately in intercultural situations based on one's intercultural knowledge, skills, and attitudes" (Deardorff, 2004, p. 194). This chapter looks at outcomes in the area of intercultural learning, which includes the development of intercultural competence, but also cultural understanding, awareness, and sensitivity, cross-cultural competence and adaptability and related concepts. The chapter also looks at education abroad and its impact on global-mindedness and global citizenship, which includes social responsibility, global awareness and civic engagement (Tarrant, Rubin, & Stoner, 2014).

Assessment of Intercultural Competence

Measuring and assessing intercultural competence and similar outcomes in education abroad is a major challenge for education abroad practitioners. Several measurements have been utilized in order to evaluate the intercultural learning that takes place during education abroad. Assessments are direct, indirect, or a combination thereof and can include:

- An evaluation of students' performances in real-world scenarios (Koester & Olebe, 1988).
- Observations of students (Marx & Moss, 2011).
- Discussions with instructors of the students (Bacon, 2002).
- An analysis of students' portfolios (Jackson, 2018) or other class-related work such as journals (Elola & Oskoz, 2008) or final papers (Root & Ngampornchai, 2013).
- Interviews (Czerwionka, Artamonova, & Barbosa, 2015), or questionnaires (Medina-Lopez-Portillo, 2004).
- Commercially available tools to measure concepts of intercultural competence, such as the Intercultural Development Inventory (IDI) and the Cross-Cultural Adaptability Inventory (CCAI).

The IDI (Hammer, Bennett, & Wiseman, 2003) is perhaps the most commonly used assessment tool in education abroad and it measures students' orientation regarding cultural dissimilarities based on the Developmental Model of Intercultural Sensitivity, DMIS (Bennett, 1986). In this model, students move from ethnocentric to ethnorelative stages of worldviews thereby demonstrating stronger potential for more complex intercultural encounters. This tool has been used to assess students both in long-term (Pedersen, 2009, 2010; Vande Berg, Paige, & Lou, 2012) and short-term programs (Anderson, Lawton, Rexeisen, & Hubbard, 2006; Jackson, 2008).

Based on a study by Deardorff (2006a) who surveyed 24 representative US institutions as well as a panel of 23 experts on intercultural matters, the most frequently used assessment tool for intercultural competence cited by the administrators was student interviews. The experts on intercultural competence in this study suggested a mix of qualitative and quantitative measures, which can show different degrees of ICC.

The following are assessment tools for intercultural competence:

- The Intercultural Development Inventory (IDI) developed by Hammer et al. (2003) has been used in several studies (Anderson & Lawton, 2011; Maharaja, 2018; Marx & Moss, 2011; Pedersen, 2009, 2010; Tarchi, Surian, & Daiute, 2019).
- The Cross-Cultural Adaptability Inventory (CCAI) developed by Kelley and Meyers (1995) has been used by Black and Duhon (2006); Maharaja (2018); Mapp (2012); Williams (2005); Zielinski (2007).
- The Global Perspective Inventory (GPI) developed by Braskamp, Braskamp, and Engberg (2013); Merrill, Braskamp, and Braskamp (2012) has been used by Anderson and Lawton (2011); Engberg (2013); Gaia (2015); Glass and Westmont (2014); Grigorescu (2015).
- The Intercultural Adjustment Potential Scale (ICAPS) developed by Matsumoto et al. (2001) has been used by several researchers as well (Savicki, 2012; Savicki, Downing-Burnette, Heller, Binder, & Suntinger, 2004).
- The International Education Survey (IES) developed by Zorn (1996) has been used in a few studies (Curtin, Martins, & Schwartz-Barcott, 2015; DeDee & Stewart, 2003).
- The Beliefs, Events and Values inventory (BEVI) developed by Shealy (2016) has been used by Wandschneider et al. (2015).
- The Global Competence Aptitude Assessment (GCAA) developed by Hunter (2004) has been used by Breitkreuz (2015); Schenker (2019).
- The Global-Mindedness Scale (GMS) developed by Hett (1993) has been used in several studies (Clarke, Flaherty, Wright, & McMillen, 2009; Kehl & Morris, 2008; LeCrom, Greenhalgh, & Dwyer, 2015).
- The Intercultural Sensitivity Index (ISI) developed by Olson and Kroeger (2001) has been used by several researchers (Bloom & Miranda, 2015; Clarke et al., 2009; Williams, 2005; Zarnick, 2010).

Mapp (2012) measured students' cross-cultural adaptability using the CCAI before and after a short stay abroad of between one and three weeks. The CCAI measures four components of adaptability, namely Emotional Resilience, Flexibility/Openness, Perceptual Acuity, and Personal Autonomy (Kelley & Meyers, 1995). The 87 participants in various faculty-led programs were mostly social work students and the programs often included a service-learning component. Results showed significant increases in cross-cultural adaptability with the largest change in emotional resilience (Mapp, 2012). Similarly, an investigation of US business students studying in London for four weeks also showed significant increases in all areas of the cross-cultural adaptability inventory (Black & Duhon, 2006). Similar results were found in other majors: Sports management (LeCrom et al., 2015), nursing students (Penman & Ellis, 2004), education majors (Colwell, Nielsen, Bradley, & Spearman, 2016), and business students (Rexeisen & Al-Khatib, 2009). Overall, these short-term studies show increased cultural awareness and intercultural competence as a result of time spent abroad.

Short-term programs have been shown to lead to increased intercultural knowledge, which has been interpreted as a sign of cultural adaptation (Czerwionka et al., 2015). Specifically, these short programs appear to assist students in increasing their knowledge about the host culture, also considered the cognitive aspect of ICC (Lee & Song, 2019), including the host community's history, politics, values, etc. (Czerwionka et al., 2015). Thus, even short stays abroad can lead to a deeper understanding of the host community and culture. Furthermore, short-term programs have resulted in positive changes in the affective components of intercultural competence (Lee & Song, 2019), and world-mindedness, which refers to an individual's appreciation for global perspectives (Douglas & Jones-Rikkers, 2001).

In addition to external measures of intercultural competence, students' perceptions of their development during short-term study abroad have been predominantly positive, as well. Participants in short summer education abroad noted a heightened cultural awareness in themselves, while also admitting that while noticing cultural differences they did not always understand them (Brubaker, 2007). In line with cultural awareness, short-term programs for pre-service teachers have shown participants' enhanced understanding of their own cultural identities and their effects on cultural perspectives (Byker & Putnam, 2018). Additionally, these pre-service teachers had an increased sense of the importance of incorporating and acknowledging culture in their future teaching. Similarly, pre-service teachers who spent a summer in Honduras noted their own changed perceptions about students from culturally and linguistically different backgrounds (Sharma & Phillion, 2019). These results indicate that short stays abroad can have an impact on students' cultural beliefs and perceptions.

Studies exploring whether education abroad affects cultural intelligence show generally positive results, with few studies showing no relationship between prior travel abroad and cultural intelligence (MacNab & Worthley, 2012) or showing only modest support for an increase in cultural intelligence after a five weeks abroad (Nguyen et al., 2018). R. L. Engle and Crowne (2014) compared cultural intelligence between students who participated in short-term education abroad of 7 to 14 days and those who did not go abroad and found that the education abroad students showed significant increases in cultural intelligence. Other studies also revealed that participation in short-term education abroad enhances students' cultural intelligence (Rustambekov & Mohan, 2017) and that students' social experiences during their cross-cultural adjustment may be an especially important contributing factor (Chao, Takeuchi, & Farh, 2017).

Concerns in Short-Term Programs

In spite of the many positive accounts of development in the area of intercultural competence, sensitivity and adaptability, research also shows that not all students develop equally. All in all, short-term programs have been shown to positively impact some components of intercultural competence. In their longitudinal analysis of over 1600 students over a four-year period, Salisbury, An, and Pascarella (2013) found that education abroad overall had a positive effect on intercultural competence, but this was only significant on some subscales of the intercultural competence measurement that was used. In line with these findings, a comparison of global citizenship outcomes of students in summer courses at home and abroad showed that the education abroad group was significantly more advanced only on two of the three measures of global citizenship, and neither group changed on the third measure (Tarrant et al., 2014). These findings highlight that intercultural competence development can still be maximized in education abroad, especially in short-term program.

Jackson's (2011) analysis of 11 students from Hong Kong who spent five weeks in England clearly shows that all students followed a different developmental path. Additionally, the students perceived themselves as more interculturally competent than the IDI results revealed. Anderson and Lawton confirm the individual paths in their study and conclude:

> Two students participating in the same study abroad program could each undergo a transformational experience, but see little in common between them regarding that experience. How each student internalizes their intercultural experiences is moderated by their prior experiences, both international and domestic.
>
> *(Anderson & Lawton, 2011, pp. 96–97)*

Even though much research highlights the potential positive effects of short-term abroad programs on intercultural competence, there are also cautionary results that highlight a lack of improvement, increased intercultural awareness in only some areas or for some students, or a lack of sustained improvements. In a study comparing cultural learning between Spanish language learners in a semester abroad and Spanish language learners at home, the qualitative analysis of the collaborative blogs between the groups showed that it was in fact the at-home group that expressed more interest in other people's way of life (Elola & Oskoz, 2008). Nonetheless, overall the authors found more instances of intercultural competence based on Byram's (1997) model in the blogs and questionnaires of the education abroad group. There is little argument over the fact that immersion in the host culture alone does not lead to the development of intercultural competence and many researchers emphasize that merely sending students abroad is not enough (Lou & Weber Bosley, 2012; Vande Berg, 2007).

Mixed findings were also reported by LeCrom et al. (2015), who compare the global-mindedness of alumni who had participated in a two-week trip for sports management students from the US to Western Europe to alumni who had not. They found no statistically significant difference between the groups in their overall global-mindedness which was measured using the Global-Mindedness Scale (GMS) (Hett, 1993). However, the education abroad participants showed higher levels of cultural pluralism, which is defined as an "appreciation of the diversity of cultures in the world and a belief that all have something of value to offer" (LeCrom et al., 2015, p. 72). In Zarnick's (2010) study, the intercultural sensitivity of the eleven students who completed an adapted ISI survey prior and after their one-week education abroad program showed only minimal changes. In fact, students' interest in learning more about other cultures decreased from pre- to post-survey, which leads the author to conclude that a program of one week may have very little impact. Similar concerns over short-term programs are voiced by Root and Ngampornchai (2013) who criticize the superficiality of intercultural understanding that they identified in students' reflective papers. Their analysis was based on 18 students who had traveled to a variety of countries for lengths ranging from one week to six months, with the average having studied abroad five to eight weeks. While the authors acknowledged that education abroad offers strong opportunities for cross-cultural learning, they did not see a deeper understanding and connection between observed practices and cultural values in the students' papers.

Only about a third of students who had studied in Spain for seven weeks advanced to the next level on the Developmental Model of Intercultural Sensitivity, which indicates that short-term education abroad may only be effective in fostering intercultural development for some students (Medina-Lopez-Portillo, 2004). In their analysis of US students' intercultural sensitivity after four weeks in London and Dublin, Anderson et al. (2006) found that students overall improved on their scores on the IDI, but not enough to show progression from one stage to the next. Similarly, US students who spent four weeks in Spain showed very little changes in intercultural sensitivity as measured by the ISI (Bloom & Miranda, 2015).

Even students studying abroad for one semester do not all make significant gains, as was shown in the large-scale study by Vande Berg et al. (2009) who point out that "a sizable number of students abroad did not learn significantly more than control students" (p. 25). Additionally, studies measuring students' intercultural sensitivity or competence show very different levels of gains. Comparing, for example, the IDI gains of education abroad participants from Georgetown (Vande Berg et al., 2009), the University of Minnesota (Paige, Harvey, & McCleary, 2012), the American University Center of Provence (L. Engle & Engle, 2012), the University of the Pacific (Bathurst & Brack, 2012), or The Scholar Ship program, a transnational program for students from anywhere in the world (Medina-Lopez-Portillo & Salonen, 2012), ranged from 1.32 (Georgetown) to 18.4 (American University Center of Provence). This shows that development of intercultural competence is neither guaranteed nor universal across programs but is impacted by a variety of factors.

All in all, results from short-term programs indicate that while there is the potential of these programs to enhance students' intercultural learning in some areas of intercultural competence (Lee & Song, 2019), they do not necessarily do so, especially without targeted interventions. For students to show significant changes in intercultural competence, long-term stays abroad may be necessary.

Furthermore, short-term programs are more likely to reinforce stereotypes (Allen et al., 2006; Cain & Zarate, 1996; Kortegast & Kupo, 2017) and existing cultural power relations (Kortegast & Kupo, 2017). Allen et al. (2006) found that over the course of the summer program, participants' expectations and their reporting of cultural difficulties decreased. They hypothesize that short-term programs do not give participants sufficient opportunity to experience culture and thereby shelter participants from the challenges associated with navigating a new culture and deny them the consequential development of intercultural competence.

Long-Term Program Outcomes

Studies analyzing semester- and year-long programs have consistently shown strong outcomes in intercultural competence (Alred, 2000; Behrnd & Porzelt, 2011). A study on education abroad alumni of semester- and year-long programs revealed higher levels of global-mindedness in those who had studied abroad than those who had not (Murphy et al., 2014). Long-term programs are overall more beneficial for students' cultural learning, intercultural learning, and the development of global-mindedness than short-term programs (Anderson & Lawton, 2011; Ramirez, 2016; Wolff & Borzikowsky, 2018). The ideal time frame claimed by research varies from 13 to 18 weeks (Vande Berg et al., 2009) to two years (Lou & Weber Bosley, 2012, p. 344).

Spending a year in another country has been shown to allow students not only to develop the attitudinal factor of intercultural competence, but simultaneously

pedagogy had a bigger impact on development on the IDI than program length. Furthermore, immersive experiences such as experiential learning, have a strong effect on intercultural sensitivity (Spenader & Retka, 2015). Without intercultural instruction, increases in intercultural competence are small (Vande Berg et al., 2009). Further giving credence to the idea that what is done is more important than length, Friar (2016) found no differences in global competence between long-term program participants and students in course-embedded short-term programs of 10 to 21 days which included immersion in the host culture through volunteer work and host family stays. The study did show that both short- and long-term programs helped students develop their global competence significantly more than students who did not participate in any education abroad program. Pedersen (2009) summarizes results from a study comparing a year-long education abroad course with targeted intercultural training to the same program without intervention as well as a control group who stayed at home. Her results emphasize that the year-long group with specific pedagogy and reflective activities produced the most change in intercultural sensitivity as measured by the IDI. Additionally, her study showed that even a short-term program of two weeks with targeted intervention produced more change than the year-long program that did not include guided reflection and intercultural pedagogy. Therefore, Pederson (2009) concludes that in order to foster intercultural competence development during education abroad, targeted intervention and a long program duration are key. Interventions can include the following:

Experiential learning: Spenader and Retka (2015) found positive changes in students' intercultural sensitivity in their semester-long programs which included intercultural pedagogies. In their study, differences were observed between the programs under investigation, and the authors suggest that experiential learning including service projects had the strongest measurable effect on intercultural sensitivity. Other types of experiential learning, such as individual research or cultural explorations, were not seen as effective.

Reflection: Research shows that language and intercultural gains are greatly enhanced by integrating reflection and awareness-raising tasks. In fact, some have argued that without such guided reflective tasks learning is limited or impossible (Castañeda & Zirger, 2011). Vande Berg (2007) and Pedersen (2010) emphasized that without active intervention before, during, and after education abroad, students will not develop further intercultural competence. Kortegast and Kupo (2017) argue the importance of a critical pedagogy approach in education abroad that includes critical reflection:

> it is imperative that faculty, administrators, and program directors intervene, mediate, and provide programmatic opportunities for students to reflect and make meaning of their learning, practices, and engagements. If left unmediated, short-term study-abroad may result in experiences where students reify American dominance, superiority, and perpetuate a sense of being

"good Americans" who help the underprivileged all in the name of becoming "global citizens."

(Kortegast & Kupo, 2017, p. 167)

Antonakopoulou (2013) found that the presence of reflection tasks in a curriculum made a bigger difference in a participant's sociocultural adaptation than did program length. Dunkley (2009) also confirms that without critical analyses, reflection, and guided experiential learning activities, students do not develop global citizenship. Pedersen (2010) advocates for a set of activities completed in a psychology class abroad based on Bennett's Developmental Model of Intercultural Sensitivity (DMIS). Not surprisingly Pedersen found that the group involved in the psychology course outperformed both an at-home group and another group abroad which was not participating in the course in intercultural development as measured on the IDI. Interestingly, the experimental group also showed a more accurate self-assessment of intercultural competence. She goes on to stress the importance of "just in time" learning and constructivist educational philosophies for education abroad. She concludes:

> The data from this study suggest that if intercultural effectiveness is a goal of study abroad, we need to do much more than send students abroad to study. We need to add intercultural effectiveness as a learning outcome for students in study abroad and develop curriculum (regardless of academic content) that incorporates opportunities for such learning and development in students.
>
> *(Pedersen, 2010, p. 77)*

Research suggests that experiences abroad must be augmented by reflection about their intercultural experiences for participants to benefit to their fullest. While there is uncertainty about how precisely guided reflection should look, there is general agreement on the role of guided reflection in promoting intercultural learning. In fact, Spenader and Retka (2015) emphasize that "the areas which seem most promising in their ability to account for variation in intercultural development are that of guided/structural cultural interaction and experiential learning, and the role of guided reflection on cultural experience" (p. 33). Studies have shown that students who are guided through reflection during their time abroad make stronger gains in intercultural competence (Spenader & Retka, 2015; Vande Berg et al., 2012) and students who are not lack that development (Brockington & Wiedenhoft, 2009). Blake-Campbell (2014) found positive effects of reflection activities on intercultural competence and development of global citizenship in a program that was only one week long. The program was based on Freire's critical pedagogy and Mezirow's Transformational Learning Theory and therefore tasks were focused on critical self-reflection. Similarly, Elverson and Klawiter (2018) used daily journaling in which students responded to specific prompts focusing on the questions *what, so what, and what now* to reflect on their service-learning experience in Ghana. The authors conclude that the guided reflective journaling promoted critical thinking and supported students in processing their time abroad more meaningfully. Brockington and Wiedenhoft (2009) described a program that combines service learning with reflective ethnographic work, which contributed to the development of global citizenship (self-reflection, cultural understanding, language skills, critical analysis).

Cultural sensitivity training: Greater cultural sensitivity has been found to positively influence language and culture learning gains. Hence, cultural sensitivity training should be integrated into every stage of education abroad. For example, Vande Berg et al. (2009) found that students who had a pre-departure orientation that included cultural sensitivity training had greater learning outcomes and greater satisfaction than those who did not receive such training. Aldawsari, Adams, Grimes, and Kohn (2018) found that students with a higher level of cultural competence were able to take more agency in their learning abroad and were more independent. Pre-departure training in cultural sensitivity was identified as the only variable predicting development in intercultural competence in a study of 3030 Japanese students in short- and long-term programs abroad (Hanada & Shingo, 2019). Pre-departure intercultural sensitivity training was found to lead to greater language gains (Baker-Smemoe et al., 2014). On the other hand, coursework in international studies prior to abroad does not necessarily lead to increased intercultural competence while abroad (Root & Ngampornchai, 2013; Rust et al., 2013). For example, specific international coursework did not affect outcomes in a study by Rust et al. (2013), who compared intercultural competence of students who completed specific coursework to those students without these classes. Students spent four weeks or one semester abroad and while all increased slightly in their intercultural sensitivity, the students with international coursework did not improve more strongly. That being said, without specific intercultural instruction, a large-scale study of 1050 students showed negligible increases on the IDI after a semester abroad (Vande Berg et al., 2009). With carefully designed pre-departure training, intercultural support while abroad, and re-entry assistance, students have shown much larger IDI developments that indicate students moving from one stage of development to the next (Lou & Weber Bosley, 2012).

Individual Differences and Intercultural Competence

A variety of distinct intercultural skills including intercultural sensitivity and awareness play a role in students' capacity for learning in education abroad. Some studies point to the fact that lower levels of intercultural sensitivity may prevent students from engaging with the target community members (Aveni, 2005; Isabelli-García, 2006; Pellegrino, 1998). This in turn may lead to missed opportunities for language and cultural learning and the development of global competence.

Ethnocentrism hinders progress in intercultural competence. Ethnocentrism can be defined as "an individual preference for one's native culture expressed as discomfort with novel and ambiguous settings" (Barbuto, Beenen, & Tran, 2015, p. 269). Studies have revealed that students with lower levels of ethnocentrism are more likely to participate in education abroad (R. I. Kim & Goldstein, 2005). During education abroad, ethnocentric students may be uncomfortable in their interactions with the host community and may have difficulties adjusting and accepting different cultural norms. A study which analyzed the effects of ethnocentrism on success in education abroad based on interviewing students who had spent between 3 and 36 months in another country found that students with high levels of ethnocentrism had a lower likelihood of having a successful education abroad experience (Barbuto et al., 2015).

Cultural intelligence is "the ability to adapt successfully across varied cultures" (Harrison & Brower, 2011, p. 42) or the ability "to interact, relate, adapt, and work effectively across cultures" (Mesidor & Sly, 2016, p. 265). Positive relationships between cultural intelligence and education abroad were found for metacognitive emotional intelligence (Lin, Chen, & Song, 2012), motivational cultural intelligence (Templer, Tay, & Chandrasekar, 2006), and cognitive and behavioral cultural intelligence (Ang et al., 2007). Studies also have found positive effects of cultural intelligence on students' adjustment during education abroad (Lin et al., 2012; Nguyen et al., 2018) across different scenarios and contexts, including cross-cultural work assignments (Ang et al., 2007; Templer et al., 2006) and interactional adjustment of international students (Iskhakova, 2018). Similarly, cultural intelligence positively impacts students' well-being in education abroad (Ang et al., 2007; Peng, Van Dyne, & Oh, 2015) as students with higher cultural intelligence have fewer difficulties with acculturation and depression (Gebregergis, Huang, & Hong, 2019). Furthermore, students find it easier to adjust psychologically to their new environment and are less likely to be homesick if they possess higher levels of cultural intelligence (Harrison & Brower, 2011). These factors may have implications for what type of program might be best suited for a student.

More open students have stronger appreciation of cultural learning (Cho & Morris, 2015). Openness has an impact on how students behave during their time abroad and consequently on the outcomes of their sojourn. Individuals with higher levels of openness tend to engage a lot with host community members and are more effective at cross-cultural adjustment while abroad (Caligiuri, 2000). Studies have also confirmed a strong relationship between higher levels of psychological adjustment abroad and open-mindedness as well as openness to diversity and sociocultural adjustment (Basow & Gaugler, 2017; Yakunina, Weigold, Weigold, & Hercegovac, 2012). Burke, Watkins, and Guzman (2009) identified openness as a significant predictor of adjusting to life abroad. All in all, research suggests that high levels of openness are an important factor that facilitates intercultural learning and success in education abroad.

Studies have confirmed that extroverted students develop more social and personal relationships during education abroad (Burke et al., 2009; Hasegawa, 2019). Extroverted students tend to be more active in establishing a social network while introverted students tend to stay by themselves and interact less with others (Hasegawa, 2019) though the social networks do not always include members of the host community. Burke et al. (2009) also showed that extroverted students participate more in activities with peers of the host community but also of their own culture. Overall, extroverted individuals find it easier to adjust to another culture (Swagler & Jome, 2005).

Rexeisen and Al-Khatib (2009) assessed business students' intercultural development on the IDI during a semester program and found women developed more strongly than men in several areas of the IDI. Along similar lines, female participants tend to be more open to new cultures (Kehl & Morris, 2008).

Conclusion

Overall, it can be concluded that year-long education abroad is more beneficial for the development of intercultural competence because it allows students to fully engage with the cultures, communities, and universities abroad. It may take students 3 to 5 months to transition into the culture and new educational system before they can be fully incorporated into and benefit from the host university and new environment (Bicknese, 1974b; Steinwidder, 2016). This transition period is only possible in long-term programs. Encouragingly, long-term effects in ICC were found for long-term programs.

Since a higher initial level of cultural sensitivity has been found to be beneficial for program outcomes, it is important that pre-departure orientations include a focus on cultural sensitivity training in general and specific cultural preparation for the community which the students will enter. As Kortegast and Kupo (2017) point out, pre-departure orientations often share information about cultural behaviors without a critical reflection of the origin and meaning of such practices and the participants' roles and potential impacts in these interactions: "study abroad methods to teach about culture can create a framework that promotes exploitation and positions the students as the consumer with limited benefit to the community visited" (p. 157). The impacts of gender and gender roles identified in previous research (Trentman, 2013; Walsh & DeJoseph, 2003) may not be as pronounced, if the program provides cultural sensitivity training (Davidson, 2010).

While abroad, it is crucial to support participants in their intercultural development. This requires qualified and skilled personnel as well as adequate preparation for the personnel to serve as cultural facilitators. The curriculum can be enhanced by experiential components and guided reflection. Even after education abroad reflective tasks are important to solidify the ICC development.

Chapter 2.4. Academic, Professional, and Personal Development

In addition to the linguistic and intercultural learning outcomes, there are many additional benefits for participants as the quotes at the beginning of each of the three parts of this book indicate. Garbati and Rothschild (2016) conclude that education abroad shapes education abroad participants personally and professionally.

Academic

Academic outcomes and concerns can be divided into two broad categories: Academic success and academic direction. Students often fear that participating, especially in long-term education abroad will impact their time-to-degree. Yet, students report that education abroad was the most impactful experience of their college career (Paige et al., 2007).

Academic Success

Adjusting to different academic expectations in education abroad can cause students anxiety (Garbati & Rothschild, 2016) and students fear that education abroad will have a negative impact on their GPA. However, education abroad participants on average increase their GPAs (Sutton & Rubin, 2010; Thomas & McMahon, 1998), which might be attributable to favorable conversion rates. Akande and Slawson (2000) report that IES alumni found that education abroad improved their academic performance and ability to learn. Similarly, ERASMUS alumni reported having made more academic progress during their year abroad (Teichler & Janson, 2007). In our own experience education abroad's impact on academic performance has been more varied largely depending on how well students handled the transitions to and from the host country.

Research has revealed a connection between education abroad for community college students' academic success (Raby, Rhodes, & Biscarra, 2014; Rhodes, Raby, & Biscarra, 2013); students who had studied abroad surpassed non-participants on several measures including likelihood of earning a degree, completing transfer level English or Math credits, and transferring to a four-year institution of higher learning. Gains were especially high for Hispanic community college student participants (Rhodes, Thomas, Raby, Codding, & Lynch, 2016). Norris and Gillespie (2009) as well as Akande and Slawson (2000) also found that education abroad contributed to students from four-year institutions continuing on to graduate school. Dwyer (2004b) found that education abroad resulted in higher academic attainment.

Naturally, the unfamiliar educational culture can both negatively and positively influence participants. In every cohort in the AYF program, we have students who struggle with the open deadlines, the heavy weight on one exam or paper at the end of the semester, and the expectation of more student independence. On the other hand, we also always have students who blossom, because they can more freely pursue their interests in comparison to the more rigid curricula in many US institutions. In one recent case, we had a student who discovered and profited from the German "duales System" where a college education and an apprenticeship in a company are combined. For this student, the approach worked much better than the US educational system and it resulted in her deciding to stay and pursue such a degree. She completed her trainee program and still lives and works in Germany.

Differing levels of formality and hierarchies in the education system can make the educational system abroad confusing and can increase anxiety and disorientation in participants (Garbati & Rothschild, 2016). Grading systems in different educational systems also vary greatly in the value they place on grades, and the meaning of a grade. These uncertainties can cause anxiety in students. Even though the AYF program converts grades from the German system to the US system based on previous grade transfer analysis, students still respond emotionally to the German grade and not the converted grade. Home university pressures on the GPA can increase these negative emotions and also hinder cultural integration. In their collaborative autoethnography, Garbati and Rothschild report:

> Both of us were initially concerned about our *mention assez bien* achievement, but soon learned that we were making good progress and were not as unsuccessful as we may have originally thought. Neither of us seemed prepared for the French grading system prior to our arrival in France.
>
> *(Garbati and Rothschild, 2016, n.p.)*

Program personnel need to anticipate the difficulties that differences in grading pose for students and help them better understand and interpret their evaluations.

Academic Direction

Norris and Gillespie (2009) found that education abroad contributed to students changing or expanding their major. Garbati and Rothschild (2016) also found that education abroad defined their academic direction. Our alumni as well as former education abroad participants in our alumni survey also confirmed the impact of education abroad on academic direction. We have observed that the greater academic freedom students can have especially in long-term education abroad programs can introduce them to new areas of study, which at times impacts their academic direction.

Longer education abroad programs have been found to have a greater impact on academic and professional outcomes and directions. Long-term education abroad participants are more likely to:

- Expand or change their course of study due to education abroad (Dwyer, 2004b).
- Change their career direction as a result of education abroad (Dwyer, 2004b).
- Continue with graduate education, except in medicine or law (Dwyer, 2004b).
- Have worked, interned, or done volunteering abroad, which contributes to career path and preparation including the establishment of a professional network abroad (Dwyer, 2004b).
- Have found education abroad supportive of their future careers (Bian, 2013) and earning potential (Teichler & Janson, 2007).
- Have developed language skills they still use in the workplace, which has resulted in them being more likely to receive overseas assignments or work for multinational organizations (Dwyer, 2004b).
- Have perceived education abroad benefited their job placement (Aydin, 2012; Gray et al., 2002).

In addition to length, other program design factors may a play a role. For example, several teacher education abroad programs include daily or weekly reflection guided journals to assist the pre-service teachers in better understanding their time abroad (Brindley, Quinn, & Morton, 2009; Pence & Macgillivray, 2008). The researchers conclude that reflection plays a crucial role in personal growth for the pre-service teachers and suggest that "the importance of self-reflection as a part of an international field experience cannot be overstated" (Pence & Macgillivray, 2008, p. 24). Experiential learning has to be connected to reflection to be truly transformative (Qualters, 2010).

Professional

Similarly to education abroad having an impact on academic direction and success, education abroad has been found to impact alumni's careers (DeGraaf, Slagter, Larsen, & Ditta, 2013) as was also indicated by the respondents in our survey.

Professional Direction

As we have been able to observe in our own students, education abroad often impacts students' direction for their professional career. At times, students are reaffirming their direction through internships and coursework in the subject from different cultural perspectives, other times students discover an entirely new path. Norris and Gillespie (2009) revealed that education abroad alumni have changed career plans as a result of education abroad, and established contacts while studying abroad which became professional contacts. Participants in short-term education abroad from Middlebury College responded in interviews about their experiences positively about the value of education abroad on their professional development. Students indicated that it had helped them to explore their own interests both academically and professionally (Gates, 2014). Garbati and Rothschild (2016) as well as DeGraaf et al. (2013) also found an impact of education abroad on career paths. The IES alumni study also found an impact on the career itself (Akande & Slawson, 2000). Year-long education programs were more influential on career preparation and direction than shorter programs, though there was an impact across program length (Dwyer, 2004b).

Career Placement

Education abroad is often advertised as contributing to alumni's marketability and employability. Anecdotally our alumni, especially those who participated in long-term education abroad opportunities, tell us that their experience abroad appeared to be the deciding factor in a hiring decision. This was also confirmed by alumni responding to a survey we administered. Norris and Gillespie (2009) investigated the impact of education abroad on career development and contrasted alumni with an international career and those with a domestic career. They claim that the best way to prepare students for today's global economy is through education abroad. Their study found that the majority of students benefited from the experience in their career development. A large-scale study from ERASMUS participants showed that the majority of year-long education abroad participants believed that their experience had supported them in obtaining their first job. Similarly, employers in the ERASMUS study confirmed that language proficiency and having studied abroad are important criteria in hiring decisions (Teichler & Janson, 2007).

However, not all education abroad alumni are able to strategically use their education abroad experience. Strategic planning and decision-making is required before and during education abroad, and alumni have to learn how to market their experience and the transferability of the skills acquired to potential employers. Norris and Gillespie conclude that education abroad advisors and faculty play an important role in guiding students to the appropriate program for them:

> Advisors and students need to understand not only the student's priorities for studying away from the home institution but also the student's ideas about graduate school and career. Students with international or intercultural career aspirations should be advised to consider programs that are conducted in a language other than English, run for a full academic year, include an internship component, house students with host country nationals, and/or feature courses offered by the host institution.
>
> *(Norris & Gillespie, 2009, p. 395)*

Many students who completed internships in their field of study later found careers in this area (T. B. Fryer & Day, 1993). Over the years, we have had a small but growing number of students whose internship in Freiburg contributed directly and indirectly to their career. Some students were able to continue to freelance or even work for the organization where they interned, others used the unpaid internship as a building block for gainful employment elsewhere in the same or related field.

Career Trajectory

Based on the research by IES, education abroad plays an important role in the global orientation of alumni's career trajectory. 48% of the alumni surveyed by Norris and Gillespie (2009) continued with international work/study experiences after the education abroad program. Their language development through education abroad contributed to their ability to develop their international career. "Study abroad may be the key that opens the global career door for up to a third of all participants" (p. 389). Overall they found a trend toward more international careers in education abroad alumni. The trend toward international careers was also confirmed by Dwyer (2004b) and Akande and Slawson (2000). The more immersed and engaged students were during their time abroad, the more likely they were to have an international career later (Norris & Gillespie, 2009). Norris and Gillespie (2009) found that men were more influenced in developing an international career through education abroad than women.

Personal

Students perceive a great amount of personal development as a result of short-term and long-term participation in education abroad (Gates, 2014). Spending a year in another country provides students with the unique opportunity of experiencing life in a completely different environment with big and small tasks that are involved in living abroad independently, such as navigating through an unknown city, finding an apartment, opening an account at a local bank, finding a phone provider, and many other day-to-day tasks (Johnson & McKinnon, 2018). Education abroad can also positively impact personality traits (Niehoff, Petersdotter, & Freund, 2017; Zimmermann & Neyer, 2013). Participants in year-long programs have reported positive changes in their personal development and maturation (Alred & Byram, 2002). The type of learning students engage in during long-term education abroad programs can be seen as and has been described by students themselves as transformative (Brown, 2009b; Nada, Montgomery, & Araújo, 2018). As a result of becoming more aware of cultural differences and similarities, many students gain self-awareness that leads them to grow as a person and individual. This factor is seen by some students as the most important aspect of their education abroad experience (Gray et al., 2002). Most alumni describe their education abroad experience to us as life-changing, especially if they participated in long-term education abroad. This transformation is often viewed positively by the alumni, but does at times cause challenges for them in the reintegration process.

Language Learning

It is of course not surprising that students gain language abilities while abroad, however, the developments in language learning go beyond the development of language skills. For example, Garbati and Rothschild (2016) reported that participating in education abroad and being exposed to other international students created an awareness of the processes involved in language learning and other international students became role-models. Over time the initial self-doubt in linguistic ability developed into confidence in one's own language ability (Garbati & Rothschild, 2016). Amuzie and Winke (2009) found that education abroad participants changed their language learning beliefs while abroad. The longer they participated in education abroad, the more pronounced those changes were. After education abroad, learners put more emphasis on autonomy in language learning and less emphasis on the teacher, which increases their potential to be life-long learners and users of the language.

Education abroad plays a role in language anxiety. Anxiety in education abroad can be related to a number of apprehensions, one of which may be the use of the additional language. As Horwitz, Horwitz, and Cope (1986) suggest, foreign language anxiety is a "distinct complex of self-perceptions, beliefs, feelings, and behaviors" which stem "from the uniqueness of the language learning process" (p. 128). Students with high foreign language anxiety are often afraid to speak in the language which may prevent them from engaging with community members during education abroad. Additionally, students with higher language learning anxiety have been found to be less motivated to learn the language (R. C. Gardner, Day, & MacIntyre, 1992) and these students may view education abroad as too great a challenge.

During education abroad, anxiety can arise as a result of language learning problems and cultural differences (Allen & Herron, 2003). Specifically, anxiety can stem from feeling overwhelmed with academic work in a new cultural context or inadequate in comparison to host community peers, frustration at slow language progress, or discomfort with cultural differences (Bown, Dewey, & Belnap, 2015), to name a few. Even students who may not have experienced anxiety while learning a language at the home campus may experience anxiety in the education abroad context, since the learning context is different.

However, education abroad can also have an overall positive effect on students' language learning anxiety. For example, a study of Korean students by Thompson and Lee (2014) showed that the more time they were abroad, the lower their English learning anxiety became. Similar results emerged in a study of learners of

Arabic who spent a semester in Jordan (Dewey et al., 2018). Over time, the participants in this program became less anxious in general, even if there was an initial feeling of discomfort in the host community. Due to this trend in decreased anxiety as education abroad progresses, longer programs may have an advantage over short-term stays.

Self-confidence and Risk-taking

Students often report that abroad they had to learn to make mistakes and take risks, which positively impacted their willingness to take risks and grow through errors. Students report that they gained self-confidence because of their time spent abroad (Maharaja, 2018). Not surprisingly, education abroad impacts self-esteem and confidence (De Poli et al., 2018; Dwyer, 2004b). Like education abroad students overall, community college students who participated in education abroad programs noted increased self-confidence (Brenner, 2016). Self-esteem improves through education abroad which influences the willingness to take risks (Bacon, 2002). Participants in long-term education abroad programs acquire problem-solving skills and learned how to cope with and adapt to difficult and unknown situations. This can lead to an increase in self-confidence and a discovery of their own personality and competencies (Aydin, 2012; Bacon, 2002), as well as increased self-esteem (Geeraert & Demoulin, 2013). A study on German adolescents participating in nine-month exchange programs further confirmed the effects of education abroad on self-esteem. Stronger increases in self-esteem were observed for the education abroad participants than the adolescents who remained in their home country (Hutteman, Nestler, Wagner, & Egloff, 2015). In their collaborative autoethnography, Garbati and Rothschild (2016) reported education abroad contributing to their willingness to take risks and ultimately pride in their accomplishments.

Independence and Self-efficacy

Through education abroad participants can develop their skills to navigate challenging and unfamiliar situations (Benson, Barkhuizen, Bodycott, & Brown, 2013). Garbati and Rothschild (2016) recount that having to navigate a new environment without anyone to help was tiring but ultimately led to personal growth: Growth in independence, development of courage, demonstration of pride, and a "figure it out" mentality. Through education abroad, participants can develop an increased ability to navigate the host community, which can give them courage for new situations in the future (Allen et al., 2006). Courtois (2019) found a positive impact on risk-taking and self-efficacy.

Education abroad can impact students' language self-efficacy. Analyses of students' self-perceived self-efficacy during education abroad revealed that students who spent significant amounts of time abroad perceived increases in their communication self-efficacy (Milstein, 2005). Milstein (2005) also reported a correlation between perceived challenges during education abroad and increased self-reported self-efficacy. This indicates that experiencing challenges during a time in another country does not necessarily have a negative effect on students but can, in fact, lead to increased confidence and self-efficacy perceptions.

Self-efficacy beliefs can be defined as the judgments students "hold about their capability to organize and execute the courses of action required to master academic tasks" (Mills, Pajares, & Herron, 2007, p. 417). Students with stronger self-efficacy are likely to attempt more challenging activities and tasks, which has a direct bearing on education abroad participation and success. Research has shown that strong perceived self-efficacy is correlated to higher goal setting and academic achievement (Zimmerman & Bandura, 1994; Zimmerman, Bandura, & Martinez-Pons, 1992) and leads to stronger intercultural adjustment during education abroad (Hechanova-Alampay, Beehr, Christiansen, & Van Horn, 2002; Nguyen et al., 2018). If faced with difficult communication situations, some students opt to avoid these learning opportunities rather than dealing with what they perceive to be a difficult situation (Levin, 2001). However, students with high self-efficacy in the host language are more likely to search for opportunities to interact in the host community and language (Cankaya, Liew, & de Freitas, 2018, p. 1702). Creating a supportive and encouraging environment is crucial for supporting all students, but especially those with lower levels of self-efficacy.

Compared to other factors such as motivation and anxiety, some researchers suggest that self-efficacy is the strongest predictor of academic performance (Bandura, 1997; Schunk & Pajares, 2005). Social self-efficacy during education abroad, defined as students' perceived abilities in managing and engaging in positive social interactions (Çankaya & Xing Dong, 2017), as well as their self-perceived autonomy (Cankaya et al., 2018), impact students' personal growth initiative. The more self-efficacy and autonomy students possess, the stronger their initiative and engagement in self-development becomes. High degrees of personal growth initiative are also positively correlated with cultural adjustment as a study on international students in the Netherlands revealed (Taušová, Bender, Dimitrova, & van de Vijver, 2019).

As seen in a study by Jacobone and Moro (2015), who compared the outcomes of an academic year abroad to a control group at home, the year-long sojourn abroad had strong effects on students' self-efficacy. The authors conclude that the experiences and challenges students had to overcome supported a development of higher self-efficacy and confidence in themselves. Likewise, Petersdotter, Niehoff, and Freund (2017) found that education abroad participants developed higher levels of self-efficacy than those who did not leave the home university. Additionally, more weekly contact with members of the host community was correlated to higher self-efficacy for students during education abroad.

Lopez-McGee (2018) noted that students who participated in short-term programs reported increased self-efficacy in their cross-cultural competence.

However, other areas such as problem-solving or international mindedness did not see an increase in self-efficacy and the author attributes this to the limited opportunities for interacting with the host community in short-term programs. One study found that in a five-week program abroad, students who identify with one culture made gains in self-efficacy while students who identified with more than one culture did not (Nguyen et al., 2018). Nonetheless, some positive results have been revealed for short-term education abroad and self-efficacy. For example, nursing students who participated in a two-week experiential learning program in Central America, showed a significant increase in perceived self-efficacy for the Hispanic student participants, and moderate increased for the African American, Asian, and Native American nursing students (Long, 2014). Another cohort of nursing students who had completed a short-term clinical immersion program abroad also showed higher self-efficacy than their peers who had completed the service-learning projects at home (Anita & McKenry, 1999). Cubillos and Ilvento (2012) also reported increased self-efficacy for all language skills for students on five-week and semester-long education abroad programs. With the exception of speaking, self-efficacy for all language skills increased more strongly in the semester-long education abroad program. While short-term programs have found some positive effects on students' self-efficacy, a longer stay is preferable.

Self-regulation and Agency

Self-regulation defined as "goal-directed behavior" (Hofmann, Schmeichel, & Baddeley, 2012, p. 174) can positively impact outcomes of education abroad. Research on education abroad shows that students employ a variety of self-regulation strategies in the education abroad context and that these strategies are connected to their individual goals. The majority of strategies in language-focused education abroad are language-learning strategies. But strategies to remain motivated and strategies for goal-setting can also be seen (Allen, 2013). A study on Chinese students studying abroad in the UK (Cheng, Friesen, & Adekola, 2019) revealed that students employed many emotion regulation strategies to deal with the challenges and stress they experienced. Through these emotion regulation strategies, students were able to deal with stressors they experienced in their time abroad which had arisen from language barriers, social interactions with peers, and interactions with their teachers. Emotion-regulating strategies were also an important aspect of intercultural adjustment in the study by Zheng (2017) on Chinese learners in the UK. The strategies the students employed helped them to maintain their psychological well-being which indicates that teaching students effective emotion regulation strategies can support their psychological well-being while abroad.

In connection to self-regulation, personal agency contributes to the learning outcomes of students as well. Agency can narrowly be defined as the ability to act (Lier, 2008). Research has shown a connection between autonomy and cross-cultural competence for students in education abroad. The more cross-cultural competence students possessed, the more autonomy they exhibited during their time abroad (Aldawsari et al., 2018). This means, that students who were more cross-culturally competent reported more independence in their choices and behaviors abroad. These findings emphasize the need for helping students develop cross-cultural competence as an important determinant of their autonomy and agency during education abroad.

Flexibility, Adaptability, and Creativity

Research on education abroad has also shown that time spent in another country and multicultural experiences positively impact creativity (Leung & Chiu, 2010; Leung, Maddux, Galinsky, & Chiu, 2008; Leung & Chiu, 2008; Maddux, Adam, & Galinsky, 2010). In line with creativity, time abroad can assist individuals at becoming better problem-solvers who come up with unconventional solutions to problems (Cho & Morris, 2015). Furthermore, education abroad contributes to students adaptability (De Poli et al., 2018) and relaxedness (Allison, Davis-Berman, & Berman, 2012). It is not surprising then, that education abroad helps students developed flexibility and adaptability (Bian, 2013; Williams, 2005). A study investigating 221 international graduate students and their personal growth in relation to several measures of personality showed that self-perceived autonomy impacted their curiosity which in turn led to stronger initiative and engagement in self-development, or Personal Growth Initiative (Cankaya et al., 2018). Community college students participating in education abroad reported developing curiosity and self-reflection during their education abroad program (Brenner, 2016). Maddux and Galinsky (2009) also found an impact on creativity and another study found education abroad positively impacting time-management and decision-making skills along with dependability (P. Gardner, Gross, & Steglitz, 2008). In short, education abroad contributed to participants being more adaptable, independent, and creative in facing challenges.

Psychological Well-being

Research points to the connection between students' psychological well-being and education abroad outcomes. An inability to adjust to a different culture may negatively impact students' well-being (Aldawsari et al., 2018). Psychological well-being can also be impacted by students' language skills. Studies have shown that stronger language proficiency is connected to fewer difficulties with psychological well-being during a time abroad (Jin & Wang, 2018; O'Reilly, Ruan, & Hickey, 2010; Sümer, Poyrazli, & Grahame, 2008; Tananuraksakul & Hall, 2011). Basow and Gaugler (2017) found that in their semester-program abroad, students with more social interaction with the host community members had fewer difficulties to adjust psychologically to living in a different country. Students who have traveled to other countries before, experience fewer difficulties with adjusting to the new culture and are less likely to feel depressed, stressed or psychologically unwell (Gebregergis et al., 2019). Students with intrinsic motivation are less likely to experience distress while abroad (Yang, Zhang, & Sheldon, 2018; Yu, 2010). In order to maintain psychological well-being, students also need the ability to regulate their emotions (Cheng et al., 2019; Zheng, 2017). Studies point to the importance of preparing students emotionally and psychologically for the unique challenges of education abroad.

Interestingly, Bathke and Kim (2016) showed that mental health can improve in some areas during sojourn. For example, the percentage of students feeling stressed was much higher before than during study abroad and was also lower after study abroad than before though higher than during. The study reports similar findings for feeling anxiety. They suggest that this could be indicative of the coping skills and confidence that students acquire during education abroad.

Empathy, Curiosity, and Worldview

One of the most significant and globally beneficial outcomes of education abroad are the changes to worldviews and the increased empathy that education abroad students may develop. It is not surprising that being in an uncomfortable and unfamiliar situation can impact one's ability to empathize. In fact, education abroad supports students in the development of their ability to empathize with others (Gray et al., 2002). Similarly, in research conducted on openness and agreeableness, both a semester and a year spent in another country significantly impacted adolescents' openness and agreeableness (Greischel et al., 2016; Zimmermann & Neyer, 2013). This increasing tendency was not found for the control group who did not study abroad. It is therefore also not surprising that education abroad alumni have been found to be open and tolerant (Allison et al., 2012), have greater appreciation for and openness toward diversity at home and abroad (Akande & Slawson, 2000), and greater tolerance for ambiguity (Dwyer, 2004b). Students who spend an academic year abroad have the opportunity to develop their intercultural attitudes in positive ways as well as increase their abilities for cross-cultural interaction (Alred & Byram, 2002). Additionally, students in year-long programs have increased their acceptance of other values and cultural practices (Brown, 2009b), and tolerance (Bian, 2013). What is especially beneficial about this outcome is its potential impact on diversity and inclusion in the at-home communities.

Alumni in the IES study reported that education abroad impacted their worldview as well as their political and social views (Dwyer, 2004b), which was also confirmed in our survey and matches alumni reports we receive informally. From our own experience as well as the IES study results, these changes were more pronounced in students who participated in long-term programs (Dwyer, 2004b). Alumni also reported understanding their values and biases better as a result of education abroad (Akande & Slawson, 2000). In our survey, alumni reported that education abroad changed their worldview and contributed to a better understanding of their role and their home community's role in the world.

Identity Formation

Positive changes were also revealed for students' interpersonal development (Drexler & Campbell, 2011). Education abroad is an opportunity to reflect about one's own identity and place in the world away from the familiar. For many, education abroad influences their own identity and identity development (Block, 2007; Kinginger, 2004), gives them a new sense of self and allows them to discover a new self (Akande & Slawson, 2000), and helps them define their life goals (Allison et al., 2012). Returnees often identify less with their home culture after education abroad than before (Allen et al., 2006), which can contribute to difficulties adjusting to back home as well as an international orientation later in life. On the other hand, education abroad participants also find a sense of belonging with regard to their home community (Giovanangeli & Oguro, 2016), students at times see more commonalities between themselves and others at home, when living in a different culture.

Spending a year or more studying in another culture is perceived by many participants as a way of self-discovery (Bian, 2013; Brown, 2009b) and as a life-changing experience that changed them and helped them find their own identity (Gallucci, 2014). Different effects on and paths to identity development through education abroad are described in the literature and these are impacted by host community, involvement with the host community, individual goals and ambitions (Jing-Schmidt, Chen, & Zhang, 2016). On the most basic level, education abroad challenges the learners to re-evaluate their identity culturally, linguistically, personally, academically, and professionally. They have to understand and define the connection between their own identity within and between the communities they are navigating.

LGBTQ+ students may face additional difficulties when studying in other countries, especially if those countries have different cultural norms and restrictive ideas about sexual orientation and gender identity. Some countries have laws against homosexuality, for example, and report higher numbers of hate crimes against LGBTQ+ individuals. Thus, safety concerns play a large role in the decision of LGBTQ+ students to study abroad (Bryant & Soria, 2015). Notwithstanding the added hardships that LGBTQ+ students might experience during education abroad, former participants in Europe and Asia voiced positive evaluations of their time abroad and most would not hesitate to choose education abroad again (Michl, Pegg, & Kracen, 2019; Schoenberger, 2019). Although the result of an extremely small sample, a qualitative analysis of the experiences of five members of the LGBTQ+ community who had previously studied abroad revealed that students saw their time abroad as an opportunity for reinvention (Schoenberger, 2019). Being away from their family and communities provided them with a sense of freedom and removed pressures of having to conform to anyone's expectations. As noted in the study, this freedom will be impacted by the location of the abroad program.

Women of color who studied abroad together in Africa have benefitted strongly from reclaiming their heritage, redefining sisterhood, and feeling empowered to produce change in their own communities (Morgan, Mwegelo, & Thuner, 2002). In a similar manner, heritage language learners who study abroad in a community that speaks their heritage language, perceive profound effects on their identity (Petrucci, 2007; Trentman, 2015). Self-efficacy developed more in students with ethnoracial background closer to the host community (Long, 2014). Garbati and Rothschild (2016) also commented on education abroad allowing them to connect to their heritage. Black students were more likely to invest in their learning, when they were able to use education abroad to connect to their heritage or ethnoracial identity (Anya, 2011).

International Orientation

As already alluded to, education abroad has a long-term impact on international behavior such as international friendships and international travel (Akande & Slawson, 2000; Garbati & Rothschild, 2016; Weichbrodt, 2014) and internationally-oriented leisure activities (Murphy et al., 2014). In the study by Brenner (2016), community college students reported education abroad contributing to their desire for further travel abroad. Our own experience working with alumni and research continues to show that participation in education abroad can motivate students for continued and additional language study (Akande & Slawson, 2000; Archangeli, 1999; Badstübner & Ecke, 2009; Chieffo & Zipser, 2001; M. Fryer & Roger, 2018; Ingram, 2005; Morreale, 2011) including the study of additional languages (Archangeli, 1999). Education abroad students often also continue to engage in education abroad or other international experiences. For example, many of our AYF Alumni later participate in one of the year-long abroad teaching assignments (e.g., Fulbright TAs) after they graduate. In the IES survey, Norris and Gillespie (2009) also found that alumni were more likely to study abroad again. In fact, the more international experience participants had, the more likely they were to do it again. Short-term education abroad often leads to additional and at times longer second education abroad experiences (Hackney, Boggs, & Borozan, 2012). Offering a variety of education abroad options is therefore important to still the continuing thirst for abroad experiences in our alumni. Part of post-sojourn support must then also include advising students for further international experiences – including post-graduation – and assisting students with their applications.

Program Design and Academic, Professional, and Personal Outcomes

As with other factors, program length may matter in outcomes of education abroad. Longer stays have been found to be more beneficial for the development of some individual characteristics and personal identity. The advantages in these areas of a longer stay have included:

- Stronger cultural and ethnic identification (Hamad & Lee, 2013).
- Self-discovery and identity formation (Aydin, 2012; Bacon, 2002; Brown, 2009b; Brown & Graham, 2009; Gallucci, 2014; Zimmermann & Neyer, 2013).
- Self-efficacy development (Courtois, 2019; H.-I. Kim & Cha, 2017).
- Decrease in neuroticism (Zimmermann & Neyer, 2013).
- Greater level of cultural tolerance (Dwyer, 2004b), ability to communicate with people from diverse backgrounds (Schartner, 2016), and empathy (Gray et al., 2002).
- Greater levels of autonomy, self-reliance, independence and self-confidence (Amuzie & Winke, 2009; Aydin, 2012; Bian, 2013; Brown, 2009b; Geeraert & Demoulin, 2013; Juhasz & Walker, 1987).
- Greater level of maturation (Zimmermann & Neyer, 2013).
- Ability to problem-solve, deal with stress (Brown, 2009b) and take risks (Courtois, 2019).
- More flexibility and adaptability (Bian, 2013; Williams, 2005).
- Self-management skills such as time management, decision-making and dependability (P. Gardner et al., 2008).
- Creativity (Maddux & Galinsky, 2009).

Long-term education abroad alumni are:

- More likely to have international careers later and are more globally engaged (Murphy et al., 2014; Norris & Gillespie, 2009; Wiers-Jenssen, 2017).
- More likely to have a network of global friends (Dwyer, 2004b).
- More likely to still be in touch with friends they met during their time abroad (Dwyer, 2004b).

A word of caution on these results is that they are largely based on the self-report survey results from IES. The longer the program the alumni participated in, the more likely it was that the education abroad offerings of institutions mattered when they originally made their college decision, suggesting that these students were already more internationally oriented before they even entered college (Dwyer, 2004b), which may have skewed the results.

Moving away from length, another influential program design component is the level and kind of support provided to participants. Alumni often report that the year abroad was the most important for their personal growth and developing independence (Garbati & Rothschild, 2016). As Garbati and Rothschild illustrate, the pride of learning to navigate a new place and the confidence gained through this successful managing of a struggle has a lasting impact on program participants.

While education abroad is often hailed as developing maturity and independence, this is not always possible. The expectations of parents and students of the services and protections that should be offered by programs is often counter-productive to their development of maturity and independence (AAUP, 1995; Kinginger, 2010). The challenge in education program design is striking a balance between supporting and challenging to learn. The attempts to mimic US institutional context for legal or student/parent satisfaction reasons, may have a negative impact on the often-praised development of maturity and independence of education abroad students, since they are then more guided in their experience. Naturally, such services are not available to direct-enroll participants, in which students must navigate the host community independently without facilitators from home. One of the advantages of JYA programs such as AYF is that students can take advantage of as little or as many of the program offerings as they would like. The intercultural staff at AYF can help facilitate intercultural interactions and unpack miscommunications, yet students can also explore the cultural maize independently.

Individual Factors and Academic, Professional, and Personal Outcomes

We have already discussed many different individual factors and their impact on specific outcomes. We draw our attention now to personality. Research on the effects of personality on students' choice to education abroad as well as the outcomes of their participation has revealed connections between personality traits and participation as well as outcomes in education abroad programs. The five personality traits that are commonly investigated are extraversion, agreeableness, conscientiousness, neuroticism, and openness (McCrae & John, 1992). Even though research confirms that personality traits are considered relatively stable, changes across the lifespan can occur and are affected by biological and contextual factors (Zimmermann, Hutteman, Nestler, Neyer, & Back, 2015). Importantly, transformative life changes can also impact a specific personality trait. A longer stay in another culture is a significant life event that can alter personality traits. During a time abroad, personality traits can play a role in students' programmatic preferences, for example for living arrangements. Extroverted students may prefer living in a dorm with other students, while introverted students might opt for living by themselves (Zimmermann et al., 2015). The majority of education abroad research has focused on the effects of the openness trait, but some research also exists for extraversion. So far, little research has investigated the remaining three of the big five personality traits and their connection to education abroad.

Conclusion

Not only did students report gaining maturity through their time abroad (Bian, 2013; Gray et al., 2002), but research has confirmed that long-term programs support personal maturation (Zimmermann & Neyer, 2013). A year abroad can also help language learners overcome communication apprehension (Aydin, 2012) and students after education abroad have reported increased confidence in communicating with others from diverse backgrounds (Schartner, 2016). Further benefits that students have reported as outcomes of their year abroad include finding their own strength, gaining the capacity to deal with stress, an increase in self-belief, and a sense of self-direction (Brown, 2009b), independence (Bian, 2013), as well as a new self-understanding (Brown & Graham, 2009). As alumni reported in their responses to our survey, students not only find their academic and professional direction while abroad, but also their spiritual direction and at times their spouse. In their study on alumni, Norris and Gillespie (2009) conclude: "studying abroad truly does change one's life" (p. 395) – a statement echoed by many of the testimonials and qualitative comments we have gathered through our programs and our research.

Chapter 2.5. Impact on Communities and Institutions

Beyond the individual, education abroad experience is seen as having a positive impact on national security, peace-making efforts, and the economic competitiveness of a country (Durbin, 2006) as well as the home institution (Chieffo & Zipser, 2001) and the host institution/community (Crawford & Berquist, 2020). Education abroad contributes to international exchange – in both positive as well as negative ways.

Host Community

The influence of education abroad programs in host communities is naturally mitigated through program design factors. Depending on how mindful the program designers and program leaders are about a reciprocal rather than a colonial relationship with the host community, the impacts can be more or less positive.

Community at Large

A carefully and ethically designed program can bring benefits to the host community. For example, Schnuth and Celestin (2020) describe a program in which medical students provide resources and medical services to rural communities in partnership with an NGO that operates globally in rural communities. What is important in this program is the reciprocal nature of the program; the community is provided with medical services and at the same time the participants are learning to appreciate a completely different health care system and approach to health care in those communities. All sides are learning how to provide more effective medical care. The benefit for the community can be much simpler such as an exchange of ideas or jointly solving problems. Other times the community can benefit through additional English language experience through students from the US, which can help their own population become more competitive in the global job market through language practice and experience with international students. Furthermore, education abroad alumni can become ambassadors for the host community after their return.

In long-term immersive programs, participants are residents not visitors in the community and integrate into the community (Garbati & Rothschild, 2016), through which they internationalize the community, which can be seen positively as well as negatively. The influx of international students brings income to the community, but can also make them dependent on such income or price others out of housing. For example, there are those who lament that Brighton in England used to be a beautiful beach town before it became a hub for teenage English language learners on short-term abroad experiences. When destinations become too popular, they can easily alienate the locals. Our host community in Mayen celebrates the arrival of the US students; it is almost like receiving visitors from so far away is elevating the status of the small community in the Eifel.

As Delgado and Yoder (2020) summarize, education abroad program design typically puts the focus on learning outcomes and university research – and we would add institutional financial well-being – and program designers are not (primarily) concerned with the impact on the community. This puts the host community in a potentially vulnerable position and hence a reciprocal partnership should be sought early with the host community to avoid negative impact on the community as much as possible. Service-learning can be especially delicate. For example, service learning projects can be a disservice to the community, if the participants are not qualified to perform the work (Chapman, 2016). Service learning projects also run the risk of creating power relationships that devalue the host community and/or make the host community financially or otherwise dependent on the program. Furthermore, such projects can run the risk of at least challenging local beliefs or even pushing home community beliefs on the host community. For example, Esquith (2020) discusses how participants in a service learning abroad program in Mali had to be taught to navigate their own beliefs that children should learn first in their first language with the dominant belief in the community that children are disadvantaged, if they start learning in their home language rather than the colonial language of French. To avoid these potential cultural clashes and power dynamics, Delgado and Yoder (2020) had as one of their design principles for the program to not transport the MSU culture to Costa Rica. Kortegast and Kupo (2017) as well as the authors in Crawford and Berquist (2020) provide models and recommendations for avoiding a post-colonial or consumerist impact on the host community.

Host Families and Peers

In programs that rely on host families, host families can benefit from the education abroad program. Many programs pay host families – though at times it is just to cover expenses – and this can lead to a financial benefit for the families, though it also can create a dependency and a customer-service relationship. Gutel (2008) found that some students, especially male students, viewed their host families as service providers. Di Silvio et al. (2014) summarized a variety of reasons for host families to agree to be host families from cultural exchange, to financial incentives, to language learning, to social contact, and pride in their own communities. Our own survey respondent mirrored those responses: Intercultural exchange, showing others around, delight in others being interested in their cultures, and providing opportunities to their children to practice English.

If students live in dorms or take classes with host community peers, they also contribute to an internationalization of those peers. Often, as described by alumni in our survey and also in research, the locals appreciate the opportunities to use and develop their English language skills. Yet, it simultaneously reinforces the dominance and power of English. On the positive side, the international exchange through living together can not only contribute to intercultural competence development in program participants but also their peers. Through the participants, the host community peers are able to expand their global networks through the contact with international peers.

Host Institution

Because education abroad participants work within the constraints of the educational system at home, they sometimes need to push values and practices from their home educational context onto the host institution. For example, the German university system usually has students write their research papers during the two-month break between the semesters. Due dates often fall late during that time period and professors tend to read those papers just before or at the beginning of the next semester. However, our AYF students are required to turn in papers two weeks after the semester ends and the program kindly asks professors to submit the grades as early as possible to ensure a timely credit transfer process. Another example is local teaching staff, which is subcontracted by the program and may also be teaching at the local institution. Those instructors are often asked or even required to follow the academic standards and procedures of the home institution, which can be against the cultural educational values of the host institution, the host community, and the instructor. Furthermore, the host institution often incurs additional costs such as staffing for international students, extra training for their own instructional staff, and at times office space or housing for program personnel.

Host institutions also benefit from education abroad participants. For one, it internationalizes their own student population, which can have a positive effect on appeal and ranking. Additionally, if the programs are built on a reciprocal relationship, they can be beneficial for students and potentially faculty at the host institution. For example, the AYF program is in legal terms an exchange program, which means that students from Freiburg are allowed to study at the consortium universities in the Midwest for free and AYF students can take courses in Freiburg for free. Being able to offer such international experiences to students makes universities more attractive to students and their graduates more attractive to employers.

Some education abroad programs involve faculty exchanges, which raises the international (research) profile of the faculty. In other cases, the education abroad program involves research collaboration with the host institution by faculty and/or students, which can also enhance the research profile of a university and raise the quality of the research.

Home Community

Education abroad not only impacts the host community, but also the home community. For example, education abroad participants become ambassadors for their communities abroad and they can bring what they have learned abroad back to their communities. Brux and Fry (2010) revealed that increasing participation of students of color may have a positive effect on peers, the host, and the home community. It would certainly provide a more representative picture of the US than is the case with current participation trends.

National Security

As the Lincoln Commission has laid out, education abroad creates multilingual globally competent citizens, who are prepared to deal with diplomatic challenges (Commission on the Abraham Lincoln Study Abroad Fellowship Program, 2005). The depth of language skills and intercultural competence that is required for diplomatic and national security work is unlikely developable in a purely at-home institutional context. Given that language proficiency and intercultural competence are more developed in longer program, these goals support the call in this book for reinvigorating long-term programs.

Global Prosperity

Global literacy and intercultural competence are needed for a globally competitive workforce and therefore the country's economic prosperity (Commission on the Abraham Lincoln Study Abroad Fellowship Program, 2005). Norris and Gillespie (2009) concur that preparation for a global work force requires education abroad.

Diversity

Education abroad has been found to positively impact tolerance, acceptance, empathy and diversity. For example, IES survey respondents indicated that they were seeking greater diversity of friends (Akande & Slawson, 2000). Schnuth and Celestin (2020) found that their community-engagement abroad participants were more able and interested in working with diverse and underserved communities at home after their participation abroad. Furthermore, pre-service teachers that are involved in international teaching practicums are more prepared to teach future diverse populations and thereby better support a diverse range of students and promote global-mindedness and intercultural competence (Cushner, 2009), critical consciousness and empathy (Palmer & Menard-Warwick, 2012). This is to say that working with others abroad may be necessary to develop the skills and attitudes to better support marginalized groups at home in professional and private settings.

Engagement

A study surveying University of Wisconsin alumni revealed that those who had studied abroad showed more civic engagement on issues of international importance and some issues of domestic importance, higher voluntary simplicity, and were more engaged in philanthropy in the arts, education, environment, human rights, international development, and social justice (Murphy et al., 2014). This large-scale survey study suggests that education abroad has a long-lasting impact on not just the individual studying abroad, but the community as a whole. The IES alumni survey found similar results: Akande and Slawson (2000) also found that alumni showed greater appreciation for the arts; and Dwyer (2004b) confirmed a higher level of volunteerism among alumni. Similarly, Rexeisen and Al-Khatib (2009) found positive effects of education abroad in attitudes towards the environment. Additionally, students who participate in semester-long education abroad have been shown to increase their levels of conscientiousness (Niehoff et al., 2017). The increased civic engagement of education abroad alumni multiplies the benefits of education abroad to the greater community.

Home Institution

Institution

Having students participate in education abroad increases the internationalization of the student population (Chieffo & Zipser, 2001). Furthermore, education abroad programs contribute to students selecting an institution over another (Chieffo & Zipser, 2001). In the language classes at MSU, students often report that they selected MSU among other things because of MSU's large variety of education abroad programs. Every semester, there is at least one student in our basic language program, who learned about AYF through their teacher (typically an AYF alumni) and their teachers successfully encouraged them to take German at MSU and participate in the AYF program. Faculty leaders and student participants also serve as positive ambassadors for the home institution in the host community (Moseley, 2009).

Programs can raise an institutions' prestige and visibility to other institutions and prospective students (Hanouille & Leuner, 2001), especially if programs are open to students from outside of the institution. Therefore, some programs can also be a financial gain for the institution (Hanouille & Leuner, 2001), or at least keep the monies for education abroad with the institution and not lost to another provider. Furthermore, having an education abroad program conducted by the home institution with home faculty decreases the liability of the home institutions, since at-home students and education abroad participants are following the same rules (Hanouille & Leuner, 2001).

A long-term impact of education abroad is its friend-raising potential for institutions. Students often stay connected to peers from their program even decades later (Garbati & Rothschild, 2016), which can emotionally connect them to the institution and make them more likely to donate, especially if it is connected to the education abroad program they participated in. Some institutions have started offering alumni trips for education abroad alumni.

Departments

Education abroad participation can increase the motivation to study languages (Badstübner & Ecke, 2009; Chieffo & Zipser, 2001), which contributes to language enrollments at the home institution in advanced courses. Of course, while they are abroad, students are not enrolled in home institution language courses, which may decrease enrollments as well. Some fear that education abroad takes students away from the program (Barnhart, Ricks, & Spier, 1997). However, after education abroad, students are more likely to minor or major in the language(s) of the host community (Archangeli, 1999). In addition to the more direct impact on enrollment, education abroad programs can also have an indirect impact. Through offering interdisciplinary programs, language departments can strengthen their relations with other units on campus, which can raise their profile on campus (Chieffo & Zipser, 2001) and increase enrollments.

For example, as MSU increased student participation in year-long education abroad program, more students decided to minor or upgrade from a minor to a major, but they completed those degrees in Germany, thereby not contributing to enrollments in upper level courses at home. Similarly, the strong enrollments in the summer program at Yale take away from second-year enrollments on campus but later increase enrollments in advanced classes as participants return and enroll in advanced courses. It is therefore imperative to inform students of their options for education abroad including appropriate preparatory coursework, suitable coursework while abroad, as well as appropriate coursework after education abroad.

Faculty

Education abroad contributes to faculty development (Chieffo & Zipser, 2001; Hanouille & Leuner, 2001; Moseley, 2009) and education abroad leadership enriches faculty's lives, which is demonstrated by a high level of job satisfaction (Moseley, 2009). Education abroad programs can also lead to student and faculty research collaborations, which are beneficial for both the students and the faculty members (Moseley, 2009). Education abroad leadership can also help faculty expand their international research network and collaboration (Moseley, 2009).

Faculty play an important role in all phases of education abroad. Barnhart et al. summarize faculty roles:

> Faculty have important roles to play as: members of international education policy advisory and overseas scholarship committees; general advocates of education abroad and promoters of campus-sponsored, affiliated, and other overseas programs; advisers and preapproval and transfer academic credit evaluations, in conjunction with your office and/or the registrar; resources in program development and administration, including cost analysis and budget

preparation; area-studies resources in pre-departure orientation and post-return reentry programming; international consultants to other campus committees; campus-based or overseas program directors; oversees teachers in institutional study abroad programs and exchange.

(Barnhart et al., 1997, pp. 37–38)

As student support services on the home campus have increased, students expect similar services abroad and these typically fall on the shoulders of faculty leaders. Several of these roles are high paid roles at home, but program leaders typically only receive their home salary or a small stipend for leading the program (AAUP, 1995). In conducting interviews with faculty leaders, Goode identified four dimensions of the faculty role:

Dean of Students dimension (student social life, student group dynamics, student mental health, student physical health, student safety, and student alcohol use); logistic (administrative) dimension (scheduling, administration, staff management, and budgeting); intercultural dimension (familiarity with the study abroad program sites ahead of time, and intellectual insights about the culture of the sites to share with students); academic dimension (curriculum development, teaching, grading, and academic mentoring).

(Goode, 2008, p. 155)

In addition to Goode's categories, faculty roles have been described as instructor/educator, administrator, risk and safety manager, social worker/therapist (Hornig, 1995; O'Neal & Krueger, 1995), caregiver, comforter and relationship builder (Davis & Spoljoric, 2019), and initiator, collaborator, facilitator, and advocate (Kohlbry & Daugherty, 2013).

In Goode's (2008) study, faculty leaders reported the challenge of navigating the multiple roles and the seemingly contradictory expectation of being both nurturing and occupying a position of authority. Faculty felt most prepared for the academic portion of the position and felt most supported by the international education office for the logistical aspects of the program (Goode, 2008). Unfortunately, it was also found that the Dean of Students role and the logistical responsibilities were omnipresent and so pressing, that they overwhelmed faculty leaders and distracted them from working with students on intercultural development. The varied roles faculty leaders must perform often over-extend them, but adding more staff would make the program less affordable.

Due to these numerous roles, education abroad can be a daunting assignment for program directors. A study of education abroad directors revealed three particular areas of stress (Madden, McMillan, & Madden, 2018): Time investment, financial costs, and physiological demands. Faculty explained that the time it took to prepare and lead a program was not always worth it in terms of compensation and results, sometimes even including out-of-pocket expenses that were not reimbursed. Stress and fatigue from travel and the high level of responsibility for a group of students was noted as another downside to leading education abroad. In addition to those, further issues include relational, legal and professional risks.

Programs that require participation from home campus faculty, on the other hand, are attractive features to recruit new faculty to a campus (Goode, 2008) and are more attractive to students. With time, however, institutions do struggle with finding faculty to lead programs abroad (Moseley, 2009). Informants for our book, who had repeatedly led education abroad, reported that their leadership in education abroad was not considered in their annual review or negatively impacted their annual performance review.

Moseley (2009) in a personal account, however, explained the value of leading education abroad programs, when it aligns with the research of the faculty members. He does acknowledge that some institutions see education abroad as service and may not count (as much) during annual and promotion reviews. Moseley (2009) reported that the ability to lead a research-focused education abroad program brought service, teaching, and research together; instruction-free weekends at a site that was relevant for his research allowed for field-work; preparation for the course broadened his expertise and perspective on the community in which his research is situated; the close collaboration with students meant that a subset became collaborators on his large-scale research project; the research experience resulted in publications; and the collaborative administration of the program with a local department allowed him to expand his research network. The intense experiences during education abroad often also lead to education abroad leaders feeling a stronger connection with the students and may bring more job satisfaction. We both consider our education abroad leadership opportunities as some of the most rewarding experiences of our professional life, which had a great influence on how we approach our positions at home today.

Multilingualism and Global-Connectedness

Impacts on the individual can lead to an impact on the community at large. For example, increased proficiency through year-long experience motivated students to become language teachers (Garbati & Rothschild, 2016). Another way that the impact of education abroad multiplies is through its impact on diversity as discussed earlier. Education abroad can be a valuable opportunity for students to confront their own ethnocentric views and thus has been suggested as a training tool for future teachers. Marx and Moss (2011) outline how preservice teachers spent a semester in London and had opportunities to reflect on their cultural beliefs and how these impact their teaching. The authors saw positive effects on the future teachers' intercultural competence. Ethnocentrism can negatively impact the way teachers treat students with diverse backgrounds so that lowering teacher trainees' levels of ethnocentrism is an important goal.

Informal alumni reports and survey responses indicate the pride alumni take in spreading their international orientation with their family and community. In their survey study of IES alumni, Akande and Slawson (2000) found that 29% of the older IES alumni have children and/or grandchildren who also participated in education abroad. This goes along with the finding that people who have family members who participated in education abroad are more likely to participate in education abroad (Hackney et al., 2012) and are better supported especially upon their return (Kartoshkina, 2015).

Conclusion

Alumni reports continue to show that education abroad, especially long-term education abroad has a transformative impact on the individual participating. However, the individual does not exist in a vacuum, hence we wanted to summarize some of the larger impacts on communities due to education abroad. We agree with Norris and Gillespie (2009): "If every college student today was encouraged to explore the possibility of or prepare for globally oriented work, tomorrow's world would be shaped and reshaped by minds and hearts influenced by the unique experience of education abroad" (p. 396). At the same time, it is important that programs are carefully designed not just for supporting learning outcomes for the participants, but also to avoid negative impacts on communities.

References

AAUP. (1995). Directing foreign study: The professor abroad. *Academe,* 81(5), 21–21. Retrieved from www.jstor.org/stable/40250872.

Akande, Y., & Slawson, C. (2000). Exploring the long-term impact of study abroad: A case study of 50 years of study abroad alumni. *International Educator,* 9(3), 12–17.

Aldawsari, N. F., Adams, K. S., Grimes, L. E., & Kohn, S. (2018). The effects of cross-cultural competence and social support on international students' psychological adjustment: Autonomy and environmental mastery. *Journal of International Students,* 8(2), 901–924.

Allen, H. W. (2013). Self-regulatory strategies of foreign language learners: From the classroom to study abroad and beyond. In C. Kinginger (Ed.), *Social and cultural aspects of language learning in study abroad* (pp. 47–72). Amsterdam: John Benjamins.

Allen, H. W., Dristas, V., & Mills, N. (2006). Cultural learning outcomes and summer study abroad. In M. Mantero (Ed.), *Identity and second language learning: Culture, inquiry, and dialogic activity in educational contexts* (pp. 189–215). Charlotte, NC: Information Age Publishing.

Allen, H. W., & Herron, C. (2003). A mixed-methodology investigation of the linguistic and affective outcomes of summer study abroad. *Foreign Language Annals,* 36(3), 370–385. doi:10.1111/j.1944-9720.2003.tb02120.x.

Allison, P., Davis-Berman, J., & Berman, D. (2012). Changes in latitude, changes in attitude: Analysis of the effects of reverse culture shock – a study of students returning from youth expeditions. *Leisure Studies,* 31(4), 487–503. doi:10.1080/02614367.2011.619011.

Alred, G. (2000). L'année à l'étranger. Une mise en question de l'identité. *Recherche et Formation,* 33, 27–44. doi:10.3406/refor.2000.1615.

Alred, G., & Byram, M. (2002). Becoming an intercultural mediator: A longitudinal study of residence abroad. *Journal of Multilingual and Multicultural Development,* 23(5), 339–352. doi:10.1080/01434630208666473.

Amuzie, G. L., & Winke, P. (2009). Changes in language learning beliefs as a result of study abroad. *System,* 37(3), 366–379. doi:10.1016/j.system.2009.02.011.

Anderson, P. H., & Lawton, L. (2011). Intercultural development: Study abroad vs. on-campus study. *Frontiers: The Interdisciplinary Journal of Study Abroad,* 21, 86–108.

Anderson, P. H., Lawton, L., Rexeisen, R. J., & Hubbard, A. C. (2006). Short-term study abroad and intercultural sensitivity: A pilot study. *International Journal of Intercultural Relations,* 30(4), 457–469. doi:10.1016/j.ijintrel.2005.10.004.

Ang, S., Van Dyne, L., Koh, C., Ng, K. Y., Templer, K. J., Tay, C., & Chandrasekar, N. A. (2007). Cultural intelligence: Its measurement and effects on cultural judgment and decision making, cultural adaptation and task performance. *Management and Organization Review,* 3(3), 335–371. doi:10.1111/j.1740-8784.2007.00082.x.

Anita, S. C., & McKenry, L. (1999). Preparing culturally competent practitioners. *The Journal of Nursing Education,* 38(5), 228–234.

Antonakopoulou, E. (2013). Sociocultural adaptation of US education abroad students in Greece. *Frontiers: The Interdisciplinary Journal of Study Abroad,* 23, 60–72.

Anya, U. (2011). Connecting with communities of learners and speakers: Integrative ideals, experiences, and motivation of successful black second language learners. *Foreign Language Annals,* 44(3), 441–466.

Archangeli, M. (1999). Study abroad and experiential learning in Salzburg, Austria. *Foreign Language Annals,* 32(1), 115–122. doi:10.1111/j.1944-9720.1999.tb02380.x.

Arnett, C. (2013). Syntactic gains in short-term study abroad. *Foreign Language Annals*, 46 (4), 705–712. doi:10.1111/flan.12052.

Avello, P., & Lara, A. R. (2014). Phonological development in L2 speech production during study abroad programs differing in length of stay. In C. Perez-Vidal (Ed.), *Language acquisition in study abroad and formal instruction contexts* (pp. 137–166). Amsterdam: John Benjamins.

Aveni, V. P. (2005). *Study abroad and second language use: Constructing the self*. Cambridge: Cambridge University Press.

Aydin, S. (2012). "I am not the same after my ERASMUS": A qualitative research. *The Qualitative Report*, 17(55), 1–23.

Bacon, S. M. (2002). Learning the rules: Language development and cultural adjustment during study abroad. *Foreign Language Annals*, 35(6), 637–646. doi:10.1111/j.1944-9720.2002.tb01902.x.

Badstübner, T., & Ecke, P. (2009). Student expectations, motivations, target language use, and perceived learning progress in summer study abroad program in Germany. *Die Unterrichtspraxis/Teaching German*, 42(1), 41–49.

Bae, S. Y., & Song, H. (2017). Intercultural sensitivity and tourism patterns among international students in Korea: using a latent profile analysis. *Asia Pacific Journal of Tourism Research*, 22(4), 436–448.

Baker-Smemoe, W., Dewey, D. P., Bown, J., & Martinsen, R. A. (2014). Variables affecting L2 gains during study abroad. *Foreign Language Annals*, 47(3), 464–486. doi:10.1111/flan.12093.

Bandura, A. (1997). *Self-efficacy: The exercise of control*. New York: W. H. Freeman.

Barbuto, J. E., Beenen, G., & Tran, H. (2015). The role of core self-evaluation, ethnocentrism, and cultural intelligence in study abroad success. *The International Journal of Management Education*, 13(3), 268–277. doi:10.1016/j.ijme.2015.07.004.

Barnhart, B., Ricks, T., & Spier, P. (1997). Faculty roles. In W. Hoffa & J. Pearson (Eds.), *NAFSA's guide to education abroad for advisers and administrators* (2nd ed., pp. 37–56). Washington, DC: NAFSA Association of International Educators.

Baró, À. L., & Serrano, R. S. (2011). Length of stay and study abroad: Language gains in two versus three months abroad. *RESLA*, 24, 95–110.

Barron, A. (2003). *Acquisition in interlanguage pragmatics: Learning how to do things with words in a study abroad context*. Amsterdam: John Benjamins Publishing Company.

Barron, A. (2006). Learning to say "you" in German: The acquisition of sociolinguistic competence in a study abroad context. In M. A. DuFon & E. Churchill (Eds.), *Language learners in study abroad contexts* (pp. 59–88). Clevedon: Multilingual Matters.

Basow, S. A., & Gaugler, T. (2017). Predicting adjustment of US college students studying abroad: Beyond the multicultural personality. *International Journal of Intercultural Relations*, 56, 39–51. doi:10.1016/j.ijintrel.2016.12.001.

Bathke, A., & Kim, R. (2016). Keep calm and go abroad: The effect of learning abroad on student mental health. *Frontiers: The Interdisciplinary Journal of Study Abroad*, 17, 1–16.

Bathurst, L., & Brack, B. L. (2012). Shifting the locus of intercultural learning. Intervening prior to and after student experiences abroad. In M. V. Berg, R. M. Paige, & K. H. Lou (Eds.), *Student learning abroad: What our students are learning, what they're not, and what we can do about it* (pp. 261–283). Sterling, VA: Stylus.

Beattie, J., Valls-Ferrer, M., & Pérez-Vidal, C. (2014). Listening performance and onset level in formal instruction and study abroad. In C. Pérez-Vidal (Ed.), *Language acquisition in study abroad and formal instruction contexts* (pp. 195–216). Amsterdam: John Benjamins Publishing Company.

Behrnd, V., & Porzelt, S. (2011). Intercultural competence and training outcomes of students with experiences abroad. *International Journal of Intercultural Relations*, 36(2), 213–223. doi:10.1016/j.ijintrel.2011.04.005.

Bennett, M. J. (1986). Towards ethnorelativism: A developmental model of intercultural sensitivity. In R. M. Paige (Ed.), *Cross-cultural orientation: New conceptualizations and applications* (pp. 27–70). New York: University Press of America.

Bennett, M. J. (1993). Towards ethnorelativism: A developmental model of intercultural sensitivity. In R. M. Paige (Ed.), *Education for the intercultural experience* (pp. 21–71). Yarmouth: Intercultural Press.

Benson, P., Barkhuizen, G., Bodycott, P., & Brown, J. (2013). *Second language identity in narratives of study abroad*. New York: Palgrave Macmillan.

Bhawuk, D. P. S., & Brislin, R. (1992). The measurement of intercultural sensitivity using the concepts of individualism and collectivism. *International Journal of Intercultural Relations*, 16, 413–436.

Bian, C. (2013). Study Abroad as Self-Development: An Analysis of International Students' Experience in China and France. *Frontiers of Education in China*, 8(3), 448–477. doi:10.3868/s110-002-013-0028-8.

Bicknese, G. (1971). Juniors in Germany: Effects and opinions. An experimental evaluation through student polls. Retrieved from https://files.eric.ed.gov/fulltext/ED042390.pdf

Bicknese, G. (1974a). Study abroad part I: A comparative test of attitudes and opinions. *Foreign Language Annals*, 7(3), 325–336. doi:10.1111/j.1944-9720.1974.tb02592.x.

Bicknese, G. (1974b). Study abroad part II: As the students see It: The junior year abroad reassessed. *Foreign Language Annals*, 7(3), 337–345. doi:10.1111/j.1944-9720.1974.tb02593.x.

Black, H. T., & Duhon, D. L. (2006). Assessing the impact of business study abroad programs on cultural awareness and personal development. *Journal of Education for Business*, 81(3), 140–144.

Blake-Campbell, B. (2014). More than just a sampling of study abroad: Transformative possibilities at best. *The Community College Enterprise*, 20(2), 6–71.

Block, D. (2007). *Second language identities*. New York: Continuum.

Bloom, M., & Miranda, A. (2015). Intercultural sensitivity through short-term study abroad. *Language and Intercultural Communication*, 15(4), 567–580. doi:10.1080/14708477.2015.1056795.

Bongiovanni, S., Long, A. Y., Solon, M., & Willis, E. W. (2015). The effect of short-term study abroad on second language Spanish phonetic development. *Studies in Hispanic and Lusophone Linguistics*, 8(2), 243–283.

Borras, J., & Llanes, A. (2020). L2 reading and vocabulary development after a short study abroad experience. *Vigo International Journal of Applied Linguistics*, 17, 35–55. doi:10.35869/vial.v0i17.1464.

Bown, J., Dewey, D., & Belnap, R. K. (2015). Student interactions during study abroad in Jordan. In R. Mitchell, N. Tracy-Ventura, & K. McManus (Eds.), *Social interaction, identity and language learning during residence abroad* (pp. 199–222). Amsterdam: The European Second Language Association.

Braskamp, L. A., Braskamp, D. C., & Engberg, M. E. (2013). Global perspective inventory (GPI): Its purpose, construction, potential uses, and psychometric characteristics. Retrieved http://citeseerx.ist.psu.edu/viewdoc/download?doi=10.1.1.584.9216&rep=rep1&type=pdf.

Brecht, R., Davidson, D., & Ginsberg, R. (1995). Predictors of foreign language gain during study abroad. In B. F. Freed (Ed.), *Second language acquisition in a study abroad context* (pp. 317–334). Amsterdam: John Benjamins.

Breitkreuz, K. R. (2015). Nursing student adaptation during a semester abroad. *Online Journal of Cultural Competence in Nursing and Healthcare*, 5(1), 141–162.

Brenner, A. (2016). Transformative learning through education abroad: A case study of a community college program. In R. L. Raby & E. J. Valeau (Eds.), *International education at community colleges* (pp. 293–310). New York: Palgrave Macmillan.

Briggs, J. G. (2015). Out-of-class language contact and vocabulary gain in a study abroad context. *System*, 53, 129–140. doi:10.1016/j.system.2015.07.007.

Brindley, R., Quinn, S., & Morton, M. L. (2009). Consonance and dissonance in a study abroad program as a catalyst for professional development of pre-service teachers. *Teaching and teacher education*, 25(3), 525–532.

Brockington, J. L., & Wiedenhoft, M. D. (2009). The liberal arts and global citizenship: Fostering intercultural engagement through integrative experiences and structured reflection. In R. Lewin (Ed.), *The handbook of practice and research in study abroad: Higher education and the quest for global citizenship* (pp. 117–132). New York: Routledge.

Brown, L. (2009a). A failure of communication on the cross-cultural campus. *Journal of Studies in International Education*, 13(4), 439–454. doi:10.1177/1028315309331913.

Brown, L. (2009b). The transformative power of the international sojourn. *Annals of Tourism Research*, 36(3), 502–521. doi:10.1016/j.annals.2009.03.002.

Brown, L., & Graham, I. (2009). The discovery of the self through the academic sojourn. *Existential Analysis*, 20(1), 79–93.

Brubaker, C. (2007). Six weeks in the Eifel: A case for culture learning during short-term study abroad. *Die Unterrichtspraxis/Teaching German*, 40(2), 118–123.

Brux, J. M., & Fry, B. (2010). Multicultural students in study abroad: Their interests, their issues, and their constraints. *Journal of Studies in International Education*, 14(5), 508–527.

Bryant, K. M., & Soria, K. M. (2015). College students' sexual orientation, gender identity, and participation in study abroad. *Frontiers: The Interdisciplinary Journal of Study Abroad*, 15, 91–106.

Burke, M. J., Watkins, M. B., & Guzman, E. (2009). Performing in a multi-cultural context: The role of personality. *International Journal of Intercultural Relations*, 33(6), 475–485. doi:10.1016/j.ijintrel.2009.05.005.

Byker, E. J., & Putnam, S. M. (2018). Catalyzing cultural and global competencies: Engaging preservice teachers in study abroad to expand the agency of citizenship. *Journal of Studies in International Education*, 23(1), 84–105. doi:10.1177/1028315318814559.

Byram, M. (1997). *Teaching and assessing intercultural communicative competence*. Clevedon: Multilingual Matters.

Cain, A., & Zarate, G. (1996). The role of training courses in developing openness to Otherness: From tourism to ethnography. *Language, Culture and Curriculum*, 9(1), 66–83.

Caldwell, P., & Purtzer, M. A. (2015). Long-term learning in a short-term study abroad program: "Are we really truly helping the community?". *Public Health Nursing*, 32(5), 577–583. doi:10.1111/phn.12168.

Caligiuri, P. M. (2000). Selecting expatriates for personality characteristics: A moderating effect of personality on the relationship between host national contact and cross-cultural adjustment. *MIR: Management International Review*, 40(1), 61–80. Retrieved from www.jstor.org/stable/40835867.

Cankaya, E. M., Liew, J., & de Freitas, C. P. P. (2018). Curiosity and autonomy as factors that promote personal growth in the cross-cultural transition process of international students. *Journal of International Students*, 8(4), 1694–1708.

Çankaya, E. M., & Xing Dong, J. L. (2017). An examination of the relationship between social self-efficacy and personal growth initiative in international context. *International Journal of Intercultural Relations*, 61, 88–96. doi:10.1016/j.ijintrel.2017.10.001.

Carlson, J. S., Burn, B. B., Useem, J., & Yachimowicz, D. (1991). *Study abroad: The experience of American undergraduates in Western Europe and the United States*. Westport, CT: Greenwood Press.

Carlson, J. S., & Widaman, K. F. (1988). The effects of study abroad during college on attitudes toward other cultures. *International Journal of Intercultural Relations*, 12(1), 1–17. doi:10.1016/0147-1767(88)90003-X.

Carroll, J. B. (1967). Foreign language proficiency levels attained by language majors near graduation from college. *Foreign Language Annals*, 1(2), 131–151. doi:10.1111/j.1944-9720.1967.tb00127.x.

Castañeda, M. E., & Zirger, M. L. (2011). Making the most of the "new" study abroad: Social capital and the short-term sojourn. *Foreign Language Annals*, 44(3), 544–564.

Chao, M. M., Takeuchi, R., & Farh, J. L. (2017). Enhancing cultural intelligence: The roles of implicit culture beliefs and adjustment. *Personnel Psychology*, 70(1), 257–292. doi:10.1111/peps.12142.

Chapman, D. D. (2016). The ethics of international service learning as a pedagogical development practice: a Canadian study. *Third World Quarterly*, 39(10), 1899–1922. doi:10.1080/01436597.2016.1175935.

Chen, G.-M., & Starosta, W. J. (2000). Intercultural sensitivity. In L. A. Samovar & R. E. Porter (Eds.), *Intercultural communication. A reader* (9th ed., pp. 406–414). Belmont: Wadsworth.

Cheng, M., Friesen, A., & Adekola, O. (2019). Using emotion regulation to cope with challenges: A study of Chinese students in the United Kingdom. *Cambridge Journal of Education*, 49(2), 133–145. doi:10.1080/0305764X.2018.1472744.

Chieffo, L., & Zipser, R. (2001). Integrating study abroad in the foreign language curriculum. *ADFL Bulletin*, 32, 79–85.

Cho, J., & Morris, M. W. (2015). Cultural study and problem-solving gains: Effects of study abroad, openness, and choice. *Journal of Organizational Behavior*, 36(7), 944–966. doi:10.1002/job.2028.

Clarke, I., Flaherty, T. B., Wright, N. D., & McMillen, R. M. (2009). Student intercultural proficiency from study abroad programs. *Journal of Marketing Education*, 31(2), 173–181.

Cohen, A. D., Paige, R. M., Shively, R. L., Emert, H. A., & Hoff, J. G. (2005). *Maximizing study abroad through language and culture strategies: Research on students, study abroad program professionals, and language instructors*. Final report to the International Research and Studies Program, Office of International Education, US Department of Education. Retrieved from https://carla.umn.edu/maxsa/documents/MAXSAResearchReport.pdf.

Collentine, J. (2004). The effects of learning contexts on morphosyntactic and lexical development. *Studies in Second Language Acquisition*, 26, 227–248. doi:10.1017/S0272263104262040.

Collentine, J. (2009). Study abroad research: Findings, implications and future directions. In M. H. Long & C. J. Doughty (Eds.), *The handbook of language teaching* (pp. 218–233). Malden, MA: Wiley-Blackwell.

Colwell, J., Nielsen, D., Bradley, B. A., & Spearman, M. (2016). Preservice teacher reflections about short-term summer study abroad experiences in Italy. In J. A. Rhodes & T. M. Milby (Eds.), *Advancing teacher education and curriculum development through study abroad programs* (pp. 91–111). Hershey, PA: IGI Global.

Commission on the Abraham Lincoln Study Abroad Fellowship Program. (2005). Global competence & national needs. One million Americans studying abroad. Retrieved from www.aplu.org/library/global-competence-and-national-needs-one-million-america ns-studying-abroad/file.

Conroy, M. A. (2016). Contextual factors in second language learning in a short-term study abroad programme in Australia. *The Language Learning Journal*, 1–21. doi:10.1080/ 09571736.2015.1118643.

Courtois, A. (2019). From "academic concern" to work readiness: student mobility, employability and the devaluation of academic capital on the year abroad. *British Journal of Sociology of Education*, 40(2), 190–206. doi:10.1080/01425692.2018.1522241.

Crawford, P., & Berquist, B. (2020). *Community engagement abroad. Perspectives and practices on service, engagement, and learning overseas*. East Lansing, MI: Michigan State University Press.

Cubillos, J. H. (2004). Transcending boundaries: The benefits of short-term study abroad experiences for foreign language teachers. *NECTFL Review*, 54, 24–34.

Cubillos, J. H., Chieffo, L., & Fan, C. (2008). The impact of short-term study abroad programs on L2 listening comprehension skills. *Foreign Language Annals*, 41(1), 157–186. doi:10.1111/j.1944-9720.2008.tb03284.x.

Cubillos, J. H., & Ilvento, T. (2012). The impact of study abroad on students' self-efficacy perceptions. *Foreign Language Annals*, 45(4), 494–511.

Curtin, A. J., Martins, D. C., & Schwartz-Barcott, D. (2015). A mixed methods evaluation of an international service learning program in the Dominican Republic. *Public Health Nursing*, 32(1), 58–67. doi:10.1111/phn.12117.

Cushner, K. (2009). The role of study abroad in preparing globally responsible teachers. In R. Lewin (Ed.), *The handbook of practice and research in study abroad. Higher education and the quest for global citizenship* (pp. 151–169). New York: Routledge.

Czerwionka, L., Artamonova, T., & Barbosa, M. (2015). Intercultural knowledge development: Evidence from student interviews during short-term study abroad. *International Journal of Intercultural Relations*, 49, 80–99. doi:10.1016/j.ijintrel.2015.06.012.

Davidson, D. E. (2010). Study abroad: When, how long, and with what results? New data from the Russian front. *Foreign Language Annals*, 43(1), 6–26. doi:10.1111/j.1944-9720.2010.01057.x.

Davie, J. (1996). Language skills, course development and the year abroad. *Language Learning Journal*, 13(1), 73–76. doi:10.1080/09571739685200221.

Davis, J. H., & Spoljoric, D. (2019). Comfort: Context for the study abroad faculty role. *Nursing Science Quarterly*, 32(4), 314–319. doi:10.1177/0894318419864327.

De Poli, S., Vergolini, L., & Zanini, N. (2018). The impact of a study abroad programme on learning abilities and personality traits: evidence from a randomization. *Applied Economics Letters*, 25(8), 562–566. doi:10.1080/13504851.2017.1346354.

Deardorff, D. K. (2004). In search of intercultural competence. *International Educator*, 13(2). Retrieved from http://ezproxy.msu.edu:2047/login?url=http://proquest.umi.com/p qdweb?did=772375861&Fmt=7&clientId=3552&RQT=309&VName=PQD).

Deardorff, D. K. (2006a). Assessing intercultural competence in study abroad students. In M. Byram & A. Feng (Eds.), *Living and studying abroad. Research and practice* (pp. 232–256). Clevedon: Multilingual Matters.

Deardorff, D. K. (2006b). Identification and assessment of intercultural competence as a student outcome of internationalization. *Journal of Studies in International Education*, 10(3), 241–266.

DeDee, L. S., & Stewart, S. (2003). The effect of student participation in international study. *Journal of professional nursing*, 19(4), 237–242. doi:10.1016/S8755-7223(03)00086-3.

DeGraaf, D., Slagter, C., Larsen, K., & Ditta, E. (2013). The long-term personal and professional impacts of participating in a study abroad program. *Frontiers: The Interdisciplinary Journal of Study Abroad*, 23, 42–59.

DeKeyser, R. (2007). Study abroad as foreign language practice. In R. M. DeKeyser (Ed.), *Practice in a Second Language. Perspectives from Applied Linguistics and Cognitive Psychology* (pp. 208–223). Cambridge: Cambridge University Press.

DeKeyser, R. (2010). Monitoring processes in Spanish as a second language during a study abroad program. *Foreign Language Annals*, 43(1), 80–92. doi:10.1111/j.1944-9720.2010.01061.x.

Delgado, V., & Yoder, S. (2020). Reexamining university–community partnerships in a civic engagement study-abroad program. In P. Crawford & B. Berquist (Eds.), *Community Engagement Abroad: Perspectives and Practices on Service, Engagement, and Learning Overseas* (pp. 131–144). East Lansing, MI: Michigan State University.

Demetry, C., & Vaz, R. F. (2017). Influence of an education abroad program on the intercultural sensitivity of STEM undergraduates: A mixed methods study. *Advances in Engineering Education*, 6(1), 1–32.

Dewey, D. P. (2004). A comparison of reading development by learners of Japanese in intensive domestic immersion and study abroad contexts. *Studies in Second Language Acquisition*, 26(2), 303–327. doi:10.1017/S0272263104262076.

Dewey, D. P. (2008). Japanese vocabulary acquisition by learners in three contexts. *Frontiers: The Interdisciplinary Journal of Study Abroad*, 15, 127–148.

Dewey, D. P., Belnap, R. K., & Steffen, P. (2018). Anxiety: Stress, foreign language classroom anxiety, and enjoyment during study abroad in Amman, Jordan. *Annual Review of Applied Linguistics*, 38, 140–161.

Di Silvio, F., Diao, W., & Donovan, A. (2016). The development of L2 fluency during study abroad: A cross-language study. *The Modern Language Journal*, 100(3), 610–624. doi:10.1111/modl.12343.

Di Silvio, F., Donovan, A., & Malone, M. E. (2014). The effect of study abroad homestay placements: Participant perspectives and oral proficiency gains. *Foreign Language Annals*, 47(1), 168–188.

Diaz-Campos, M. (2004). Context of learning in the acquisition of Spanish second language phonology. *Studies in Second Language Acquisition*, 26(2), 249–273.

Dings, A. (2012). Native speaker/nonnative speaker interaction and orientation to novice/expert identity. *Journal of Pragmatics*, 44(11), 1503–1518.

Dings, A. (2014). Interactional competence and the development of alignment activity. *The Modern Language Journal*, 98(3), 742–756. doi:10.1111/modl.12120.

Douglas, C., & Jones-Rikkers, C. G. (2001). Study abroad programs and American student worldmindedness: An empirical analysis. *Journal of Teaching in International Business*, 13(1).

Douthit, T. L., Schaake, S. L., Hay, M. M. R., Grieger, D. M., & Bormann, J. M. (2015). *Student blogs and journals as assessment tools for faculty-led study abroad trips NACTA Journal*, 59(3), 213–218.

Drexler, D. S., & Campbell, D. F. (2011). Student development among community college participants in study abroad programs. *Community College Journal of Research and Practice*, 35(8), 608–619. doi:10.1080/10668920801901258.

Du, H. (2013). The development of Chinese fluency during study abroad in China. *The Modern Language Journal*, 97(1), 131–143. doi:10.1111/j.1540-4781.2013.01434.x.

Dunkley, M. (2009). *What students are actually learning on study abroad and how to improve the learning experience.* Paper presented at the 20th ISANA International Education Association Conference Proceeding, Canberra (Australia).

Duperron, L., & Overstreet, M. H. (2009). Preparedness for study abroad: Comparing the linguistic outcomes of short-term Spanish program by third, fourth and sixth semester L2 learners. *Frontiers: The Interdisciplinary Journal of Study Abroad*, 18, 147–179.

Durán Martínez, R., Gutiérrez Almarza, G., Beltrán Llavador, F., & Martínez Abad, F. (2016). The impact of an Erasmus placement in students' perception of their intercultural communicative competence. *Journal of Intercultural Communication Research*, 45(4), 338–354. doi:10.1080/17475759.2016.1186721.

Durbin, R. J. (2006). The Lincoln Commission and the future of study abroad. *International Educator*, 15(1), 4–6.

Dwyer, M. M. (2004a). Charting the impact of studying abroad. *International Educator*, 13 (1), 14–20.

Dwyer, M. M. (2004b). More is better: The impact of study abroad program duration. *Frontiers: The Interdisciplinary Journal of Study Abroad*, 10, 151–163.

Dyson, P. (1988). *The year abroad.* London: Central Bureau for Educational Visits and Exchanges.

Ellwood, C. (2011). Undoing the knots: Identity transformations in a study abroad programme. *Educational Philosophy and Theory*, 43(9), 960–978. doi:10.1111/j.1469-5812.2009.00559.x.

Elola, I., & Oskoz, A. (2008). Blogging: Fostering intercultural competence development in foreign language and study abroad contexts. *Foreign Language Annals*, 41(3), 454–477. doi:10.1111/j.1944-9720.2008.tb03307.x.

Elverson, C. A., & Klawiter, R. (2018). Using guided reflection to link cultural and service learning in a study abroad course. *Journal of professional nursing*, 35(3), 181–186. doi:10.1016/j.profnurs.2018.11.004.

Engberg, M. E. (2013). The influence of study away experiences on global perspective-taking. *Journal of College Student Development*, 54(5), 466–480. doi:10.1353/csd.2013.0073.

Engberg, M. E., & Jourian, T. J. (2015). Intercultural wonderment and study abroad. *Frontiers: The Interdisciplinary Journal of Study Abroad*, 25.

Engle, L., & Engle, J. (2004). Assessing language acquisition and intercultural sensitivity development in relation to study abroad program design. *Frontiers: The Interdisciplinary Journal of Study Abroad*, 10, 219–236.

Engle, L., & Engle, J. (2012). Beyond immersion. The American University Center of Provence experiment in holistic intervention. In M. V. Berg, R. M. Paige, & K. H. Lou (Eds.), *Student learning abroad. What our students are learning, what they're not, and what we can do about it* (pp. 284–307). Sterling, VA: Stylus.

Engle, R. L., & Crowne, K. A. (2014). The impact of international experience on cultural intelligence: An application of contact theory in a structured short-term programme. *Human Resource Development International*, 17(1), 30–46. doi:10.1080/13678868.2013.856206.

Esquith, S. L. (2020). Civic engagement's challenges for study abroad: An ethical and political perspective. In P. Crawford & B. Berquist (Eds.), *Community Engagement Abroad: Perspectives and Practices on Service, Engagement, and Learning Overseas* (pp. 145–156). East Lansing, MI: Michigan State University.

Evans, M., & Fisher, L. (2005). Measuring gains in pupils' foreign language competence as a result of participation in a school exchange visit: the case of Y9 pupils at three comprehensive schools in the UK. *Language Teaching Research*, 9(2), 173–192. doi:10.1191/1362168805lr162oa.

Fantini, A. E. (2000). Assessing intercultural competence: A YOGA form. In *SIT Occasional Papers Series: Addressing International Education, Training & Service* (pp. 34–42). Brattleboro, VT: School for International Training.

Faretta-Stutenberg, M., & Morgan-Short, K. (2017). The interplay of individual differences and context of learning in behavioral and neurocognitive second language development. *Second Language Research*, 34(1), 67–101. doi:10.1177/0267658316684903.

Félix-Brasdefer, J. C. (2013). Interlanguage refusals: Linguistic politeness and length of residence in the target community. *Language Learning*, 54(4), 587–653. doi:10.1111/j.1467-9922.2004.00281.x.

Foster, P. (2009). Lexical diversity and native-like selection: The bonus of studying abroad. In B. Richards, M. Daller, D. Malvern, P. Meara, J. Milton, & J. Treffers-Daller (Eds.), *Vocabulary studies in first and second language acquisition* (pp. 91–106). Basingstoke: Palgrave Macmillan.

Freed, B. F. (1990). Language Learning in a study abroad context: The effects of interactive and noninteractive out-of-class contact on grammatical achievement and oral proficiency. In J. E. Alatis (Ed.), *Linguistics, language teaching and language acquisition: The interdependence of theory, practice and research the interdependence of theory, practice and research* (pp. 459–477). Washington, DC: Georgetown University Press.

Freed, B. F. (1995a). Language learning and study abroad. In B. F. Freed (Ed.), *Second language acquisition in a study abroad context* (pp. 3–34). Amsterdam: John Benjamins.

Freed, B. F. (1995b). What makes us think that students who study abroad become fluent? In B. F. Freed (Ed.), *Second language acquisition in a study abroad context* (pp. 123–149). Amsterdam: John Benjamins.

Freed, B. F., Segalowitz, N., & Dewey, D. P. (2004). Comparing regular classroom, study abroad, and intensive domestic immersion programs. *SSLA*, 26, 275–301.

Freed, B. F., So, S., & Lazar, N. A. (2003). Language learning abroad: How do gains in written fluency compare with gains in oral fluency in French as a second language? *ADFL Bulletin*, 34(3), 34–40.

Friar, S. (2016). Global citizenship development: Comparing long-term study abroad, course-embedded study abroad, and non-study abroad students. Doctor of Education dissertation, Edgewood College. ProQuest 10158442.

Fryer, M., & Roger, P. (2018). Transformations in the L2 self: Changing motivation in a study abroad context. *System*, 78, 159–172. doi:10.1016/j.system.2018.08.005.

Fryer, T. B., & Day, J. T. (1993). Foreign language curricular needs of students preparing for an internship abroad. *The Modern Language Journal*, 77(3), 277–288. doi:10.2307/329097.

Fuller, T. L. (2007). Study abroad experiences and intercultural sensitivity among graduate theological students: A preliminary and exploratory investigation. *Christian Higher Education*, 6(4), 321–332. doi:10.1080/15363750701268319.

Gaia, A. C. (2015). Short-term faculty-led study abroad programs enhance cultural exchange and self-awareness. *International Education Journal: Comparative Perspectives*, 14(1), 21–31.

Gallucci, S. (2014). Negotiating second-language identities in and through border crossing. *Compare: A Journal of Comparative and International Education*, 44(6), 916–937.

Garbati, J. F., & Rothschild, N. (2016). Lasting impact of study abroad experiences: A collaborative autoethnography. *Forum Qualitative Sozialforschung/Forum: Qualitative Social Research*, 17(2), 1–18. doi:10.17169/fqs-17.2.2387.

Gardner, P., Gross, L., & Steglitz, I. (2008). Unpacking your study abroad experience: Critical reflection for workplace competencies. *Collegiate Employment Research Institute Research Brief*, 1(1). Retrieved from https://files.eric.ed.gov/fulltext/ED509854.pdf.

Gardner, R. C., Day, J. B., & MacIntyre, P. D. (1992). Integrative motivation, induced anxiety, and language learning in a controlled environment. *Studies in Second Language Acquisition*, 14(2), 197–214. doi:10.1017/S0272263100010822.

Gates, L. (2014). The impact of international internships and short-term immersion programs. In A. Highum (Ed.), *Undergraduate global education: Issues for faculty, staff, and students* (pp. 33–40). San Francisco, CA: Jossey-Bass.

Gebregergis, W. T., Huang, F., & Hong, J. (2019). Cultural intelligence, age and prior travel experience as predictors of acculturative stress and depression among international students studying in China. *Journal of International Students*, 9(2), 511–534.

Geeraert, N., & Demoulin, S. (2013). Acculturative stress or resilience? A longitudinal multilevel analysis of sojourners' stress and self-esteem. *Journal of Cross-Cultural Psychology*, 44(8), 1241–1262. doi:10.1177/0022022113478656.

George, A. (2019). Study abroad homestay versus dormitory: Extralinguistic factors and regional features. *Spanish in Context*, 16(1), 77–103. doi:10.1075/sic.00027.geo.

Giovanangeli, A., & Oguro, S. (2016). Cultural Responsiveness: a framework for rethinking students' interculturality through study abroad. *Intercultural Education*, 27(1), 70–84.

Glass, C. R., & Westmont, C. M. (2014). Comparative effects of belongingness on the academic success and cross-cultural interactions of domestic and international students. *International Journal of Intercultural Relations*, 38, 106–119. doi:10.1016/j.ijintrel.2013.04.004.

Godfrey, L., Treacy, C., & Tarone, E. (2014). Change in French second language writing in study abroad and domestic contexts. *Foreign Language Annals*, 47(1), 48–65. doi:10.1111/flan.12072.

Goertler, S., & the 369ers. (2019). Understanding the people and the language around you: Using awareness-raising action research in undergraduate education abroad. *Die Unterrichtspraxis/Teaching German*, 52(1). doi:10.1111/tger.12083.

Gomes da Costa, B., Smith, T. M. F., & Whiteley, D. (1975). *German language attainment: A sample survey of universities and colleges in the UK*. Heidelberg: Julios Groos.

Goode, M. L. (2008). The role of faculty study abroad directors: A case study. *Frontiers: The Interdisciplinary Journal of Study Abroad*, 15, 149–172.

Grass, S. (2014). An evaluation of an international service experience and students' intercultural competence. Doctor of Education dissertation, Florida State University. ProQuest 3681724.

Gray, K. S., Murdock, G. K., & Stebbins, C. D. (2002). Assessing study abroad's effect on an international mission. *Change*, 34(3), 45–51.

Greischel, H., Noack, P., & Neyer, F. J. (2016). Sailing uncharted waters: Adolescent personality development and social relationship experiences during a year abroad. *Journal of Youth and Adolescence*, 45(11), 2307–2320. doi:10.1007/s10964-016-0479-1.

Grey, S., Cox, J. G., Serafini, E. J., & Sanz, C. (2015). The role of individual differences in the study abroad context: Cognitive capacity and language development during short-term intensive language exposure. *The Modern Language Journal*, 99(1), 137–157. doi:10.1111/modl.12190.

Grieve, A. M. (2015). The impact of host family relations and length of stay on adolescent identity expression during study abroad. *Multilingua*, 34(5), 623–657.

Grigorescu, C. (2015). Undergraduate students' perceptions of study abroad and their level of achievement of global learning outcomes. Doctor of Education dissertation, Florida International University. ProQuest 3721483.

Gullekson, N. L., & Tucker, M. L. (2012). An examination of the Rrelationship between emotional intelligence and intercultural growth for students studying abroad. *Journal of the Academy of Business Education*, 13, 162–178.

Gutel, H. (2008). The home stay: A gendered perspective. *Frontiers: The Interdisciplinary Journal of Study Abroad*, 15, 173–188.

Gutiérrez Almarza, G., Durán Martínez, R., & Beltrán Llavador, F. (2015). Identifying students' intercultural communicative competence at the beginning of their placement: towards the enhancement of study abroad programmes. *Intercultural Education*, 26(1), 73–85. doi:10.1080/14675986.2015.997004.

Haas, B. W. (2018). The impact of study abroad on improved cultural awareness: a quantitative review. *Intercultural Education*, 29(5–6),571–588. doi:10.1080/14675986.2018.1495319.

Hackney, K., Boggs, D., & Borozan, A. (2012). An empirical study of student willingness to study abroad. *Journal of Teaching in International Business*, 23(2), 1123–1144.

Halenko, N., & Jones, C. (2017). Explicit instruction of spoken requests: An examination of pre-departure instruction and the study abroad environment. *System*, 68, 26–37. doi:10.1016/j.system.2017.06.011.

Hamad, R., & Lee, C. M. (2013). An assessment of how length of study-abroad programs influences cross-cultural adaptation. *Journal of Human Behavior in the Social Environment*, 23(5), 661–674. doi:10.1080/10911359.2013.788461.

Hammer, M., Bennett, M. J., & Wiseman, R. (2003). Measuring intercultural sensitivity: The intercultural development inventory. *International Journal of Intercultural Relations*, 27, 421–443.

Hampel, R., & Hauck, M. (2004). Towards an effective use of audio conferencing in distance language courses. *Language Learning & Technology*, 8(1), 66–82.

Han, J.-I., Hwang, J.-B., & Choi, T.-H. (2011). The acquisition of phonetic details: Evidence from the production of English reduced vowels by Korean learners. *Second Language Research*, 27(4), 535–557. Retrieved from www.jstor.org/stable/43103878.

Hanada, S., & Shingo, H. (2019). A quantitative assessment of Japanese students' intercultural competence developed through study abroad programs. *Journal of International Students*, 9(4), 1015–1037.

Hanouille, L., & Leuner, P. (2001). Island programs: Myths and realities in international education. *E World Education News & Review*, 14(1), 1–6.

Hardison, D. M. (2014). Changes in second-language learners' oral skills and socio-affective profiles following study abroad: A mixed-methods approach. *The Canadian Modern Language Review*, 70(4), 415–444.

Harrison, J. K., & Brower, H. H. (2011). The impact of cultural intelligence and psychological hardiness on homesickness among study abroad students. *Frontiers: The Interdisciplinary Journal of Study Abroad*, 21, 41–62. Retrieved from http://search.ebscohost.com/login.aspx?direct=true&db=ehh&AN=74609042&site=ehost-live&scope=site.

Hasegawa, A. (2019). *The social lives of study abroad: Understanding second language learners' experiences through social network analysis and conversation analysis*. New York: Routledge.

Hassall, T. (2013). Pragmatic development during short-term study abroad: The case of address terms in Indonesian. *Journal of Pragmatics*, 55, 1–17.

Hechanova-Alampay, R., Beehr, T. A., Christiansen, N. D., & Van Horn, R. K. (2002). Adjustment and strain among domestic and international student sojourners: A longitudinal study. *School Psychology International*, 23(4), 458–474. doi:10.1177/0143034302234007.

Henry, A. (2014). The development and implementation of a pre-international experience course: A cultural intervention in a university setting. Doctor of Education dissertation, Arizona State University. ProQuest 3619380.

Hernández, T. A. (2010a). Promoting speaking proficiency through motivation and interaction: The study abroad and classroom learning contexts. *Foreign Language Annals*, 43(4), 650–670. doi:10.1111/j.1944-9720.2010.01107.x.

Hernández, T. A. (2010b). The relationship among motivation, interaction, and the development of second language oral proficiency in a study-abroad context. *Modern Language Journal*, 94(4), 600–617.

Hernández, T. A. (2016). Short-term study abroad: Perspectives on speaking gains and language contact. *Applied Language Learning*, 26(1), 39–64.

Hessel, G. (2017). A new take on individual differences in L2 proficiency gain during study abroad. *System*, 66, 39–55. doi:10.1016/j.system.2017.03.004.

Hett, E. J. (1993). The development of an instrument to measure global mindedness. Doctor of Education dissertation, University of San Diego. ProQuest 9408210.

Hoffa, W. W. (2007). *A history of US study abroad: Beginnings to 1965*. Carlisle, PA: Frontiers.

Hoffa, W. W., & DePaul, S. C. (2010). *A history of US study abroad: 1965–present*. Carlisle, PA: Frontiers.

Hoffman-Hicks, S. (1999). The longitudinal development of French foreign language pragmatic competence: Evidence from study abroad participants. Doctor of Philosophy dissertation, Indiana University. ProQuest 9962710.

Hofmann, W., Schmeichel, B. J., & Baddeley, A. D. (2012). Executive functions and self-regulation. *Trends in Cognitive Sciences*, 16(3), 174–180.

Holtbrügge, D., & Engelhard, F. (2016). Study abroad programs: Individual motivations, cultural intelligence, and the mediating role of cultural boundary spanning. *Academy of Management Learning & Education*, 15(3), 435–455. doi:10.5465/amle.2015.0128.

Hornig, J. F. (1995). The toughest job you'll ever love: Faculty find rewards - and responsibilities - in study abroad programs. *Academe*, 81(5), 22–26. doi:10.2307/40250873.

Horwitz, E. K., Horwitz, M. B., & Cope, J. (1986). Foreign language classroom anxiety. *The Modern Language Journal*, 70(2), 125–132. doi:10.1111/j.1540-4781.1986.tb05256.x.

Howard, M. (2008). On the role of naturalistic and classroom exposure in the acquisition of socio-phonological variation: A longitudinal study of French liaison. *Journal of Applied Linguistics*, 5(2), 159–179. doi:10.1558/japl.v5i2.159.

Huebner, T. (1995). The effects of overseas language programs: Report on a case study of an intensive Japanese course. In B. F. Freed (Ed.), *Second language acquisition in a study abroad context* (pp. 171–194). Amsterdam: John Benjamins.

Huensch, A., & Tracy-Ventura, N. (2017). L2 utterance fluency development before, during, and after residence abroad: A multidimensional investigation. *The Modern Language Journal*, 101(2), 275–293. doi:10.1111/modl.12395.

Hunter, W. D. (2004). Knowledge, skills, attitudes, and experiences necessary to become globally competent. Doctor of Education dissertation, Lehigh University. ProQuest 3147319.

Hutteman, R., Nestler, S., Wagner, J., & Egloff, B. (2015). Wherever I may roam: Processes of self-esteem development from adolescence to emerging adulthood in the context of international student exchange. *Journal of Personality and Social Psychology*, 108 (5), 767–783. doi:10.1037/pspp0000015.

Ife, A., Vives, G., & Meara, P. (2000). The impact of study abroad on the vocabulary development of different proficiency groups. *Spanish Applied Linguistics: A Forum for Theory and Research*, 4(1), 55–84.

Iino, M. (2006). Norms of interaction in a Japanese homestay setting: Toward a two-way flow of linguistic and cultural resources. In M. A. DuFon & E. E. Churchill (Eds.), *Language learners in study abroad contexts* (pp. 151–176). Clevedon: Multilingual Matters.

Ingram, M. (2005). Recasting the foreign language requirement through study abroad: A cultural immersion program in Avignon. *Foreign Language Annals*, 38(2), 211–222. doi:10.1111/j.1944-9720.2005.tb02486.x.

Isabelli-García, C. (2004). Study abroad for advanced foreign language majors: Optimal duration for developing complex structure. In H. Byrnes & H. Maxim (Eds.), *Advanced foreign language learning: A challenge to college programs*. Boston, MA: Heinle.

Isabelli-García, C. (2006). Study abroad social networks, motivation and attitudes: Implications for second language acquisition. In M. A. DuFon & E. Churchill (Eds.), *Language learners in study abroad contexts* (pp. 231–259). Clevedon: Multilingual Matters.

Isabelli-García, C. (2007). Development of the Spanish subjunctive by advanced learners: Study abroad followed by at-home instruction. *Foreign Language Annals*, 40(2), 330–341.

Iskhakova, M. (2018). Does cross-cultural competence matter when going global: Cultural intelligence and its impact on performance of international Sstudents in Australia. *Journal of Intercultural Communication Research*, 47(2), 121–140. doi:10.1080/17475759.2018.1437463.

Ismail, B., Morgan, M., & Hayes, K. (2006). Effect of short study abroad course on student openness to diversity. *Journal of Food Science Education*, 5(1), 15–18. doi:10.1111/j.1541-4329.2006.tb00070.x.

Iwasaki, N. (2007). Assessing progress towards advanced level Japanese after a year abroad: Focus on individual learners. *Japanese Language and Literature*, 41(2), 271–296. doi:10.2307/30198038.

Jackson, J. (2008). Globalization, internationalization, and short-term stays abroad. *International Journal of Intercultural Relations*, 32, 349–358.

Jackson, J. (2011). Host language proficiency, intercultural sensitivity, and study abroad. *Frontiers: The Interdisciplinary Journal of Study Abroad*, 21, 167–188.

Jackson, J. (2018). Optimizing intercultural learning and engagement abroad through online mentoring. In J. Jackson & S. Oguro (Eds.), *Intercultural interventions in study abroad* (pp. 119–136). New York: Routledge.

Jacobone, V., & Moro, G. (2015). Evaluating the impact of the Erasmus programme: Skills and European identity. *Assessment and Evaluation in Higher Education*, 40(2), 309–328. doi:10.1080/02602938.2014.909005.

Jin, L., & Wang, C. D. C. (2018). International students' attachment and psychological well-being: the mediation role of mental toughness. *Counselling Psychology Quarterly*, 31 (1), 59–78. doi:10.1080/09515070.2016.1211510.

Jing-Schmidt, Z., Chen, J.-Y., & Zhang, Z. (2016). Identity development in the ancestral homeland: A Chinese heritage perspective. *The Modern Language Journal*, 100(4), 797–812. doi:10.1111/modl.12348.

Johnson, P., & McKinnon, S. (2018). Positioning year-long study abroad at the centre of the modern languages curriculum: Supporting and assessing learning. In J. L. Plews & K. Misfeldt (Eds.), *Second language study abroad: Programming, pedagogy, and participant engagement* (pp. 24–47). Cham: Palgrave Macmillan.

Juan-Garau, M. (2014). Oral accuracy growth after formal instruction and study abrod. In C. Pérez-Vidal (Ed.), *Language acquisition in study abroad and formal instruction contexts* (pp. 87–111). Amsterdam: John Benjamins.

Juhasz, A. M., & Walker, A. M. (1987). The impact of study abroad on university students' perceptions of self. *ERIC Document: ED341916.*

Kartoshkina, Y. (2015). Bitter-sweet reentry after studying abroad. *International Journal of Intercultural Relations*, 44, 35–45. doi:10.1016/j.ijintrel.2014.11.001.

Kehl, K., & Morris, J. (2008). Differences in global-mindedness between short-term and semester-long study abroad participants at selected private universities. *Frontiers: The Interdisciplinary Journal of Study Abroad*, 15, 67–79.

Kelley, C., & Meyers, J. (1995). *CCAI Cross Cultural Adaptability Inventory manual.* Minneapolis, MN: National Computer Systems.

Kim, H.-I., & Cha, K. A. (2017). Effects of experience abroad and language proficiency on self-efficacy beliefs in language learning. *Psychological Reports*, 120(4), 670–694. doi:10.1177/0033294117697088.

Kim, J., Dewey, D. P., Baker-Smemoe, W., & Ring, S. (2015). L2 development during study abroad in China. *System*, 55, 123–133. doi:10.1016/j.system.2015.10.005.

Kim, R. I., & Goldstein, S. B. (2005). Intercultural attitudes predict favorable study abroad expectations of US college students. *Journal of Studies in International Education*, 9(3), 265–278. doi:10.1177/1028315305277684.

Kinginger, C. (2004). Alice doesn't live here anymore: Foreign language learning and identity reconstruction. In A. Pavlenko & A. Blackledge (Eds.), *Negotiation of identities in multilingual contexts* (pp. 219–242). Clevedon: Multilingual Matters.

Kinginger, C. (2008). Language learning in study abroad: Case studies of Americans in France. *The Modern Language Journal*, 92(1), 1–124. doi:10.1111/j.1540-4781.2008.00821.x.

Kinginger, C. (2009). *Language learning and study abroad: A critical reading of research.* New York: Palgrave Macmillan.

Kinginger, C. (2010). American students abroad: Negotiation of difference? *Language Teaching*, 43(2), 216–227. doi:10.1017/S0261444808005703.

Kishino, H., & Takahashi, T. (2019). Global citizenship development: Effects of study abroad and other factors. *Journal of International Studies*, 9(2), 535–559. doi:10.32674/jis.v9i2.390.

Klapper, J., & Rees, J. (2012). University residence abroad for foreign language students: Analysing the linguistic benefits. *Language Learning Journal*, 40(3), 335–358.

Knight, S. M., & Schmidt, R. (2004). The homestay component of study abroad: Three perspectives. *Foreign Language Annals*, 37(2), 254–262.

Koester, J., & Olebe, M. (1988). The behavioral assessment scale for intercultural communication effectiveness. *International Journal of Intercultural Relations*, 12, 233–246.

Kohlbry, P., & Daugherty, J. (2013). Nursing faculty roles in international service-learning projects. *Journal of professional nursing*, 29(3), 163–167. doi:10.1016/j.profnurs.2012.04.018.

Kortegast, C., & Kupo, V. L. (2017). Deconstructing underlying practices of short-term study abroad: Exploring issues of consumerism, postcolonialism, cultural tourism, and commodification of experience. *The International Journal of Critical Pedagogy*, 8(1), 149–172.

Kruse, J., & Brubaker, C. (2007). Successful study abroad: tips for student preparation, immersion, and postprocessing. *Die Unterrichtspraxis/Teaching German*, 40(2), 147–152.

Kuo, Y.-H. (2011). Language challenges faced by international graduate students in the United States. *Journal of International Students*, 1(2), 38–42.

Lafford, B. (2004). The effect of the context of learning on the use of communication strategies by learners of Spanish as a second language. *Studies in Second Language Acquisition*, 26(2), 201–225. doi:10.1017/S0272263104262039.

Lafford, B., & Collentine, J. (2006). The effects of study abroad and classroom contexts on the acquisition of Spanish as a second language: From research to application. In R. Salaberry & B. Lafford (Eds.), *The art of teaching Spanish: Second language acquisition from research to praxis* (pp. 103–126). Washington, DC: Georgetown University Press.

Lapkin, S., Hart, D., & Swain, M. (1995). A Canadian interprovincial exchange: Evaluating the linguistic impact of a three-month stay in Quebec. In B. F. Freed (Ed.), *Second language acquisition in a study abroad context* (pp. 67–94). Amsterdam: John Benjamins.

Lara, R., Mora, J. C., & Pérez-Vidal, C. (2015). How long is long enough? L2 English development through study abroad programmes varying in duration. *Innovation in Language Learning and Teaching*, 9(1), 46–57. doi:10.1080/17501229.2014.995764.

LeCrom, C. W., Greenhalgh, G., & Dwyer, B. (2015). Seeing the world differently: An analysis of the impact of a sport-related study abroad program on global mindedness. *Journal of Applied Sport Management*, 7(2), 60–82.

Lee, J., & Song, J. (2019). Developing intercultural competence through study abroad, telecollaboration, and on-campus language study. *Language Learning & Technology*, 23(3), 178–198.

Leonard, K. R., & Shea, C. E. (2017). L2 speaking development during study abroad: Fluency, accuracy, complexity, and underlying cognitive factors. *The Modern Language Journal*, 101(1), 179–193. doi:10.1111/modl.12382.

Leung, A. K.-Y., & Chiu, C.-Y. (2010). Multicultural experience, idea receptiveness, and creativity. *Journal of Cross-Cultural Psychology*, 41(5), 723–741. doi:10.1177/0022022110361707.

Leung, A. K.-Y., Maddux, W. W., Galinsky, A. D., & Chiu, C.-Y. (2008). Multicultural experience enhances creativity: The when and how. *The American Psychologist*, 63(3), 169–181. doi:10.1037/0003-066X.63.3.169.

Leung, A. K. Y., & Chiu, C. Y. (2008). Interactive effects of multicultural experiences and openness to experience on creative potential. *Creativity Research Journal*, 20(4), 376–382. doi:10.1080/10400410802391371.

Levin, D. M. (2001). Language learners' sociocultural interaction in a study abroad context. Doctor of Philosophy dissertation, Indiana University. ProQuest 3005426.

Lier, L. v. (2008). Agency in the classroom. In J. P. Lantolf & M. E. Poehner (Eds.), *Sociocultural theory and the teaching of second languages* (pp. 163–186). London: Equinox.

Lin, Y.-c., Chen, A. S.-y., & Song, Y.-c. (2012). Does your intelligence help to survive in a foreign jungle? The effects of cultural intelligence and emotional intelligence on cross-cultural adjustment. *International Journal of Intercultural Relations*, 36(4), 541–552. doi:10.1016/j.ijintrel.2012.03.001.

Lindseth, M. U. (2010). The development of oral proficiency during a semester in Germany. *Foreign Language Annals*, 43(2), 246–268. doi:10.1111/j.1944-9720.2010.01077.x.

Lindseth, M. U. (2016). The effects of form-focused instruction on subject-verb inversion in German. *Foreign Language Annals*, 49(1), 10–22. doi:10.1111/flan.12174.

Llanes, À. (2011). The many faces of study abroad: An update on the research on L2 gains emerged during a study abroad experience. *International Journal of Multilingualism*, 8(3), 189–215. doi:10.1080/14790718.2010.550297.

Llanes, À., & Muñoz, C. (2009). A short stay abroad: Does it make a difference? *System*, 37 (3), 353–365. doi:10.1016/j.system.2009.03.001.

Lokkesmoe, K. J., Kuchinke, K. P., & Ardichvili, A. (2016). Developing cross-cultural awareness through foreign immersion programs. *European Journal of Training and Development*, 40(3), 155–170. doi:10.1108/EJTD-07-2014-0048.

Lombardi, M. (2011). A study on students' intercultural learning through short-term study abroad programs. Doctor of Education dissertation, Northeastern University. ProQuest 3498297.

Long, T. (2014). Influence of international service-learning on nursing student self-efficacy toward cultural competence. *Journal of Nursing Education*, 53(8), 474–478. doi:10.3928/01484834-20140725-02.

Lopez-McGee, L. D. (2018). Examining undergraduate students' goals and self-efficacy beliefs in study abroad programs. Doctor of Philosophy dissertation, George Mason University. ProQuest 10841769.

Lou, K. H., & Weber Bosley, G. (2012). Facilitating intercultural learning abroad. The intentional, targeted intervention model. In M. V. Berg, R. M. Paige, & K. H. Lou (Eds.), *Student learning abroad. What our students are learning, what they're not, and what we can do about it* (pp. 335–359). Sterling, VA: Stylus.

Lutterman-Aguilar, A., & Gingerich, O. (2002). Experiential pedagogy for study abroad: Educating for global citizenship. *Frontiers: The Interdisciplinary Journal of Study Abroad*, 8, 41–82.

MacIntyre, P. D., Noels, K. A., & Clément, R. (1997). Biases in self-ratings of second language proficiency: The role of language anxiety. *Language Learning*, 47(2), 265–287. doi:10.1111/0023-8333.81997008.

MacNab, B. R., & Worthley, R. (2012). Individual characteristics as predictors of cultural intelligence development: The relevance of self-efficacy. *International Journal of Intercultural Relations*, 36(1). doi:10.1016/j.ijintrel.2010.12.001.

Madden, T. M., McMillan, A., & Madden, L. T. (2018). This Is not a vacation: The shadow side of study abroad programs for faculty. *Journal of Management Education*, 43(2), 185–199. doi:10.1177/1052562918815212.

Maddux, W. W., Adam, H., & Galinsky, A. D. (2010). When in Rome … learn why the Romans do what they do: How multicultural learning experiences facilitate creativity. *Personality & Social Psychology Bulletin*, 36(6), 731–741. doi:10.1177/0146167210367786.

Maddux, W. W., & Galinsky, A. D. (2009). Cultural borders and mental barriers: The relationship between living abroad and creativity. *Journal of Personality and Social Psychology*, 96(5), 1047–1061. doi:10.1037/a0014861.

Magnan, S. S., & Back, M. (2007). Social interaction and linguistic gain during study abroad. *Foreign Language Annals*, 40(1), 43–61. doi:10.1111/j.1944-9720.2007.tb02853.x.

Maharaja, G. (2018). The impact of study abroad on college students' intercultural competence and personal development. *International Research and Review: Journal of Phi Beta Delta Honor Society for International Scholars*, 7(2), 18–41.

Malone, M. E., Rifkin, B., Christian, D., & Johnson, D. E. (2003). *Attaining high levels of proficiency: Challenges for language education in the United States*. Paper presented at the Conference on Global Challenges and US Higher Education, Duke University, Durham, NC.

Mapp, S. C. (2012). Effect of short-term study abroad programs on students' cultural adaptability. *Journal of Social Work Education*, 48(4), 727–737. doi:10.5175/JSWE.2012.20110010.

Marqués-Pascual, L. (2011). Study abroad, previous language experience, and Spanish L2 development. *Foreign Language Annals*, 44(3), 565–582.

Martin, D., Katz-Buonincontro, J., & Livert, D. (2015). Understanding the role of openness to experience in study abroad students. *Journal of College Student Development*, 56(6), 619–625.

Martinsen, R. A. (2010). Short-term study abroad: Predicting changes in oral skills. *Foreign Language Annals*, 43(3), 504–530. doi:10.1111/j.1944-9720.2010.01095.x.

Martinsen, R. A. (2011). Predicting changes in cultural sensitivity among students of Spanish during short-term study abroad. *Hispania*, 94(1), 121–141.

Marx, H. A., & Moss, D. M. (2011). Please mind the culture gap: Intercultural development during a teacher education study abroad program. *Journal of Teacher Education*, 62(1), 35–47. doi:10.1177/0022487110381998.

Masuda, K. (2011). Acquiring interactional competence in a study abroad context: Japanese language learners' use of the interactional particle "ne." *The Modern Language Journal*, 95(4), 519–540. doi:10.1111/j.1540-4781.2011.

Matsumoto, D., LeRoux, J., Ratzlaff, C., Tatani, H., Uchida, H., Kim, C., & Araki, S. (2001). Development and validation of a measure of intercultural adjustment potential in Japanese sojourners: the Intercultural Adjustment Potential Scale (ICAPS). *International Journal of Intercultural Relations*, 25(5), 483–510. doi:10.1016/S0147-1767(01)00019-0.

Matsumura, S. (2001). Learning the rules for offering advice: A quantitative approach to second language socialization. *Language Learning*, 51(4), 635–679. doi:10.1111/0023-8333.00170.

Matsumura, S. (2003). Modelling the relationships among interlanguage pragmatic development, L2 proficiency, and exposure to L2. *Applied lLnguistics*, 24(4), 465–491. doi:10.1093/applin/24.4.465.

McCabe, L. T. (1994). The development of a global perspective during participation in Semester at Sea: A comparative global education program. *educational Review*, 46(3), 275–286.

McCrae, R. R., & John, O. P. (1992). An introduction to the five-factor model and its applications. *Journal of Personality* 60(2), 175–215. doi:10.1111/j.1467-6494.1992.tb00970.x.

Meara, P. (1994). The year abroad and its effects. *Language Learning Journal*, 10(1), 32–38. doi:10.1080/09571739485200351.

Medina-Lopez-Portillo, A. (2004). Intercultural learning assessment: The link between program duration and the development of intercultural sensitivity. *Frontiers: The Interdisciplinary Journal of Study Abroad*, 10, 179–199.

Medina-Lopez-Portillo, A., & Salonen, R. (2012). Developing a global learning and living community: A case study of intercultural experiences on The Scholar Ship. In M. V. Berg, R. M. Paige, & K. H. Lou (Eds.), *Student learning abroad: What our students are learning, what they're not, and what we can do about it* (pp. 360–382). Sterling, VA: Stylus.

Meier, G., & Daniels, H. (2013). "Just not being able to make friends": Social interaction during the year abroad in modern foreign language degrees. *Research Papers in Education*, 28(2), 212–238. doi:10.1080/02671522.2011.629734.

Menard-Warwick, J., & Palmer, D. (2012). Bilingual development in study-abroad journal narratives: Three case studies from a short-term program in Mexico. *Multilingua*, 31(1), 381–412. doi:10.1515/multi-2012-0018.

Merrill, K. C., Braskamp, D. C., & Braskamp, L. A. (2012). Assessing individual's global perspective. *Journal of College Student Development*, 53(2), 356–360. doi:10.1353/csd.2012.0034.

Mesidor, J. K., & Sly, K. F. (2016). Factors that contribute to the adjustment of international students. *Journal of International Studies*, 6(1), 262–282.

Miano, A., Bernhardt, E. B., & Brates, V. (2016). Exploring the effects of a short-term Spanish immersion program in a postsecondary setting. *Foreign Language Annals*, 49(2), 287–301.

Michl, T., Pegg, K., & Kracen, A. (2019). Gender × Culture: A pilot project exploring the study abroad experiences of trans and gender expansive students. *Frontiers: The Interdisciplinary Journal of Study Abroad*, 31(2), 32–50.

Milleret, M. (1991). Assessing the gain in oral proficiency from summer foreign study. *ADFL Bulletin*, 22(3), 39–43.

Mills, N., Pajares, F., & Herron, C. (2007). Self-efficacy of college intermediate French students: Relation to achievement and motivation. *Language Learning*, 57(3), 417–442. doi:10.1111/j.1467-9922.2007.00421.x.

Milstein, T. (2005). Transformation abroad: Sojourning and the perceived enhancement of self-efficacy. *International Journal of Intercultural Relations*, 29(2), 217–238. doi:10.1016/j.ijintrel.2005.05.005.

Milton, J., & Meara, P. (1995). How periods abroad affect vocabulary growth in a foreign language. *International Journal of Applied Linguistics*, 107(8), 17–34. doi:10.1075/itl.107-108.02mil.

Mitchell, R., McManus, K., & Tracy-Ventura, N. (2015). Placement type and language learning during residence abroad. In R. Mitchell, N. Tracy-Ventura, & K. McManus (Eds.), *Social interaction, identity and language learning during residence abroad* (pp. 115–138). Amsterdam: The European Second Language Association.

Mitchell, R., Tracy-Ventura, N., & McManus, K. (2017). *Anglophone students abroad: Identity, social relationships and language learning*. New York: Routledge.

Mora, E. I., Piñero, L. Á.-O., & Díaz, B. M. (2019). Developing intercultural competence in Seville outside the classroom. *Learning and Teaching: The International Journal of Higher Education in the Social Sciences*, 12(3), 73–87. doi:10.3167/latiss.2019.120305.

Morais, D. B., & Ogden, A. (2011). Initial development and validation of the global citizenship scale. *Journal of Studies in International Education*, 15(5), 445–466. doi:10.1177/1028315310375308.

Morgan, R. M., Mwegelo, D. T., & Thuner, L. N. (2002). Black women in the African diaspora seeking their cultural heritage through studying abroad. *NASPA Journal*, 39, 333–353.

Morreale, S. G. (2011). The relationship between study abroad and motivation, attitude and anxiety in university students learning a foreign language. Doctor of Philosophy dissertation, Wayne State University. ProQuest 3445246.

Moseley, W. G. (2009). Making study abroad a win–win opportunity for pre-tenure faculty. *Frontiers: The Interdisciplinary Journal of Study Abroad*, 18, 231–240.

Murphy, D., Sahakyan, N., Yong-Yi, D., & Magnan, S. S. (2014). The impact of study abroad on the global engagement of university graduates. *Frontiers: The Interdisciplinary Journal of Study Abroad*, 24, 1–24.

Mystkowska-Wiertelak, A., & Pawlak, M. (2017). *Willingness to communicate in instructed second language acquisition: Combining a macro- and micro-perspective*. Bristol: Multilingual Matters.

Nada, C., Montgomery, C., & Araújo, H. C. (2018). "You went to Europe and returned different": Transformative learning experiences of international students in Portugal. *European Educational Research Journal*, 17(5), 696–713. doi:10.1177/1474904118765334.

Nguyen, A.-M. D., Jefferies, J., & Rojas, B. (2018). Short term, big impact? Changes in self-efficacy and cultural intelligence, and the adjustment of multicultural and mono-cultural students abroad. *International Journal of Intercultural Relations*, 66, 119–129. doi:10.1016/j.ijintrel.2018.08.001.

Niehoff, E., Petersdotter, L., & Freund, P. A. (2017). International sojourn experience and personality development: Selection and socialization effects of studying abroad and the Big Five. *Personality and Individual Differences*, 112, 55–61. doi:10.1016/j.paid.2017.02.043.

Norris, E. M., & Gillespie, J. (2009). How study abroad shapes global careers: Evidence from the United States. *Journal of Studies in International Education*, 13(3), 382–397. doi:10.1177/1028315308319740.

O'Brien, I., Segalowitz, N., Freed, B., & Collentine, J. (2007). Phonological memory predicts second language oral fluency gains in adults. *Studies in Second Language Acquisition*, 29(4), 557–581. doi:10.1017/S027226310707043X.

O'Brien, M. G. (2003). Longitudinal development of second language German vowels. Doctor of Philosophy dissertation, University of Wisconsin. ProQuest 3089612.

Olson, C. L., & Kroeger, K. R. (2001). Global competency and intercultural sensitivity. *Journal of Studies in International Education*, 5, 1–23.

Omachinski, K. M. (2013). Communication and cultural implications of short-term study-abroad experiences on engineering students. *Connexions: International Professional Communication Journal*, 1(2), 43–77.

O'Neal, J. C., & Krueger, R. L. (1995). Directing a program abroad. *Academe*, 81(5), 28–34. doi:10.2307/40250874.

O'Reilly, A., Ruan, D., & Hickey, T. (2010). The psychological well-being and socio-cultural adaptation of short-term international students in Ireland. *Journal of College Student Development*, 51(5), 584–598. doi:10.1353/csd.2010.0011.

Ozer, S. (2015). Predictors of international students' psychological and sociocultural adjustment to the context of reception while studying at Aarhus University, Denmark. *Scandinavian Journal of Psychology*, 56(6), 717–725. doi:10.1111/sjop.12258.

Paige, R. M., Cohen, A. D., Kappler, B., Chi, J. C., & Lassegard, J. P. (2002). *Maximizing study abroad: A students' guide to strategies for language and culture learning and use*. Minneapolis, MN: Center for Advanced Research on Language Acquisition, University of Minnesota.

Paige, R. M., Fry, G., Stallman, E., Horne, A., La Brack, B., & Josic, J. (2007). *SAGE survey*. Minneapolis, MN: University of Minnesota.

Paige, R. M., Harvey, T. A., & McCleary, K. S. (2012). The maximizing study abroad project: Toward a pedagogy for culture and language learning. In M. V. Berg, R. M. Paige, & K. H. Lou (Eds.), *Student learning abroad: What our students are learning, what they're not, and what we can do about it* (pp. 308–334). Sterling, VA: Stylus.

Palmer, D. K., & Menard-Warwick, J. (2012). Short-term study abroad for Texas pre-service teachers: On the road from empathy to critical awareness. *Multicultural Education*, 19(3), 17–26.

Pearson, L., Fonseca-Greber, B., & Foell, K. (2006). Advanced proficiency for foreign language teacher candidates: What can we do to help them achieve this goal? *Foreign Language Annals*, 39(3), 507–519.

Pedersen, P. J. (2009). Teaching towards an ethnorelative worldview through psychology study abroad. *Intercultural Education*, 20(suppl. 1), S73–S86. doi:10.1080/14675980903370896.

Pedersen, P. J. (2010). Assessing intercultural effectiveness outcomes in a year-long study abroad program. *International Journal of Intercultural Relations*, 34(1), 70–80. doi: doi:10.1016/j.ijintrel.2009.09.003.

Pellegrino, V. A. (1998). Student perspectives on language learning in a study abroad context. *Frontiers: The Interdisciplinary Journal of Study Abroad*, 4(2), 91–120.

Pence, H. M., & Macgillivray, I. K. (2008). The impact of an international field experience on preservice teachers. *Teaching and teacher education*, 24(1), 14–25.

Peng, A. C., Van Dyne, L., & Oh, K. (2015). The influence of motivational cultural intelligence on cultural effectiveness based on study abroad. *Journal of Management Education*, 39(5), 572–596. doi:10.1177/1052562914555717.

Penman, J., & Ellis, B. J. (2004). Philippine academic visit: brief but life-changing. *International Journal of Nursing Education Scholarship*, 1(1), 1–12.

Pérez-Vidal, C., & Juan-Garau, M. (2009). The effect of study abroad (SA) on written performance. In L. Roberts, D. Veronique, M. Tellier, & A. Nilsson (Eds.), *EUROSLA Yearbook* (Vol. 9, pp. 269–295). Amsterdam: John Benjamins.

Petersdotter, L., Niehoff, E., & Freund, P. A. (2017). International experience makes a difference: Effects of studying abroad on students' self-efficacy. *Personality and Individual Differences*, 107, 174–178. doi:10.1016/j.paid.2016.11.040.

Petrucci, P. R. (2007). Heritage scholars in the ancestral homeland: An overlooked identity in study abroad research. *Sociolinguistic Studies*, 1(2), 275–296. doi:10.1558/sols.v1i2.275.

Petzold, K., & Moog, P. (2018). What shapes the intention to study abroad? An experimental approach. *Higher Education*, 75(1), 35–54. doi:10.1007/s10734-017-0119-z.

Pizziconi, B. (2017). Japanese vocabulary development in and beyond study abroad: The timing of the year abroad in a language degree curriculum. *Language Learning Journal*, 45(2), 133–152. doi:10.1080/09571736.2013.786119.

Polanyi, L. (1995). Language learning and living abroad: Stories from the field. In B. F. Freed (Ed.), *Second language acquisition in a study abroad context* (pp. 271–291). Amsterdam: John Benjamins.

Putra, K. A. (2014). The effect of study abroad on grammatical accuracy of Indonesian students' oral and written performance. *Parole: Journal of Linguistics and Education*, 3(2), 84–94. doi:10.14710/parole.v3i2%20Okt.5391.

Qualters, D. M. (2010). Making the most of learning outside the classroom. *Experiential Education*, 124, 95–99. doi:10.1002/tl.427.

Raby, R. L., Rhodes, G. M., & Biscarra, A. (2014). Community college study abroad: implications for student success. *Community College Journal of Research and Practice*, 38(2–3),174–183. doi:10.1080/10668926.2014.851961.

Ramirez, R., E. (2016). Impact on intercultural competence when studying abroad and the moderating role of personality. *Journal of Teaching in International Business*, 27(2/3), 88–105.

Rees, J., & Klapper, J. (2008). The longitudinal study of advanced L2 capacities: Issues in the quantitative longitudinal measurement of second language progress in the study abroad context. In L. Ortega & H. Byrnes (Eds.), *The longitudinal study of advanced L2 capacities* (pp. 89–105). New York: Routledge.

Regan, V. (1995). The acquisition of sociolinguistic native speech norms: Effects of a year abroad on second language learners of French. In B. Freed (Ed.), *Second language acquisition in a study abroad context* (pp. 245–267). Amsterdam: John Benjamins.

Regan, V. (2005). From speech community back to classroom: what variation analysis can tell us about the role of context in the acquisition of French as a foreign language. In J.-M. Dewaele (Ed.), *Focus on French as a Foreign Language* (pp. 191–209). Clevedon: Multilingual Matters.

Regan, V., Howard, M., & Lemée, I. (2009). *The acquisition of sociolinguistic competence in a study abroad context*. Bristol: Multilingual Matters.

Rexeisen, R. J., & Al-Khatib, J. (2009). Assurance of learning and study abroad: A case study. *Journal of Teaching in International Business*, 20(3), 192–207. doi:10.1080/08975930903099077.

Rexeisen, R. J., Anderson, P. H., Lawton, L., & Hubbard, A. C. (2008). Study abroad and intercultural development: A longitudinal study. *Frontiers: The Interdisciplinary Journal of Study Abroad*, 17, 1–20.

Reynolds-Case, A. (2013). The value of short-term study abroad: An increase in students' cultural and pragmatic competency. *Foreign Language Annals*, 46(2), 311–322. doi:10.1111/flan.12034.

Rhodes, G. M., Raby, R. L., & Biscarra, A. (2013). Student outcomes from participating in California community college education abroad programs. *Education and Society*, 31 (3), 23–40. doi:10.7459/es/31.3.03.

Rhodes, G. M., Thomas, J. M., Raby, R. L., Codding, A. G., & Lynch, A. (2016). Community college study abroad and implications for student success: Comparing California and New Jersey community colleges. In R. L. Raby & E. J. Valeau (Eds.), *International education at community colleges* (pp. 281–292). New York: Palgrave Macmillan.

Richter, A. (2012). *Auslandsaufenthalte während des Studiums - Stationen, Bewältigungsstrategien und Auswirkungen. Eine qualitative Studie*. Stuttgart: ibidem-Verlag.

Rivers, W. P. (1998). Is being there enough? The effects of homestay placements on language gain during study abroad. *Foreign Language Annals*, 31(4), 492–500.

Robson, G. (2015a). A model of situational willingness to communicate (WTC) in the study abroad context. *International Education Studies*, 8(10), 114–125.

Robson, G. (2015b). The relationship between WTC and oral proficiency measurements in the study abroad context. *International Education Studies*, 8(12), 56–69.

Rommal, L., & Byram, M. (2018). Becoming interculturally competent through study and experience abroad. In M. Wagner, D. C. Perugini, & M. Byram (Eds.), *Teaching intercultural competence across the age range. From theory to practice* (pp. 155–169). Bristol: Multilingual Matters.

Root, E., & Ngampornchai, A. (2013). "I came back as a new human being": Student descriptions of intercultural competence acquired through education abroad experiences. *Journal of Studies in International Education*, 17(5), 513–532. doi:10.1177/1028315312468008.

Roskvist, A., Harvey, S., Corder, D., & Stacey, K. (2014). "To improve language, you have to mix": teachers' perceptions of language learning in an overseas immersion environment. *The Language Learning Journal*, 42(3), 321–333. doi:10.1080/09571736.2013.785582.

Rust, K. G., Forster, B., Niziolek, A., & Morris, C. M. (2013). Study abroad and intercultural coursework: Their effects on change in intercultural competence. *International Research and Review*, 3(1), 3–13.

Rustambekov, E., & Mohan, R. (2017). Cultural immersion trip to Southeast Asia: A study of cross-cultural intelligence. *Journal of Teaching in International Business*, 28(2), 87–103. doi:10.1080/08975930.2017.1359768.

Salisbury, M. H., An, B. P., & Pascarella, E. T. (2013). The effect of study abroad on intercultural competence among undergraduate college students. *Journal of Student Affairs Research and Practice*, 50(1), 1–20.

Sasaki, M. (2004). A multiple-data analysis of the 3.5-year development of EFL student writers. *Language Learning*, 54(3), 525–582. doi:10.1111/j.0023-8333.2004.00264.x.

Sasaki, M. (2009). Changes in English as a foreign language students' writing over 3.5 years: A sociocognitive account. In R. Manchón (Ed.), *Writing in foreign language contexts: Learning, teaching, and research* (pp. 49–76). Clevedon: Multilingual Matters.

Sasaki, M. (2011). Effects of varying lengths of study abroad experiences on Japanese EFL students' L2 writing ability and motivation: A longitudinal study. *TESOL Quarterly*, 45(1), 81–105.

Savage, B. L., & Hughes, H. Z. (2014). How does short-term foreign language immersion stimulate language learning? *Frontiers: The Interdisciplinary Journal of Study Abroad*, 24(2), 103–120.

Savicki, V. (2012). The effects of affect on study abroad students. *Frontiers: The Interdisciplinary Journal of Study Abroad*, 22, 131–147.

Savicki, V., Downing-Burnette, R., Heller, L., Binder, F., & Suntinger, W. (2004). Contrasts, changes, and correlates in actual and potential intercultural adjustment. *International Journal of Intercultural Relations*, 28(3–4),311–329. doi:10.1016/j.ijintrel.2004.06.001.

Savicki, V., & Price, M. V. (2015). Student reflective writing: Cognition and affect before, during, and after study abroad. *Journal of College Student Development*, 56(6), 587–601. doi:10.1353/csd.2015.0063.

Scally, J. (2015). Intercultural competence development in three different study abroad program types. *Intercultural Communication Studies*, 24(2), 35–60.

Schartner, A. (2016). The effect of study abroad on intercultural competence: A longitudinal case study of international postgraduate students at a British university. *Journal of Multilingual and Multicultural Development*, 37(4), 402–418. doi:10.1080/01434632.2015.1073737.

Schauer, G. A. (2007). Finding the right words in the study abroad context: The development of German learners' use of external modifiers in English. *Intercultural Pragmatics*, 4(2), 193–220. doi:10.1515/IP.2007.011.

Schenker, T. (2018). Making short-term study abroad count - Effects on German language skills. *Foreign Language Annals*, 51(2), 411–419.

Schenker, T. (2019). Fostering global competence through short-term study abroad. *Frontiers: The Interdisciplinary Journal of Study Abroad*, 31(2), 139–157.

Schnabel, D. (2015). Intercultural competence: Development and validation of a theoretical framework, a cross-cultural multimethod test, and a collaborative assessment intervention. Doctor of Philosophy dissertation, Eberhard Karls Universität Tübingen,

Schnuth, R., & Celestin, C. (2020). Leadership in medicine for the underserved: Making it real. In P. Crawford & B. Berquist (Eds.), *Community engagement abroad: Perspectives and practices on service, engagement, and learning overseas* (pp. 85–100). East Lansing, MI: Michigan State University.

Schoenberger, L. K. (2019). Who am I? The LGBTQ+ student experience during study abroad. Doctor of Education dissertation, The Florida State University. ProQuest 13427004.

Schunk, D. H., & Pajares, F. (2005). Self-efficacy and competence beliefs in academic functioning. In A. J. Elliot, C. S. Dweck, & D. S. Yeager (Eds.), *Handbook of competence and motivation* (pp. 85–104). New York: Guilford Press.

Segalowitz, N., & Freed, B. F. (2004). Context, contact and cognition in oral fluency acquisition. *Studies in Second Language Acquisition*, 26(2), 173–199. doi:10.1017/S0272263104262027.

Serrano, R., Llanes, À., & Tragant, E. (2011). Analyzing the effect of context of second language learning: Domestic intensive and semi-intensive courses vs. study abroad in Europe. *System*, 39(2), 133–143. doi:10.1016/j.system.2011.05.002.

Serrano, R., Llanes, À., & Tragant, E. (2016). Examining L2 development in two short-term intensive programs for teenagers: Study abroad vs. "at home". *System*, 57, 43–54. doi:10.1016/j.system.2016.01.003.

Serrano, R., Tragant, E., & Llanes, À. (2012). A longitudinal analysis of the effects of one year abroad. *The Canadian Modern Language Review*, 68(2), 138–163. doi:10.3138/cmlr.68.2.138.

Sharma, S., & Phillion, J. (2019). How study abroad experiences develop multicultural awareness in preservice teachers: An eleven-year multiple case study. In M. Fuchs, S. Rai, & Y. Loiseau (Eds.), *Study abroad: Traditions and new directions* (pp. 63–78). New York: The Modern Language Association of America.

Shealy, C. N. (2016). *Making sense of beliefs and values: Theory, research, and practice*. New York: Springer.

Shiri, S. (2015). Intercultural communicative competence development during and after language study abroad: Insights from Arabic. *Foreign Language Annals*, 48(4), 541–569.

Shively, R. L. (2010). From the virtual world to the real world: A model of pragmatics instruction for study abroad. *Foreign Language Annals*, 43(1), 105–137.

Shively, R. L. (2015). Developing interactional competence during study abroad: Listener responses in L2 Spanish. *System*, 48, 86–98. doi:10.1016/j.system.2014.09.007.

Slimbach, R. (2010). *Becoming world wise: A Guide to global learning*. Sterling, VA: Stylus.

Sobkowiak, P. (2019). The impact of studying abroad on students' intercultural competence: An interview study. *Studies in Second Language Learning and Teaching*, 9(4), 681–710. doi:10.14746/ssllt.2019.9.4.6.

Spenader, A. J. (2011). Language learning and acculturation: Lessons from high school and gap-year exchange students. *Foreign Language Annals*, 44(2), 381–398. doi:10.1111/j.1944-9720.2011.01134.x.

Spenader, A. J., & Retka, P. (2015). The role of pedagogical variables in intercultural development: A study of faculty-led programs. *Frontiers: The Interdisciplinary Journal of Study Abroad*, 25, 20–36.

Steinwidder, S. (2016). EFL learners' post-sojourn perceptions of the effects of study abroad. *Comparative and International Education*, 45(2), 1–20.

Stewart, J. A. (2010). Using e-journals to assess students' language awareness and social identity during study abroad. *Foreign Language Annals*, 43(1), 138–159.

Sümer, S., Poyrazli, S., & Grahame, K. (2008). Predictors of depression and anxiety among international students. *Journal of Counseling and Development*, 86(4), 429–437. doi:10.1002/j.1556-6678.2008.tb00531.x.

Sunderman, G., & Kroll, J. F. (2009). When study-abroad experience fails to deliver: The internal resources threshold effect. *Applied Psycholinguistics*, 30(1), 79–99. doi:10.1017/S0142716408090048.

Sutton, R. C., & Rubin, D. L. (2010). *Documenting the academic impact of study abroad: Final report of the GLOSSARI project*. Paper presented at the NAFSA Annual Conference, Kansas City, Missouri. http://glossari.uga.edu/datasets/pdfs/FINAL.pdf.

Swagler, M. A., & Jome, L. M. (2005). The effects of personality and acculturation on the adjustment of North American sojourners in Taiwan. *Journal of Counseling Psychology*, 52 (4), 527–536. doi:10.1037/0022-0167.52.4.527.

Swender, E. (2003). Oral proficiency testing in the real world: Answers to frequently asked questions. *Foreign Language Annals*, 36(4), 520–526. doi:10.1111/j.1944-9720.2003.tb02141.x.

Taguchi, N. (2008). Cognition, language contact, and the development of pragmatic comprehension in a study-abroad context. *Language Learning*, 58(1), 33–71. doi:10.1111/j.1467-9922.2007.00434.x.

Taguchi, N. (2011). The effect of L2 proficiency and study-abroad experience on pragmatic comprehension. *Language Learning*, 61(3), 904–939. doi:10.1111/j.1467-9922.2011.00633.x.

Taguchi, N. (2015). *Developing interactional competence in a Japanese study abroad context*. Clevedon: Multilingual Matters.

Taguchi, N. (2016). Cross-cultural adaptability and development of speech act production in study abroad. *International Journal of Applied Linguistics*, 25(3), 343–365. doi:10.1111/ijal.12073.

Tanaka, K. (2007). Japanese students' contact with English outside the classroom during study abroad. *New Zealand Studies in Applied Linguistics*, 13, 36–54.

Tanaka, K., & Ellis, R. (2003). Study-abroad, language proficiency, and learner beliefs about language learning. *JALT Journal*, 25(1), 63–85.

Tananuraksakul, N., & Hall, D. (2011). International students' emotional security and dignity in an Australian context: An aspect of psychological well-being. *Journal of Research in International Education*, 10(2), 189–200. doi:10.1177/1475240911410784.

Tarchi, C., Surian, A., & Daiute, C. (2019). Assessing study abroad students' intercultural sensitivity with narratives. *European Journal of Psychology of Education*, 34, 873–894. doi:10.1007/s10212-019-00417-9.

Tarrant, M. A., Rubin, D. L., & Stoner, L. (2014). The added value of study abroad: Fostering a global citizenry. *Journal of Studies in International Education*, 18(2), 141–161. doi:10.1177/1028315313497589.

Taušová, J., Bender, M., Dimitrova, R., & van de Vijver, F. (2019). The role of perceived cultural distance, personal growth initiative, language proficiencies, and tridimensional acculturation orientations for psychological adjustment among international students. *International Journal of Intercultural Relations*, 69, 11–23.

Teichler, U., & Janson, K. (2007). The professional value of temporary study in another European country: Employment and work of former ERASMUS students. *Journal of Studies in International Education*, 11(3/4), 486–495. doi:10.1177/1028315307303230.

Templer, K. J., Tay, C., & Chandrasekar, N. A. (2006). Motivational cultural intelligence, realistic job preview, realistic living conditions preview, and cross-cultural adjustment. *Group and Organization Management*, 31(1), 154–173. doi:10.1177/1059601105275293.

Thomas, S. L., & McMahon, M. E. (1998). Americans abroad: Student characteristics, pre-departure qualifications and performance abroad. *The International Journal of Educational Management*, 12(2), 57–64. doi:10.1108/09513549810204432.

Thompson, A. S., & Lee, J. (2014). The impact of experience abroad and language proficiency on language learning anxiety. *TESOL Quarterly*, 48(2), 252–274. Retrieved from www.jstor.org/stable/43268051.

Tompkins, A., Cook, T., Miller, E., & LePeau, L. A. (2017). Gender influences on students' study abroad participation and intercultural competence. *Journal of Student Affairs Research and Practice*, 54(2), 204–216.

Towell, R., Hawkins, R., & Bazergui, N. (1996). The development of fluency in advanced learners of French. *Applied Linguistics*, 17(1), 84–119. doi:10.1093/applin/17.1.84.

Tracy-Ventura, N. (2017). Combining corpora and experimental data to investigate language learning during residence abroad: A study of lexical sophistication. *System*, 71, 35–45. doi:https://doi.org/10.1016/j.system.2017.09.022.

Trentman, E. (2013). Arabic and English during study abroad in Cairo, Egypt: Issues of access and use. *The Modern Language Journal*, 97(2), 457–473. doi:10.1111/j.1540-4781.2013.12013.

Trentman, E. (2015). Arabic heritage learners abroad: Language use and identity negotiation. *Al-'Arabiyya*, 48, 141–156. Retrieved from www.jstor.org/stable/44654042.

Tullock, B., & Ortega, L. (2017). Fluency and multilingualism in study abroad: Lessons from a scoping review. *System*, 71, 7–21. doi:10.1016/j.system.2017.09.019.

Valls-Ferrer, M., & Mora, J. C. (2014). L2 fluency development in formal instruction and study abroad. In C. Pérez-Vidal (Ed.), *Language acquisition in study abroad and formal instruction contexts* (pp. 111–137). Amsterdam: John Benjamins.

Vande Berg, M. (2007). Intervening in the learning of US students abroad. *Journal of Studies in International Education*, 11(3/4), 392–399.

Vande Berg, M., Connor-Linton, J., & Paige, R. M. (2009). The Georgetown consortium project: Interventions for student learning abroad. *Frontiers: The Interdisciplinary Journal of Study Abroad*, 18, 1–75.

Vande Berg, M., Paige, R. M., & Lou, K. H. (Eds.). (2012). *Student learning abroad: what our students are learning, what they're not, and what we can do about it.* Sterling, VA: Stylus.

Walsh, L. V., & DeJoseph, J. (2003). "I saw it in a different light": International learning experiences in baccalaureate nursing education. *The Journal of Nursing Education*, 42(6), 266–272.

Wandschneider, E., Pysarchik, D. T., Sternberger, L. G., Ma, W., Acheson, K., Baltensperger, B., … Hart, V. (2015). The forum BEVI project: Applications and implications for international, multicultural, and transformative learning. *Frontiers: The Interdisciplinary Journal of Study Abroad*, 25, 150–228.

Wang, C. (2010). Toward a second language socialization perspective: Issues in study abroad research. *Foreign Language Annals*, 43(1), 50–63. doi:10.1111/j.1944-9720.2010.01059.x.

Warga, M., & Schölmberger, U. (2007). The acquisition of French apologetic behavior in a study abroad context. *Intercultural Pragmatics*, 4(2), 221–251. doi:10.1515.

Watson, J. R., Siska, P., & Wolfel, R. L. (2013). Assessing gains in language proficiency, cross-cultural competence, and regional awareness during study abroad: A preliminary study. *Foreign Language Annals*, 46(1), 62–79. doi:10.1111/flan.12016.

Watson, J. R., & Wolfel, R. (2015). The intersection of language and culture in study abroad: Assessment and analysis of study abroad outcomes. *Frontiers: The Interdisciplinary Journal of Study Abroad*, 25, 57–72.

Weichbrodt, M. (2014). Learning mobility: High-school exchange programs as a part of transnational mobility. *Children's Geographies*, 12(1), 9–24. doi:10.1080/14733285.2013.850852.

Wiers-Jenssen, J. (2017). Does higher education attained abroad lead to international jobs? *Journal of Studies in International Education*, 12(2), 101–130. doi:10.1177/1028315307307656.

Wilkinson, S. (1998). On the nature of immersion during study abroad: Some participant perspectives. *Frontiers: The Interdisciplinary Journal of Study Abroad*, 4(2), 121–138.

Williams, T. R. (2005). Exploring the impact of study abroad on students' intercultural communication skills: Adaptability and sensitivity. *Journal of Studies in International Education*, 9(4), 356–371. doi:10.1177/1028315305277681.

Wolff, F., & Borzikowsky, C. (2018). Intercultural competence by international experiences? An investigation of the impact of educational stays abroad on intercultural competence and its facets. *Journal of Cross-Cultural Psychology*, 49(3), 488–514. doi:10.1177/0022022118754721.

Wortman, T. I. (2002). Psychosocial effects of studying abroad: Openness to diversity. Doctor of Philosophy dissertation, The Pennsylvania State University. ProQuest 3060033.

Wright, C. (2013). An investigation of working memory effects on oral grammatical accuracy and fluency in producing questions in English. *TESOL Quarterly*, 47(2), 352–374. Retrieved from www.jstor.org/stable/43267795.

Wright, C., & Schartner, A. (2013). "I can't … I won't?" International students at the threshold of social interaction. *Journal of Research in International Education*, 12(2), 113–128. doi:10.1177/1475240913491055.

Wynveen, C. J., Kyle, G. T., & Tarrant, M. A. (2011). Study abroad experiences and global citizenship: Fostering proenvironmental behavior. *Journal of Studies in International Education*, 16(4), 334–352. doi:10.1177/1028315311426782.

Xu, W., Case, R. E., & Wang, Y. (2009). Pragmatic and grammatical competence, length of residence, and overall L2 proficiency. *System*, 37(2), 205–216. doi:10.1016/j.system.2008.09.007.

Yager, K. (1998). Learning Spanish in Mexico: The effect of informal contact and student attitudes on language gain. *Hispania*, 81(4), 898–913. doi:10.2307/345798.

Yakunina, E. S., Weigold, I. K., Weigold, A., & Hercegovac, S. (2012). The multicultural personality: Does it predict international students' openness to diversity and adjustment? *International Journal of Intercultural Relations*, 36(4), 533–540. doi:10.1016/j.ijintrel.2011.12.008.

Yang, Y., Zhang, Y., & Sheldon, K. M. (2018). Self-determined motivation for studying abroad predicts lower culture shock and greater well-being among international students: The mediating role of basic psychological needs satisfaction. *International Journal of Intercultural Relations*, 63, 95–104. doi:10.1016/j.ijintrel.2017.10.005.

Yashima, T., Zenuk-Nishide, L., & Shimizu, K. (2004). The influences of attitudes and affect on willingness to communicate and second language communication. *Language Learning*, 54(1), 119–152. doi:10.1111/j.1467-9922.2004.00250.x.

Yu, B. (2010). Learning Chinese abroad: The role of language attitudes and motivation in the adaptation of international students in China. *Journal of Multilingual and Multicultural Development*, 31(3), 301–321. doi:10.1080/01434631003735483.

Zarnick, B. E. (2010). Short-term study abroad programs and the development of intercultural sensitivity. Master of Arts dissertation. Retrieved from https://ecommons.luc.edu/luc_theses/512.

Zheng, W. (2017). Beyond cultural learning and preserving psychological well-being: Chinese international students' constructions of intercultural adjustment from an emotion management perspective. *Language and Intercultural Communication* 17(1), 9–25. doi:10.1080/14708477.2017.1261673.

Zielinski, B. A. Z. (2007). Study abroad length of program influence on cross-cultural adaptability. Master of Arts thesis. Retrieved from http://scholar.lib.vt.edu/theses/available/etd-04302007-105204.

Zimmerman, B. J., & Bandura, A. (1994). Impact of self-regulatory influences on writing course attainment. *American Educational Research Journal*, 31(4), 845–862. doi:10.2307/1163397.

Zimmerman, B. J., Bandura, A., & Martinez-Pons, M. (1992). Self-motivation for academic attainment: The role of self-efficacy beliefs and personal goal setting. *American Educational Research Journal*, 29(3), 663–676. doi:10.2307/1163261.

Zimmermann, J., Hutteman, R., Nestler, S., Neyer, F. J., & Back, M. (2015). Und wenn sie zurückkommen, sind sie plötzlich erwachsen …?! Auslandserfahrungen als Kontext der Persönlichkeitsentwicklung. *Forum Jugendarbeit International 2013–2015, 2013–2015*, 203–213.

Zimmermann, J., & Neyer, F. J. (2013). Do we become a different person when hitting the road? Personality development of sojourners. *Journal of Personality and Social Psychology*, 105(3), 515–530. doi:10.1037/a0033019.

Zorn, C. R. (1996). The long-term impact on nursing students of participation in international education. *Journal of professional nursing*, 12, 106–110.

PART 3
BEST PRACTICES IN
EDUCATION ABROAD

Working in education abroad means that your office is a microcosm of the university [...].

Every day is different, so be adaptable and ready to communicate.

And never forget who your work is for: students.

—*Education abroad administrator and survey respondent*

Chapter 3.1. Maximizing Inclusion, Diversity, and Equity in Education Abroad

Education abroad provides a myriad of benefits including increased intercultural competence (Shiri, 2015), global-mindedness (Kehl & Morris, 2008), and language skills (Isabelli-García, Bown, Plews, & Dewey, 2018), enhanced employability (Farrugia & Sanger, 2017), stronger communication skills and academic performance (Luo & Jamieson-Drake, 2015), higher graduation rates (Posey, 2003), and personal development (Zimmermann & Neyer, 2013). Due the range of positive outcomes associated with education abroad as well as the high demand for members of society with global experience and language proficiency, it is important to make education abroad more accessible to all students.

Motivating students to participate in education abroad must include highlighting the value of such endeavors so that prospective participants understand the benefits. To make education abroad a worthwhile undertaking, we have to help students and the stakeholders who advise and influence them see how education abroad can fit into academic and post-college careers. Motivating students also includes removing perceived barriers to education abroad. This includes more than making education abroad financially affordable for students. Students have to see that they can study abroad without falling behind in their degree completion and that time abroad can enhance – not impede – their academic achievements and employability. This chapter makes concrete suggestions for increasing participation in education abroad by diversifying participation through reaching underrepresented student groups including students of color, students with disabilities, students from certain majors, community college students, and male students.

Factors Impacting Participation

Previous research has identified factors that make it more likely for students to select education abroad options. These include:

- Perceiving personal and professional benefits.
- High levels of self-efficacy and intrinsic motivation.
- Friends or family with international experience.
- Previous international experience.
- Language proficiency.
- Identity markers.
- No strong personal and family commitments at home (Hackney, Boggs, & Borozan, 2012).
- Low levels of ethnocentrism.
- Interest in foreign languages.
- Low intercultural communication apprehension (R. I. Kim & Goldstein, 2005).

- Majoring in the social sciences.
- Higher socio-economic background (Salisbury, Umbach, Paulsen, & Pascarella, 2009).

Student motivations for choosing education abroad are varied and their actual participation depends on their perceptions of programs, their intercultural awareness, perceived benefits and value for improving career prospects and life or academic skills, program duration, cost, demographic factors (Bandyopadhyay & Bandyopadhyay, 2015), as well as their overall expectations of the experience (Goldstein & Kim, 2006). Strong motivators are a desire for travel, other cultures and new experiences (Jacobone & Moro, 2015). Importance is often given to improving job prospects, content knowledge, and language skills. Based on an analysis by Goel, De Jong, and Schnusenberg (2010), behavioral beliefs are the strongest incentives for students and are more important than cost, family and academic support. Students who select short-term programs often have different motivations and one study identified a desire for international travel as the strongest motivator for those students (Nyaupane, Paris, & Teye, 2010). Once students have decided to participate in education abroad, factors including cost (Albers-Miller, Prenshaw, & Straughan, 1999), program length (Hackney et al., 2012), program location (Albers-Miller et al., 1999), and relevance for the major appear to be most important in selecting a particular program.

The main deterrent for studying abroad is cost (S. Doyle et al., 2010; Naffziger, Bott, & Mueller, 2010; Walker, 2015; Warnick, Call, & Davies, 2018). Other barriers include:

- Anxiety-related obstacles (Quraeshi, Luqmani, & Veeck, 2012).
- Not wanting to leave friends and family (S. Doyle et al., 2010).
- Safety concerns (Vernon, Moos, & Loncarich, 2017).
- Fear of travel (Amani & Kim, 2018).
- Worries over being in an unknown environment (Naffziger et al., 2010).
- Work or family responsibilities (Amani & Kim, 2018; Chieffo & Griffiths, 2009).
- Concerns over graduating on time (Warnick et al., 2018).
- Difficulties with transferring credits (Stern, 2004).
- Worries over academic performance (Vernon et al., 2017).
- Lack of family support (Minton, 2016).
- Lack of target language skills (Austin & Rust, 2015).

Underrepresented Groups in Education Abroad

Students of color, community college students, students with disabilities and/or mental health disorders, LGBTQ+ students, first-generation college students, STEM and pre-professional majors, and male students remain underrepresented in education abroad (Scheib & Mitchell, 2008; Sweeney, 2013). Some of the above groups share the same reasons for lower participation rates whereas there are also distinct obstacles that require targeted strategies. The following sections first outline specific barriers to education abroad for underrepresented groups, followed by a discussion of recommendations to diversify participation, to be concluded by specific strategies to target individual underrepresented groups.

Students of Color

Participation of people of color in education abroad continues to remain low, although slight increases have been noted (Stallman, Woodruff, Kasravi, & Comp, 2010). In spite of low participation rates, most research shows that there is no discrepancy between intent to study abroad between students of color and White students (Goldstein & Kim, 2006; Lingo, 2019; Simon & Ainsworth, 2012; Stroud, 2010), though some research points to lower intent for Asian students (Luo & Jamieson-Drake, 2015; Salisbury, Paulsen, & Pascarella, 2010).

Overall, research on students of color in education abroad is scarce and mostly focuses on barriers to participation or the goal of heritage seeking. Barriers include financial constraints, family concerns, lack of support, work commitments, historical attitudes and patterns of study abroad (Brux & Fry, 2010), fear of discrimination or racism (Covington, 2017), lack of mentors (Ali, 2015), difficulties of aligning it with their major requirements (Key, 2018) or academic program (Van Der Meid, 2003), lack of relevant programs (McClure, Szelenyi, Niehaus, Anderson, & Reed, 2010) in relevant locations with meaningful content (Calhoon, Wildcat, Annett, Pierotti, & Griswold, 2003), and racism during the decision-making process and fear of racism abroad (Simon & Ainsworth, 2012).

Students of color often choose destinations where they have ancestral links which has been shown to contribute to their identity development (Beausoleil, 2008; Comp, 2008; Penn & Tanner, 2009; Raymondi, 2005). Women of color who studied abroad together in Africa, for example, have benefitted strongly from reclaiming their heritage, redefining sisterhood, and feeling empowered to produce change in their own communities (Morgan, Mwegelo, & Thuner, 2002).

In spite of the added difficulties that students of color may face during education abroad, research has shown that they report the same positive outcomes of education abroad as other participants (Guerrero, 2006; Willis, 2015), in addition to a better understanding of their own racial identities (J. Lee & Green, 2016; Tolliver, 2000), and higher graduation rates (Posey, 2003). Increasing participation of students of color in education abroad should be prioritized not only in order to support more equity, inclusion, and diversity, but because there are distinct benefits for the students, their peers, communities, and host and home countries (Brux & Fry, 2010).

Students with Disabilities and Mental Health Issues

Education abroad admission criteria, cultural attitudes, and misperceptions about disabilities cause the underrepresentation of students with disabilities (physical or cognitive) and mental health diagnoses (Morse, Spoltore, & Galvinhill, 2017; Shames & Alden, 2005). Intent to participate in education abroad is impacted by severity and type of disability (Sarcletti, Heißenberg, & Poskowsky, 2018); students with visual impairments show stronger intent while those with dyslexia, dyscalculia, or mental illness show lower intent to participate.

In addition to the barriers most students perceive, students with disabilities face distinct obstacles to and challenges in education abroad, including a lack of assistive devices and academic support, and inadequate support services (Hameister, Matthews, Hosley, & Groff, 1999; Heirweg, 2020). Similarly, students with mental health illnesses have to overcome specific barriers such as possible discontinuity of their mental health care or reduced services abroad (McCabe, 2005). While abroad, students with disabilities have to tackle social and physical barriers including lack of accessible buildings and feeling separated from peers without disabilities (Prohn, Kelley, & Westling, 2016). Students with disabilities prefer inclusive education abroad programs in their junior year (Matthews, Hameister, & Hosley, 1998) and inclusive programs have been shown to be beneficial for all participants and for fostering a sense of community (Prohn et al., 2016).

Education abroad staff and instructors should keep in mind, that "Students with disabilities are first and foremost students. […] the same issues that concern all students concern students with disabilities" (Hameister et al., 1999, p. 95). By planning ahead, consulting with the accessibility office and education abroad staff, and showing flexibility, accommodations for most needs can be found (Emery, 2008).

LGBTQ+ Students

There is a dearth of research on LGBTQ+ students in education abroad and their needs need to be better addressed (Seay, 2014). LGBTQ+ participants may have safety concerns due to the target culture and laws (Bryant & Soria, 2015) but in spite of added difficulties, a large-scale study of LGBTQ+ students revealed that they were not less likely to participate in education abroad than their peers but in fact even more likely to participate in certain types of programs (Bryant & Soria, 2015) which they may see as an opportunity to redefine themselves (Schoenberger, 2019).

Students from Community Colleges

Although education abroad programs have existed at community colleges since 1969 and have seen a large increase in offerings after 2000 (Raby & Valeau, 2007), internationalization efforts at the majority of community colleges remain comparatively low (Green & Siaya, 2005) and there is little interest in an international education among community college students (Robertson, 2015, 2017).

In 2017/2018, community college students made up only 1.7% of the total education abroad population (Institute of International Education, 2019). Education abroad has distinct challenges for students at two-year institutions, due to the students' age, diversity, work/family obligations and less state funding (Raby, 2020). Factors impacting community college students' decision to go abroad include the opportunity to strengthen a transfer application to a four-year institution, timing of the program, faculty encouragement, family support, and traveling with a group of peers (Amani & Kim, 2018). Positive outcomes of education abroad for community college students include: Improved language abilities (Brenner, 2016); academic success (Raby, Rhodes, & Biscarra, 2014; Rhodes, Raby, & Biscarra, 2013); degree completion and continuation at a university (Rhodes, Thomas, Raby, Codding, & Lynch, 2016); and interpersonal development (Drexler & Campbell, 2011). Increasing access to education abroad for community college students is even more important because it expands access for low-income and minoritized students (Raby & Valeau, 2007).

Students in STEM Majors & Pre-Professional Majors

The particular obstacles encountered by STEM and pre-professional majors include rigorous degree requirements, sequencing of courses, and lack of appropriate science classes at host institutions (DeWinter, 1997). Additionally, the plan to go on to medical school adds more requirements to students' schedules and leaves little room for education abroad especially when credit transfer and course acceptance abroad is difficult (Niehaus & Inkelas, 2016).

In spite of only slight differences in education abroad intent (Niehaus & Inkelas, 2016; Stroud, 2010), overall, "pre-professional majors such as engineering, education, and the health sciences are significantly underrepresented compared to overall participation rate" (Salisbury et al., 2009, p. 121). The discrepancies in participation by different majors is also impacted by available education abroad offerings that are targeted to their field of study or compatible with the often strict schedules of STEM and pre-professional majors.

Male Students

Statistics show that across time more women have participated in education abroad than men both from the US (Stallman et al., 2010) and from Europe (Böttcher et al., 2016) and the gap is widening. One explanation for this could lie in predominant views of education abroad as mostly for women, academically insignificant, cultural enrichment without serious learning (Gore, 2005). Men tend to prefer programs that include internships and other outcome-oriented activities (Thirolf, 2014). In an attempt to better understand the gender gap, Salisbury et al. (2010) conducted a study including incoming students at 21 institutions of higher learning and revealed that "while intent to study abroad among women seems to be affected by influential authority figures and educational contexts, intent to study abroad among men seems to be primarily shaped by emerging personal values, experiences, and peer influence" (p. 635). However, other studies did not find gender differences in motivators and barriers to participation between men and women (Lindsay, 2014; Shirley, 2006).

In an effort to explain the gender gap, Hurst (2019) suggests to consider class as an underlying factor. Her study of 2012 graduates of 17 liberal arts colleges in the US revealed that populations with a higher socio-economic background showed a greater gender difference. The notion that education abroad is for "wealthy women from wealthy institutions" (Gore, 2005, p. 52) has persisted in the US in spite of evidence to show that this is not true.

First-Generation College Students

First-generation students along with ethnic and racial minority students (J. Engle & Tinto, 2008) are proportionally underrepresented in education abroad programs (Rausch, 2017). Like many other groups, they worry about cost and potential graduation delays and are influenced by their family's opinions and concerns. Additionally, many first-generation college students hold jobs and take fewer credits, and because many live off campus they are often less involved in extracurricular activities as well as volunteering (Pascarella, Pierson, Wolniak, & Terenzini, 2004; Terenzini et al., 1994) which can prevent them from participating in certain programs abroad.

However, research also suggests that this group has much to contribute to education abroad programs due to their resilience and experience of navigating unknown educational contexts (Rausch, 2017), and many of these students do actively participate in academic and co-curricular activities including studying abroad (Demetriou, Meece, Eaker-Rich, & Powell, 2017).

Recommendations for Diversifying Participation in Education Abroad

Increase Funding and Keep Costs Low

Perhaps the most important step to increasing participation of many of the underrepresented groups in education abroad is to increase funding. Although research suggests that more scholarships are not enough to remove obstacles (Salisbury et al., 2009), scholarships, grants and financial support are nonetheless important in supporting low-income students (Engel, 2017), many of which are first-generation college students, students of color, and working students from community colleges (Chen & Nunnery, 2019).

More open scholarships need to be available for underrepresented student groups. Cost can be kept low by subsidizing costs incurred by education abroad that are above what a student would pay for on-campus study, which is done at

The University of Denver through the Cherrington Global Scholars program (Shirley, 2006). Several scholarships already exist to support underrepresented groups, such as the NAFSA Tamara H. Bryant Memorial Scholarship and the Benjamin A. Gilman International Scholarship Program, which is intended for low-income undergraduates and sponsored by the US State Department (West, 2019). The number of ethnic minority students who received financial aid through this program rose to 64% in 2014–2015 (Engel, 2017). Scholarships are also crucial to support students with disabilities who may incur additional costs with education abroad if special accommodations are required while abroad (Twill & Guzzo, 2012). While allowing students with disabilities to bring along a personal assistant can mean the difference between whether a student can or cannot go abroad, the additional cost of this is often not covered by universities so providing grants for students to use for this purpose is important.

An interesting approach to supporting scholarships is implementing a general international education fee for all education abroad programs and using this fee to start a fund for students who need financial assistance (West, 2019). In order to reap the benefits of available scholarships and awards, it is important to actively and publicly disseminate information about available funding and the possibilities of continuing the scholarships students already hold. Information sessions where students can learn about financing options and receive individual support can be far more effective than merely providing students a link to a website for finding funding. Developing brochures with information about the scholarships along with a well-designed website for finding more resources is recommended. One informant suggested reducing barriers to financial assistance by removing application procedures and automatically consider education abroad applicants for education abroad scholarships.

Another problem stems from a lack of general funding and lower endowments at community colleges and Historically Black Colleges and Universities (HBCUs) which make the development of education abroad grants for their students difficult. Additionally, these financial differences mean that these colleges often do not want to send students abroad for semester or year-long programs and lose their tuition money (Esmieu et al., 2016). Community colleges as well as HBCUs need more federal funding in order to expand their education abroad options (Mullen, 2014).

In addition to increasing funding through scholarships, awards and grants, carefully considering programmatic decisions such as program location and time of travel can help to lower costs. Off-season programs will mean lower prices for airfare, lodging and activities, for example. In some cases, using travel agencies can be cost-saving because of their competitive rates (Rusnak, Peek, Orriola, & Makut, 2019). Working with consortia schools helps to share administrative costs and expands program options for students (Brux & Fry, 2010).

As the Lincoln Commission reported, at MSU, more than half of the education abroad programs, including AYF, are kept at costs at or lower than an equivalent to the same amount of credits taken on the home campus. This means that the vast majority of students only have the added expense of the flight; international and out-of-state students can actually save money through AYF. An important task for language faculty members and program staff is to make it very clear how education abroad costs differ from a year at home with special attention played to all costs and not just tuition and program fees. For example, students in the AYF program often comment that housing, grocery, and health care costs were much lower than at home. Education abroad may incur costs that students are not aware of including application fees, immunizations, visa and passport fees. Keeping application fees low or rolling these into program fees if students go abroad and providing grants for supporting up-front costs can incentivize underrepresented students to apply for education abroad programs.

Ease Academic Barriers

In order to encourage students from underrepresented majors to study abroad, universities need to find solutions to credit-transfer problems, show flexibility in the order of degree completion requirements, and allow students to take required courses abroad. Programs should work with students to find alternative paths to acquire the necessary content knowledge. Advisors can help students design a curriculum that allows for a year abroad even in STEM and pre-professional majors and the earlier students engage their advisors in such conversations, the more likely that they will be able to complete a program without sacrificing time to degree. Sometimes it may require taking some courses early and taking other courses a bit later, or it may require doing more research about the target institution's offerings to find equivalencies to what the students need to take at home. For some it may mean going on a year abroad in their final year, for others in their second year of university studies. During education abroad, students can often fulfill some of their general education requirements, but it is also important to help them find courses that count toward their major (Sideli, Dollinger, & Doyle, 2003). The initiatives undertaken to globalize science learning at Emory University are excellent and successful examples how academic barriers can be overcome and education abroad can be integrated into science curricula (Wainwright, Ram, Teodorescu, & Tottenham, 2009).

Institutions often have a limit on the number of outside courses students are allowed to count for their major which discourages students from selecting long-term education abroad. To diversify education abroad participation, universities should remove or at least minimize the limits placed on the number of abroad courses that students can use for their major (Marcum, 2001). US institutions are encouraged to include information about pre-approved courses at their partner universities abroad on their education abroad websites with the option for students to petition for other courses to count for credit that are not yet on this list.

Students likely will need the support of advisors to find solutions especially when courses are slightly different from equivalent courses at the home campus.

Many students worry how time abroad might affect their GPA (Minton, 2016; Vernon et al., 2017; Walker, 2015) and especially male students are concerned about graduation delays (Shirley, 2006). However, students who studied abroad were actually shown to increase their GPAs (Sutton & Rubin, 2010; Thomas & McMahon, 1998). Because grading criteria and systems sometimes vary drastically between countries, universities may want to include pass/fail options for students when working with overseas transcripts. In addition, showing flexibility in deadlines may be necessary because of the different academic calendars (Gordon, Patterson, & Cherry, 2014). Furthermore, home institutions should conduct periodic grade analyses to determine whether a certain program may result in a lower GPA for students. If that is the case across several cohorts, the conversion rate may need to be adjusted.

US institutions of higher education need to begin to collaborate more strongly and effectively with institutions abroad in order to establish better frameworks for education abroad, credit transfer, and course recognition. The European ERASMUS program provides an excellent example of how to simplify credit transfer, awarding double degrees and diploma supplements. The latter helps ERASMUS participants in their future applications because employers can easily identify how courses taken abroad were relevant for a student's degree or gave the student additional expertise (Kehm, 2005). Strong relationships between the host institution and the institutions at home can help in identifying appropriate courses but formal agreements can be especially useful in easing credit-transfer issues (Turlington, Collins, & Porcelli, 2002).

Improve Outreach, Advising, Marketing, and Mentoring

Increasing outreach efforts, strengthening individual student advising and mentoring, as well as improving marketing strategies and materials are crucial measures for diversifying education abroad participation. For example using an Inclusive Excellence Scorecard, as recommended by Sweeney (2013), can help education abroad offices evaluate the representation of students of color in their programs. She includes several examples of such scorecards that can be adapted to assess how minoritized groups are represented in programs, marketing materials, and outreach efforts.

Promotional materials such as flyers, brochures, and websites need to be more diverse and represent all students, including students of color, LGBTQ+ and male students, students with and without disabilities. Similarly, education abroad fairs and info sessions benefit from including alumni from all underrepresented groups to provide successful examples and mentorship. This could help dispel stereotypes that education abroad is merely a feminine endeavor (Thirolf, 2014), which is often the message sent by marketing materials (Redden, 2009). Marketing materials can highlight the many ways in which new friendships are formed in education abroad in order to help minoritized students with the concern of traveling alone (Yankey, 2014).

In addition, strategies used to attract different groups of students to education abroad need to be adjusted to account for their different motivations. For example, "promoting study abroad as an opportunity to challenge oneself and test one's limits" (Yankey, 2014, p. 223) can be a way to attract more men to education abroad. Since many male students participate in education abroad if they perceive benefits for their major or future career (Lucas, 2009), it is important to highlight these benefits in information sessions and promotional materials. Many students may be unaware of the variety of skills they can develop in education abroad and how they can increase their own marketability. According to a study by Salisbury et al. (2010), marketing also needs to include pre-college contexts, so that a positive foundation for participating in a variety of educational opportunities can be laid early on.

Promoting education abroad programs specifically to students of color (Eidson, 2015), clubs, fraternities, or organizations on campus can also help to create a culture of education abroad that challenges any negative perceptions and can make students see that they are not the only one in their group of friends to consider the option (TerraDotta, 2019). It is also important to pay attention to the language used in outreach materials to make sure it is inclusive (Butler, Madden, & Smith, 2018); it was found that language for reaching the LGBTQ+ community was at times dated and it is crucial to regularly update language so all students feel included (Hipple, Soltis, & Hyers, 2020). Clearly outlining and advertising the outcomes of education abroad could result in a better understanding of the potential benefits for students' personal, academic and career development.

Gore (2005) suggests that since gender-related stereotypes seem to be preventing male students from education abroad, making sure that there are male advisors who successfully participated in and benefitted from an education abroad experience can convince male students to give education abroad a chance. This recommendation holds true for all underrepresented groups who need advisors and peer mentors who participated in global experiences themselves.

Research has identified advising as a crucial component in students' education abroad intentions and decisions (Martinez, Ranjeet, & Marx, 2009). Therefore, the importance of getting faculty buy-in for education abroad cannot be overstated. This can include, for example, inviting faculty of color, faculty with disabilities, faculty representing the LGBTQ+ community, and faculty from STEM majors as guest speakers to discuss their own international experiences and how they shaped their lives and careers. Representatives from underrepresented student groups, for example faculty of color, are often more influential on students' decisions, especially in the Black student community (Penn & Tanner, 2009; Perdue, 2018; Scheib & Mitchell, 2008). Mentorship programs through which either former education abroad participants of color or faculty provide encouragement to students who are unsure about education abroad are ideal. Students look up to peers and faculty who are similar to them more so than advisors and peers with whom they cannot identify. Furthermore, peers and faculty similar to the student's profile can better prepare students for the particular challenges they might encounter.

Participation in education abroad can be diversified by matching "returning students with prospects on the basis of gender, race and academic discipline" (Gordon et al., 2014, p. 83). Moreover, if participants keep a blog about their experiences abroad, those blogs can be read by prospective students to get a better idea of what a semester or year abroad means. Info sessions with returnees have been proven to be a successful strategy as well. Student panel discussions on the topic of underrepresented groups and education abroad with former participants, guest speakers and even Fulbright Scholars can be used to advertise programs to students of color (Picard, Bernardino, & Ehigiator, 2009). Sharing information about what education abroad alumni are doing now and where their career paths took them, can make students aware of the opportunities that will open up through education abroad.

Diversifying who is involved in the process of advising and mentoring students is a crucial measure because students need to have positive role models that will encourage them to participate in education abroad and can properly advise them for their situation. Staff in education abroad offices, therefore, need to represent more diversity and include people of color, men and women with and without disabilities, and members of the LGBTQ+ community. Including student workers and volunteers with disabilities and from other underrepresented groups can also help to create a more inclusive environment. Growing numbers of education abroad offices hire education abroad returnees in peer advisor positions; these peers are often the first point of contact for students interested in education abroad opportunities.

Diversify Program Types

An important strategy to attract underrepresented students to education abroad programs is by diversifying the types of education abroad programs through (1) designing effective short-term programs, and (2) adding experiential learning components to existing programs or creating new ones. Research has shown that diversifying program offerings supports all underrepresented groups: STEM-majors often prefer short-term programs during the summer which do not interfere with their regular academic schedule or internships and research opportunities with direct relevance for their major and job prospects (Warnick et al., 2018). Similarly, male students tend to prefer outcome-oriented programs, such as internships, with value for their résumés (Thirolf, 2014). For community college students and students of color, short-term programs are often a more manageable

and sometimes the only available option because of their work and family obligations. Students with disabilities, depending on type and severity of their disability,
find short-term programs more manageable as well. Helping students "balance their
personal, familial, academic, and professional responsibilities with the requirements
and timing of a study abroad program" (Amani & Kim, 2018, p. 689) is especially
important for community college students as well as non-traditional adult learners
(Peppas, 2005). Short-term programs are well suited for that and can take place
during winter or spring break or in the summer semester. Even though there are
limitations to learning outcomes in short-term programs, well-designed short
sojourns abroad still have the potential to affect students' worldviews and global-
mindedness and are a viable option when long-term programs are unavailable
(Blake-Campbell, 2014).

Additionally, offering education abroad programs that enhance students' job
prospects by including experiential learning components can help attract students
of color (Lu, Reddick, Dean, & Pecero, 2015) and STEM-majors. Since many
male students also choose education abroad based on its relevance for their academic development and job prospects, incorporating internships, research
opportunities, or service-learning components can be a great strategy for increasing participation by many of the underrepresented groups. Adding international
field study courses to their education abroad offerings more than tripled participation rates at Fox Valley Technical College, likely because these programs gave
students practical experience relevant to their majors (Bartzis, Kirkwood, &
Mulvihill, 2016).

Combining semester- or year-long education abroad programs with internships
can be a strong pull for students from all majors and can convince students to give
long-term education abroad a chance. He and Qin (2017) outline a semester-long
program in China which includes internships for each participant as well as
weekly community service. The program attracts students from all majors,
including STEM, and students reported that the internships had been very relevant for their academic fields of interest. Likewise, internships in locations that are
desirable for students of color due to their interest in connecting with their
heritage are a suitable option for better addressing the interests and needs of this
population. Summer internships in Ghana, for example, are an attractive choice
and the widespread use of English there also eases students' concerns about lacking additional language knowledge (Steeves, 2006).

Lastly, combining education abroad with undergraduate research can be another
step for diversifying participation. Many students are eager to improve their research
skills. Research projects can support the acquisition of discipline-specific knowledge,
which is often valued by students, especially by STEM-majors (Bender, Wright, &
Lopatto, 2009). However, field research also requires prior knowledge and preparation, for example background in statistics, and not all students have the necessary
training for in-depth research abroad (Houlihan, 2007) which must be considered
when advising students for education abroad.

can find a program that fits their specific interests. Especially for short-term programs, non-traditional locations are gaining popularity. Some of the less popular destinations outside of Europe can be a valuable alternative for students because cost of living may be lower in these places. This would help to keep the costs of education abroad down (Covington, 2017).

Apart from meeting the interests of students of color, education abroad in locations that are culturally more different to the US may provide more opportunities for developing intercultural competence. In fact, one study found some support for this argument: Students' world mindedness increased more in destinations that were more culturally different from their home country (Douglas & Jones-Rikkers, 2001). Thus, removing students from their comfort zones may help them grow personally and gain cultural awareness, especially when programs are designed with targeted reflective interventions. Wells (2006) suggests, that the "worldview that could develop from an experience in a country on the periphery of the modern global system will be broader than one formed in a country that holds a position of global power similar to that of the United States" (p. 121). Additionally, these locations lend themselves to learning more about the interconnectedness of the world, and can serve both the students', the institutions' and the society's goals for an international education.

Developing more programs in nontraditional locations can be a valuable contribution for universities that sets them apart from peer institutions. Nonetheless, as Wells (2006) reminds us, this does not imply a decreased focus on traditional locations. On the contrary, "increasing the number of students studying in nontraditional locations may instead be part of a larger concerted effort to increase the overall numbers of students studying abroad" (p. 125).

Develop Holistic Admissions Criteria

Most institutions have GPA requirements for education abroad programs. This disadvantages many students, and is based on the inaccurate assumption that students' learning at the home institution is a direct mirror for how they will learn abroad (Vande Berg, Connor-Linton, & Paige, 2009). Such a generalized view does not account for differences in learning contexts and the motivating role education abroad can play on students' capacity for academic performance nor does it consider the impact of specific interventions included in well-designed education abroad programs that include individual mentoring, reflective practice, and academic support. Institutions are encouraged to carefully examine and reevaluate their current education abroad application criteria and components in order to ensure that they are inclusive and fair.

Admission to programs traditionally based solely on students' GPA can instead be more holistic. Materials can include "several equally weighted factors such as an in-depth interview, a personal essay outlining educational history and motivation for participation, references from advisors, teachers or other educational professionals" (Shames & Alden, 2005, p. 24). Yet, application materials that are easier to complete are easier to process for students who are already unsure whether education abroad is the right choice for them.

In order to diversify participation in education abroad it is also important that all admissions materials and information are accessible and inclusive and use language that is non-discriminatory and makes all students feel welcome. Optional sections on the application form where students can identify topics they personally wish to discuss with an advisor can make students feel better supported (Butler et al., 2018).

Increase Collaborations between Campus Support Offices and with other Institutions

There are several ways that smaller institutions can make year-long programs available to their students through third-party vendor programs, direct enrollment, joining consortia, or sending their students on a program with one of the larger universities. Undoubtedly one of the most effective strategies for diversifying participation in education abroad is to utilize already existing partnerships with other universities (Rusnak et al., 2019) or establish new connections. Especially for community colleges, partnering with other institutions is an important step to internationalizing their campus (Opp & Gosetti, 2014). Becoming members of consortia can increase education abroad opportunities (Korbel, 2007), and can help to expand program options at four-year institutions, with sharing the financial burden, benefitting from the expertise of faculty from member schools, and, adding programs with discipline-specific content or foci of interest to minoritized students (DeWinter, 1997). Sadly, in spite of their benefits, at many community colleges, memberships in consortia are not always maintained due to budget cuts (Raby & Valeau, 2007). A renewed investment in consortia and inter-institutional collaborations could be beneficial for prioritizing international education at community colleges.

AYF, for example, is open to students from all US institutions but not many students from other institutions participate. When trying to expand the reach of the AYF to students from other institutions several challenges occurred, for example when institutions with existing direct-enroll programs charge their students extra for participating, or when schools have exclusivity contracts with a third-party vendor. More negotiations with the home institutions can be necessary and the process of enrolling in a program from another university is generally more cumbersome. That being said, once a program opens their door to other institutions and actively recruits at those institutions, systems can be put in place to better support the students.

In addition to leveraging existing or establishing new partnerships between institutions, it is also important to increase collaborations between different offices on campus. The education abroad office has to work closely with the admissions office, the financial aid office, the University Physician, the disabilities office, and any other offices that exist to support students on campus. Particularly in supporting students with disabilities, the education abroad office has a lot to gain by working closely with the experts at the disability office who can help identify how best to accommodate different disabilities in an education abroad context. Collaborating with the equivalent offices at the host institutions is equally important. It has to be acknowledged again that not all destinations have such offices and accommodations might need to be more ad-hoc. Through regular site visits, faculty and advisors can have a better understanding of how students can be accommodated and which locations are best suited for students with certain disabilities (Hameister et al., 1999).

Develop Global Certificates

An interesting strategy for motivating more diverse students to participate in an education abroad program is for colleges and universities to develop global certificates. These certificates could be included on students' diplomas and attest to the students' engagement in global learning. One part of the certificate can be an international experience, whether a semester or year abroad, or a short-term experiential learning program.

Several colleges have developed such certificates, for example Santa Fe College whose International Studies Certificate was designed to promote global literacy and led to increases in course offerings with global content, as well as foreign languages. The certificate requires "twenty credits in courses with international content, including eight credits in a foreign language," along with participation in "a series of international events, clubs, and activities, with the option and encouragement to study abroad" (Rodriguez, 2016, p. 225). Students also complete an e-portfolio in which they reflect on their international experiences. Since the development of the certificate, the college has seen an increase in interest and participation in global activities on campus as well as in education abroad. Similar initiatives have been developed at other institutions and have been proven to be an incentive for students to consider a study or service-learning opportunity abroad. Universities which already have a global learning certificate should consider making a stay abroad a required component of the program to encourage more students to go abroad.

Some institutions have developed specific certificates for certain disciplines which include international experiences, for example engineering programs. These address the need for increasing STEM major participation in education abroad. For example, Montana State University has an International Engineering Certificate, which requires among other things at least a two-week education abroad experience. The International Engineering Program at the University of Rhode Island is a five-year program in which students spend the entire fourth year abroad. The Global Minor at the College of Engineering at Purdue

University requires both a semester abroad, and a three-month international internship in addition to language study. Though not a certificate, The International Science and Technology Initiatives at MIT includes paid international internships for students, which is a very attractive option for students (Paxton, Sherick, & Marley, 2012). As Rodriguez rightfully points out, "global Certificate programs present an all-encompassing alternative to curricular internationalization alone and function as an umbrella under which international initiatives coalesce and gain intentionality and exposure" (Rodriguez, 2016, p. 226).

Pay Attention to Group Set-Up for Education Abroad

Students prefer traveling with peers. Many students find the prospect of traveling to another country by themselves daunting and feel more comfortable if friends are joining the program. Creating opportunities for minoritized students to travel together has been seen as an important incentive – students from underrepresented groups feel safer and more secure if they are not the only person from their community in an education abroad cohort. Programs where students can go with other classmates and experience a semester or year abroad together, such as the AYF, are one option. Short-term programs designed for groups of students from the same university are another way to solve this. Collaborations with other universities can also work, if students are given time for interactions and meetings before the trip starts (Vernon et al., 2017).

Several researchers point to the necessity of paying attention to the racial and social group composition for education abroad programs in which students travel together (Blake et al., 2019; Willis, 2015). As Blake et al. explain: "such a strategy might reduce the frequency with which students from these backgrounds experience prejudice within their programs and enrich the learning experience of all participants by including more diverse voices as these groups navigate and analyze their host countries" (Blake et al., 2019, p. 8). Ensuring that group travel includes diverse participants will also help students feel more comfortable and serve as encouragement for minoritized students to participate. Diverse groups typically create a space in which minoritized students feel like they are better understood and especially students of color prefer having other peers who can help them challenge negative experiences abroad (V. Doyle, 2018; Willis, 2015).

Moreover, "creating a more diverse environment within the study abroad programs would limit the associated reproduction of inequality" (Simon & Ainsworth, 2012, p. 18). Focusing on the racial set-up of education abroad groups should, therefore, be prioritized, not only because minoritized students feel safer if they are not the only person who has a disability or is a student of color or a member of the LGBTQ+ community within an education abroad cohort, but also because it is a crucial step in ensuring equal access to education abroad. Lastly, group cohesion also benefits from a diverse racial composition of the education abroad group (Willis, 2012).

Alleviate Fears, Correct Misperceptions, Change the General Perception of Education Abroad

Many students from underrepresented groups ultimately do not participate in education abroad, even if interested, because they have fears related to potential discrimination, racism, or lack of accessibility in another country, concerns over their own language abilities, and incomplete or even inadequate information about the target culture. Even smaller concerns over the food and access to certain products can become an obstacle. It is crucial to better inform students about the target communities in order to help them see that many of their fears are unfounded (Gordon et al., 2014) and to listen more carefully to their concerns.

Students who are afraid of racism abroad can benefit from speaking with peers or faculty of color who have spent time in the country of choice (Lu et al., 2015). Similarly, students with disabilities will benefit from speaking with other students who already went abroad and learning from how their disabilities were accommodated (Scheib & Mitchell, 2008). Advisors play an important role in helping students with disabilities find resources beforehand so that they can better understand how they will be able to function in the host community and what additional supports might have to be put into place for them.

While certain concerns over discrimination, racism, and sexism are not unfounded, they do not have to prevent students from deciding to participate. Instead, advisors can help students find an appropriate education abroad program that meets the students' interests and goals while keeping the host community's ideologies in mind. For members of the LGBTQ+ community, countries where homosexuality is still considered illegal should be considered carefully and alternatives explored. Education abroad staff can still help students feel safer abroad by ensuring that they have single rooms and bathrooms abroad so they do not run into problems due to segregated housing which can be an issue for trans and gender expansive students (Michl, Pegg, & Kracen, 2019). Additionally, and perhaps more importantly, students have to be equipped with the tools to deal with any potential instances of racism, sexism, or discrimination (Willis, 2015). Researching affinity groups abroad in advance can ease students' worries as well. Pre-departure orientation thus, plays a crucial role for any student participating in education abroad.

While lack of language abilities has been cited as one deterrent to education abroad (Austin & Rust, 2015), research shows that students with low proficiency are able to make tremendous gains during education abroad. This should be used in recruiting students who may be hesitant to participate because they have not studied a language long enough. Many courses at universities abroad, especially in Europe, are also taught in English. Students who are concerned about language skills can attend these classes, or even select an education abroad location where English is widely spoken. Additionally, if students spend an entire year abroad, they can use the first semester for intensive language study and the second semester for taking courses in their major.

The overall image of education abroad has to be changed so it is no longer seen as "an insignificant pursuit by wealthy women" (Gore, 2005, p. 41). Predominant views of education abroad are still that of "cultural enrichment for women with no concern for professional preparation and no interest in significant academic experiences" (Gore, 2005, p. 58), a view which makes male students, low-income and students of color feel as though education abroad is not meant for them. Changing these historical perceptions by highlighting the value and diverse benefits of education abroad can assist students in understanding the academic, personal, linguistic, and intercultural gains they can make by studying in another country.

Increase Faculty Support and Training

The support of faculty is one of the most important factors impacting students' decisions to participate in education abroad, just as lack of this support is one of the largest barriers (Loberg, 2012). In fact, "increased involvement of the faculty may well hold the key to tackling barriers to student participation in study abroad" (Paus & Robinson, 2008, p. 45). Advisors who downplay the value of an international experience or emphasize the difficulties of fitting it into a full schedule can have a negative impact on students' choices. On the contrary, faculty members who actively show students how time abroad can positively connect to students' academic futures, careers, and personal development, can be the deciding factor in students' decisions.

In order to be able to complete this crucial role, faculty need to be better informed about education abroad options and their benefits (Brux & Fry, 2010). Implementing training and support for faculty is also important to motivate them to develop new education abroad programs as well as to help them better address the needs of diverse students. Through training, faculty and staff can be better prepared to understand issues of race, gender and sexuality, and provide stronger support for all students (Goldoni, 2017).

Institutions of higher learning are encouraged to provide incentives for faculty to become actively involved in internationalization efforts and in designing new programs or participating in existing ones (Yucas, 2003). Incentives could include teaching releases after leading education abroad programs, higher compensation, administrative assistance for the planning and running of the program, or providing funds to develop new and innovative programs. Curriculum development funds could be provided to support the re-design of existing courses in order to make their content more relevant and inclusive. Faculty should also receive opportunities to conduct research and attend conferences abroad in order to increase faculty interest in and enthusiasm for international experiences which will often translate into stronger advocacy for education abroad (Green, 2002).

Further Recommendations

Inclusion of students with disabilities, mental health disorders, and other under-represented groups has to become an institutional priority (Ablaeva, 2012). When setting up homestay families, for example, program designers should include families with a variety of ethnic backgrounds, and families that include members with disabilities (Sygall, 1995). In order to make education abroad truly inclusive, institutional attitudes toward international experiences have to be changed and diversity needs to be normalized (Scheib & Mitchell, 2008).

Institutional support for education abroad is crucial and "must be a priority.[...] Support, both financial and other, at all levels within the institution, must be provided to domestic students to encourage study abroad" (Gordon et al., 2014, p. 85). It is important to also keep in mind that no one approach will work for all students. In order to diversify participation, specific strategies will have to be applied based on the needs of the underrepresented student group (Garver & Divine, 2007). Individual strategies also include considering processes to increase student participation based on class level of students (Quraeshi et al., 2012). This could mean encouraging students to select short-term programs during their first year, and a longer program abroad later on, with the addition of a service-learning, internship or field placement. To achieve this "it is helpful to develop a range of upgraded and unique education abroad programs that are closely connected to a student's academic development and to the shifting interests and expectations of students at each of the different student levels" (Quraeshi et al., 2012, p. 86).

Lastly, in order to diversify education abroad, it is crucial to get families on board. Family encouragement and support plays an indispensable role in students' intent and actual choice to participate. One way to get families to buy into the idea of education abroad is by sending them information about the benefits of an international stay (Gordon et al., 2014) or education abroad brochures as part of admissions materials, inviting them to education abroad fairs on campus, and having dedicated pages on education abroad websites for parents. "Study abroad must broaden beyond the middle class White, female demographic to include more socioeconomic representation, greater gender balance, and sharp increases in minority student participation" (Picard et al., 2009, p. 342) and in order to achieve this goal, institutional and faculty support, and family buy-in are vital.

Chapter 3.2. Maximizing Language Learning

In spite of the many positive effects of education abroad on students' language skills, it must be kept in mind that "study abroad is not a magic formula or a cure-all for language-learning problems. Study abroad can advance language learning but does not instantly transform students into simulacra of native speakers" (Kinginger, 2009b, p. 210). This chapter, therefore, suggests concrete ways to maximize language learning in education abroad. Suggestions are not in any particular order.

Prepare Students for their Time Abroad

Before students embark on their adventures to another country and culture, it is important to prepare them to make the most of their time abroad (Goldoni, 2015). Preparatory sessions that teach students skills of observation can be helpful. Additionally, students should be given time to write down their language learning goals before they leave. They can check in on these goals with their program director while they are abroad and adjust their behaviors accordingly. At the end of their sojourns, they can reflect on which linguistic goals they achieved or did not achieve and why. Studies have indicated the benefits for students of having clear language goals for education abroad (Iwasaki, 2007; Larson, 1999).

In order to help students engage in meaningful interactions with members of the target community, it is recommended to have students practice talking to speakers of the host community language before going abroad (Kinginger, 2011). Ideally, this type of practice is included as regular component of their language instruction, for example through virtual exchanges (Schenker, 2013a, 2013b). Additionally, role-plays and simulations can be included prior to going abroad to help students try out some of the typical situations they may encounter during their time abroad and ensure that they have the necessary vocabulary to navigate these situations. Reading the local newspaper before education abroad, also helps students understand the important topics in town and provides them with the vocabulary to engage in those discussions.

Teach Language Before, During, and After Education Abroad

Preparing students linguistically for their time abroad is a crucial step in ensuring that they have the necessary foundations in the language in order to benefit from immersion in the target community. As DeKeyser (2007) explains, "the quality of the students' learning experience abroad depends to a large extent on their preparation at home" (p. 217). This preparation includes teaching students rules for communicating in the host language(s), as well as assisting them in acquiring functional knowledge of the grammar so that they can use the time abroad to make noticeable progress. Students need to be at least somewhat comfortable in using the language so that they will not shy away from communicating with host community members while abroad (Davie, 1996). Especially the domain of listening comprehension needs to receive enough attention before students go abroad as they often struggle to understand and hence participate in conversations abroad. In addition, training students in pragmatics can be a good preparation, for example by teaching phrases and strategies for holding conversations, and emphasizing differences or similarities in communicative norms of their first language(s) and the host community language(s) (Pryde, 2014).

Research has shown that prior coursework in the host community language(s) is a predictor of linguistic gain during education abroad (Freed, 1995; Magnan & Back, 2007). Ensuring that students have taken at least a few classes in the language before going abroad can help students succeed linguistically during their sojourn. Ideally, faculty should "integrate the study abroad experience – deliberately and systematically, in terms of both linguistic and cultural preparation – into the FL curriculum" (Redman, 2009, p. 86). One way to do this is to purposefully integrate teaching about destinations that offer education abroad programs for the specific language at one's institution prior to studying abroad (Goertler & McEwen, 2018).

Even in long-term education abroad programs, the amount of language practice that students receive is often not as high as it should be (DeKeyser, 2007). Students need more language practice and more quality input, opportunities for output, interaction as well as targeted feedback. Therefore, students should be encouraged to continue taking language classes while they are abroad so they can build on the foundational knowledge from their classes back home and expand their out-of-class learning while abroad. Language teachers are in an ideal position to help students make sense of their linguistic encounters, interpret misunderstandings, and help them acquire further linguistic abilities.

Students should be encouraged to continue taking language classes once they return from education abroad in order to build on the skills they developed abroad and avoid language attrition. Studies indicate that students benefit from language classes taken after education abroad and may even benefit more than students who had not previously studied abroad (Isabelli-García, 2007; Marqués-Pascual, 2011). As Kinginger (2009a) summarizes, education abroad helps students to "increase their social interactive abilities and become better prepared for instruction in the finer points of grammar and literacy" (p. 85) when they return home. There are also certain domains of language proficiency that do not develop as much during education abroad or require a substantial duration of time spent abroad, such as phonological development. Further instruction after time spent abroad is needed for students to develop in these areas (J. C. Mora, 2014).

After education abroad, specific courses are best suited for returnees, such as courses focusing on discourse and advanced grammar concepts, or content-based courses that connect to students' majors and interests (Kinginger, 2009a). In addition to courses that complement the education abroad experience, universities could organize sessions in which returnees present the research that they conducted abroad. Peer mentoring programs are also a great way to help students continue to expand their language skills. In addition to continuing with language classes, finding ways to maintain students' contact with the host community can be a great way to support their language development after their return.

Teach Communication Strategies

Communication strategies are verbal and non-verbal techniques used to overcome communication problems (Dörnyei, 1995). Non-verbal communication strategies can help education abroad participants overcome linguistic short-comings, for example while participating in sports or other leisure activities (Montero, 2019; Tarone, 1981). Encouraging students to participate in extracurricular activities while abroad may therefore be an effective way in helping them develop their communication strategies naturally.

Teaching students circumlocution, appealing for help, replacement skills and other communication strategies can be helpful either before or while students are abroad. Some suggestions for teaching communication strategies are made by Dörnyei (1995) and include:

- Making students aware of strategies they use in their L1 and L2.
- Motivating students to take risks without fear of making errors.
- Showing models of strategies used by native speakers.
- Teaching linguistic terms to discuss strategies.
- Comparing cross-cultural differences in communication strategies.
- Offering opportunities for trying out communication strategies in practice.

For more ideas of how to teach communication strategies, several ideas are listed in the articles by Ogane (1998) and Maleki (2010), in the student self-guide *Communication Strategies: Study Guide* (GTS Learning, 2013), and the *Maximizing Study Abroad* guide (Paige, Cohen, Kappler, Chi, & Lassegard, 2002).

Teach Language Learning Strategies

Teaching participants language learning strategies helps them maximize their linguistic development during their time abroad (Hernández, 2010a). According to Chamot (2005), "explicit instruction includes the development of students' awareness of their strategies, teacher modeling of strategic thinking, identifying the strategies by name, providing opportunities for practice and self-evaluation" (p. 123). Language classes at home are an ideal context for teaching language learning strategies. In the absence of strategy training in language courses, pre-departure training for education abroad participants should include some strategy instruction, for example through using the *Strategy Inventory for Language Learning* (Oxford, 1990), which, though originally designed for learners of English, can be adapted to be used for other language learners.

Language learning strategy training should continue while students are abroad. The book *Maximizing Study Abroad* (Paige et al., 2002) contains a great collection of activities for before, during, and after education abroad with which students can enhance their language learning strategies. They include tasks for becoming better listeners, vocabulary acquisition techniques, strategies for improving oral skills, reading comprehension, and writing development, and translation strategies. Another important strategy students should acquire is the ability to identify how they can increase their exposure to the language while abroad (Paige et al., 2002). One way to do this, for example, is by having students research their destination and local environment more in-depth at a pre-departure meeting. Students can find out about local clubs, organizations and events that may be of interest to them where they will be exposed to the language.

Language learning strategies are especially important for success in year-long education abroad programs in countries where students' L1 is not the primary language of communication. Meta-analyses of studies focusing on language learning strategies revealed moderate to large effects of interventions that teach language learning strategies and suggests that language learning strategy training may be more effective beyond the novice level (Ardasheva, Wang, Adesope, & Valentine, 2017; Plonksy, 2019). Based on these findings, including training for language learning strategies can be especially beneficial during education abroad, especially since most of the participants are intermediate or even advanced learners of the language.

Language learning strategies can "assist learners in becoming more responsible for their efforts in learning and using the target language" (Cohen, 2011, p. 139). As part of teaching language learning strategies, efforts should be made to raise students' language learning awareness. As Pyper and Slagter (2015) summarize, "helping students become aware of their attitudes and perceptions is a first step toward helping them modify behaviors to enable them to improve their L2 acquisition" (p. 84).

Increase Contact with Members of the Host Community

Lack of engagement with the host community has been identified as one of the strongest hindrances to language acquisition during education abroad. Kinginger (2011) emphasizes that, if students do not make strong linguistic gains during education abroad, "it is because they do not become sufficiently or meaningfully engaged in the practices of their local host communities or because they lack guidance in interpreting their observations" (p. 67). Reasons for this lack of integration are varied and often include too much reliance on social media, insufficient preparation for education abroad, or an emphasis of non-language related goals.

Interactions with members of the host community can be arranged through joining religious organizations, sports clubs, or academic activities offered by the host university (Trentman, 2013). Because different activities provide different access to host community members, it is important to help students find and try out a variety of programs. Some students were successful in integrating into the host community by pursuing a personal talent or hobby which brought them in contact with native-speaking peers (Goldoni, 2013). Helping students explore ways to pursue their hobbies while abroad can therefore be a crucial step in assisting them in using the target language meaningfully.

A buddy program or tandem partner has been shown to be an effective way to help students interact more in the community language(s). Ideally this program is set up by someone directly (e.g., education abroad leader) or indirectly (e.g., host university's International Student Office) connected to the program and all students can sign up for it. Students often find buddy programs which can include weekly conversation practice to be helpful for their language learning (Hennings & Tanabe, 2018; Pyper & Slagter, 2015) as well as for their overall adjustment (J. H. Lee, 2018). Similarly to a buddy system, students can benefit from tutors who help them with classwork and assignments (J. Kim, Dewey, Baker-Smemoe, & Ring, 2015). This is especially useful for beginning language learners who may struggle to adjust to academic coursework abroad.

Another way to increase contact with members of the target community is by designing and implementing specific tasks that require interaction. Since students often shy away from seeking out these connections on their own, program staff can help by assigning homework that requires meaningful interactions (Cadd, 2012; DeKeyser, 2007). These can be part of the coursework students complete or can be expectations for the particular education abroad program. For example, students can be given the task to interview members of the community with a specific set of questions (Archangeli, 1999). The responses can then be shared with other members of the education abroad cohort, if there is one, or reflected upon in individual journals or blogs. Travers (1980) designed a series of tasks for students that forced them to interact with strangers while abroad. These included asking for directions, ordering food, finding out train times, and others, and pushed students to use their language skills in a natural environment. While these tasks focused largely on survival activities, they can be adjusted to the particular contexts of the education abroad program of the students.

In an effort to increase contact with host community members, Cadd (2012) developed twelve tasks which students had to complete while abroad. These included, for example, identifying a typical dish and talking to a restaurant about it, or attending a public event and speaking with other attendees about the event. These tasks helped students become less nervous in interacting with host community members, increased their fluency and their willingness to communicate.

The host university can play a crucial role in promoting use of the host language(s) by organizing social events for international and local students. Joint

shown that interacting and conversing in the host language with peers from the home country can be beneficial as well (Freed, Segalowitz, & Dewey, 2004), for example for advancing vocabulary knowledge (Dewey, 2008). However, it is often difficult for peers of the same home language to speak the host language together and a language pledge can be a motivator for students to stick to the L2. Furthermore, interactions do not have to be exclusively in the host language and may more realistically include multilingual communications common to the host community.

Concerns have been voiced over students' use of technology during education abroad which can prevent them from fully immersing themselves in the host community. On the extreme end would be a media pledge, as suggested by Huesca (2013), that would limit students' use of their mobile devices for streaming in their L1, for example. However, technology can also serve language learning purposes when abroad. Guichon (2019), for example, suggests the use of a mobile app for tracking students' learning abroad. In the app, students can take pictures and write comments about their experiences and it has been shown to help students in keeping track of their own learning outside the classroom. Thus, students can use their mobile devices for daily journaling in the L2, for photo-blogging, or creating virtual tours of their locations (Godwin-Jones, 2016). Linguistic landscape projects are another great way to use technology productively while abroad and these could be incorporated in courses to show students how language works in the signs around them (Cenoz & Gorter, 2008). Mobile devices can be a big help for navigating unknown cities, and students could be shown how to use mapping apps, apps for finding local attractions or events, or using the web for looking up information such as opening hours of buildings (Durbidge, 2019). Additionally, since research has found a connection between motivation and use of L2 through technology (Seibert Hanson & Dracos, 2016), keeping students motivated remains a priority for education abroad programs.

Having students reflect on their use of the host language(s) can help them realize if they are availing themselves of all opportunities for language learning while abroad. To that end, it is helpful to have students complete a language log, such as the online Linguafolio through The Center for Applied Second Language Studies (CASLS) at the University of Oregon (CASLS, 2020), or by using the printable worksheets from the National Council of State Supervisors for Languages (NCSSFL, 2020). These tools allow students to keep track of their goals and assess their own progress. Simple language contact profiles, such as the one in the study by Martinsen (2010), the chart used by Martinsen, Baker, Dewey, and Bown (2010), or the listening log introduced by Kemp (2010) can also be used to have students keep track of and analyze their use of their languages every week. Using these types of language logs can help students manage their learning independently (Lomartire, 2018).

In order to use the language outside of the classroom, establishing a strong social network is crucial. Research has shown that "the development of social networks may be a key to whether or not students are able to improve their L2 proficiency while studying abroad" (Baker-Smemoe, Dewey, Bown, & Martinsen, 2014, p. 468). Establishing a social network is often more difficult for female students, especially in certain locations (Kinginger, 2004; Polanyi, 1995), and in general is easier for students living close to or with peers of the target community (Dewey, Ring, Gardner, & Belnap, 2013). To help students understand their own social networks, they can be encouraged to complete the Study Abroad Social Interaction Questionnaire (Ring, Gardner, & Dewey, 2013), in which they track their interaction with others during their sojourn. The program director can use the questionnaire to assist the student in identifying ways in which the social network can be expanded. Because stronger social networks have been shown to help students advance their language skills, especially in vocabulary (Dewey, 2008) and speaking (Du, 2013; Isabelli-García, 2006), efforts must be made to assist students in building such networks.

Incorporate Service-Learning or Internships

Another way to increase students' language learning during education abroad is to provide them with internship or service-learning placements that puts them in direct contact with people and institutions in the host communities (Ducate, 2009). Service, volunteer encounters and internships can be an important source of language learning outside of the classroom (He & Qin, 2017; Hernández, 2016; S.-L. Wu, 2017) that results in stronger linguistic gains (Fraser, 2002; Whitworth, 2006).

In many places volunteer opportunities are available for students that can connect them to the community, for example through after-school activities or language courses for the community (Goldoni, 2013), soup kitchens, senior living homes, hospitals, historical sites, or homeless shelters (Kinginger, 2009a). Placements in schools where students might help teach their first language(s) can also provide opportunities for observing the L2 in use (C.-H. Wu, 2018). Depending on where students are volunteering, the activity can allow them to get to know other dialects, host community members of different ages and backgrounds, and work with other volunteers who are often peers their age (Grimes-MacLellan, 2018). Volunteer work allows students to use the language in authentic contexts which can help boost their confidence (Curtin, Martins, Schwartz-Barcott, DiMaria, & Ogando, 2013). Setting up volunteer placements can be time-consuming and students may need specific preparation depending on what type of volunteer work they will perform. Some recommendations for designing and finding volunteer opportunities for students in education abroad are made by Grimes-MacLellan (2018) and include, for example finding partner institutions for collaborations, identifying a contact person, and getting information about possibilities from former participants in the desired location.

An intermediate level of language proficiency may be required for students to succeed in internships abroad (He & Qin, 2017). Lower proficiency can prevent students from communicating in the host language(s) at the workplace. Internships offer opportunities for acquiring discipline-specific vocabulary and help students gain a better command of the language overall (DeWinter, 2007). When selecting internships for students, the potential placement site should be chosen carefully. Some companies abroad operate with a lot of English and may not give students as many opportunities for using the L2 (Kurasawa & Nagatomi, 2006), a concern if language learning is the goal. Internships that are embedded into coursework can be especially beneficial as class-time can be used for analyzing the experience and discussing any language questions that arose during the placements (Brown, 2014). Several education abroad programs are now including optional or mandatory internships or service-learning projects during or after students' semester or year abroad which expand students' language learning tremendously (Davidson & Lekic, 2012; Vahlbusch, 2003). Internships, volunteer and service-learning opportunities can provide students access to a larger social network (Goldoni, 2013; Isabelli-García, 2006; Martinsen et al., 2010) which is crucial for their development of language skills.

Maintain High Levels of Motivation

Motivation plays an important role in the sociocultural adjustment and language learning of education abroad participants, especially in long-term programs. Assisting students to remain motivated during education abroad depends on the length and type of their education abroad experience as well as a variety of internal and external factors such as program types, language proficiency, and personality. Motivational issues during education abroad are often related to difficulties experienced due to inadequate language skills and lack of contact with peers from the community. Remaining motivated to learn the language requires an ability to deal with challenges, lack of progression, and even what might appear as setbacks in language development. Ushioda (2014) suggests that students need resilience and determination in order to remain focused on language learning even when they experience difficulties, but that students also need strategies for overcoming language learning challenges. Specifically, at earlier stages of language learning students need cognitive strategies such as how to memorize, repeat and rehearse information, but at more advanced language learning stages, Ushioda (2014) suggests that metacognitive knowledge is necessary. For example, students can be taught how to scaffold their thinking by the teacher modeling an approach of self-verbalization when thinking through a problem. Students might then use these same questions for themselves when working through a language problem or challenge. In addition to self-verbalization modeling, which may on its own not lead to the development of strategies for the students, Ushioda (2014) recommends using conceptual questions, as well as verbal encouragement and praise. She also underlines the importance of the teacher relinquishing their role and giving students the power to regulate their own thinking.

Since research has emphasized the role of the instructor in motivating students both to begin and continue with language study, instructors remain an important resource for students before, during and after education abroad. A study by Awad (2014) revealed that students felt motivated if the language classes provided enjoyment as well as serious tasks, and if their instructor supported them in their language learning endeavors. During education abroad, instructors both at the home campus and those accompanying students during their sojourn, need to continue to support students in a variety of ways both inside and outside of the classroom. Be it an informal e-mail to check in on students' progress abroad, or a get together over coffee on the ground – small gestures can go a long way to help students feel supported and thereby maintain their learning motivation.

Motivation issues may also stem from an inability to find friends or contact with local peers which may cause a sense of loneliness and isolation and may lead students to question the utility of their stay abroad. Helping students find opportunities to connect with other students is, again, one of the main steps to be taken to support them in their time abroad. Because changes in motivation can occur when students lack meaningful interactions (Isabelli-García, 2006), helping students establish a good social network and offering them opportunities for interacting with others is crucial.

Helping students build on their education abroad experience and keeping them motivated to continue with the study of language and international issues requires careful post-sojourn support and training. Some recommendations for how this can be achieved can be found in the guidebook *Maximizing Study Abroad* (Paige et al., 2002). Thus, when students return home, it is imperative that they are encouraged to make use of their newly acquired skills and knowledge in advanced language and content courses and even in interdisciplinary courses. Students will need advice on selecting appropriate courses and assistance in finding opportunities for using the language in extracurricular contexts.

Promote Reflection and Observation

In a review of previous research, Kinginger (2011) points out that "Observation, participation, and reflection or introspection are among the main modes of learning languages in study abroad settings" (p. 68). Since these three modes are also part of ethnography, Kinginger promotes the use of ethnographic research by students during their time abroad. She suggests that "explicit focus on ethnographic techniques might help some students to appreciate the relevance of observation, formal and informal participation (e.g., in interviews or in conversations), and introspection for language learning" (Kinginger, 2009a, pp. 45–46). In her guidebook, Kinginger includes activities that can be completed with students before they go abroad to teach them how to observe language use. Ethnographic projects have been incorporated successfully in many education

For successful and transformative student reflection, Savicki and Price (2018) caution that reflection should not overgeneralize, lack detail or context, remove emotions or focus only on emotions. Effective reflection, then, provides enough detail and context to allow students to find alternative interpretations of events and perspectives, and connects the students' personal experiences to the reflection. Critical reflection not just on culture but also on national identity can help students move toward global citizenship (Dolby, 2007).

Even before leaving their home institution, reflective activities can be integrated in pre-departure training. During time abroad, reflective activities can take many shapes, and blogging during time abroad is a favorite activity in many programs (Douthit, Schaake, Hay, Grieger, & Bormann, 2015; Dressler & Tweedie, 2016; L. Lee, 2011; Rubesch, 2017; Savicki & Price, 2017; Tonkin & Coudray, 2016). Using web 2.0 or 3.0 technologies is helpful to encourage reflection because they can "produce a virtual 'third space' where students could better reflect on cultural differences, sharpen their own intercultural skills, and gain the metacognitive skills necessary to become life-long learners from experience" (Downey & Gray, 2012, p. 1). By using categories for their blog entries, students can begin to see overlaps and similarities in their own experiences and those of their peers abroad. Incorporating photographs into their blogs is another way to encourage introspection of cultural differences and similarities. Similarly to individual blogging, dialogic journaling in which students and instructors establish a mutual exchange can promote reflection. While abroad, dialogic journaling can support the establishment of positive teacher-student relationships (Dressler & Tweedie, 2016). However, this type of reflective activity requires a lot of time commitment from the instructor. Without prompting students to reflect on cultural aspects, their diary entries are likely to remain descriptive and un-reflected (Vogt, 2020) or superficial, especially in short-term programs (Tonkin & Coudray, 2016). By systematically incorporating reflective reports with targeted prompts, students can engage in stronger intercultural learning processes. Vogt (2020) suggests a procedure for pre-service teachers in education abroad that includes student observations, describing the observed, reflecting on the observed, and concluding the reflection.

Adding a dialogical or discussion component can be crucial in getting students to think more deeply about the topics and moving beyond the superficial. It may be necessary for instructors to become involved by giving feedback, posing further questions, and helping students think more critically (Tonkin & Coudray, 2016). Additionally, scheduling regular debriefing sessions or group discussions between members of an education abroad cohort can help students support each other and find alternative ways of understanding their cultural experiences (Dorsett, 2019). Reflective assignments that promote students' interaction with the culture and each other can help students test generalizations and form hypothesis about their experiences (Lou & Weber Bosley, 2012). All in all, feedback is paramount to help students in their reflections and avoid over-generalized conclusions.

Apart from journaling, other types of reflective activities include free writing sessions during class (Savicki & Price, 2018), digital storytelling (Hamilton, Rubin, Tarrant, & Gleason, 2019; Perry et al., 2015), PhotoVoice projects (Homeyer, Leggette, McKim, & Walker, 2017; Ingle & Johnson, 2019), role playing and drama activities (Savicki & Price, 2018), working with linguistic landscapes (Lomicka & Ducate, 2019), or creating a portfolio (Penman & Ratz, 2015). Working with critical incidents (Williams, 2017) is another option. Follow-up discussions can help students find meaning and better understand cross-cultural differences.

An interesting approach to foster reflection is the PRISM method, which stands for helping "students get Prepared, make it Relevant, get Involved, make Sense, and make it Matter" (Williams, 2017, p. 24). For this approach, students watch videos to prepare them, read texts to make the videos relevant, then get involved in the community through specific assignments before using guiding questions to structure the evaluation of their experiences. Using this approach has shown to help students become more interculturally competent than students who participated in unstructured reflection.

After study abroad, workshops (Downey & Gray, 2012), co-curricular experiences (Salisbury, 2011), or essays (Maharaja, 2018) can serve to build on what students learned during their sojourn and further promote reflection.

Implement Pre-departure Training

If possible, students should take a class on intercultural communication before their time abroad. While specific course objectives may vary depending on program type and goals, the three main goals of a pre-departure course summarized by Martin (1989) can be applied to almost any context: Providing students with conceptual frameworks for intercultural learning, teaching them strategies for adjusting to and interacting in a different culture, and preparing them for functioning in the host community. Theories of intercultural competence and development should be included, as well as an exploration of students' own and the target culture (Dunlap & Mapp, 2017). Courses, such as the University of Pacific's *Cross-Cultural Training* (Bathurst & Brack, 2012), focus on cultural concepts and critical incidents. In addition to culture and communication topics, pre-departure can also draw from psychology to help students understand relevant concepts that impact outcomes of education abroad (Goldstein, 2017). Through these courses, instructors can "minimize the risk of shallow student learning, while also helping them to navigate important logistic concerns" (Dunlap & Mapp, 2017, p. 894).

In the absence of a pre-departure course, some pre-departure training should nevertheless be conducted. Orientation sessions that merely address logistics are insufficient. Instead, "structured preparation needs to include opportunities to reflect on one's own culture and identify possible challenges associated with cultural adjustment before embracing notions of other cultures and the impact of experiencing cultural difference" (Campbell & Walta, 2015, p. 13). Pre-departure training could include aspects of the following:

- Reflection on one's own identity, home culture, and personality (Moloney & Genua-Petrovic, 2012), for example through writing a cultural auto-biography (Goldoni, 2015).
- Discussion of critical incidents and cultural practices (Goldoni, 2015).
- Reflection on stereotypes and prejudices (Goldoni, 2015).
- Discussion of possible challenges connected to adjusting to a new culture (Campbell & Walta, 2015).
- Learning frameworks of intercultural competence and giving them the vocabulary needed to describe their experiences (Deardorff, 2011).
- Addressing preconceived notions about the host community (D. S. Jackson & Nyoni, 2012).
- Simulations (Goertler & McEwen, 2018).
- Specific culture-related reading assignments (Dunlap & Mapp, 2017).
- Strategies for cultural adjustment and critical cultural awareness (Chamot & Harris, 2019).

Another type of pre-departure training can take place through courses or workshops that focus on intercultural effectiveness and diversity, as suggested by Pedersen (2010). Many of the activities outlined in *Maximizing Study Abroad* (Paige et al., 2002) can be integrated into pre-departure preparation for students to help them understand how they will be able to make the most out of their time abroad.

Programs with limited resources or few faculty members involved in education abroad may not have the capacity to develop full classes or even extended training modules to prepare students for education abroad. Online tools may be of use here, such as the intercultural training modules *What's up with culture* (La Brack, 2003) suggested by Bathurst and Brack (2012). Another tool to consider for implementation pre-departure training is the *Culture Matters Peace Corps Workbook* (Peace Corps, 2011). Instructors and study abroad staff can also make use of the book *Maximizing Study Abroad* (Paige et al., 2002) which includes activities that can be used in pre-departure modules. These can serve as a great starting point for helping students think about intercultural learning and their upcoming stays abroad. Further examples of activities for pre-departure training are introduced as part of the Intercultural Education Resources for Erasmus Students and their Teachers, which can be found online (www.ierest-project.eu) (Atabong et al., 2015). This guide includes three modules for preparing students for their sojourns intended for approximately 48 hours of training. These fully developed units can easily be implemented by any instructor wishing to better prepare students before departure. Another valuable resource is the PluriMobil project, which was also developed in Europe and includes activities, lesson plans, and a handbook for enhancing intercultural learning of education abroad participants of different levels (elementary through higher education) and can be found online (https://plurimobil.ecml.at) (European Centre for Modern Languages, 2015).

Implement Training during Education Abroad

Research has shown that students experience stronger intercultural competence benefits by participating in courses on intercultural learning while they are abroad. These in-country opportunities should include:

> notions of culture, enculturation, transition shock and adaptation, adjusting to differing cultures of teaching and learning, intercultural relationship-building, L2 use in academic and social situations, intercultural conflict resolution, intercultural interaction and identity change, stereotyping and otherization, re-entry/ reverse culture shock, intercultural (communicative) competence, global identity/citizenship, and the marketing of international experience/intercultural/L2 communication skills.
>
> *(J. Jackson, 2018a, p. 376)*

The courses can be offered face-to-face or online (J. Jackson, 2018b) and can draw on textbooks on intercultural communication, such as Jackson's *Introducing Language and Intercultural Communication* (J. Jackson, 2014), or *Preparing to Study Abroad: Learning to Cross Cultures* (Duke, 2014) or the aforementioned *Maximizing Study Abroad* (Paige et al., 2002). Through targeted feedback from the instructor, students are encouraged to "think more deeply and critically about their intercultural attitudes and actions" (J. Jackson, 2018a, p. 377). Courses need to teach cultural content and frameworks and foster self-reflection while pushing students to explore values and beliefs and practice their analytical skills through readings and research (L. Engle & Engle, 2012).

When offering a full course is not possible, shorter modules can be included in classes several times throughout students' time abroad. Almeida, Fantini, Simões, and Costa (2016) suggest eight modules to be incorporated into language courses that focus, among others, on the topics what is culture, cultural relativism, living in another culture, and intercultural education. Within these modules the host culture can be "used as a basis for reflecting about the objective and subjective dimensions of culture and contrasting the multiples identities in the language classroom" (p. 523).

In addition to targeted pre-departure preparation and training while abroad, fostering intercultural competence development should extend to the time after students' return to their home country. At a minimum, post-return support should include debriefing sessions and discussions about students' experiences (Moloney & Genua-Petrovic, 2012).

Immersion in the Host Community

Research has indicated the need for fully immersing students in the host community as one of the most effective tools for intercultural learning. Immersion is crucial, because "students must interact in the culture to receive the gain of increased intercultural communication skills" (Williams, 2005, p. 370). In fact, without immersive opportunities, programs have led to a lack of intercultural development or even negative outcomes (More & Greenwood, 2019). A homestay component can promote immersion; host families can provide a safe space for students to try the language and get to know the culture (Castañeda & Zirger, 2011). As such, the families make students feel comfortable, which can also translate into "opportunities within the community for the students to constantly be engaged in language and culture learning" (Castañeda & Zirger, 2011, p. 557). Students who spent more time with their host families or other people from the host community and less time with peers from home improve their intercultural competence more strongly (Vande Berg et al., 2009), although homestays do not always lead to interaction and can also be negative experiences for students.

In order to maximize the learning that takes place through the homestays, it is helpful not only to carefully select the host families based on their own goals for participating, but also to train and prepare them for their guest, when appropriate. They could be taught fundamentals of active learning, and be encouraged to serve as cultural mentors and information source for their visiting guest (E. I. Mora, Piñero, & Díaz, 2019). Naturally, these suggestions and expectations have to be balanced with the desire to have reciprocal relationship with host families and not treating them as service providers. In programs that do not include a homestay component, students' intercultural learning can be enhanced by connecting them to local families (Almeida et al., 2016). Connecting students to the community can also include the organization of international dinners or movie nights to which local students or families are invited (Almeida et al., 2016).

Immersion can also be maximized through shared living arrangements with local university students or through engaging in activities with members of the host community. Supporting students in forming social networks with speakers of the host language(s) is crucial in offering them a stronger immersion experience. Since it may be challenging for students, especially those with limited language proficiency, to find opportunities for interacting with others, programs should help students connect with others by providing access to networks, organizing joint programs, and supporting students in finding clubs or activities in their areas of interest. Engaging in activities with members from the host community can lead to new friendships and offer many opportunities for further immersion experiences (Lofflin, 2007). Joining a sports club, choir, or dance group can be an excellent way of becoming more immersed and extending one's social network while abroad (Mitchell, 2015). Tandem partners or language exchange partners are another excellent opportunity for students to engage with community members.

Immersion also includes providing students with different opportunities for exploring the local city and country: "exposure to new places, cultures, and learning environments where a students' preconceived and established notions and beliefs are tested, may act as the catalyst or impetus for bringing forth a transformative experience" (Perry, Stoner, & Tarrant, 2012, p. 282). Immersion in the culture thus extends to cultural exploration during the program. Cultural excursions can expand classroom learning and should be connected to course content.

E. I. Mora et al. (2019) emphasize the value of moving beyond a tourist approach to sightseeing and instead allowing students to be integrated in the culture and visit places that locals also frequent. Finding members of the community to serve as guides as opposed to instructor-led tours is one step in this direction. Coffee shops, bookstores, religious sites and other places where locals meet can be included as destinations and can enhance students' insights into the host culture.

Include Service-Learning and Community Engagement

Research has shown that including service-learning projects in semester- and year-long education abroad program enhances the intercultural learning outcomes of participants (E. I. Mora et al., 2019). While students are abroad, service-learning opportunities with local businesses can support both the goal of immersion as well as the development of intercultural competence (Brandauer & Hovmand, 2013). Community-based, experiential learning activities maximize cultural immersion thereby fostering intercultural learning (L. Engle & Engle, 2012).

While host families can provide a great tool for immersion, deeper connections to other members in the community are needed to truly help students develop their intercultural competence. As E. I. Mora et al. (2019) noted, "the lack of local contacts often resulted in fundamental ignorance about Sevillian culture and society and led to the perpetuation of some stereotypes that students never overcame" (p. 75). Service-learning projects in the community can help solve this problem as they help students to move outside of their comfort zone, learn about the society in which they are studying, and move beyond stereotypical understandings of the culture.

Experiential learning can take many forms such as weekly volunteer work in local organizations, carefully selected to support the overall program goals (E. I. Mora et al., 2019). The experiential learning activities ideally are embedded within the overall programmatic objectives and coursework as much as possible. For example, students could be expected to write a reflective essay about their experience. Another option is to have students volunteer in local schools for a few hours a week (Palmer & Menard-Warwick, 2012). Students can also be involved in interviewing members of the community as part of experiential learning (Archangeli, 1999).

Internships are another option that can maximize intercultural learning during education abroad. They fit especially well with certain fields of study, for example health internships for nursing students (Evanson & Zust, 2004), consulting practicums for business students (Hawkins & Weiss, 2005), or teaching practicums for pre-service teachers (Byker & Putnam, 2018). Through these work experiences, students can be guided "along a path (which often presents a number of obstacles) through these sectors of social and human engagement so that they are exposed to the true dynamics of the changes" in the host society (Biagi, Bracci, Filippone, & Nash, 2012, p. 27). As such, experiential learning provides a unique addition to education abroad.

Service learning has to be carefully planned and implemented, especially in the case of short-term community service in developing countries where it should not be conducted only for the benefits of the students. Ethical issues ensuing from underqualified students working in settings such as healthcare or instruction might be a disservice to the community and "an unintended consequence of our actions is that people in need will end up being taken advantage of for our own ends" (Chapman, 2016, p. 1915).

Provide Mentors

Even the most qualified and well-prepared students will likely encounter difficulties and experience conflicts as they navigate their time away, especially in long-term programs. Having a mentor who can listen to their thoughts and problems can be an ideal way to support students' learning while abroad (Bacon, 2002; Root & Ngampornchai, 2013). Studies have confirmed that having a mentor while abroad is positively correlated to gains in intercultural competence (Almeida et al., 2016; Campbell & Walta, 2015; Vande Berg et al., 2009). Either an individual mentor, or group mentoring sessions can improve the intercultural outcomes (Paige & Berg, 2012).

A mentor, or cultural facilitator (Scally, 2015), can help students not only make sense of the various experiences and ups and downs that are part of a year abroad, but can also offer advice in decision-making and navigation of students' daily responsibilities. In order for effective cultural mentoring to take place, instructors need to be properly trained and possess knowledge about concepts of culture and intercultural competence (Paige & Goode, 2009). They also need to have adequate intercultural competence themselves, because "faculty with monocultural worldviews can become a hindrance for student development" (Medina-Lopez-Portillo & Salonen, 2012, p. 379). A mentor while abroad can also help students to "confront liminality, deal with disruption and dislocation, reflect on encounters with the 'other', and support them in exploring intercultural awareness" (Starr-Glass, 2020, p. 46). Another model of cultural mentoring includes having a faculty member from the home institution who meets with the participants virtually. This faculty member should be an expert in the language and culture and can offer support and advice as well as guide students through assessment tasks that foster reflection (Giovanangeli, Oguro, & Harbon, 2018).

Ideally, mentoring for education abroad is two-fold: Students should have both an experienced faculty member as cultural guide as well as a peer mentor from the host community. Several programs make use of a buddy system which pairs local students with international ones to help them not only with settling into the new environment but also with cultural differences. If the buddy program includes targeted activities which the partners complete together, it can be a mutual intercultural learning experience. For example, the partners could complete a service project together such as volunteering in the community (Wilson-Forsberg, Power, Kilgour, Darling, & Laurier, 2018).

Connecting incoming and outgoing international students can be useful if their times in the host community overlap. For example, in the AYF program students in Freiburg meet the students, who will be studying at their respective home universities in the upcoming year. Those students then are part of orientation and social events at the home university to prepare students for study in Freiburg. Peer-group activities could be an important learning opportunity for those that are new to the country as well as those who are about to return home (Tonkin & Coudray, 2016).

Provide Support from the Home and Host University

The university abroad plays an important role in supporting students in their journey to become global citizens and develop their intercultural competence. They can help students establish their social network by offering activities for international and local students or implementing specific programs such as buddy programs, mentoring services, language tandems, etc. Additionally, the host university can provide access to community resources for students (Perez-Encinas, 2016). In order to create an inclusive environment that embraces diversity, the host university is encouraged to organize specific events that integrate the international students and highlight the diverse cultures represented on campus (H.-p. Wu, Garza, & Guzman, 2015).

The host university can help students adjust not just academically, but also socially and culturally (Ammigan, 2019). This can include helping students find student organizations to join or campus activities to try (H.-p. Wu et al., 2015). Studies have shown that students highly value support in establishing connections to local students (Ammigan, 2019). Other possible support services include orientation weeks, offering language courses or culture adaptation courses (Perez-Encinas, Rodriguez-Pomeda, & Josek, 2017).

Along with host university administrative support and support from offices for international students, faculty also supports students' adjustment and intercultural growth. Whenever possible, home and host institutions should make counselling services available to students which can help with acculturation stress, adjustment problems, and other difficulties that advisors or education abroad staff may not be qualified to handle (Lértora, Sullivan, & Croffie, 2017). Students' mental and physical well-being has to be a priority so they can gain the benefits of inter-cultural learning during their time abroad. The specific support services needed to help students with their cultural adjustment depend on the length of the pro-gram, student background, and individual factors; there is not one-size-fits-all approach. The best support is tailored to the individual needs of the students.

Engage Students in Research

Another strategy for enhancing intercultural competence is to engage students in research or ethnographic projects. Having students complete original research while abroad allows them to combine the skills they learned during their semester or year abroad and produce an analytic and reflective final project that showcases their abilities and cultural learning (More & Greenwood, 2019). Its compilation fosters deeper intercultural learning and enables students to reflect on what they have learned over the course of their time abroad. Action research projects can be a great way for students to learn more about topics they find particularly inter-esting in the context of the host language and/or culture. Goertler and the 369ers (2019) showed how action research prompts students to notice differences between what they learned about the culture and language at home and what they actually perceived abroad.

Students who study abroad for an entire year have sufficient time and can begin their research during the first semester, begin collecting data, and use the second semester for analyzing their topic related to culture in their target country. The research can be supervised by a faculty member at their home institution remotely (Oguro, 2016) if there is no faculty member abroad with them. Smaller ethnographic projects as part of coursework also have the benefit of promoting openness toward learning about other cultures (Bateman, 2002). Similarly, eth-nographic research can help students pay more attention to their surroundings, thereby getting to know the culture more in-depth (J. Jackson, 2006b). Ethno-graphic interviews with members of the community can be a great source of learning on which students can reflect in additional course assignments such as their blogs or journals (L. Lee, 2012).

In order to truly get to know another culture and gain intercultural awareness, students have to possess language proficiency that allows them to interact with the members of the community and participate as much as possible in all aspects of life abroad. Therefore, fostering language skills is an important step in promoting the development of intercultural competence. One way to support language learning is by incorporating a language pledge (L. Engle & Engle, 2012) which can be espe-cially useful for island programs where students interact primarily with members of their own community. Specific suggestions for promoting language learning during education were outlined in the previous chapter.

Chapter 3.4. Maximizing Program Design

Introduction

This book set out to provide stakeholders with research- and practice-informed information on how to maximize the effectiveness of education abroad programs, diversify participation, and reinvigorate the JYA. While education abroad programs are increasing, there is still room for reaching a more diverse audience and making education abroad more inclusive and equitable. Program design has also changed driven by political and educational developments as well as the market and financial concerns. With the diversification of the student population, destinations, and program types came a prioritization of goals. In the following, we discuss program design features that maximize education abroad's impact.

A first step in improving program design is considering the *Study Abroad Matters Guide* (Institute of International Education & AIFS, 2018) with its eight recommendations:

- Start outreach in the student's first year.
- Foster collaboration between education abroad and career services.
- Improve communication between college and industry.
- Keep employability skills in mind when designing programs.
- Expand and promote internship offerings abroad.
- Encourage underrepresented students to participate.
- Recruit STEM students.
- Track employment outcomes.

The *Study Abroad Matters Guide* has a heavy focus on employability and no mention of language and intercultural competence or community impact. As language educators, our primary focus for education abroad is on language and intercultural competence development. Hence, with our book we hope to build and expand from those recommendations to also address humanistic and community goals.

Designing Education Abroad

We applaud the trend in education abroad to greater diversity in all aspects of program design. To maximally support students, it is important to provide access to a variety of program types and properly advise students for the best choice. It is unrealistic for smaller universities and colleges to have the same diversity of programs as an institution like MSU. We therefore encourage large universities to make their programs available to students from other institutions and encourage small universities to remove barriers for students to participate in those programs and market them to their students.

As advocates for education abroad, we urge institutions to make education abroad a core and integrated component of the institution's educational mission. Expanding from others, we recommend the following guiding design principles of education abroad:

- Intentional design.
- Integrated curriculum.
- Structured reflection.
- Experiential and immersive curricular and co-curricular components.
- Intensive and reciprocal relationships with the community.
- Iterative program evaluation involving a multitude of stakeholders using quantitative and qualitative measures.
- Equity, inclusion, accessibility and diversity.

Destination

Destinations have diversified and can still be diversified further. MSU recently changed its education abroad office's structure from being organized geographically to being organized disciplinarily. Students should be motivated and advised to select programs based on their academic interests, needs, and professional goals and not their consumer interests. This shift to thinking about destinations based on goals not only informs students' program selection, but also program designers' destination choices.

In program design, ideally destinations are selected carefully to address the learning goals and needs of the student population. We discourage institutions from focusing solely on major tourist hubs. Yet, at times a trip to a major tourist attraction in the country/region might need to be included to make the program more attractive. Destinations should be selected with a focus on maximizing the local resources, expertise and opportunities while mitigating the risk of a negative impact on the community.

Program Type

It is important to offer different program types and advise students appropriately. For example, students who are and need more independence and have good language proficiency in the language(s) of the community, can be encouraged to participate in a direct-enroll program; whereas students with less language proficiency and more service needs might be better suited by a short-term faculty-led program. Introverted students might be better suited by a long-term program than a short-term program.

Reciprocal Partnerships

Education abroad has the potential of having a negative impact on the host community through reinforcing power hierarchies, viewing the destination from an ethnocentric perspective, and treating the local community from a consumerist perspective. Kortegast and Kupo (2017) as well as the authors in Crawford and Berquist (2020) provide guidelines for designing ethical programs focusing on a two-way relationship.

Housing

Since participants have different circumstances, needs, and goals, whenever feasible it is good to strive to provide different housing types and scenarios to be more inclusive and equitable.

Living with members of the local community whether in dorms or host families is beneficial for the development of linguistic and intercultural competences and especially in long-term programs results in life-long friendships. Living with host community members has also been found beneficial for psychological well-being (O'Reilly, Ryan, & Hickey, 2010). However, simply living with community members is not enough. Several recommendations have been made to improve the effectiveness of living situations:

- Carefully select and match living situations and families/peers whenever possible.
- Remind participants that host families are not service providers.
- Prepare students for the homestay (Benson, 2017; Goode, 2008; Mitchell et al., 2015).
- Teach students agency and their role in creating communicative situations in culturally sensitive ways.
- Provide guidelines and training to host families/roommates on how to support student learning (Castañeda & Zirger, 2011) and also provide the family with agency.
- Create a buddy system for the dorms (Di Silvio et al., 2014).
- Create and require interaction and engagement activities with the people the participants live with (Knight & Schmidt-Rinehart, 2010; Vande Berg et al., 2009).

For more detail, Di Silvio et al. (2014) provide a great set of recommendations to maximize host family experiences.

While we can set up access to the local community through living arrangements, we cannot control how the community responds. For students placed with host families that relationship invariably plays a significant role in their experience abroad and subsequent learning outcomes. For example, programs who value immersion and cultural interaction will seek families who view students as part of the family instead of as lodgers paying rent. More engagement will lead to more learning (Vande Berg et al., 2009). Despite pre-screening and the possibility that the family or family members and the student simply do not get along, there may be cultural issues around family life in the education abroad site that may limit or enhance interaction and thereby learning in quantity and in quality (Collentine, 2009; Iino, 2006; Tanaka, 2007; Wilkinson, 1998). Programs can use pre-departure orientations to share cultural expectations in living situations. Yet not all families will match these assumed expectations or may apply different expectations to a guest from another culture. Programs may need to provide handbooks and tasks to facilitate reciprocal and meaningful interactions and relationships.

For students placed in dorms, the program may have limited control over the choice of room and our roommates/flatmates. Participants may live primarily with other international students or members of the host community with no interest in communicating with peers who are only there for a limited amount of time. While programs cannot control the flatmates, they are able to teach participants strategies to engage with others in the dorm complex. Similar to the assertion that simply being abroad is not enough for language gains, Trentman (2013) found that living in dorms does not automatically lead to increased interaction. Especially when students share dorm rooms or apartments with members of their own culture or other international students comfortable in English, there are often limited opportunities for practicing the L2 (George, 2019). However, staying in a residence hall can lead to increased language learning when students establish positive relationships with their roommates (Kinginger & Wu, 2018). Social networks are easier to establish for students who live with peers from the host community (Ring et al., 2013).

When interviewing AYF students (all of whom live in dorms) about their connection with the community, we found unexpected patterns. As Resident Director, Senta Goerter assumed that students who lived with other students from the program would have a harder time connecting with their flatmates, who were not from the program. However, in interviewing students, it became clear that many students found the comfort of having another student from the program helped them venture into the common area and then also connect with the non-program flatmates. In several cases, the AYF students were able to negotiate a misunderstanding or a communication challenge with the assistance of the other program member. Similarly, in one dorm that had a surprisingly high number of flatmates who were mostly not home, successful students utilized another AYF student in the same dorm who lived in a more interactive environment to gain access to host community members. This is to say that we typically cannot control who the students live with, but we can teach them how to use a buddy system to increase their social network.

Curriculum

In education abroad curriculum design goes far beyond individual courses during the program. Here are the guiding principles for curriculum design:

- Make education abroad a core of the degree program.
- Integrate and articulate at-home curricula pre- and post-education abroad with those in the host community abroad.
- Include transition components both before (e.g., language and culture training, logistics workshops, ethnographic skills, preparing for culture-shock, telecollaboration with abroad community; etc.) and after (e.g., unpacking the experience, marketing experience, dealing with reverse culture shock, capstone paper, etc.). A great example of integrated intercultural curriculum that includes pre-departure and post-departure activities is described by Bathurst and Brack (2012).
- Integrate curricular (coursework) with co-curricular experiences (service learning, field trips, internships, etc.).
- Follow a just-in-time pedagogy that stays flexible to the developments and experiences of students before during and after education abroad.
- Create opportunities for inter-, trans- and multidisciplinary learning
- Include experiential and immersive learning activities
- Adjust the curriculum to different academic disciplines, language proficiency levels, and academic skills through subcontracting special sheltered immersion interdisciplinary courses.
- Think locally and act globally: create a hyper local curriculum with a global impact. Offer discipline-specific program components with localized and globally relevant experiential components (e.g., lectures by experts, clinical experiences, research projects, etc.)

Kortegast and Kupo (2017) provide excellent critical reflection questions and tasks for ethical program design and implementation. The tasks are as follows:

- Identify and employ a pedagogy that disrupts postcolonial practices, commodification, and cultural tourism.
- Create/adopt a framework that acknowledges the impact of power, oppression, tourism, and community on the participant, community members, and overall learning experience.
- Identify opportunities to role model ways to intervene, ask questions, make meaning, and complicate conversations about their experiences.
- Focus learning outcomes on measurable outcomes that include intercultural learning and country appropriate cultural expectations and values.
- Broaden conversations about expectations and experiences to include purpose of the experience, biases, and in-country expectations.
- Build reflection and small group interactions into the curriculum.
- Provide participants opportunities to engage with their daily experiences and encourage reflection and learning.
- Provide writing and discussion prompts that include opportunities to think about and process personal values, biases, and experiences.

These prompts should provide opportunities to engage students in different ways (writing, small group/large group discussions, group projects, etc.).

- Engage in conversations that address issues of power, privilege, consumerism, and representation of knowledge.
- Create opportunities for participants to develop group projects that will be presented once back in country.
- Provide experiences that go beyond reunion type activities.
- Structured interactions regarding re-entry issues, sharing experiences (in-country and post-study abroad), and personal interactions should be included.
- Develop opportunities for students to engage in meaning-making opportunities that encourage reflection. Engagement should include articulation of emerging knowledge, skills, and competencies developed during study abroad experience.
- Support opportunities for presentations to campus and local communities that focus on in-country experiences. These presentations can include photo essays and research projects.

(Kortegast & Kupo, 2017, pp. 165–166)

Experiential Learning

Experiential learning opportunities such as internships, excursions/field trips, service-learning/community-engagement projects, immersion tasks, and research projects enhance education abroad. Whenever possible, these activities should be designed with the students' and the community's goals and needs in mind and fully integrated into the curriculum.

Two long-standing effective service-learning education abroad projects are: (1) The ethnography project at Earlham College; and (2) the K-Project – the Integrative Cultural Research Project at Kalamazoo College. In both cases, students participate in service projects in the host community or communities. At Earlham, students are taught ethnographic skills and asked to complete ethnographic tasks culminating in an ethnography. The Kalamazoo students are asked to make DIVE (describe, interpret, verify, evaluate) observations culminating in a research presentation. Service learning can help students "understand specific social problems and the process of lending assistance" while at the same time increasing their "interest in service, the host country, and its people" (Sachau, Brasher, & Fee, 2010, p. 656).

In pre-professional programs service-learning can take on the form of clinical experiences. Nursing students in a two-week experiential program in Central America significantly increased their perceived self-efficacy and felt more confident in working with diverse individuals (Long, 2014). Anita and McKenry (1999) compared students completing a short-term clinical experience at home versus abroad and found the abroad students showed higher self-efficacy development.

Some internships operate in English (Kurasawa & Nagatomi, 2006), which may not always be known or desired by the program or the participant – though there is some research that suggests that students prefer internships where host language skills are not needed (Steeves, 2006). Students report most positively about internships that allow them to work collaboratively and where they felt comfortable given their language proficiency (He & Qin, 2017). In addition to the language issues, there are also cultural issues that influence the internship placement. For example, in the German education system an unpaid internship must be tied to an educational program. In the case of the AYF that means that we offer an internship course, in which we unpack the internship experience. In overseeing the internship program in the AYF program, Senta Goerter found that many conflicts between internship hosts and education abroad participants could be traced to the cultural value of "Eigenverantwortung" (responsibility and initiative for oneself). For example, one participant continuously reported not having anything to do and projects being taken away from her. She was frustrated that the internship supervisors were not teaching her and not providing her with learning opportunities. At the same time, the internship supervisors were frustrated that the intern asked too many questions and never solved issues on her own, and that she did not see things that needed to get done. This conflict between the student expecting to be taught, guided, and provided with opportunities and the hosts expecting interns to be independent and taking charge was seen to varying degrees in almost all internships. As a consequence, we integrated materials that introduced students to expectations of interns and internship providers in the German context, with one of those elements being "Eigenverantwortung."

When designing community-engagement projects, a few design principles need to be taken into consideration (expanded from the authors in Crawford & Berquist, 2020):

- Collaboratively designed with the partners.
- Bidirectional.
- Reciprocal.
- Community voices respected and recognized.
- Preparation for the project prior to departure.
- Facilitation, reflection, and guidance throughout the project.

Immersion, Reflection, and Guidance

The effectiveness of education abroad experiences in regard to intercultural and language development often depends on the relationship with community members in the host community. When programs maximize the curricular and co-curricular opportunities that engage learners with the community, language learning is positively impacted (Castañeda & Zirger, 2011). Many programs leave it up to the students to create those opportunities or assume by simply connecting the students to community members through housing arrangements, tandem partnerships, field trips, etc. the students will be able to develop relationships that lead to language and culture learning. As Castañeda and Zirger (2011) point out, such relationships may or may not materialize without facilitation. Furthermore, simply increasing the quantity of L2 use may not positively contribute to language learning gains, as the quality of such interactions is more important than the quantity of interactions (Baker-Smemoe et al., 2014). Experiential and immersive experiences can come in different formats. They can be co-curricular components such as communication tasks or the main component of a program such as the research projects, internships, or work obligations.

Tasks designed to encourage interaction with the host community have a positive impact on intercultural outcomes (Antonakopoulou, 2013). Archangeli (1999) found that students conducting interviews with native speakers gave learners more self-confidence to interact with native speakers, increased their willingness to seek opportunities to converse with host community members, and forced them to expand their linguistic repertoire beyond that in a casual conversation. It was important that these tasks were integrated into the regular curriculum. Baker-Smemoe et al. (2014) found that providing access to community members and teaching strategies how to create and maintain a social network improved language and culture immersion. They hypothesized that the explicit requirement for learners to interact with NS (presumably made available by the program) was helpful.

Cadd (2012) suggests that students must have incentives to interact with community members and lays out a series of 12 tasks that encouraged students to purposefully and actively engage with host community members. The tasks decreased anxiety, increased willingness to speak, deepened understanding of culture, increased fluency and the ability to circumlocute according to self-report data, which contributed to their self-efficacy. Buddy programs with peers from the community can have a positive impact on language learning (Hennings & Tanabe, 2018; Pyper & Slagter, 2015) and cultural adjustment (J. H. Lee, 2018). Social events organized by the program are more successful in immersing students than expecting students to seek their own social opportunities (Surtees, 2018).

Some immersive tasks include more components than simply completing a communicative task with host community members. For example, in the program described by Prokhorov and Therkelsen (2015), students work in teams to produce a film, interview local community members, and research their selected topic. In the process they develop media literacy, Russian proficiency, and research competencies.

The quality and quantity of immersive and experiential experiences of an education abroad program design has an impact on participants' learning outcomes and the community. However, simply including such experiences in the curriculum might still be insufficient. Engberg and Jourian (2015) found that beyond mere participation in co-curricular activities during education abroad and in community experiences, discussing their experiences, using the language outside of the classroom, and having faculty support were all important for developing cultural competence.

Reflection and raising awareness are critical to development of intercultural competence. These activities are most effective when integrated into coursework or other mandatory program components. Language courses can be an important place for students to reflect on their education abroad and not only process what they experienced but also further their understanding through targeted readings (Kruse & Brubaker, 2007). In order to facilitate reflection, students can be given cultural and language concepts which can help them better understand what they are experiencing abroad (Paige, Harvey, & McCleary, 2012). Reflection can be integrated in education abroad programs of all lengths in a variety of ways. Regular guidance and meaningful reflection at multiple points before, during, and after education abroad are crucial for students' intercultural learning (Pilon, 2017).

It must be emphasized that reflective activities in and of themselves do not lead to increases in intercultural competence (Paige & Berg, 2012). Students also have to be guided and supported in their reflections in order to benefit from the integration of such activities in education abroad, because "unexamined cultural experiences do not facilitate intercultural competence development" (Hammer, 2012, p. 131).

According to Grimes-MacLellan (2018) experiential learning has the potential to be a transformative experience for students if "students are embedded in authentic activity in the host country that promotes deep and extended engagement with host country nationals" (p. 166). As summarized by Montrose (2002), an experiential education abroad program should include the key principles of: Intention, authenticity, planning, clarity, monitoring and assessment, reflection, evaluation, and acknowledgment. When these principles are followed, experiential learning in education abroad adds an invaluable dimension because it can "foster growth in intercultural competence, reinforce and deepen classroom learning about host societies, and contribute to students' fluency in the target languages" (Steinberg, 2002, p. 222).

Many experiential learning opportunities also promote community building among students (Convertini, 2019). Experiential learning abroad "engages students in a deliberate process of hands-on problem solving and critical thinking" (Montrose, 2002, p. 3.). Adding experiential learning opportunities to education abroad programs is seen as an effective way to foster global citizenship (Tarrant, Rubin, & Stoner, 2014), problem-solving skills (Hawkins & Weiss, 2005), soft skills and sensitivity (Zamastil-Vondrova, 2005), and cross-cultural awareness (Malewski, Sharma, & Phillion, 2012). What is important to remember is that these outcomes are all only potentials and require careful program design.

To improve reflection, immersion, and guidance in education abroad:

- Provide strategy training to participants (see for example the *Maximizing Study Abroad Guide*: Paige, Cohen, Kappler, Chi, & Lassegard, 2002).
- Include immersion tasks before, during, and after education abroad (see for example Cadd, 2012).
- Include reflection and awareness-raising tasks before, during, and after education abroad. (good example for during: Pedersen, 2010; good example for after: Allison, Davis-Berman & Berman, 2011).
- Provide opportunities for individual as well as group reflection (Allison, Davis-Berman & Berman, 2012).
- Conduct reflective progress checks throughout facilitated and supported in mentoring sessions (Watson & Wolfel, 2015)
- Provide guidance and facilitations before, during, and after education abroad.
- Organize social activities with community members.
- Provide tutors, peer mentors, and buddies as cultural facilitators and tandem partners.
- Require community-based ethnographic research.

Preparing and Supporting Faculty

Faculty roles in education abroad are varied and are expansive for education abroad faculty-leaders. They can be conduits of program information through simple announcements in classes (90% of students participating in language classes reported that they gained at least some information about the education abroad through their language instructor), class visits, special presentations, and individual advising sessions (Chieffo & Zipser, 2001). Faculty program leaders can prepare and support students for logistical, health and safety, cultural, linguistic, and academic issues and assist them when these issues arise. Faculty leaders play important roles before, during, and after education abroad to design, implement, assess, and promote programs.

Faculty training for education abroad often centers on risk management and laws, the dominant themes from a liability standpoint. This leaves faculty unprepared for many of the other roles (Barnhart, Ricks, & Spier, 1997; Goode, 2008) and they often do not have adequate support for the various tasks they have to perform (Hornig, 1995; O'Neal & Krueger, 1995).

Goode (2008) summarizes research pointing to the lack of formal training and preparation for education abroad leaders. It is not surprising that the faculty leaders interviewed also expressed that their degree programs did not prepare them for being an education abroad leader. Faculty typically only receive one workshop from the education abroad unit, which often focuses on logistics, health, and safety. However, they viewed the workshops positively and reported benefiting from the logistical tips and the advice from more experienced education abroad leaders. Faculty feel underprepared to fulfill the role of a Dean of Students (Goode, 2008), since at home the faculty member would send referrals to that office, but not actually oversee the handling of issues better left to experts. Faculty leaders in Goode's (2008) study stressed the importance of faculty planning for logistical issues far in advance and yet building in enough flexibility to adjust to changing conditions and circumstances. Faculty leaders are also often given generic and program-specific handbooks which serve as resources for tasks from pre-departure to re-entry (e.g., Goode, 2008). From our own experience and mirroring the reports from the faculty in Goode's studies, while newcomers benefit from workshops and handbooks, true learning often does not happen until one is in the position and faculty therefore clearly need support while they are abroad and after they return.

Program leaders may themselves not be adequately trained and skilled in intercultural competence, which may hinder their ability to support their students' development (Goode, 2008). Faculty with limited intercultural competence negatively impact the students' ability to further develop their intercultural competence (Medina-Lopez-Portillo & Salonen, 2012; Paige & Goode, 2009). Faculty understand that having some knowledge about the program site and having insights about the culture are part of the faculty leader role (Goode, 2008), yet a one-time pre-program site visit alone is not enough to help faculty understand the cultural complexities of the host community and are thereby inadequate without additional preparation. Moseley (2009) speaks of the importance of preparing hyper-localized curricula to not just prepare students but also the faculty member for the cultural context. While the director of the education abroad office in Goode's (2008) study reported that intercultural development was a topic covered in the faculty workshop, the faculty did not appear to have noticed such preparation. Faculty leaders also reported that their own previous intercultural experiences – be it at home or abroad – had prepared them for their roles. Yet only five of the eight faculty leaders reported having had specific intercultural experiences prior to departure and these varied greatly in quality and quantity. Goode (2008) investigated education abroad leader's intercultural development using the IDI and found them mostly to be in the ethnocentric dimension, while perceiving themselves in the first stages of ethnorelativism. Kinginger (2010) also hints that leaders can be ethnocentric. She points out:

> it may be that in some cases, the very people who are charged with providing insight on international education are blinded by illusions of national superiority and contribute to the construction of dominant discourses in which education of true quality can only be found in the United States.
>
> (Kinginger, 2010, p. 223)

We agree with Goode (2008) that education abroad offices should include more training for faculty directors on intercultural development to both develop their ICC and their ability to support students in their intercultural development.

In many cases current levels of preparation, support, and compensation/ rewards for faculty leaders are insufficient. Given the variety of roles that education abroad leaders take on before, during, and after education abroad, they need to be prepared for and supported in dealing with:

- Logistics.
- Health and safety.
- Language proficiency.
- Intercultural competence and (reverse) culture shock.
- Conduct, policies, and laws.
- Supporting and working with diverse students.
- Pedagogy of education abroad (including a focus on language and ICC development, equity, inclusion, diversity, and accessibility).
- The emotional labor involved in such an intensive experience, especially with supporting students in mental health crises.

In short, faculty need to be prepared for and supported in their wider roles. A good resource guide for faculty – though older – is provided by Barnhart et al. (1997). Handbooks, trainings, and a mentor network can be helpful for education abroad leaders.

The American Association of University Professors (1995) suggests that accompanying faculty should be tenured faculty members to avoid abuse and ensure long-term understanding of and investment in the institution. Pre-tenured faculty members leading education abroad might slow their progress towards tenure. One informant, who had led education abroad during his pre-tenure time, expressed that his mentors discouraged him from leading education abroad. Yet, like Moseley, he was able to justify his participation by combining his research with the education abroad leadership and including undergraduate participants as collaborators on his research at the education abroad site.

Faculty leaders' compensation must be appropriate with the expanded role, ideally without passing those costs on to the education abroad participants. Similarly, education abroad leadership needs to be aligned with other job and promotion requirements, so that the experience counts for promotion and annual review at home. Preparation of faculty must include a realistic discussion of the time, resources, energy, and emotional commitment required so that faculty can negotiate sustainable circumstances and adequate compensation and recognition.

Moseley provides the following policy suggestions:

> providing small amounts of funding for faculty and student research done within the context of study abroad programs; consideration of involvement

with study abroad programs as a positive contribution when reviewing a faculty member's tenure portfolio; support of publications based on faculty-student collaborative research which evolves out of study abroad programming; and greater recognition that junior faculty who become involved with study abroad programs may have different needs than more senior faculty (such as time for research and writing, responsibilities related to young children, etc.).

(Moseley, 2009, p. 237)

To not overwhelm faculty leaders, it might be advantageous to find local partners to provide some of the services that students are used to from home and look to the faculty leader to fulfill (e.g., writing center, tutoring, mental health support, student activities, etc). This might also help with the dilemma of wanting faculty and staff to be adequately compensated while at the same time keeping programs affordable. Sharing expenses with other institutions or including direct-enroll or third-party programs or third-party support might also help cut costs and reduce workloads. Naturally, one must then keep in mind that faculty and staff hired locally might be unfamiliar with US (educational) culture and might require extra preparation (Goode, 2008).

Recruiting Participants

The role that education abroad plays in the overall educational experience of students starts with how such experiences are portrayed in marketing materials. Programs, especially from third party vendors, economically depend on enrollments. The marketing materials often look like travel brochures "with promises of adventure and opportunities to experience new cultures" (Kortegast & Kupo, 2017, p. 155). Chieffo and Zipser (2001) describe the university programs at Delaware differently:

We take care to portray our programs not as a vacation or a trip abroad but rather as a serious scholastic endeavor. A good recruiter has the ability to persuade students that study abroad can be both an enjoyable experience and a worthwhile academic activity.

(Chieffo & Zipser, 2001p. 81)

How programs are marketed influences what students expect and the attitude they have toward their education abroad experience and the community (Kortegast & Kupo, 2017).

In order to encourage more students to consider education abroad and adequately prepare them, a concerted effort is needed to internationalize K–12 schools in an equitable and accessible way. Language instruction should not be a luxury item, but home language support and additional language instruction need to be available for all students if we want to make education abroad more accessible. At MSU, we have a Community Language School (CLS) that offers language instruction to children as young as 3 years old all the way to adults. The CLS offers classes both on campus as well as conducts outreach in schools. Such programs can play an important role in both expanding the reach of language instruction and diversifying the language offerings.

In addition to language preparation, fostering intercultural competence and a curiosity about other communities can positively contribute to students' preparation for and willingness to participate in education abroad. Some ideas to diversify schools are: An increase of communities covered and discussed in the curriculum (their histories, culture, arts, literature, etc.), integration of people from a variety of cultural backgrounds on all levels of schools. Planting a seed of curiosity about other communities, is an important step in opening students to the possibility of education abroad.

If general college recruitment visits and materials include education abroad information (including debunking some of the myths about education abroad), prospective students might factor in the education abroad offerings in their consideration for selecting a college. The earlier the students make a decision to participate in education abroad, the more carefully their educational trajectory can be planned to maximize the efficient and effective integration of education abroad in their degree program. We encourage education abroad administrators to form partnerships with feeder schools to identify students with a predisposition for education abroad before they even enter college.

Recruitment and preparation for education abroad starts as soon as students commit to the university. Hossler and Gallagher (1987, as cited in Hackney, Boggs, & Borozan, 2012) define three stages of decision-making for education abroad: "(a) the development of the pre-disposition or intent to study abroad, (b) the search for a suitable program, and (c) the selection of and departure for a specific location and program" (p. 124). We have argued above that the first phase can or should be during K–12.

During the active recruitment period after students arrived on campus, it is important to offer targeted support and preparation for students. Students with different backgrounds, abilities, and needs require different types of support before, during, and after education abroad. For example, students with disabilities depend on specific support structures and mentoring already at the planning stage and when selecting an education abroad destination (Ablaeva, 2012). Advisors can help find a program that can accommodate their needs (Soneson & Cordano, 2009). Students of color and other minoritized students in education abroad also depend on different support structures, but more research is needed to provide specific guidelines (Sweeney, 2013). It is clear, however, that individual differences, contexts and goals impact which programs are best for students and they need help in identifying those programs and preparing for them.

Expanding from the recommendations in Chapter 3.1 and based on information from practitioners and research, we make the following additional recommendations for recruitment:

- Use values-based recruitment materials that advertise programs as an enjoyable scholarly experience not a fun trip.
- Include information about the education abroad programs, the communities and community members in the regular curriculum.
- Identify appropriate feeder classes, go on class visits, and follow up with personalized emails and conversations which include instructors, advisors, and guardians when appropriate.
- Identify students who have already gone abroad or have language skills in the host language(s) as they are more likely to participate.
- Have faculty advocate for education abroad in their classes.
- Include a variety of alumni in recruitment to showcase stories of success and also help the alumni further reflect and process their experiences.
- Provide accurate information for informed decision-making.
- Debunk misinformation and break down fears.
- Involve all stakeholders.
- Upsell: encourage longer experiences or more immersive experiences as they fit with the prospective participant's goals and needs.

Preparing Participants

Preparation starts with peeking a student's curiosity about education abroad – potentially long before they come to our campuses via general recruitment brochures or targeted mailing to applicants. Preparing students includes special mentions of education abroad in the curriculum at the home campus or even assignments that explore the history, culture, language, and significance of the education abroad locations. It also includes the more common elements, such as pre-departure orientation and intensive language courses. People involved with preparation include the family and support networks of participants, academic advisors and regular faculty members, program leaders, peer mentors, financial aid and scholarship staff, and the support and administrative staff in an Education Abroad Office. It may also include professionals in campus health and counseling services.

To prepare and support students for education abroad, we recommend:

- Communicate with and prepare the student and their support network.
- Build relationships with advisors across campus to determine plans to work within graduation requirements and learning goals.
- Build strong relationships with financial aid and donors to make more funding accessible to students.

- Identify requirements that can and requirements that cannot be fulfilled abroad or through education abroad.
- Provide collaborative academic planning that includes home advisors as well as program representatives.
- Bring the target community already to the students (e.g., virtual tandem partnerships).
- Before abroad, connect students with international students on campus.
- Prepare students for common challenges.
- Help students develop agency.
- Teach emotional regulation strategies.
- Assist students with the logistics and emotions of transitioning abroad.

In addition to resources mentioned in the previous chapters, Highum (2014) also provided a good resource for pre-departure.

Preparation for education abroad is important in the curriculum. For example, service learning with reflection before going abroad can be beneficial. Brockington and Wiedenhoft (2009) describe the integration of service learning into the overall curricula at two liberal arts colleges (Earlham and Kalamazoo Colleges). Their description of the experiences of students suggest that experience with co-curricular activities that require reflection as well as service-learning activities prior to participation in an education abroad program, allows learners to more effectively and ethically engage in the global aspects of a service-learning project abroad. They conclude:

> There should be a rigorous on-campus program that promotes: understanding diverse cultures and understanding cultures as diverse; developing intercultural skills; understanding global processes; preparing for citizenship, both local and global. A study abroad program that is integrated into an on-campus curriculum and that also seeks to integrate and support students in new intercultural settings will do much to produce global citizens who are home in the world.
>
> *(Brockington & Wiedenhoft, 2009, p. 131)*

In addition to general cultural sensitivity, students also benefit from being prepared for common challenges in education abroad and to be taught strategies to take agency in their own learning and experience (Pyper & Slagter, 2015).

Chieffo and Zipser (2001) found that students in language classes were more informed about the programs and the destinations than those not in those classes. In the German program at MSU, we have revised our curriculum in the Basic Language Program to include units on our education abroad destination to assist with recruitment and preparation (Goertler & McEwen, 2018). The curriculum, for example, includes an activity in which students compare information about different living situations in one education abroad program and then argue which one would be best for them and why. Students reported having found that helpful in both imagining possible education abroad participation as well as making an actual decision on housing when they did decide on AYF. Another form of preparing students for abroad is through engaging them in online communities in the host community prior to education abroad, which helps students get ready, spark their interest, and builds their confidence. Another effective preparation technique is to train students in ethnographic research, which helps them process their experiences while abroad (Allen & Dupuy, 2013).

It is important that students develop agency in the learning process. They must be encouraged to be active participants in their relationships and provided with the tools to navigate their identities and roles:

> students should be encouraged to clearly demonstrate their interest in engaging with their host families and to be proactive in pursuing interactions and activities. It is critical that students understand that extensive interaction with native speakers does not happen automatically during study abroad, but rather requires a personal commitment to generating and taking advantage of speaking opportunities.
>
> *(Di Silvio et al., 2014, p. 180)*

Before departing, students need to be made aware of how to maximize their learning while abroad, for example by providing strategies for integrating with the host community. Even before they leave their home countries, students need assistance in gaining learner autonomy (Meier & Daniels, 2013). Pre-departure workshops can better prepare students to both deal with potential challenges they may encounter abroad as well as help them better understand intercultural issues (Penman & Ratz, 2015). Creating agency in students, so that they become active contributors in their interactions abroad is an important design feature of effective education abroad programs (Allen & Dupuy, 2013).

With a diversification of participants, it is crucial to work with students individually to maximize their learning outcomes in relation to their goals. For example, teach students how to use technology to support their education abroad and caution them about ways that it hinders their education abroad experience (Hofer, Thebodo, Meredith, Kaslow, & Saunders, 2016). Butler (2019) points out that in order to maximize learning from education abroad, "students must be appropriately supported in their cognitive, psychosocial, and emotional development" (p. 146). In long-term programs, it is advantageous to reduce the involvement and support from staff as students become more comfortable in the environment to ultimately allow them to navigate the place independently.

Course options and pedagogical experiences vary greatly by program type. If students are engaged in service learning, internships, research, or community engagement, a strong disciplinary background will allow them to be a true contributor to those experiences. Furthermore, students who intend to take coursework in the host community will perform better, if they already have a solid disciplinary background in the courses chosen. For example, a student in a program led by Senta Goerter selected a number of STEM courses in Germany, despite limited language proficiency. To the program leadership's surprise, the student did very well in the courses and attributed their strong disciplinary preparation at home to their success abroad.

Supporting Participants

It takes a large network to recruit, prepare, and support education abroad participants before, during, and after education abroad. This support network benefits from frequent and transparent communication and the more experienced and expert members of that network providing support not just to the students but the other members. In most programs there is room to enhance and expand communication among the network. This network may include: Education abroad office staff, education abroad leaders and personnel, advisors, professors, administrators, host institution staff and faculty, peers, parents/guardians, family members, employers, etc. Preparation and support needs to start long before students come to college and continue after they graduate. We suggest involving peer mentors and faculty and support personnel at-home and in the host community working together. It is worth acknowledging that today's parents are more involved in their students' lives and it might be necessary and/or advantageous to include parents and guardians in all phases of education abroad.

When programs diversify their student population, it is important that program spokespeople communicate openly, frequently, effectively, and appropriately with the new population and with their faculty and academic advisors. It could be advantageous for programs to conduct needs analyses to better understand the needs and goals of the (new) students and their academic units. Since circumstances and populations change, we recommend that programs continuously evaluate their programs in respect to the needs and goals set forth by the students, their academic programs, and the education abroad program itself. Such information can then also lead to providing accurate information about the opportunities, expectations, services, and curriculum of the program to the students and their support network. For example, practitioners perceive an increased need in mental wellness and programs would want to be upfront about what they can and cannot offer. Ideally mental wellness preparation starts pre-departure (Allen & Herron, 2003; Elemo & Turkum, 2019) and continues while abroad in both individual as well as group settings (Binder, Schreier, Kühnen, & Kedzior, 2013; Pan, Ng, Young, & Caroline, 2017). Support networks play an important role in recruiting students and supporting them before, during, and after education abroad.

Before Education Abroad

Regular communication among the local program staff at the host institution, the relevant departments at the home institution, and the international education office at the host institution and at the home institution, if such an office exists, is essential. For example, program leaders need something as simple as timely updates on applicant lists from the office tracking that information (Chieffo & Zipser, 2001). With them they can begin interacting with applicants and continue recruiting those who have not yet applied. Communication with a student's advisor is also key prior, during, and after education abroad to ensure a smooth credit transfer and progress toward degree. Furthermore, early in the process reliable information about available financial assistance is important, since students often see cost as an obstacle to education abroad.

The students' at-home social network can play an important role in their experience before, during, and after education abroad. Often it is discouragement in the form of worry and resistance from friends and family that students list as the primary reason for their reluctance to participate in education abroad. First-generation college students are more influenced by their families than students whose family had gone to college. First-generation students may receive less encouragement for participating in education abroad opportunities due to their families' (likely) unfamiliarity with education abroad (Mitic, 2019). Simon and Ainsworth's 2012 study found family unfamiliarity to be more common with students of color than other students. Students with an at-home network that includes supportive peers and a faculty leader are more likely to participate in programs abroad (Hackney et al., 2012). Additional support and resources may be needed for some students to support them and their at-home social network before, during, and after education abroad.

During Education Abroad

In addition to the at-home support network, there are also various support networks that the program can establish in the host community. We already mentioned the importance of tutors as well as the benefits of a buddy or tandem program. In addition, peer mentors from the host community who serve as cultural facilitators, when they are properly trained (Paige & Goode, 2009) have a positive impact on participants' intercultural competence development (Almeida et al., 2016; Campbell & Walta, 2015; Paige & Berg, 2012; Scally, 2015; Starr-Glass, 2020; Vande Berg et al., 2009).

Students typically have access to a social network in the home community as well as the host community while abroad. There is an impact of the amount of time spent with members of these groups in the home culture versus time spent with host community members. Especially in the later stages of education abroad, spending more time with members of one's own culture has been correlated with reduced cultural adjustment and more stress (Geeraert, Demoulin, & Demes, 2014). Studies have shown that students with little social support in education abroad are more likely to report depressive symptoms (M. Jackson, Ray, & Bybell, 2013; Sümer, Poyrazli, & Grahame, 2008). Similarly, a study analyzing the psychological well-being of international students in the US revealed a relationship between support and students' environmental mastery (Aldawsari, Adams, Grimes, & Kohn, 2018). According to the authors, social support assists international students in maintaining control and dealing with challenges during education abroad. Thus, it is important for instructors and/or education abroad directors to check in with students about their social support systems and to provide opportunities for them to expand their social support network. This can be done through offering access to activities with other international students as well as members in the host community, and availability of instructors and mentors for conversations, discussions and advice.

While the students are abroad, their at-home social network can be both a distraction and an important resource. With the availability of various technology tools, it is much easier for students to stay connected to their families and friends, which may counter any worry about being separated from them by going abroad. Yet once abroad, some students rely so heavily on their home social network that it hampers engagement with the community they are in. Furthermore, if persons in their social network at home have no or little experience with education abroad and/or this particular community, they may misinterpret problems and mislead the participant. Education abroad websites now often include parent and family sections that go beyond providing logistical information to also providing information on how to support their student.

Kinginger (2008, 2009b) discourages extended visits from family and friends from home as well as extended communication with friends and family back home. On the other hand, families and friends who visit students abroad and take a genuine interest in learning about their lives abroad, contribute to students developing a sense of pride over their new life and development (Garbati & Rothschild, 2016). Family and friends' own experience with education abroad plays an important role in their ability to support students during the challenging reintegration phase (Kartoshkina, 2015) as well as during preparation (Simon & Ainsworth, 2012). We have started inviting families to orientation sessions, so that we can answer their questions and educate them on how to best support their student abroad. Every year at least one parent takes us up on the offer and other parents reach out to us on the phone. Most often their questions center around financial questions and wanting to learn more about, how their student's life will look like abroad. It is up to the students' support network, whether they take advantage of the resources and what they do with them.

The program can identify and recommend important support structures that are already in place at home and in the abroad context before, during, and after education abroad. This is particularly important as students preparing to study abroad are concerned about institutional support abroad (J.-y. Lee & Ciftci, 2014). As with all of the contextual aspects, it is one thing whether these support systems exist and quite another if they work. For example, the AYF program has a list of counselors and other health professionals, who have come recommended by alumni and typically speak English. Yet, not all students find them a good fit given the more limited number of available counselors. Another example is that AYF offers tandem partner matching to the students. Some of those tandem partnerships turn into long-lasting friendships that foster linguistic and inter-cultural competence, others do not work out.

Application procedures, orientation sessions, team-building activities can all contribute to fostering a good relationship within a cohort. However, even with the same effort on the program's part, some years the cohort comes together well in support of one another and other years the peers are not supporting one another or are even actively sabotaging one another. In addition to the group dynamics, there are other cohort factors that can influence education abroad. For example, one of the years Senta Goerter led AYF several cohort members experienced emergencies and program staff had to focus on those participants leaving less support for other participants. In one year that Senta Goerter led the program, the cohort was exceptionally well prepared (e.g., high language skills, previous abroad experience, excellent academic records, excellent self-manage-ment and time-management strategies), which meant that program staff had more time for students with greater support needs. On the other hand, students whose language proficiency was more typical for the program, had a lower self-con-fidence as they were comparing themselves with their peers from that cohort. Due to the high group proficiency level, more communication was done in German than in a usual year and not all students were comfortable with that.

A strong in-country social network improves language development (Baker-Smemoe et al., 2014; Dewey, 2008; Dewey et al., 2013; Ring et al., 2013; Trentman, 2013), especially in speaking (Du, 2013; Isabelli-García, 2006). It is not easy for students to establish an in-country social network on their own and it is therefore important that program design includes a place for some facilitators who can help (e.g., tutors, cultural facilitators, peer mentors, tandem partners). As one would expect, the more intense the relationships are and the more diverse the social network is, the greater the language learning gains (Baker-Smemoe et al., 2014). Participants who engage with sympathetic interlocutors and/or friends with high English proficiency do better (Dewey et al., 2013).

It may help to provide students with a mentor during their time abroad with whom they can discuss their experiences (Bacon, 2002). In addition, organized social events may be necessary for helping students find connection with the local community (Surtees, 2018). Support from the local university may be equally important as social support from peers, friends, and family to help students accli-mate to their new environment. Bai (2016) found that support from advisors, faculty and classmates plays an important role in the acculturation process of international students and can help students feel less stressed during education abroad. Students may also initiate connection on their own by building social networks through clubs, religious groups, and host university interest groups (Trentman, 2013) or by pursuing hobbies (Goldoni, 2013). Faculty at the host institution play an important role in supporting students, yet not all are properly trained for the needs of international students (Garbati & Rothschild, 2016). As a program all it can do is provide a diverse range of opportunities for such connections to its students. One relies on program staff to identify organizations and clubs that are particularly open to international students or to create a list of faculty members at the local institution, who have been more or less supportive of international students.

After Return

The program support often ends with the students leaving the program, however, much more support is needed for them to successfully and efficiently transfer their credits, reintegrate into the home community and home institution, and continue to maximize the benefits of education abroad. There are two main challenges in education abroad post-sojourn that are often not addressed in the program design and communications: (1) Reverse culture shock and other issues of re-entry; and (2) attrition of learning outcomes. Education abroad returnees often feel more connected to their education abroad peers than the community at home and therefore can experience isolation (Allison et al., 2012) and reverse culture shock. The Kalamazoo Project discussed earlier as well as the *Maximizing Study Abroad* guide (Paige, Cohen, Kappler, Chi, & Lassegard, 2002) are two curricular models that help with unpacking the abroad experience to counter these common occurrences. In addition, the *Maximizing Study Abroad* guide provides activities for continued learning.

Reverse Culture Shock

Reverse culture shock and reintegration in the home community are often difficult experiences for returning students (Allison et al., 2012; Gaw, 2000; Wielkiewicz & Turkowski, 2010). Re-entry is often described as bitter-sweet, it is the return home and yet the worldview of the student has changed. Students often experience grief upon their return (Butcher, 2002). Kartoshkina (2015) lists psychological challenges such as anxiety, loneliness, isolation, frustration, apathy, anger, hostility, helplessness, depression, dissonance, discomfort, and boredom and social challenges such as difficulty in relationships with friends and family. She suggests re-entry workshops that help participants reflect on their experiences, re-entry excitements and challenges, and what they have learned. Some students report feeling disconnected and different from their friends and relatives at home which also leads to difficulties falling back into their daily routines, feeling overwhelmed and having to experience negative emotions (Pitts, 2016). Therefore, it is important to prepare students for their return (Arthur, 2003) and to help them readjust once they are back (Dykhouse & Bikos, 2019).

Especially once students have returned, it is crucial to assist them in their psychological readjustment due to the significance of the reentry effects on students' psychological well-being (Martin & Harrell, 2004). Pitts (2016) suggests that "access to a socially supportive and understanding interpersonal network is necessary for the return to psychological health" (p. 23). One way to achieve this is by enabling students to remain in contact with other education abroad students as well as friends they made while abroad. Interaction and communication with others is key to successful reentry (Martin, 1986). Students may benefit from workshops that teach them how to talk about their experiences with others who have not had a similar experience and how to connect with other people who share their experiences and emotions.

Academic Reintegration and Credit Transfer

The procedural success of education abroad depends on academic reintegration and the credit transfer process. If students are not able to transfer credits smoothly, it may extend time to degree, associated with additional costs, and/or lead to a time of uncertainty over remaining course requirements.

Another student concern upon return can be the struggle to reintegrate into the home institution's academic culture. For example, university education abroad can rely much more on student independence and self-motivation than the academic culture in the US. Additionally, especially in programs which follow a strict cohort model, students may find themselves without their cohort upon their return or their disciplinary knowledge gained abroad does not match the knowledge their peers gained at home.

To smooth the credit transfer and avoid delays in time to degree, we recommend the following strategies:

- Communicate between host and home institution before and throughout the experience to receive pre-approval of credit transfer.
- Create flexible credit transfer policies (Gordon et al., 2014).
- Create a credit transfer database that has a record of past courses and their equivalences. Such a database can allow students to select equivalencies or initiate new ones, if the information in the database does not match their needs.
- Develop mechanisms to speed up the grade processing in the host community. If that is not a possibility, prepare template statements explaining the students' situation to graduate schools, scholarship agencies/financial aid, and employers.

Attrition

In order to help students maintain gains in intercultural competence and in language, programs should strive to design post-sojourn elements that help students transition to being independent, continuous learners, users of the language, and participants in multilingual communities.

Relatively few studies have looked at the long-term effects of education abroad and even fewer have investigated the attrition of learning outcomes after education abroad. Rexeisen, Anderson, Lawton, and Hubbard (2008) investigated the long-term effects of a semester-long education abroad program with a service component and found positive effects on intercultural development at the end of the program, yet those effects were reversed at a later follow-up. They posit: "Educators must therefore question whether their responsibility to their students ends when the term is over or whether they should be trying to develop a longer-term if not life-long learning partnership" (p. 15). As is often the case with learning, if we do not continue to apply and build on what we have learned, the gains in learning go away. This means that students need more support post-return (Barnhart et al., 1997).

Strengthening re-entry support and post-education abroad training has been shown to be beneficial for the development of intercultural competence in students (Rexeisen et al., 2008). Rexeisen and colleagues suggest that "academic programs give further thought to what additional resources (e.g., post-study-abroad programming) might be developed to help students continue the constructive integration of their study abroad experiences" (p. 17).

To assist reintegration and retain learning, we recommend the following:

- Prepare students for reverse culture shock.
- Teach students strategies to talk to relatives and friends who do not have similar intercultural experiences (Kartoshkina, 2015).
- Connect returnees with people who had similar experiences.
- Provide reentry workshops.
- Provide opportunities to critically reflect on how the experiences have impacted their identity and worldviews including their attitudes toward their home culture.
- Encourage returnees to reflect on challenges and successes in reentry (Kartoshkina, 2015).
- Raise students' awareness of new skills.
- Develop continuing learning and engagement strategies creating a life-long partnership for learning (Rexeisen et al., 2008).
- Teach students how to market their new skills and apply them at home.

Young (2014) provides a good resource for re-entry support. Preparation and debriefing are especially important for program types not as closely tied to the home institution such as direct-enroll programs or independent internships. Departments and universities may also want to consider providing a course series through the home campus for each phase of education abroad (the semester before, during, and the semester after).

Dream Program

Based on the research discussed in this book and our own experiences, we, in collaboration with students in a graduate seminar on education abroad, have come up with our dream program. It is an example of an ideal – though rather wishful – degree program that fully integrates education abroad:

- **First Year Experience:** a short-term program in a desirable destination led by a faculty member with great support. This program should be before or during the first year in college. We recommend a home-stay, immersion tasks and guided reflection tasks to enhance learning.
- **Years 1–2:** Preparation at home through coursework and other forms of learning to develop language skills, ICC, and academic knowledge and skills. Whenever possible such learning experiences would include a focus on the host community. Furthermore, they may include both a research project about as well as virtual engagement with the host community.
- **Year 2:** Service-learning or community-engagement projects supported by a course on ethical civic engagement, training in ethnographic research, and guided reflections.
- **Year 3:** JYA: A year abroad with continued formal and informal learning opportunities to improve language proficiency, ICC, academic skills and knowledge, and professional preparation. The nature of such learning opportunities will need to depend on students' readiness. To enhance the learning, we suggest program-wide immersion and guided reflection tasks and a year-long ethnographic research project. To deepen the learning, we recommend an internship, community-engagement, or research project during the second semester facilitated by a faculty member from the home institution familiar with the local context. Students might also be asked to blog about their experiences and those blogs can become part of the curriculum for years 1 and 2.
- **Year 4:** Return to home with continued formal and informal learning opportunities to develop language proficiency, ICC, academic skills and knowledge, and professional preparation. These learning opportunities ideally include tasks to unpack the experience, workshops on how to market the education abroad experience, re-entry courses, public presentation of the ethnographic project from year 3, and an additional community-engagement project or internship working with a group at home that is different from the student. To enhance learning through the community engagement, an expert faculty member can facilitate guided reflection. To support learning of all students, returnees may serve as peer mentors for students in years 1–3.

Chapter 3.5. Invigorating the Junior Year Abroad: Sustainability and Adaptability

Invigorating the Junior Year Abroad

We have outlined general ways to make programs more effective, however, as indicated throughout the book a variety of learning outcomes are only possible in long-term programs and those that offer independence as well as facilitation. As Steinwidder (2016) has argued, it might take three to five months to transition to a new environment before participants can truly benefit. Hence, we argue that education abroad pay closer attention to long-term education abroad, especially the JYA.

The JYA is 100 years old (Hoffa, 2007) and it has not aged well in all cases. The JYA was the first attempt at combining language and culture learning in an immersive environment with course credit at the home institution. One of the earlier Open Doors Reports (Institute of International Education, 1967) notes that 24,900 US students were enrolled in year-long academic programs abroad in the 1965/1966 academic year, the height of JYAs. According to the US Department of Education's National Center for Education Statistics (2016), there has been a strong increase in the number of US undergraduates studying abroad, but a decline in year-long program participation. While in 2005/2006 5.3% of students selected academic year abroad programs, in 2015/2016 only 2.3% of students participated in year-long programs. While in 1996/1997 year-long programs abroad still attracted 10.7% of students (US Department of Education's National Center for Education Statistics, 2018), this number has declined year after year. The JYA will likely never be the program with the highest participation again, but due to its advantages in program design and the benefits of long-term education abroad, we argue to invigorate JYA using the following principles:

- Diversify participation.
- Improve accessibility and inclusion of programs to better accommodate diverse student populations.
- Work with pre-professional programs and STEM programs to create or modify JYA programs that fit those program and student needs.
- Be more flexible with allowing students to take online courses at home while also participating in a JYA, so that they can take some essential classes with the at-home cohort.
- Form partnerships with community colleges and other two-year institutions to utilize a JYA as a transition to a four-year institution.
- Form partnerships with HBCUs to support diversity and inclusion at home and abroad.
- Take advantage of partnerships and consortia.

- Provide family programming or housing for students with partners and/or children.
- Have a focus in the program (e.g., sustainability in Freiburg, international relations in Brussels, wildlife preservation in Namibia).
- Include internships – ideally paid or sponsored by scholarships – supported through a course either in country or at home.
- Keep costs comparable to an at-home year or even cheaper to make them more attractive.

Sustainability and Adaptability

Because the context and the stakeholders' needs and goals are always changing, all programs not just a JYA must be prepared to adjust to the times while maintaining their high-quality standards.

Sustaining Outcomes

There is very little research on long-term outcomes of education abroad and how to sustain the outcomes. The research that is available tends to be based on self-report data. More research needs to be done on long-term outcomes using iterative program assessment involving quantitative and qualitative measures and multiple stakeholders. These evaluation-adaptation cycles done by qualified personnel, should investigate short-term and long-term effects. A comparison of short-term and long-term effects can point to areas of attrition in learning outcomes. Interventions for better retention of learning outcomes can be designed and evaluated in subsequent cycles.

Sustaining Programs

In order stand the test of time, programs need to be designed with flexibility, so that they can adjust to the ever changing educational and political global landscape. To keep programs financially viable, a variety of strategies can be applied such as:

- Right-size the program: What are the minimum and maximum number of participants to maximally support learning? How much personnel is needed to support the students in their development? What resources are needed?
- Form partnerships on campus and beyond to increase the recruitment pool and support students by personnel not paid for by the program.
- Diversify the partner institutions and recruit students from institutions that typically do not send students or do not have their own offerings.
- Strengthen alumni relations for both supporting the students and for fundraising. Connecting alumni with the program rather than the alma mater is important especially in programs that are based on partnerships. For example,

the funds raised for education abroad at the AYF consortium institutions can only be used for students from that particular institution, which creates inequities across consortium universities and excludes participants who join from other institutions. Therefore, AYF created a US-based and a Germany-based alumni association, who can fundraise and distribute the funds according to needs and merit equitably across the entire program.

Sustainable Development

From the environment to the communities, education abroad leaves an impact. Thus far we have focused on mostly the positive impacts of education abroad. Yet, there is no question that education abroad leaves a carbon footprint and has the potential of being harmful for the community. We would like to see programs designed or re-designed with the UN's 17 Sustainable Development Goals in mind:

(1) no poverty, (2) zero hunger, (3) good health and well-being, (4) quality education, (5) gender equality, (6) clean water and sanitation, (7) affordable and clean energy, (8) decent work and economic growth, (9) industry, innovation, and infrastructure, (10) reduced inequalities, (11) sustainable cities and communities, (12) responsible consumption and production, (13) climate action, (14) life below water, (15) life on land, (16) peace, justice, and strong institutions, and (17) partnerships for the goals.

(United Nations, 2020)

Adapting to Global Educational and Political Climates

As international relations change and educational cultures and systems change at home and in the host communities, our programs have to adjust. The most noticeable recent trends have been the increase in English-medium classes in a variety of countries. Very recently education abroad has been impacted by travel restrictions and visa restrictions. Programs need a flexible design and contingency plans to adjust to the changing landscape. While it is impossible to be prepared for all eventualities, the pandemic of 2020 showed us that contingency plans are important in all locations.

The Future of Education Abroad

We share the concern reported in research about education abroad and its future and that the increase in short-term island programs is contributing to a consumerist approach of education abroad. There is a need for well-designed short-term programs and invigorated long-term programs. We hope that an eye to the UN's Agenda 2030 in program (re-)design can help education abroad be a positive global change agent rather than reinforcing existing power relations.

We also share the concern raised by our survey participants, that the 2020 pandemic is going to leave a long-term dent in education abroad participation and a possible increase in program closures. At the same time, we hope that this moment of restructuring can be used to rethink our current trends in education abroad, to provide more financial support for education abroad, to diversify participation especially in long-term programs, to increase awareness of ethical considerations in program design and act accordingly.

While some researchers have raised concern over the prevalence of English around the world, especially English-medium instruction, as a detriment to education abroad's benefits, we join Tullock and Ortega (2017) in embracing the fact that many locations are multilingual communities. Rather than seeing English playing a role in the host community as a hindrance, we encourage programs to acknowledge the reality that global communication is multilingual and involves translanguaging. For example, we should take advantage of English-medium courses to a reasonable extent, so that lower language proficiency students can mingle with others and advance their academic understanding. We also remind readers that Dewey, Bown, Baker, and Martinsen (2014) found that host community members with a high level of English proficiency had a positive impact on language learning success for program participants. Most importantly, paying attention to the linguistic landscape in the host community provides a platform to think critically about globalization and one's own place in the world.

In closing, education abroad can have a transformative impact on an individual and change both the host and the home community. To summarize some of those advantageous, we close here with excerpts from one survey respondent reflecting on their JYA experience:

- I was truly fortunate to be able to fully immerse myself in a new culture.
- I was able to take university courses alongside native students and be held to their standards.
- I was able to develop new ways of thinking about problems and get differing perspectives on topics ranging from political theory to history and expand my worldview.
- I felt that I was able to expand my empathy for others, as an outsider who was quickly accepted and helped through the rough transition to a country whose customs and way of doing things I had not had direct experience with.
- I feel that my compassion for the immigrant experience was greatly enhanced and my understanding of the complex, gray areas of the world would be impossible without studying abroad.
- Personally, I was able to create amazing friendships, people who challenged me to grow into a more complete human being.
- I gained an amazing amount of confidence in who I am as a person and what I can accomplish.

- Selfishly, I feel that without studying abroad I never could have improved my language skills to the degree that I did, which I take great pride in (despite the deterioration of those skills over the years) and which have led to personal success and advancement in the workplace.
- Moving to a new country has many challenges, just not knowing the cultural norms, how to go about daily life activities that you take for granted (shopping for groceries was at first a unique endeavor!), finding a social group as a young adult and the sense of belonging that brings and of course communicating with depth and complexity. However, those challenges were to varying degrees easy to overcome.
- I had great support from my program in doing things like opening a bank account, enrolling in classes and language testing.
- I was pushed but always with the knowledge that I had a support system I could turn to.
- My depth of knowledge of the language also allowed me to communicate more freely than some, providing me with many native friends who could assist in my cultural assimilation and fill gaps in my need for close relationships and social bonding.
- I was also lucky to be in a dorm situation with students from all over the world, which helped ease the transition, including an old high school friend who happened to be in the same university but with a different program (totally by happenstance!). I think that bit of familiarity truly helped me succeed.

References

AAUP. (1995). Directing foreign study: The professor abroad. *Academe*, 81(5), 21–21. Retrieved from www.jstor.org/stable/40250872.

Ablaeva, Y. S. (2012). Inclusion of students with disabilities in study abroad: Current practices and student perspectives. Master of Arts dissertation, University of Oregon. ProQuest 1516785.

Albers-Miller, N. D., Prenshaw, P. J., & Straughan, R. D. (1999). Study abroad programs: An exploratory study of student perceptions. *American Marketing Association. Conference Proceedings*, 10, 65–72.

Aldawsari, N. F., Adams, K. S., Grimes, L. E., & Kohn, S. (2018). The effects of cross-cultural competence and social support on international students' psychological adjustment: Autonomy and environmental mastery. *Journal of International Students*, 8(2), 901–924.

Ali, B. (2015). African American students are underrepresented in study abroad. Retrieved from https://sites.ed.gov/whieeaa/files/2015/11/Bakar-Ali-International-Studies-Paper1.pdf.

Allen, H. W., & Dupuy, B. (2013). Study abroad, foreign language use, and the communities standard. *Foreign Language Annals*, 45(4), 468–493.

Allen, H. W., & Herron, C. (2003). A mixed-methodology investigation of the linguistic and affective outcomes of summer study abroad. *Foreign Language Annals*, 36(3), 370–385. doi:10.1111/j.1944-9720.2003.tb02120.x.

Allison, P., Davis-Berman, J., & Berman, D. (2012). Changes in latitude, changes in attitude: Analysis of the effects of reverse culture shock – a study of students returning from youth expeditions. *Leisure Studies*, 31(4), 487–503. doi:10.1080/02614367.2011.619011.

Almeida, J., Fantini, A. E., Simões, A. R., & Costa, N. (2016). Enhancing the intercultural effectiveness of exchange programmes: Formal and non-formal educational interventions. *Intercultural Education*, 27(6), 517–533. doi:10.1080/14675986.2016.1262190.

Amani, M., & Kim, M. M. (2018). Study abroad participation at community colleges: Students' decision and influential factors. *Community College Journal of Research and Practice*, 42(10), 678–692. doi:10.1080/10668926.2017.1352544.

Ammigan, R. (2019). Institutional satisfaction and recommendation: What really matters to international students? *Journal of International Students*, 9(1), 262–281. doi:10.32674/jis.v9i1.260.

Anita, S. C., & McKenry, L. (1999). Preparing culturally competent practitioners. *The Journal of Nursing Education*, 38(5), 228–234.

Antonakopoulou, E. (2013). Sociocultural adaptation of US education abroad students in Greece. *Frontiers: The Interdisciplinary Journal of Study Abroad*, 23, 60–72.

Anya, U. (2011). Connecting with communities of learners and speakers: Integrative ideals, experiences, and motivation of successful black second language learners. *Foreign Language Annals*, 44(3), 441–466.

Archangeli, M. (1999). Study abroad and experiential learning in Salzburg, Austria. *Foreign Language Annals*, 32(1), 115–122. doi:10.1111/j.1944-9720.1999.tb02380.x.

Ardasheva, Y., Wang, Z., Adesope, O. O., & Valentine, J. C. (2017). Exploring effectiveness and moderators of language learning strategy instruction on second language and self-regulated learning outcomes. *Review of Educational Research*, 87(3), 544–582. doi:10.3102/0034654316689135.

Arthur, N. (2003). Preparing international students for the re-entry transition. *Canadian Journal of Counselling*, 37(3), 173–185.

Atabong, A., Baten, L., Bavieri, L., Beaven, A., Borghetti, C., Čebron, N., ... Vassilicos, B. (2015). Intercultural education resources for Erasmus students and their teachers. Retrieved from https://eprint.ncl.ac.uk/file_store/production/243192/E3C6E785-B3A4-4F1D-9B23-CB8E7C3C4F96.pdf

Austin, J. M., & Rust, D. Z. (2015). Developing an experiential learning program: Milestones and challenges. *International Journal of Teaching and Learning in Higher Education*, 27 (1), 143–153.

Awad, G. (2014). Motivation, persistence, and cross-cultural awareness: A study of college students learning foreign languages. *Academic of Educational Leadership Journal*, 18(4), 97–116.

Bacon, S. M. (2002). Learning the rules: Language development and cultural adjustment during study abroad. *Foreign Language Annals*, 35(6), 637–646. doi:10.1111/j.1944-9720.2002.tb01902.x.

Bai, J. (2016). Perceived support as a predictor of acculturative stress among international students in the United States. *Journal of International Students*, 6(1), 93–106.

Baker-Smemoe, W., Dewey, D. P., Bown, J., & Martinsen, R. A. (2014). Variables affecting L2 gains during study abroad. *Foreign Language Annals*, 47(3), 464–486. doi:10.1111/flan.12093.

Bandyopadhyay, S., & Bandyopadhyay, K. (2015). Factors influencing student participation in college study abroad programs. *Journal of International Education Research*, 11(2), 87–94.

Barnhart, B., Ricks, T., & Spier, P. (1997). Faculty roles. In W. Hoffa & J. Pearson (Eds.), *NAFSA's guide to education abroad for advisers and administrators* (2nd ed., pp. 37–56). Washington, DC: NAFSA Association of International Educators.

Bartzis, O. L., Kirkwood, K. J., & Mulvihill, T. M. (2016). Innovative approaches to study abroad at Harper College and Fox Valley Technical College. In R. L. Raby & E. J. Valeau (Eds.), *International education at community colleges* (pp. 237–246). New York: Palgrave Macmillan.

Bateman, B. E. (2002). Promoting openness toward culture learning: Ethnographic interviews for students of Spanish. *The Modern Language Journal*, 86(3), 318–331.

Bathurst, L., & Brack, B. L. (2012). Shifting the locus of intercultural learning. Intervening prior to and after student experiences abroad. In M. V. Berg, R. M. Paige, & K. H. Lou (Eds.), *Student learning abroad. What our students are learning, what they're not, and what we can do about it* (pp. 261–283). Sterling, VA: Stylus.

Beausoleil, A. (2008). Understanding heritage and ethnic identity development through study abroad: The case of South Korea. Doctor of Education dissertation, University of California. ProQuest 333041.

Belnap, R. K., Bown, J., Dean, E. M., Dewey, D. P., Schouten, L. J., Smith, A. K., ... Taylor, J. R. (2015). Project perseverance and Arabic study abroad. *Al-'Arabiyya: Journal of the American Association of Teachers of Arabic*, 48, 1–21.

Bender, C., Wright, D., & Lopatto, D. (2009). Students' self-reported changes in intercultural knowledge and competence associated with three undergraduate science experiences. *Frontiers: The Interdisciplinary Journal of Study Abroad*, 18(1), 307–322.

Benson, P. (2017). Sleeping with strangers: Dreams and nightmares in experiences of homestay. *Study Abroad Research in Second Language Acquisition and International Education*, 2(1), 1–20. doi:10.1075/sar.2.1.01ben.

Biagi, F., Bracci, L., Filippone, A., & Nash, E. J. (2012). Instilling reflective intercultural competence in education abroad experiences in Italy: The FICCS approach + reflective education. *Italica*, 89(1), 21–33. Retrieved from www.jstor.org/stable/41440493.

Binder, N., Schreier, M., Kühnen, U., & Kedzior, K. K. (2013). Integrating international students into tertiary education using intercultural peer-to-peer training at Jacobs University Bremen, Germany. *Journal of Education and Training Studies*, 1(2), 273–285. doi:10.11114/jets.v1i2.170.

Blake, D., Gasman, M., Esmieu, P. L., & Samayoa, A. s. C. (2019). Culturally relevant study abroad for students of color: Lessons from the Frederick Douglass global fellowship in London. *Journal of Diversity in Higher Education*. doi:10.1037/dhe0000112.

Blake-Campbell, B. (2014). More than just a sampling of study abroad: Transformative possibilities at best. *The Community College Enterprise*, 20(2), 6–71.

Böttcher, L., Araújo, N. A. M., Nagler, J., Mendes, J. F. F., Helbing, D., & Herrmann, H. J. (2016). Gender gap in the ERASMUS mobility program. *PLos ONE*, 11(2), 1–8. doi:10.1371/journal.pone.014951.

Brandauer, S. C., & Hovmand, S. (2013). Preparing business students for the global workplace through study abroad: A case study of the Danish Institute for Study Abroad. *Journal of International Education in Business*, 6(2), 107–121. doi:10.1108/JIEB-05-2013-0018.

Brenner, A. (2016). Transformative learning through education abroad: A case study of a community college program. In R. L. Raby & E. J. Valeau (Eds.), *International education at community colleges* (pp. 293–310). New York: Palgrave Macmillan.

Brockington, J. L., & Wiedenhoft, M. D. (2009). The liberal arts and global citizenship: Fostering intercultural engagement through integrative experiences and structured reflection. In R. Lewin (Ed.), *The handbook of practice and research in study abroad: Higher education and the quest for global citizenship* (pp. 117–132). New York: Routledge.

Brown, N. A. (2014). Foreign language study coupled with internship experience as an entrée to professional opportunities. *Russian Language Journal*, 64, 71–81. Retrieved from www.jstor.org/stable/43669251.

Brux, J. M., & Fry, B. (2010). Multicultural students in study abroad: Their interests, their issues, and their constraints. *Journal of Studies in International Education*, 14(5), 508–527.

Bryant, K. M., & Soria, K. M. (2015). College students' sexual orientation, gender identity, and participation in study abroad. *Frontiers: The Interdisciplinary Journal of Study Abroad*, 15, 91–106.

Burkhart, B., Hexter, H., & Thompson, D. (2001). Why TRIO students need to study abroad. Retrieved from www.pellinstitute.org/downloads/trio_clearinghouse-Burkart_Hexter_Thompson_April_2001.pdf

Butcher, A. (2002). A grief observed: Grief experiences of East Asian international students returning to their countries of origin. *Journal of Studies in International Education*, 6(4), 354–368. doi:10.1177/102831502237641.

Butler, P. E. (2019). Learning to navigate. Lessons from student development. In E. Brewer & A. C. Ogden (Eds.), *Education abroad and the undergraduate experience. Critical perspectives and approaches to integration with student learning and development* (pp. 132–148). Sterling, VA: Stylus.

Butler, P. E., Madden, M., & Smith, N. (2018). Undocumented student participation in education abroad: An institutional analysis. *Frontiers: The Interdisciplinary Journal of Study Abroad*, 15(2), 1–31.

Byker, E. J., & Putnam, S. M. (2018). Catalyzing cultural and global competencies: Engaging preservice teachers in study abroad to expand the agency of citizenship. *Journal of Studies in International Education*, 23(1), 84–105. doi:10.1177/1028315318814559.

Cadd, M. (2012). Encouraging students to engage with native speakers during study abroad. *Foreign Language Annals*, 45(2), 229–245. doi:10.1111/j.1944-9720.2012.01188.x.

Calhoon, J. A., Wildcat, D., Annett, C., Pierotti, R., & Griswold, W. (2003). Creating meaningful study abroad programs for American Indian postsecondary students. *Journal of American Indian Education*, 42(1), 46–57. Retrieved from www.jstor.org/stable/24398471.

Campbell, C. J., & Walta, C. (2015). Maximising intercultural learning in short term international placements: Findings associated with orientation programs, guided reflection and immersion. *Australian Journal of Teacher Education*, 40(10), 1–15. doi:10.14221/atje.2015v40n10.1.

CASLS. (2020). What is LinguaFolio Online? Retrieved from https://linguafolio.uoregon.edu.

Castañeda, M. E., & Zirger, M. L. (2011). Making the most of the "new" study abroad: Social capital and the short-term sojourn. *Foreign Language Annals*, 44(3), 544–564.

Cenoz, J., & Gorter, D. (2008). The linguistic landscape as an additional source of input in second language acquisition. *International Review of Applied Linguistics in Language Teaching*, 46(3), 267–287. doi:10.1515/IRAL.2008.012.

Chamot, A. U. (2005). Language learning strategy instruction: Current issues and research. *Annual Review of Applied Linguistics*, 25, 112–130. doi:10.1017/S0267190505000061.

Chamot, A. U., & Harris, V. (2019). Language learning strategy instruction for critical cultural awareness. In A. U. Chamot & V. Harris (Eds.), *Learning strategy instruction in the language classroom* (pp. 123–139). Bristol: Multilingual Matters.

Chang, A. (2017). "Call me a little critical if you will": Counterstories of Latinas studying abroad in Guatemala. *Journal of Hispanic Higher Education*, 16(1), 3–23. doi:10.1177/1538192715614900.

Chapman, D. D. (2016). The ethics of international service learning as a pedagogical development practice: A Canadian study. *Third World Quarterly*, 39(10), 1899–1922. doi:10.1080/01436597.2016.1175935.

Chen, X., & Nunnery, A. (2019). Profile of very low- and low-income undergraduates in 2015–16. Retrieved from https://nces.ed.gov/pubs2020/2020460.pdf.

Chieffo, L., & Griffiths, L. (2009). Here to stay: Increasing acceptance of short-term study abroad programs. In R. Lewin (Ed.), *The handbook of practice and research in study abroad* (pp. 365–380). New York: Routledge.

Chieffo, L., & Zipser, R. (2001). Integrating study abroad in the foreign language curriculum. *ADFL Bulletin*, 32, 79–85.

Cohen, A. D. (2011). *Strategies in learning and using a second language.* London & New York: Routledge.

Cohen, A. D. (2019). Strategy instruction for learning and performing target language pragmatics. In A. U. Chamot & V. Harris (Eds.), *Learning strategy instruction in the language classroom* (pp. 140–152). Bristol: Multilingual Matters.

Collentine, J. (2009). Study abroad research: Findings, implications and future directions. In M. H. Long & C. Doughty (Eds.), *The handbook of language teaching* (pp. 218–233). Malden, MA: Wiley-Blackwell.

Comp, D. (2007). What we know about diversity in education abroad: State of the research. In C. A. Herrin, S. Dadzie, & S. A. MacDonald (Eds.), *Proceedings for the colloquium on diversity in education abroad: How to change the picture* (pp. 48–52). Washington, DC: Academy for Educational Development.

Comp, D. (2008). US heritage-seeking students discover minority communities in Western Europe. *Journal of Studies in International Education*, 12(1), 29–37. doi:10.1177/1028315307299417.

Convertini, T. (2019). The city as the classroom: Maximizing learning abroad through language and culture experiential strategies. In M. Fuchs, S. Rai, & Y. Loiseau (Eds.), *Study abroad: Traditions and new directions* (pp. 38–51). New York: The Modern Language Association of America.

Covert, H. H. (2014). Stories of personal agency: Undergraduate students' perceptions of developing intercultural competence during a semester abroad in Chile. *Journal of Studies in International Education*, 18(2), 162–179. doi:10.1177/1028315313497590.

Covington, M. (2017). If not us, then who? Exploring the role of HBCUs in increasing Black student engagement in study abroad. *College Student Affairs Leadership*, 4(1), article 5. Retrieved from http://scholarworks.gvsu.edu/csal/vol4/iss1/5.

Crawford, P., & Berquist, B. (2020). *Community engagement abroad. Perspectives and practices on service, engagement, and learning overseas*. East Lansing, MI: Michigan State University Press.

Curtin, A. J., Martins, D. C., Schwartz-Barcott, D., DiMaria, L., & Ogando, B. M. S. (2013). Development and evaluation of an international service learning program for nursing students. *Public Health Nursing*, 30, 548–556.

Davidson, D. E., & Lekic, M. D. (2012). Comparing heritage and non-heritage learning outcomes and target-language utilization in the overseas immersion context: A preliminary study of the Russian flagship. *Russian Language Journal*, 62, 47–78.

Davie, J. (1996). Language skills, course development and the year abroad. *Language Learning Journal*, 13(1), 73–76. doi:10.1080/09571739685200221.

Dawson, N. J. (2000). Study abroad and African American college students at Southern Illinois University at Carbondale. *African Issues*, 28(1), 124–129. doi:10.2307/1167074.

Deardorff, D. K. (2011). Assessing intercultural competence. *New Directions for Institutional Research*, 149, 65–79. doi:10.1002/ir.381.

DeKeyser, R. (2007). Study abroad as foreign language practice. In R. M. DeKeyser (Ed.), *Practice in a second language: Perspectives from applied linguistics and cognitive psychology* (pp. 208–223). Cambridge: Cambridge University Press.

Demetriou, C., Meece, J., Eaker-Rich, D., & Powell, C. (2017). The activities, roles, and relationships of successful first-generation college students. *Journal of College Student Development*, 58(1), 19–36. doi:10.1353/csd.2017.0001.

Dewey, D. P. (2008). Japanese vocabulary acquisition by learners in three contexts. *Frontiers: The Interdisciplinary Journal of Study Abroad*, 15, 127–148.

Dewey, D. P., Bown, J., Baker, W., & Martinsen, R. A. (2014). Language use in six study abroad programs: An exploratory analysis of possible predictors. *Language Learning*, 64(1), 36–71.

Dewey, D. P., Ring, S., Gardner, D., & Belnap, R. K. (2013). Social network formation and development during study abroad in the Middle East. *System*, 41(2). doi:10.1016/j.system.2013.02.004.

DeWinter, U. J. (1997). Science and engineering education abroad: An overview. *Frontiers: The Interdisciplinary Journal of Study Abroad*, 3, 181–197.

DeWinter, U. J. (2007). Study abroad: An open door to language learning. *ADFL Bulletin*, 38(1–2),22–26. doi:10.1632/adfl.38.1.22.

Di Silvio, F., Donovan, A., & Malone, M. E. (2014). The effect of study abroad homestay placements: Participant perspectives and oral proficiency gains. *Foreign Language Annals*, 47(1), 168–188.

Dolby, N. (2007). Reflections on nation: American undergraduates and education abroad. *Journal of Studies in International Education*, 11(2), 141–156. doi:10.1177/1028315306291944.

Dörnyei, Z. (1995). On the teachability of communication strategies. *TESOL Quarterly*, 29(1), 55–85. doi:10.2307/3587805.

Dorsett, P. (2019). Transformative intercultural learning: A short-term international study tour. *Jounal of Social Work Education*, 55(3), 565–578. doi:10.1080/10437797.2018.1548984.

Douglas, C., & Jones-Rikkers, C. G. (2001). Study abroad programs and American student worldmindedness: An empirical analysis. *Journal of Teaching in International Business*, 13(1).

Douthit, T. L., Schaake, S. L., Hay, M. M. R., Grieger, D. M., & Bormann, J. M. (2015). *Student blogs and journals as assessment tools for faculty-led study abroad trips NACTA Journal*, 59(3), 213–218.

Downey, G., & Gray, T. (2012). Blogging with the Facebook generation: Studying abroad with gen Y. Retrieved from www.researchgate.net/publication/257483917_Blogging_with_the_Facebook_Generation_Studying_abroad_with_Gen_Y

Doyle, S., Gendall, P., Meyer, L. H., Hoek, J., Tait, C., McKenzie, L., & Loorparg, A. (2010). An investigation of factors associated with student participation in study abroad. *Journal of Studies in International Education*, 14(5), 471–490. doi:10.1177/1028315309336032.

Doyle, V. (2018). *The African American experience on study abroad: A closer look at the student perspective*. SIT Graduate Institute, Capstone Collection. Retrieved from https://digitalcollections.sit.edu/capstones/3092.

Dressler, R., & Tweedie, M. G. (2016). Dialogue Journals in Short-Term Study Abroad: "Today I Wrote My Mind." *TESOL Journal*, 7(4), 939.

Drexler, D. S., & Campbell, D. F. (2011). Student development among community college participants in study abroad programs. *Community College Journal of Research and Practice*, 35(8), 608–619. doi:10.1080/10668920801901258.

Du, H. (2013). The development of Chinese fluency during study abroad in China. *The Modern Language Journal*, 97(1), 131–143. doi:10.1111/j.1540-4781.2013.01434.x.

Ducate, L. (2009). Service learning in Germany: A four-week summer teaching program in Saxony-Anhalt. *Die Unterrichtspraxis/Teaching German*, 42(1), 32–40.

DuFon, M. A., & Churchill, E. (2006). Evolving threads in study abroad research. In M. A. DuFon & E. Churchill (Eds.), *Language learners in study abroad contexts* (pp. 1–30). Clevedon: Multilingual Matters.

Duke, S. T. (2014). *Preparing to study abroad: Learning to cross cultures*. Sterling, VA: Stylus.

Dunkley, M. (2009). *What students are actually learning on study abroad and how to improve the learning experience*. Paper presented at the 20th ISANA International Education Association Conference Proceeding, Canberra (Australia).

Dunlap, A., & Mapp, S. C. (2017). Effectively preparing students for international field placements through a pre-departure class. *Social Work Education*, 36(8), 893–904. doi:10.1080/02615479.2017.1360858.

Durbidge, L. (2019). Technology and L2 engagement in study abroad: Enabler or immersion breaker? *System* 80, 224–234.

Dykhouse, E. C., & Bikos, L. H. (2019). Re-entry friction: The curious effects of cultural dislocation on outcomes for global service learning returnees. *International Journal of Intercultural Relations*, 72, 96–108. doi:10.1016/j.ijintrel.2019.07.004.

Eidson, K. (2015). *Increasing minority participation in study abroad programs*. Paper presented at the The 2nd Annual Universality of Global Education Conference, The Woodlands, Texas. Retrieved from https://pdfs.semanticscholar.org/b5b8/506f03c92e4d1e73e2180c26a bc706cb4a80.pdf.

Elemo, A. S., & Turkum, A. S. (2019). The effects of psychoeducational intervention on the adjustment, coping self-efficacy and psychological distress levels of international students in Turkey. *International Journal of Intercultural Relations*, 70, 7–18. doi:10.1016/j.ijintrel.2019.02.003.

Elola, I., & Oskoz, A. (2008). Blogging: Fostering intercultural competence development in foreign language and study abroad contexts. *Foreign Language Annals*, 41(3), 454–477. doi:10.1111/j.1944-9720.2008.tb03307.x.

Emery, E. (2008). Cédez le passage: A chronicle of traveling in France with a disability. In T. Berberi, E. C. Hamilton, & I. Sutherland (Eds.), *Worlds apart? Disability and foreign language learning* (pp. 181–200). New Haven, CT: Yale University Press.

Engberg, M. E., & Jourian, T. J. (2015). Intercultural wonderment and study abroad. *Frontiers: The Interdisciplinary Journal of Study Abroad*, 25.

Engel, L. C. (2017). *Underrepresented students in US study abroad: Investigating impacts*. IIE Research and Policy Brief Series. New York: IIE.

Engle, J., & Tinto, V. (2008). *Moving beyond access: College success for low-income, first-generation students*. Washington, DC: The Pell Institute.

Engle, L., & Engle, J. (2012). Beyond immersion: The American University Center of Provence experiment in holistic intervention. In M. V. Berg, R. M. Paige, & K. H. Lou (Eds.), *Student learning abroad: What our students are learning, what they're not, and what we can do about it* (pp. 284–307). Sterling, VA: Stylus.

Esmieu, P., Mullen, S., Samayoa, A. s. C., Gasman, M., Perkins, C., Wolff, M., ... Beazley, M. (2016). Increasing diversity abroad: Expanding opportunities for students at minority-serving institutions. Retrieved from https://cmsi.gse.upenn.edu/sites/default/files/MSI_StdyAbrdRprt_R4fin.pdf.

European Centre for Modern Languages. (2015). Plurilingual and intercultural learning through mobility: Practical resources for teachers and teacher trainers. Retrieved from https://plurimobil.ecml.at.

Evanson, T. A., & Zust, B. L. (2004). The meaning of participation in an international service experience among baccalaureate nursing students. *International Journal of Nursing Education scholarship*, 1(1), 0–14. doi:10.2202/1548-923x.1070.

Farrugia, C., & Sanger, J. (2017). Gaining an employment edge: The impact of study abroad on 21st century skills & career prospects in the United States, 2013–2016. Retrieved from https://educationabroad.wvu.edu/files/d/fbd30891-5f37-4309-a9b9-9bde74bd52bf/gaining-an-employment-edge-the-impact-of-study-abroad.pdf.

Fraser, C. (2002). Study abroad: An attempt to measure the gains. *German as a Foreign Language 2002*(1), 45–65.

Freed, B. F. (1995). What makes us think that students who study abroad become fluent? In B. F. Freed (Ed.), *Second language acquisition in a study abroad context* (pp. 123–149). Amsterdam: John Benjamins.

Freed, B. F., Segalowitz, N., & Dewey, D. P. (2004). Comparing regular classroom, study abroad, and intensive domestic immersion programs. *SSLA*, 26, 275–301.

Garbati, J. F., & Rothschild, N. (2016). Lasting impact of study abroad experiences: A collaborative autoethnography. *Forum Qualitative Sozialforschung/Forum: Qualitative Social Research*, 17(2), 1–18. doi:10.17169/fqs-17.2.2387.

Garver, M. S., & Divine, R. L. (2007). Conjoint analysis of study abroad preferences: Key attributes, segments and implications for increasing student participation. *Journal of Marketing for Higher Education*, 17(2), 189–215. doi:10.1080/08841240801912427.

Gaw, K. F. (2000). Reverse culture shock in students returning from overseas. *International Journal of Intercultural Relations*, 24(1), 83–104. doi:10.1016/S0147-1767(99)00024-3.

Gearhart, R. (2005). Taking American race relations on the road ... to Africa. *African studies quarterly*, 8(2), 70–83.

Geeraert, N., Demoulin, S., & Demes, K. A. (2014). Choose your (international) contacts wisely: A multilevel analysis on the impact of intergroup contact while living abroad. *International Journal of Intercultural Relations*, 38, 86–96. doi:10.1016/j.ijintrel.2013.08.001.

George, A. (2019). Study abroad homestay versus dormitory: Extralinguistic factors and regional features. *Spanish in Context*, 16(1), 77–103. doi:10.1075/sic.00027.geo.

Giovanangeli, A., Oguro, S., & Harbon, L. (2018). Mentoring students' intercultural learning during study abroad. In J. Jackson & S. Oguro (Eds.), *Intercultural interventions in study abroad* (pp. 88–102). New York: Routledge.

Godwin-Jones, R. (2016). Emerging technologies: Integrating technology into study abroad. *Language Learning and Technology*, 20(1), 1–20.

Goel, L., De Jong, P., & Schnusenberg, O. (2010). Toward a comprehensive framework of study abroad intentions and behaviors. *Journal of Teaching in International Business*, 21(4), 248–265. doi:10.1080/08975930.2010.526011.

Goertler, S. (2015). Study abroad and technology: Friend or enemy? *FLTMag*. Retrieved from https://fltmag.com/study-abroad-and-technology/.

Goertler, S., & McEwen, K. (2018). Closing the GAP for generation study abroad: Achieving goals, improving articulation, and increasing participation. *ADFL Bulletin*, 44 (41–55).

Goertler, S., & the 369ers. (2019). Understanding the people and the language around you: Using awareness-raising action research in undergraduate education abroad. *Die Unterrichtspraxis/Teaching German*, 52(1). doi:10.1111/tger.12083.

Goldoni, F. (2013). Students' immersion experiences in study abroad. *Foreign Language Annals*, 46(3), 359–376. doi:10.1111/flan.12047.

Goldoni, F. (2015). Preparing students for studying abroad. *Journal of the Scholarship of Teaching and Learning*, 15(4), 1–20. doi:10.14434/josotl.v15i4.13640.

Goldoni, F. (2017). Race, ethnicity, class and identity: Implications for study abroad. *Journal of Language, Identity, and Education*, 16(5), 328–341. doi:10.1080/15348458.2017.1350922.

Goldstein, S. B. (2017). Teaching a psychology-based study abroad pre-departure course. *Psychology learning and teaching*, 16(3), 404–424. doi:10.1177/1475725717718059.

Goldstein, S. B., & Kim, R. I. (2006). Predictors of US college students' participation in study abroad program: A longitudinal study. *International Journal of Intercultural Relations*, 30(4), 507–521.

Goode, M. L. (2008). The role of faculty study abroad directors: A case study. *Frontiers: The Interdisciplinary Journal of Study Abroad*, 15, 149–172.

Gordon, P. J., Patterson, T., & Cherry, J. (2014). Increasing international study abroad rates for business students. *Academy of Educational Leadership Journal*, 18(3), 77–86.

Gore, J. E. (2005). *Dominant beliefs and alternative voices: Discourse, belief, and gender in American study abroad*. New York: Routledge.

Green, M. F. (2002). Joining the world: The challenge of internationalizing undergraduate education. *Change*, 34(3), 12–21. Retrieved from www.jstor.org/stable/40177335.

Green, M. F. (2007). Internationalizing community colleges: Barriers and strategies. *New Directions for Community Colleges, 2007*(138), 15–24. doi:10.1002/cc.277.

Green, M. F., & Siaya, L. M. (2005). *Measuring internationalization at community colleges*. Washington, DC: American Council on Education.

Grimes-MacLellan, D. (2018). Increasing student engagement during study abroad through service learning: A view from Japan. In J. L. Plews & K. Misfeldt (Eds.), *Second language study abroad: Programming, pedagogy, and participant engagement* (pp. 165–192). Cham: Palgrave Macmillan.

GTS Learning. (2013). *Communication strategies: Study guide.* London: GTS Learning.

Guerrero, E., Jr. (2006). The road less traveled: Latino students and the impact of studying abroad. Doctor of Education dissertation, The University of California.

Guichon, N. (2019). A self-tracking study of international students in france: Exploring opportunities for language and cultural learning. *ReCALL*, 31(3), 276–292. doi:10.1017/S0958344019000090.

Hackney, K., Boggs, D., & Borozan, A. (2012). An empirical study of student willingness to study abroad. *Journal of Teaching in International Business*, 23(2), 1123–1144.

Hameister, B., Matthews, P., Hosley, N., & Groff, M. (1999). College students with disabilities and study abroad: Implications for international education staff. *Frontiers: The Interdisciplinary Journal of Study Abroad*, 5(2), 81–100.

Hamilton, A., Rubin, D., Tarrant, M., & Gleason, M. (2019). Digital storytelling as a tool for fostering reflection. *Frontiers: The Interdisciplinary Journal of Study Abroad*, 31(1), 59–73.

Hammer, M. R. (2012). The intercultural development inventory: A new frontier in assessment and development of intercultural competence. In M. V. Berg, R. M. Paige, & K. H. Lou (Eds.), *Student learning abroad: What our students are learning, what they're not, and what we can do about it* (pp. 115–136). Sterling, VA: Stylus.

Hawkins, D. E., & Weiss, B. L. (2005). Experiential education in graduate tourism studies. *Journal of Teaching in Travel & Tourism*, 4(3), 1–29. doi:10.1300/J172v04n03_01

He, Y., & Qin, X. (2017). Students' perceptions of an internship experience in China: A pilot study. *Foreign Language Annals*, 50(1), 57–70. doi:10.1111/flan.12246.

Heirweg, S. (2020). Study abroad programmes for all? Barriers to participation in international mobility programmes perceived by students with disabilities. *International Journal of Disability, Development and Education*, 67(1), 73–91. doi:10.1080/1034912X.2019.1640865.

Hennings, M., & Tanabe, S. (2018). Study abroad objectives and satisfaction of international students in Japan. *Journal of International Students*, 8(4), 1914–1925. doi:10.5281/zenodo.1472920.

Hernández, T. A. (2010a). Promoting speaking proficiency through motivation and interaction: The study abroad and classroom learning contexts. *Foreign Language Annals*, 43(4), 650–670. doi:10.1111/j.1944-9720.2010.01107.x.

Hernández, T. A. (2010b). The relationship among motivation, interaction, and the development of second language oral proficiency in a study-abroad context. *Modern Language Journal*, 94(4), 600–617.

Hernández, T. A. (2016). Short-term study abroad: Perspectives on speaking gains and language contact. *Applied Language Learning*, 26(1), 39–64.

Highum, A. (2014). Predeparture services for students studying abroad. In A. Highum (Ed.), *Undergraduate global education: Issues for faculty, staff, and students* (pp. 51–57). San Francisco, CA: Jossey-Bass.

Hipple, E., Soltis, D. E., & Hyers, L. (2020). Queering study abroad: Web-based outreach to LGBTQ+ university students by study abroad programs. *Frontiers: The Interdisciplinary Journal of Study Abroad*, 32(2), 175–186. doi:10.36366/frontiers.v32i2.473.

Hofer, B. K., Thebodo, S. W., Meredith, K., Kaslow, Z., & Saunders, A. (2016). The long arm of the digital tether: Communication with home during study abroad. *Frontiers: The Interdisciplinary Journal of Study Abroad*, 28, 24–41.

Hoffa, W. W. (2007). *A history of US study abroad: Beginnings to 1965.* Carlisle, PA: Frontiers.

Hoffman-Hicks, S. (1999). The longitudinal development of French foreign language pragmatic competence: Evidence from study abroad participants. Doctor of Philosophy dissertation, Indiana University. ProQuest 9962710.

Homeyer, M., Leggette, H. R., McKim, b., & Walker, J. (2017). Visualizing connection: Using photovoice to understand students' study away experience. *NACTA Journal*, 61 (2), 113–120. Retrieved from https://link.gale.com/apps/doc/A498129775/AONE?u= 29002&sid=AONE&xid=008aefbc.

Hornig, J. F. (1995). The toughest job you'll ever love: Faculty find rewards – and responsibilities – in study abroad programs. *Academe*, 81(5), 22–26. doi:10.2307/ 40250873.

Houlihan, P. (2007). Supporting undergraduates in conducting field-based research: A perspective from on-site faculty and staff. *Frontiers: The Interdisciplinary Journal of Study Abroad*, 14, 9–16.

Huesca, R. (2013). How Facebook can ruin study abroad. *Chronicle of Higher Education.* Retrieved from www.chronicle.com/article/How-Facebook-Can-Ruin-Study/ 136633/.

Hurst, A. L. (2019). Class and gender as predictors of study abroad participation among US liberal arts college students. *Studies in Higher Education*, 44(7), 1–15. doi:10.1080/ 03075079.2018.1428948.

Iino, M. (2006). Norms of interaction in a Japanese homestay setting: Toward a two-way flow of linguistic and cultural resources. In M. A. DuFon & E. E. Churchill (Eds.), *Language learners in study abroad contexts* (pp. 151–176). Clevedon: Multilingual Matters.

Ingle, W. K., & Johnson, D. (2019). Photovoices of urban educational leadership students abroad in Peru. *Frontiers: The Interdisciplinary Journal of Study Abroad*, 21(1), 74–110.

Institute of International Education. (1967). *Report on international exchange.* New York: Institute of International Education.

Institute of International Education. (2019). Profile of US study abroad students, 2005/06– 2017/18. Retrieved from www.iie.org/Research-and-Insights/Open-Doors/Data/ US-Study-Abroad/Student-Profile.

Institute of International Education & AIFS. (2018). Study abroad matters: Linking higher education to the contemporary workforce through international experience. Retrieved from https://p.widencdn.net/zfaw8t/Study-Abroad-Matters-White-Paper.

Isabelli-García, C. (2006). Study abroad social networks, motivation and attitudes: Implications for second language acquisition. In M. A. DuFon & E. Churchill (Eds.), *Language learners in study abroad contexts* (pp. 231–259). Clevedon: Multilingual Matters.

Isabelli-García, C. (2007). Development of the Spanish subjunctive by advanced learners: Study abroad followed by at-home instruction. *Foreign Language Annals*, 40(2), 330–341.

Isabelli-García, C., Bown, J., Plews, J. L., & Dewey, D. P. (2018). Language learning and study abroad. *Language Teaching*, 51(4), 439–484. doi:10.1017/S026144481800023X.

Iwasaki, N. (2007). Assessing progress towards advanced level Japanese after a year abroad: Focus on individual learners. *Japanese Language and Literature*, 41(2), 271–296. doi:10.2307/30198038.

Jackson, D. S., & Nyoni, F. P. (2012). Reflections on study abroad education: Guidelines on study abroad preparation and process. *Journal of Human Behavior in the Social Environment*, 22(2), 201–212. doi:10.1080/10911359.2011.647480.

Jackson, J. (2006a). Ethnographic pedagogy and evaluation in short-term study abroad. In M. Byram & A. Feng (Eds.), *Living in studying abroad: Research and practice* (pp. 134–157). Clevedon: Multilingual Matters.

Jackson, J. (2006b). Ethnographic preparation for short-term study and residence in the target culture. *International Journal of Intercultural Relations*, 30(1), 77–98. doi:10.1016/j. ijintrel.2005.07.004.

Jackson, J. (2011). Host language proficiency, intercultural sensitivity, and study abroad. *Frontiers: The Interdisciplinary Journal of Study Abroad*, 21, 167–188.

Jackson, J. (2014). *Introducing language and intercultural communication*. New York: Routledge.

Jackson, J. (2018a). Intervening in the intercultural learning of L2 study abroad students: From research to practice. *Language Teaching*, 51(3), 365–382. doi:10.1017/S0261444816000392.

Jackson, J. (2018b). Optimizing intercultural learning and engagement abroad through online mentoring. In J. Jackson & S. Oguro (Eds.), *Intercultural interventions in study abroad* (pp. 119–136). London & New York: Routledge.

Jackson, M., Ray, S., & Bybell, D. (2013). International students in the US: Social and psychological adjustment. *Journal of International Students*, 3(1), 17–28.

Jacobone, V., & Moro, G. (2015). Evaluating the impact of the Erasmus programme: Skills and European identity. *Assessment and Evaluation in Higher Education*, 40(2), 309–328. doi:10.1080/02602938.2014.909005.

Jurasek, R., Lamson, H., & O'Maley, P. (1996). Ethnographic learning while studying abroad. *Frontiers: The Interdisciplinary Journal of Study Abroad*, 2(1), 23–44.

Kartoshkina, Y. (2015). Bitter-sweet reentry after studying abroad. *International Journal of Intercultural Relations*, 44, 35–45. doi:10.1016/j.ijintrel.2014.11.001.

Kehl, K., & Morris, J. (2008). Differences in global-mindedness between short-term and semester-long study abroad participants at selected private universities. *Frontiers: The Interdisciplinary Journal of Study Abroad*, 15, 67–79.

Kehm, B. M. (2005). The contribution of international student mobility to human development and global understanding. *US–China Education Review*, 2(1), 18–24.

Kemp, J. (2010). The listening log: Motivating autonomous learning. *ELT Journal*, 64(4), 385–395. doi:10.1093/elt/ccp099.

Key, S. (2018). Black American undergraduates studying abroad: What are their intentions and behaviors? Doctor of Education dissertation, University of Pittsburgh. ProQuest 13819828.

Kim, J., Dewey, D. P., Baker-Smemoe, W., & Ring, S. (2015). L2 development during study abroad in China. *System*, 55, 123–133. doi:10.1016/j.system.2015.10.005.

Kim, R. I., & Goldstein, S. B. (2005). Intercultural attitudes predict favorable study abroad expectations of US college students. *Journal of Studies in International Education*, 9(3), 265–278. doi:10.1177/1028315305277684.

Kinginger, C. (2004). Alice doesn't live here anymore: Foreign language learning and identity reconstruction. In A. Pavlenko & A. Blackledge (Eds.), *Negotiation of identities in multilingual contexts* (pp. 219–242). Clevedon: Multilingual Matters.

Kinginger, C. (2008). Language learning in study abroad: Case studies of Americans in France. *The Modern Language Journal*, 92(1), 1–124. doi:10.1111/j.1540-4781.2008.00821.x.

Kinginger, C. (2009a). *Contemporary study abroad and foreign language learning: An activist's guidebook*. University Park, PA: Center for Advanced Language Proficiency Education and Research (CALPER).

Kinginger, C. (2009b). *Language learning and study abroad: A critical reading of research*. New York: Palgrave Macmillan.

Kinginger, C. (2010). American students abroad: Negotiation of difference? *Language Teaching*, 43(2), 216–227. doi:10.1017/S0261444808005703.

Kinginger, C. (2011). Enhancing language learning in study abroad. *Annual Review of Applied Linguistics*, 31, 58–73. doi:10.1017/S0267190511000031.

Kinginger, C., & Wu, Q. (2018). Learning Chinese through contextualized language practices in study abroad residence halls: Two case studies. *Annual Review of Applied Linguistics*, 38, 102–121. doi:10.1017/S0267190518000077.

Knight, S. M., & Schmidt-Rinehart, B. C. (2010). Exploring conditions to enhance student/host family interaction abroad. *Foreign Language Annals*, 43(1), 64–71. doi:10.1111/j.1944-9720.2010.01060.x.

Korbel, L. A. (2007). In union there is strength: The role of state global education consortia in expanding community college involvement in global education. *New Directions for Community Colleges, 2007*(138), 47–55. doi:10.1002/cc.281.

Kortegast, C., & Kupo, V. L. (2017). Deconstructing underlying practices of short-term study abroad: Exploring issues of consumerism, postcolonialism, cultural tourism, and commodification of experience. *The International Journal of Critical Pedagogy*, 8(1), 149–172.

Kruse, J., & Brubaker, C. (2007). Successful study abroad: tips for student preparation, immersion, and postprocessing. *Die Unterrichtspraxis/Teaching German*, 40(2), 147–152.

Kurasawa, I., & Nagatomi, A. (2006). Study abroad and internship programs: Reflection and articulation for lifelong learning. *Global Business Languages*, 11, 23–30.

La Brack, B. (2003). What's up with culture? Retrieved from www2.pacific.edu/sis/culture/.

Larson, P. (1999). "Doing" language: Making new links. *ADFL Bulletin*, 30(3), 28–31.

Lee, J., & Green, Q. (2016). Unique opportunities: Influence of study abroad on Black students. *Frontiers: The Interdisciplinary Journal of Study Abroad*, 18, 61–77.

Lee, J.-y., & Ciftci, A. (2014). Asian international students' socio-cultural adaptation: Influence of multicultural personality, assertiveness, academic self-efficacy, and social support. *International Journal of Intercultural Relations*, 38(1), 97–105. doi:10.1016/j.ijintrel.2013.08.009.

Lee, J. H. (2018). The effects of short-term study abroad on L2 anxiety, international posture, and L2 willingness to communicate. *Journal of Multilingual and Multicultural Development*, 39(8), 703–714.

Lee, L. (2011). Blogging: Promoting Learner Autonomy and Intercultural Competence through Study Abroad. *Language Learning & Technology*, 15(3), 87–109.

Lee, L. (2012). Engaging study abroad students in intercultural learning through blogging and ethnographic interviews. *Foreign Language Annals*, 45(1), 7–21. doi:10.1111/j.1944-9720.2012.01164.x.

Lértora, I. M., Sullivan, J. M., & Croffie, A. L. (2017). They are here, now what do we do? Recommendations for supporting international student transitions. *VISTAS Online*, 1–12.

Lindsay, A. (2014). *The gender gap in study abroad*. SIT Graduate Institute, Capstone Collection. Retrieved from https://digitalcollections.sit.edu/capstones/2734.

Lingo, M. D. (2019). Stratification in study abroad participation after accounting for student intent. *Research in Higher Education*, 1–29. doi:10.1007/s11162-019-09545-z.

Loberg, L. (2012). Exploring factors that lead to participation in study abroad. Doctor of Education dissertation, University of California. ProQuest 3541468.

Lofflin, S. E. (2007). *Adventures abroad: The student's guide to studying overseas*. New York: Kaplan.

Lomartire, S. (2018). The Italian electronic language log: A critical evaluation. In R. Biasini & A. Proudfoot (Eds.), *Using digital resources to enhance language learning – case studies in Italian* (pp. 55–65). Voillans, France: Research-publishing.net.

Lomicka, L., & Ducate, L. (2019). Using technology, reflection, and noticing to promote intercultural learning during short-term study abroad. *Computer Assisted Language Learning*, 1–31. doi:10.1080/09588221.2019.1640746.

Long, T. (2014). Influence of international service-learning on nursing student self-efficacy toward cultural competence. *Journal of Nursing Education*, 53(8), 474–478. doi:10.3928/01484834-20140725-02.

Lou, K. H., Vande Berg, M., & Paige, R. M. (2012). Intervening in student learning abroad. Closing insights. In M. V. Berg, R. M. Paige, & K. H. Lou (Eds.), *Student learning abroad: What our students are learning, what they're not, and what we can do about it* (pp. 411–419). Sterling, VA: Stylus.

Lou, K. H., & Weber Bosley, G. (2012). Facilitating intercultural learning abroad: The intentional, targeted intervention model. In M. V. Berg, R. M. Paige, & K. H. Lou (Eds.), *Student learning abroad: What our students are learning, what they're not, and what we can do about it* (pp. 335–359). Sterling, VA: Stylus.

Lu, C., Reddick, R., Dean, D., & Pecero, V. (2015). Coloring up study abroad: Exploring black students' decision to study in China. *Journal of Student Affairs Research and Practice*, 52(4), 440–451. doi:10.1080/19496591.2015.1050032.

Lucas, J. M. (2009). Where are all the males? A mixed methods inquiry into male study abroad participation. Doctor of Philosophy dissertation, Michigan State University. ProQuest 3381358.

Luo, J., & Jamieson-Drake, D. (2015). Predictors of study abroad intent, participation, and college outcomes. *Research in Higher Education*, 56(1), 29–56.

Magnan, S. S., & Back, M. (2007). Social interaction and linguistic gain during study abroad. *Foreign Language Annals*, 40(1), 43–61. doi:10.1111/j.1944-9720.2007.tb02853.x.

Maharaja, G. (2018). The impact of atudy abroad on college students' intercultural competence and personal development. *International Research and Review: Journal of Phi Beta Delta Honor Society for International Scholars*, 7(2), 18–41.

Maleki, A. (2010). Techniques to teach communication strategies. *Journal of Language Teaching and Research*, 1(5), 640–646. doi:10.4304/jltr.1.5.640-646.

Malewski, E., Sharma, S., & Phillion, J. (2012). How international field experiences promote cross-cultural awareness in preservice teachers through experiential learning: Findings from a six-year collective case study. *Teachers College Record*, 114, 1–44.

Marcum, J. A. (2001). Eliminate the roadblocks. *The Chronicle of Higher Education*, 18. Retrieved from www.chronicle.com/article/Eliminate-the-Roadblocks/21807.

Marqués-Pascual, L. (2011). Study abroad, previous language experience, and Spanish L2 development. *Foreign Language Annals*, 44(3), 565–582.

Martin, J. N. (1986). Communication in the intercultural reentry: Student sojourners' perceptions of change in reentry relationships. *International Journal of Intercultural Relations*, 10(1), 1–22.

Martin, J. N. (1989). Predeparture orientation: Preparing college sojourners for intercultural interaction. *Communication Education*, 38(3), 249–258.

Martin, J. N., & Harrell, T. (2004). Intercultural reentry of students and professionals: Theory and practice. In D. Landis, J. M. Bennett, & M. J. Bennett (Eds.), *Handbook of intercultural training* (pp. 309–337). Thousand Oaks, CA: Sage.

Martinez, M. D., Ranjeet, B., & Marx, H. A. (2009). Creating study abroad opportunities for first-generation college students. In R. Lewin (Ed.), *The handbook of practice and research in study abroad: Higher education and the quest for global citizenship*. New York: Routledge.

Martinsen, R. A. (2010). Short-term study abroad: Predicting changes in oral skills. *Foreign Language Annals*, 43(3), 504–530. doi:10.1111/j.1944-9720.2010.01095.x.

Martinsen, R. A., Baker, W., Dewey, D. P., & Bown, J. (2010). Exploring diverse settings for language acquisition and use: Comparing study abroad, service learning abroad, and foreign language housing. *Applied Language Learning*, 20(1–2),45–69.

Matthews, P. R., Hameister, B. G., & Hosley, N. S. (1998). Attitudes of college students toward study abroad: Implications for disability service providers. *Journal of Postsecondary Education and Disability*, 13(2), 67–77.

McCabe, L. (2005). Mental health and study abroad: Responding to the concern. *International Educator* (November–December), 52–57. Retrieved from www.nafsa.org/_/File/_/InternationalEducator/EducationAbroadNovDec05.pdf.

McClure, K. R., Szelenyi, K., Niehaus, E., Anderson, A. A., & Reed, J. (2010). "We just don't have the possibility yet": US Latina/o narratives on study abroad. *Journal of Student Affairs Research and Practice*, 47(3), 367–387.

Medina-Lopez-Portillo, A., & Salonen, R. (2012). Developing a global learning and living community: A case study of intercultural experiences on The Scholar Ship. In M. V. Berg, R. M. Paige, & K. H. Lou (Eds.), *Student learning abroad. What our students are learning, what they're not, and what we can do about it* (pp. 360–382). Sterling, VA: Stylus.

Meier, G., & Daniels, H. (2013). "Just not being able to make friends": Social interaction during the year abroad in modern foreign language degrees. *Research Papers in Education*, 28(2), 212–238. doi:10.1080/02671522.2011.629734.

Michl, T., Pegg, K., & Kracen, A. (2019). Gender x Culture: A pilot project exploring the study abroad experiences of trans and gender expansive students. *Frontiers: The Interdisciplinary Journal of Study Abroad*, 31(2), 32–50.

Minton, M. R. (2016). Trio-eligible students and study abroad: Influential factors, barriers, and benefits. Doctor of Philosophy dissertation, Illinois State University. ProQuest 10131421.

Mitchell, R. (2015). The development of social relations during residence abroad. *Innovation in Language Learning and Teaching*, 9(1), 22–33. doi:10.1080/17501229.2014.995762.

Mitchell, R., McManus, K., & Tracy-Ventura, N. (2015). Placement type and language learning during residence abroad. In R. Mitchell, N. Tracy-Ventura, & K. McManus (Eds.), *Social interaction, identity and language learning during residence abroad* (pp. 115–138). Amsterdam: The European Second Language Association.

Mitic, R. R. (2019). Learning abroad and engagement at home for first-generation college students: The relationship of study abroad participation to civic outcomes. Doctor of Philosophy dissertation, New York University. ProQuest 13880006.

Moloney, R., & Genua-Petrovic, R. (2012). "In bare feet with my journal": promoting the intercultural development of young exchange students. *Babel*, 47(1), 14–24.

Montero, L. (2019). Developing effective L2 communication strategies abroad and at home. *The Language Learning Journal*, 47(5), 642–652. doi:10.1080/09571736.2017.1357744.

Montrose, L. (2002). International study and experiential learning: The academic context. *Frontiers: The Interdisciplinary Journal of Study Abroad*, 8, 1–15.

Mora, E. I., Piñero , L. Á.-O., & Díaz, B. M. (2019). Developing intercultural competence in Seville outside the classroom. *Learning and Teaching: The International Journal of Higher Education in the Social Sciences*, 12(3), 73–87. doi:10.3167/latiss.2019.120305.

Mora, J. C. (2014). The role of onset level on L2 perceptual phonological development after formal instruction and study abroad. In C. Pérez-Vidal (Ed.), *Language acquisition in study abroad and formal instruction contexts* (pp. 167–194). Amsterdam: John Benjamins.

More, E. I., & Greenwood, D. J. (2019). Active learning and intercultural competence. *Learning and Teaching: The International Journal of Higher Education in the Social Sciences*, 12 (3), 1–17. doi:10.3167/latiss.2019.120302.

Morgan, R. M., Mwegelo, D. T., & Thuner, L. N. (2002). Black women in the African diaspora seeking their cultural heritage through studying abroad. *NASPA Journal*, 39, 333–353.

Morse, C. C., Spoltore, J. D., & Galvinhill, P. (2017). College/university counseling centers supporting study away: Challenges and opportunities. *Journal of College Student Psychotherapy*, 31(4), 325–335. doi:10.1080/87568225.2017.1313690.

Moseley, W. G. (2009). Making study abroad a win–win opportunity for pre-tenure faculty. *Frontiers: The Interdisciplinary Journal of Study Abroad*, 18, 231–240.

Mullen, S. (2014). Study abroad at HBCUs: Challenges, trends, and best practices. In M. Gasman & F. Commodore (Eds.), *Opportunities and challenges at historically Black colleges and universities* (pp. 139–164). New York: Palgrave.

Naffziger, D. W., Bott, J. P., & Mueller, C. B. (2010). Study abroad: Validating the factor analysis of student choices. *International Business: Research, Teaching and Practice*, 4(1), 72–81.

NCSSFL. (2020). *LinguaFolio for Learners*. Retrieved from https://ncssfl.org/lingua folio2020/linguafolio2020-learners/.

Niehaus, E., & Inkelas, K. K. (2016). Understanding stem majors' intent to study abroad. *College Student Affairs Journal*, 34(1), 70–84. Retrieved from http://search.ebscohost.com/login.aspx?direct=true&db=ehh&AN=118904660&site=ehost-live&scope=site.

Nyaupane, G. P., Paris, C. M., & Teye, V. (2010). Why do students study abroad? Exploring motivations beyond earning academic credits. *Tourism Analysis*, 15, 263–267. doi:10.3727/108354210X12724863327920.

Obaid, L. B. (2015). Increasing cultural competence for Saudi English language learners in the UK. *Procedia – Social and Behavioral Sciences*, 192, 695–702. doi:10.1016/j.sbspro.2015.06.108.

Ogane, M. (1998). Teaching Communication strategies. *ERIC document (ED 419384)*. Retrieved from https://files.eric.ed.gov/fulltext/ED419384.pdf.

Oguro, S. (2016). Facilitating students' interaction and engagement with the local society during study abroad. In B. Kürsteiner, L. Bleichenbacher, & R. Frehner (Eds.), *Teacher education in the 21st century: A focus on convergence* (pp. 247–262). Cambridge: Cambridge Scholars.

O'Neal, J. C., & Krueger, R. L. (1995). Directing a program abroad. *Academe*, 81(5), 28–34. doi:10.2307/40250874.

Opp, R. D., & Gosetti, P. P. (2014). The role of key administrators in internationalizing the community college student experience. *New Directions for Community Colleges, 2014* (165), 67–75. doi:10.1002/cc.20092.

O'Reilly, A., Ryan, D., & Hickey, T. (2010). The psychological well-being and sociocultural adaptation of short-term international students in Ireland. *Journal of College Student Development*, 51(5), 584–598. doi:10.1353/csd.2010.0011.

Oxford, R. (1990). *Language learning strategies: What every teacher should know*. Boston, MA: Heinle.

Paige, R. M., & Berg, M. V. (2012). Why students are and are not learning abroad. A review of recent research. In M. V. Berg, R. M. Paige, & K. H. Lou (Eds.), *Student learning abroad. What students are learning, what they're not, and what we can do about it* (pp. 29–58). Sterling, VA: Stylus.

Paige, R. M., Cohen, A. D., Kappler, B., Chi, J. C., & Lassegard, J. P. (2002). *Maximizing study abroad: A students' guide to strategies for language and culture learning and use.* Minneapolis, MN: Center for Advanced Research on Language Acquisition, University of Minnesota.

Paige, R. M., & Goode, M. L. (2009). Cultural mentoring: International education professionals and the development of intercultural competence. In D. K. Deardorff (Ed.), *The SAGE handbook of intercultural competence* (pp. 333–349). Thousand Oaks, CA: Sage.

Paige, R. M., Harvey, T. A., & McCleary, K. S. (2012). The maximizing study abroad project: Toward a pedagogy for culture and language learning. In M. V. Berg, R. M. Paige, & K. H. Lou (Eds.), *Student learning abroad: What our students are learning, what they're not, and what we can do about it* (pp. 308–334). Sterling, VA: Stylus.

Palmer, D. K., & Menard-Warwick, J. (2012). Short-term study abroad for Texas preservice teachers: On the road from empathy to critical awareness. *Multicultural Education,* 19(3), 17–26.

Pan, J.-Y., Ng, P., Young, D. K.-W., & Caroline, S. (2017). Effectiveness of cognitive behavioral group intervention on acculturation: A study of students in Hong Kong from mainland China. *Research on Social Work Practice,* 27(1), 68–79. doi:10.1177/1049731516646857.

Pascarella, E. T., Pierson, C. T., Wolniak, G. C., & Terenzini, P. T. (2004). First-generation college students: Additional evidence on college experiences and outcomes. *Journal of Higher Education,* 75(3), 249–284. Retrieved from https://link.gale.com/apps/doc/A117112010/AONE?u=29002&sid=AONE&xid=08514140.

Paus, E., & Robinson, M. (2008). Increasing study abroad participation: The faculty makes the difference. *Frontiers: The Interdisciplinary Journal of Study Abroad,* 17, 33–49.

Paxton, J., Sherick, H., & Marley, R. (2012). Work in progress: An International Engineering: Certificate: Incentivizing engineering students to pursue global experiences. Retrieved from https://ieeexplore.ieee.org/stamp/stamp.jsp?tp=&arnumber=6462305.

Peace Corps. (2011). Culture matters. The Peace Corps cross-cultural workbook. Retrieved from https://files.peacecorps.gov/multimedia/pdf/library/T0087_culturematters.pdf.

Peckenpaugh, K. (2016). Erwerb interkultureller Kompetenz in Kurzzeitauslandsprogrammen. *Zeitschrift für Interkulturellen Fremdsprachenunterricht,* 21(1), 209–226.

Pedersen, P. J. (2009). Teaching towards an ethnorelative worldview through psychology study abroad. *Intercultural Education,* 20(suppl. 1), S73–S86. doi:10.1080/14675980903370896.

Pedersen, P. J. (2010). Assessing intercultural effectiveness outcomes in a year-long study abroad program. *International Journal of Intercultural Relations,* 34(1), 70–80. doi:10.1016/j.ijintrel.2009.09.003.

Pellegrino Aveni, V. (2005). *Study abroad and second language use: Constructing the self.* Cambridge: Cambridge University Press.

Penman, C., & Ratz, S. (2015). A module-based approach to foster and document intercultural process before and during the residence abroad. *Intercultural Education,* 26(1), 49–61. doi:10/1080/14675986.2015.993529.

Penn, E. B., & Tanner, J. (2009). Black students and international education: An assessment. *Journal of Black Studies,* 40(2), 266–282.

Peppas, S. C. (2005). Business study abroad tours for non-traditional students: An outcomes assessment. *Frontiers: The Interdisciplinary Journal of Study Abroad,* 11, 143–163.

Perdue, J. (2018). Black students, passports, and global citizenship: Developing research-based strategies to increase black student interest and participation in global learning on university campuses. *The College Student Affairs Journal*, 36(1), 80–93. doi:10.1353/csj.2018.0005.

Perez-Encinas, A. (2016). Support services at Spanish and US institutions: A driver for international student satisfaction. *Journal of International Students*, 6(4), 984–998.

Perez-Encinas, A., Rodriguez-Pomeda, J., & Josek, M. (2017). Problematic areas of host university support services for short-term mobility students. *Journal of International Students*, 7(4), 1030–1047. doi:10.5281/zenodo.1035959.

Perry, L., Stoner, L., Schleser, M., Stoner, K. R., Wadsworth, D., Page, R., & Tarrant, M. A. (2015). Digital media as a reflective tool: Creating appropriate spaces for students to become introspective. *Compare: A Journal of Comparative and International Education*, 45 (2), 323–330. doi:10.1080/03057925.2014.993237.

Perry, L., Stoner, L., & Tarrant, M. (2012). More than a vacation: Short-term study abroad as a critically reflective, transformative learning experience. *Creative education*, 3(5), 679–683. doi:10.4236/ce.2012.35101.

Picard, E., Bernardino, F., & Ehigiator, K. (2009). Global citizenship for all: Low minority student participation in study abroad—Seeking strategies for success. In R. Lewin (Ed.), *The handbook of practice and research in study abroad: Higher education and the quest for global citizenship* (pp. 321–345). London: Routledge.

Pilon, S. (2017). Developing intercultural learning among students in short-term study abroad. *NECTFL Review*, 79, 133–153.

Pitts, M. J. (2016). Sojourner reentry: a grounded elaboration of the integrative theory of communication and cross-cultural adaptation. *Communication Monographs*, 83(4), 419–445. doi:10.1080/03637751.2015.1128557.

Plonksy, L. (2019). Language learning strategy instruction: Recent research and future directions. In A. Uhl Chamot & V. Harris (Eds.), *Learning strategy instruction in the language classroom* (pp. 3–21). Bristol: Multilingual Matters.

Polanyi, L. (1995). Language learning and living abroad: Stories from the field. In B. F. Freed (Ed.), *Second language acquisition in a study abroad context* (pp. 271–291). Amsterdam: John Benjamins.

Posey, J. T., Jr. (2003). Study abroad: Educational and employment outcomes of participants versus non participants. Doctor of Philosophy dissertation, The Florida State University. ProQuest 3137474.

Prohn, S. M., Kelley, K. R., & Westling, D. L. (2016). Studying abroad inclusively: Reflections by college students with and without intellectual disability. *Journal of Intellectual Disabilities*, 20(4), 341–353.

Prokhorov, A., & Therkelsen, J. (2015). Visualizing St. Petersburg: Using documentary production in a short-term study abroad program to enhance oral proficiency, media literacy, and research skills. *Journal of Film and Video*, 67(3/4), 112–124.

Pryde, M. (2014). Conversational patterns of homestay hosts and study abroad students. *Foreign Language Annals*, 47(3), 487–506. doi:10.1111/flan.12100.

Pyper, M. J., & Slagter, C. (2015). Competing priorities: Student perceptions of helps and hindrances to language acquisition during study abroad. *Frontiers: The Interdisciplinary Journal of Study Abroad*, 26, 83–106.

Quraeshi, Z. A., Luqmani, M., & Veeck, A. (2012). Advancing the participation of business students in study abroad programs. *Global Journal of Management and Business Research*, 12(11), 81–92.

Raby, R. L. (2020). Unique characteristics of US community college education abroad. *College and university*, 95(1), 41–46.

Raby, R. L., Rhodes, G. M., & Biscarra, A. (2014). Community college study abroad: implications for student success. *Community College Journal of Research and Practice*, 38(2–3),174–183. doi:10.1080/10668926.2014.851961.

Raby, R. L., & Valeau, E. J. (2007). Community college international education: Looking back to forecast the future. *New Directions for Community Colleges, 2007*(138), 5–14. doi:10.1002/cc.276.

Raschio, R. A. (2001). Integrative activities for the study-abroad setting. *Hispania*, 84(3), 534–541. doi:10.2307/3657819.

Rausch, K. (2017). First-generation strength: Supporting first-generation college students in study abroad. Doctor of Education dissertation, Arizona State University. ProQuest 10273637.

Raymondi, M. D. (2005). Latino students explore racial and ethnic identity in a global context. Doctor of Education dissertation, State University of New York at Binghamton. ProQuest 3153765.

Redden, E. (2009). Women abroad and men at home. *Inside Higher Ed*. Retrieved from www.insidehighered.com/news/2008/12/04/women-abroad-and-men-home.

Redman, J. (2009). Embedding preparation in language courses. In E. Brewer & K. Cummingham (Eds.), *Integrating study abroad into the curriculum: Theory and practice across disciplines* (pp. 85–102). Sterling, VA: Stylus.

Rexeisen, R. J., Anderson, P. H., Lawton, L., & Hubbard, A. C. (2008). Study abroad and intercultural development: A longitudinal study. *Frontiers: The Interdisciplinary Journal of Study Abroad*, 17, 1–20.

Rhodes, G. M., Raby, R. L., & Biscarra, A. (2013). Student outcomes from participating in California community college education abroad programs. *Education and Society*, 31 (3), 23–40. doi:10.7459/es/31.3.03.

Rhodes, G. M., Thomas, J. M., Raby, R. L., Codding, A. G., & Lynch, A. (2016). Community college study abroad and implications for student success: Comparing California and New Jersey community colleges. In R. L. Raby & E. J. Valeau (Eds.), *International education at community colleges* (pp. 281–292). New York:Palgrave Macmillan.

Ring, S. A., Gardner, D., & Dewey, D. P. (2013). Social network development during study abroad in Japan. In K. Kondo-Brown, Y. Saito-Abbott, S. Satsutani, M. Tsutsui, & A. Wehmeyer (Eds.), *New perspectives on Japanese language learning, linguistics, and culture* (pp. 95–121). Honolulu, HI: University of Hawai'i, National Foreign Language Resource Center.

Robertson, J. J. (2015). Student interest in international education at the community college. *Community College Journal of Research and Practice*, 39(5), 473–484. doi:10.1080/10668926.2013.879377.

Robertson, J. J. (2017). Community college student perceptions of their experiences related to global learning: Understanding the impact of family, faculty, and the curriculum. *Community College Journal of Research and Practice*, 41(11), 697–718.

Rodgers, C. (2002). Defining reflection: Another look at John Dewey and reflective thinking. *Teachers College Record*, 104(4), 842–866.

Rodriguez, P. (2016). Global certificates: Bringing intentionality and ownership to comprehensive internationalization. In R. L. Raby & E. J. Valeau (Eds.), *International education at community colleges* (pp. 223–236). New York:Palgrave Macmillan.

Root, E., & Ngampornchai, A. (2013). "I came back as a new human being": Student descriptions of intercultural competence acquired through education abroad experiences. *Journal of Studies in International Education*, 17(5), 513–532. doi:10.1177/1028315312468008.

Rubesch, T. (2017). Study abroad reflection through guided blogging with social networking services. *Kwansei Gakuin University Humanities Review*, 22, 125–131.

Rusnak, L., Peek, J. T., Orriola, D., & Makut, M. B. (2019). Integrating diverse study abroad opportunities into public health curricula: Three distinct strategies to address common barriers. *Frontiers in Public Health*, 7(29), 1–10. doi:10.3389/fpubh.2019.00029.

Sachau, D., Brasher, N., & Fee, S. (2010). Three models for short-term study abroad. *Journal of Management Education*, 34(5), 645–670. doi:10.1177/1052562909340880.

Salisbury, M. H. (2011). The effect of study abroad on intercultural competence among undergraduate college students. Doctor of Philosophy dissertation, University of Iowa.

Salisbury, M. H., Paulsen, M. B., & Pascarella, E. T. (2010). To see the world or stay at home: Applying an integrated student choice model to explore the gender gap in the intent to study abroad. *Research in Higher Education*, 51(7), 615–640.

Salisbury, M. H., Umbach, P. D., Paulsen, M. B., & Pascarella, E. T. (2009). Going global: Understanding the choice process of the intent to study abroad. *Research in Higher Education*, 50(2), 119–143. doi:10.1007/s11162-008-9111-x.

Sarcletti, A., Heißenberg, S., & Poskowsky, J. (2018). Auslandsmobilität Studierender mit studienrelevanten Beeinträchtigungen. In K. Becker & S. Heißenberg (Eds.), *Dimensionsen studentischer Vielfalt. Empirische Befunde zu heterogenen Studien- und Lebensarrangements* (pp. 28–59). Hannover: WBV.

Savicki, V., & Price, M. V. (2017). Components of reflection: A longitudinal analysis of study abroad student blog posts. *Frontiers: The Interdisciplinary Journal of Study Abroad*, XXIX(2), 51–62.

Savicki, V., & Price, M. V. (2018). Guiding reflection on cultural experience: Before, during, and after study abroad. In S. L. Pasquarelli, R. A. Cole, & M. J. Tyson (Eds.), *Passport to change: Designing academically sound, culturally relevant, short-term, faculty-led study abroad programs* (pp. 60–77). Sterling, VA: Stylus.

Scally, J. (2015). Intercultural competence development in three different study abroad program types. *Intercultural Communication Studies*, 24(2), 35–60.

Scheib, M., & Mitchell, M. (2008). Awaiting a world experience no longer: It's time for all students with disabilities to go overseas. In T. Berberi, E. C. Hamilton, & I. Sutherland (Eds.), *Worlds Apart?: Disability and Foreign Language Learning* (pp. 202–217). New Haven, CT: Yale University Press.

Schenker, T. (2013a). The effects of a virtual exchange on students' interest in learning about culture. *Foreign Language Annals*, 46(3), 491–507. doi:10.1111/flan.12041.

Schenker, T. (2013b). Virtual exchanges in the foreign language classroom. *The FLTmag*. Retrieved from http://fltmag.com/virtual-exchanges-in-the-foreign-language-classroom/.

Schenker, T. (2019). Fostering global competence through short-term study abroad. *Frontiers: The Interdisciplinary Journal of Study Abroad*, 31(2), 139–157.

Schmidt-Rinehart, B. C., & Knight, S. M. (2004). The homestay component of study abroad: Three perspectives. *Foreign Language Annals*, 37(2), 254–262.

Schoenberger, L. K. (2019). Who am I? The LGBTQ+ student experience during study abroad. Doctor of Education dissertation, The Florida State University. ProQuest 13427004.

Seay, A. (2014). *Pushing forward: The climate for LGBTQ student advising in study abroad of South Carolina*. SIT Graduate Institute Capstone Collection. Retrieved from https://digitalcollections.sit.edu/capstones/2674 (2674)

Segalowitz, N., & Freed, B. F. (2004). Context, contact and cognition in oral fluency acquisition. *Studies in Second Language Acquisition*, 26(2), 173–199. doi:10.1017/S0272263104262027.

Seibert Hanson, A. E., & Dracos, M. J. (2016). Motivation and technology use during second-language study abroad in the digital age. *Canadian Journal of Applied Linguistics*, 19(2), 64–84.

Shames, W., & Alden, P. (2005). The impact of short-term study abroad on the identity development of college students with learning disabilities and/or AD/HD. *Frontiers: The Interdisciplinary Journal of Study Abroad*, 11, 1–31.

Shiri, S. (2015). Intercultural communicative competence development during and after language study abroad: Insights from Arabic. *Foreign Language Annals*, 48(4), 541–569.

Shirley, S. W. (2006). The gender gap in post-secondary study abroad: Understanding and marketing to male students. Doctor of Philosophy dissertation, University of North Dakota. ProQuest 3233968.

Shively, R. L. (2010). From the virtual world to the real world: A model of pragmatics instruction for study abroad. *Foreign Language Annals*, 43(1), 105–137.

Sideli, K., Dollinger, M., & Doyle, S. (2003). Successful recruitment of business students for study abroad through program development, curricular integration and marketing. In G. T. M. Hult & E. C. Lashbrooke (Eds.), *Study abroad. Perspectives and experiences from business schools* (pp. 37–58). Oxford: Elsevier Science.

Simon, J., & Ainsworth, J. W. (2012). Race and socioeconomic status differences in study abroad participation: The role of habitus, social networks, and cultural capital. *ISRN Education*, 2012, article 413896. doi:10.5402/2012/413896.

Soneson, H. M., & Cordano, R. J. (2009). Universal design and study abroad: (Re-)designing programs for effectiveness and access. *Frontiers: The Interdisciplinary Journal of Study Abroad*, 18, 269–288.

Spenader, A. J., & Retka, P. (2015). The role of pedagogical variables in intercultural development: A study of faculty-led programs. *Frontiers: The Interdisciplinary Journal of Study Abroad*, 25, 20–36.

Stallman, E., Woodruff, G. A., Kasravi, J., & Comp, D. (2010). The diversification of the student profile. In W. W. Hoffa & S. C. DePaul (Eds.), *A history of US study abroad: 1965–present* (pp. 115–160). Carlisle, PA: Frontiers.

Starr-Glass, D. (2020). Intercultural awareness and short-term study abroad programs: An invitation to liminality. In D. M. Velliaris (Ed.), *Academic mobility programs and engagement: Emerging research and opportunities* (pp. 31–56). Hershey, PA: IGI Global.

Steeves, H. (2006). Experiencing international communication: An internship program in Ghana, West Africa. *Journalism & Mass Communication Educator*, 60(4), 360–375.

Steinberg, M. (2002). "Involve me and I will understand": Academic quality in experiential programs abroad. *Frontiers: The Interdisciplinary Journal of Study Abroad*, 8, 207–229.

Steinwidder, S. (2016). EFL learners' post-sojourn perceptions of the effects of study abroad. *Comparative and International Education*, 45(2), 1–20.

Stern, G. M. (2004). Credit transference a key barrier to study abroad: Recommendations in new ACE report can ease path. *The Hispanic Outlook in Higher Education*, 14(25), 26–31.

Stroud, A. H. (2010). Who plans (not) to study abroad? An examination of US student intent. *Journal of Studies in International Education*, 14(5), 491–507.

Sümer, S., Poyrazli, S., & Grahame, K. (2008). Predictors of depression and anxiety among international students. *Journal of Counseling and Development*, 86(4), 429–437. doi:10.1002/j.1556-6678.2008.tb00531.x.

Surtees, V. (2018). Peer language socialization in an internationalized study abroad context: Norms for talking about language. Doctor of Philosophy dissertation, The University of British Columbia. Open Collection UBC Theses and Dissertations. Retrieved from http s://open.library.ubc.ca/cIRcle/collections/ubctheses/24/items/1.0375711.

Sutton, R. C., & Rubin, D. L. (2010). *Documenting the academic impact of study abroad: Final report of the GLOSSARI project.* Paper presented at the NAFSA Annual Conference, Kansas City, Missouri. Retrieved from http://glossari.uga.edu/datasets/pdfs/FINAL.pdf.

Sweeney, K. (2013). Inclusive excellence and underrepresentation of students of color in study abroad. *Frontiers: The Interdisciplinary Journal of Study Abroad*, 13, 1–21.

Sygall, S. (1995). Facilitating exchange: Including persons with disabilities in international programs. *Transitions Abroad*, 18(5), 87–89.

Tanaka, K. (2007). Japanese students' contact with English outside the classroom during study abroad. *New Zealand Studies in Applied Linguistics*, 13, 36–54.

Tarone, E. (1981). Some thoughts on the notion of "communication strategy." *TESOL Quarterly*, 15, 285–295.

Tarrant, M. A., Rubin, D. L., & Stoner, L. (2014). The added value of study abroad: Fostering a global citizenry. *Journal of Studies in International Education*, 18(2), 141–161. doi:10.1177/1028315313497589.

Terenzini, P. T., Rendon, L. I., Upcraft, M. L., Millar, S. B., Allison, K. W., Gregg, P. L., & Jalomo, R. (1994). The transition to college: Diverse students, diverse stories. *Research in Higher Education*, 35(1), 57–73. Retrieved from www.jstor.org/stable/40196060.

TerraDotta. (2019). Getting more males to study abroad. Retrieved from www.terradotta. com/articles/article-Getting-More-Males-to-Study-Abroad.pdf.

Thirolf, K. Q. (2014). Male college student perceptions of intercultural and study abroad programs. *Journal of Student Affairs Research and Practice*, 51(3), 246–258. doi:10.1515/jsarp-2014-0026.

Thomas, S. L., & McMahon, M. E. (1998). Americans abroad: Student characteristics, pre-departure qualifications and performance abroad. *The International Journal of Educational Management*, 12(2), 57–64. doi:10.1108/09513549810204432.

Tolliver, D. E. (2000). Study abroad in Africa: Learning about race, racism, and the racial legacy of America. *African Issues*, 28(1/2), 112–116. doi:10.2307/1167071.

Tonkin, K., & Coudray, C. B. d. (2016). Not blogging, drinking: Peer learning, sociality and intercultural learning in study abroad. *International Education*, 15(2), 106–119. doi:10.1177/1475240916647600.

Travers, C. S. (1980). Learning through survival: An approach to foreign language teaching. *The French Review*, 53(3), 389–401. Retrieved from www.jstor.org/stable/390490.

Trentman, E. (2013). Arabic and English during study abroad in Cairo, Egypt: Issues of access and use. *The Modern Language Journal*, 97(2), 457–473. doi:10.1111/j.1540-4781.2013.12013.

Tullock, B., & Ortega, L. (2017). Fluency and multilingualism in study abroad: Lessons from a scoping review. *System*, 71, 7–21. doi:10.1016/j.system.2017.09.019.

Turlington, B., Collins, N. F., & Porcelli, M. (2002). *Where credit is due: Approaches to course and credit recognition across borders in US higher education institutions.* Washington, DC: American Council on Education Center for Institutional and International Initiatives.

Twill, S. E., & Guzzo, G. R. (2012). Lessons learned from a disabilities accessible study abroad trip. *Journal of Postsecondary Education and Disability*, 25(1), 81–86.

United Nations. (2020). The sustainable development agenda. Retrieved from www.un. org/sustainabledevelopment/development-agenda/.

US Department of Education's National Center for Education Statistics. (2016). Table 310.10. Number of US students studying abroad and percentage distribution, by sex, race/ethnicity, and other selected characteristics: Selected years, 2000–01 through 2014–15. *Digest of Education Statistics*. Retrieved from https://nces.ed.gov/programs/digest/d16/tables/dt16_310.10.asp.

US Department of Education's National Center for Education Statistics. (2018). Table 233. Number of US students studying abroad and percentage distribution, by sex, race/ethnicity, academic level, host region, and duration of stay: 1996–97 through 2007–08. *Digest of Education Statistics*. Retrieved from https://nces.ed.gov/programs/digest/d10/tables/dt10_233.asp.

Ushioda, E. (2014). Motivation, autonomy and metacognition: Exploring the interactions. In D. Lasagabaster, A. Doiz, & J. M. Sierra (Eds.), *Motivation and foreign language learning* (pp. 31–49). Amsterdam: John Benjamin.

Vahlbusch, J. (2003). Experiential learning in the University of Wisconsin-Eau Claire's program in Wittenberg, Germany. *ADFL Bulletin*, 34(2), 33–35. doi:10.1632/adfl.34.2.33.

Van Der Meid, S. J. (2003). Asian Americans: Factors influencing the decision to study abroad. *Frontiers: The Interdisciplinary Journal of Study Abroad*, 9, 71–110.

Vande Berg, M., Connor-Linton, J., & Paige, R. M. (2009). The Georgetown consortium project: Interventions for student learning abroad. *Frontiers: The Interdisciplinary Journal of Study Abroad*, 18, 1–75.

Vande Berg, M., Paige, R. M., & Lou, K. H. (Eds.). (2012). *Student learning abroad: What our students are learning, what they're not, and what we can do about it*. Sterling, VA: Stylus.

Vernon, A., Moos, C., & Loncarich, H. (2017). Student expectancy and barriers to study abroad. *Academy of Educational Leadership Journal*, 21(1), 1–9.

Vogt, K. (2020). Towards a culturally reflective practitioner: Pre-service student teachers in teaching practicums abroad. In D. M. Velliaris (Ed.), *Academic mobility programs and engagement: Emerging research and opportunities* (pp. 143–197). Hershey, PA: IGI Global.

Wainwright, P., Ram, P., Teodorescu, D., & Tottenham, D. (2009). Going global in the sciences: a case study at Emory University. In R. Lewin (Ed.), *The handbook of practice and research in study abroad: higher education and the quest for global citizenship* (pp. 381–398). New York: Routledge.

Walker, J. (2015). Student perception of barriers to study abroad. Honors in the Major Program in Marketing, University of Central Florida. Retrieved from http://stars.library.ucf.edu/honorstheses1990-2015/1890.

Warnick, G. M., Call, M. S., & Davies, R. (2018). *Understanding engineering and technology student perceptions: Barriers to study abroad participation*. Paper presented at the ASEE Annual Conference & Exposition, Salt Lake City, UT.

Watson, J. R., & Wolfel, R. (2015). The intersection of language and culture in study abroad: Assessment and analysis of study abroad outcomes. *Frontiers: The Interdisciplinary Journal of Study Abroad*, 25, 57–72.

Wells, R. (2006). Nontraditional study abroad destinations: Analysis of a trend. *Frontiers: The Interdisciplinary Journal of Study Abroad*, 13, 113–133.

West, C. (2019). Breaking barriers to study abroad. *International Educator*, 28(4), 30–35.

Whitworth, K. F. (2006). Access to learning during study abroad: The roles of identity and subject positioning. Doctor of Philosophy dissertation, The Pennsylvania State University. ProQuest 3229461.

Wielkiewicz, R. M., & Turkowski, L. W. (2010). Reentry issues upon returning from study abroad programs. *Journal of College Student Development*, 51(6), 649–664.

Wilkinson, S. (1998). Study abroad from the participants' perspective: a challenge to common beliefs. *Foreign Language Annals*, 31(1), 23–39.

Williams, T. R. (2005). Exploring the impact of study abroad on students' intercultural communication skills: Adaptability and sensitivity. *Journal of Studies in International Education*, 9(4), 356–371. doi:10.1177/1028315305277681.

Williams, T. R. (2017). Using a PRISM for reflecting: Providing tools for study abroad students to increase their intercultural competence. *Frontiers: The Interdisciplinary Journal of Study Abroad*, 29(2), 18–34.

Willis, T. Y. (2012). Rare but there: An intersectional exploration of the experiences and outcomes of Black women who studied abroad through community college programs. Doctor of Education dissertation, California State University. ProQuest 3533746.

Willis, T. Y. (2015). "And still we rise ...": Microaggressions and intersectionality in the study abroad experiences of Black women. *Frontiers: The Interdisciplinary Journal of Study Abroad*, 16, 209–230.

Wilson-Forsberg, S., Power, P., Kilgour, V., Darling, S., & Laurier, W. (2018). From class assignment to friendship: Enhancing the intercultural competence of domestic and international students through experiential learning. *Comparative and International Education*, 47(1), 1–18.

Woolf, M. (2007). Impossible things before breakfast: Myths in education abroad. *Journal of Studies in International Education*, 11(3–4),496–509. doi:10.1177/1028315307304186.

Wu, C.-H. (2018). Intercultural citizenship through participation in an international service-learning program: A case study from Taiwan. *Language Teaching Research*, 22(5), 517–531. doi:10.1177/1362168817718573.

Wu, H.-p., Garza, E., & Guzman, N. (2015). International student's challenge and adjustment to college. *Education Research International, 2015*, 1–9. doi:10.1155/2015/202753.

Wu, S.-L. (2017). The planning, implementation, and assessment of an international internship program: An exploratory case study. *Foreign Language Annals*, 50(3), 567–583. doi:10.1111/flan.12280.

Yankey, J. B. (2014). Dude, where's my passport? An exploration of masculine identity of college men who study abroad. Doctor of Philosophy dissertation, Iowa State University. ProQuest 3627526.

Young, G. E. (2014). Reentry: Supporting students in the final stage of study abroad. *New Directions for Student Services*, 146. doi:10.1002/ss.20091.

Yucas, A. (2003). The important role of faculty involvement in study abroad. In G. T. M. Hult & E. C. Lashbrooke (Eds.), *Study abroad: Perspectives and experiences from business schools* (pp. 99–114). Oxford: Elsevier.

Yuksel, P. (2018). Breaking barriers: Developing faculty-led international trips for underserved students. *Scholarship of Teaching and Learning in Psychology*, 4(3), 189–197. doi:10.1037/stl0000120.

Zamastil-Vondrova, K. (2005). Good faith or hard data? Justifying short-term programs. *International Educator*, 14(1), 44–49.

Zimmermann, J., & Neyer, F. J. (2013). Do we become a different person when hitting the road? Personality development of sojourners. *Journal of Personality and Social Psychology*, 105(3), 515–530. doi:10.1037/a0033019.

INDEX